Illinois Central College
Learning Resource Center

Escape to Utopia

BOOKS BY EVERETT WEBBER

LOUISIANA CAVALIER
BACKWOODS TEACHER
(UNDER THE NAME OF JOSEPH NELSON)
ESCAPE TO UTOPIA

With
Olga Webber

RAMPART STREET
BOUND GIRL

AMERICAN PROCESSION SERIES
Already Published:

NEW GREEN WORLD
JOHN BARTRAM AND THE EARLY NATURALISTS
BY JOSEPHINE HERBST

THE BUFFALO HUNTERS
THE STORY OF THE HIDE MEN
BY MARI SANDOZ

TINKERS AND GENIUS
THE STORY OF THE YANKEE INVENTORS
BY EDMUND FULLER

WILDERNESS FOR SALE
THE STORY OF THE FIRST WESTERN LAND RUSH
BY WALTER HAVIGHURST

THE WILD JACKASSES
THE AMERICAN FARMER IN REVOLT
BY DALE KRAMER

THE CATTLEMEN
BY MARI SANDOZ

ESCAPE TO UTOPIA
BY EVERETT WEBBER

In Preparation:

LOUISIANA PURCHASE
BY HENRY G. ALSBERG

★

★

★

AMERICAN PROCESSION SERIES

★ HENRY G. ALSBERG

GENERAL EDITOR

★

★

★

★

ESCAPE TO UTOPIA

The Communal Movement in America

BY
EVERETT WEBBER

HASTINGS HOUSE PUBLISHERS NEW YORK 22

Published simultaneously in Canada
by S. J. Reginald Saunders, Publishers, Toronto 2B

Library of Congress Catalog Card Number: 58–12525

Printed in the United States of America

FOR OLGA

AUTHOR'S NOTE AND

ACKNOWLEDGMENTS

This book began somewhat by accident through browsings in off-trail American history, but for the first several years of reading on the subject—beginning about 1945—I had no intention of using the material as in the present work. However, since then on several occasions, between other writings, I returned to the subject with the idea of producing this volume. Unfortunately, at one time I decided to drop the whole thing and a great deal of correspondence with people who had been helpful in supplying information was destroyed so that I am unable now to make some acknowledgments that I should, although the information itself was preserved in note files. There was, for instance, correspondence with several Strangite Mormons concerning their prophet. Other people were helpful concerning the legendary Cyrus Spragg. It is a matter of regret and embarrassment that these and others may not be publicly thanked.

Besides professional researchers who have made numerous reports from primary material that could not be lent, various librarians have been of assistance by locating and procuring material from libraries and historical societies. These are: Mrs. Hazel Deal, Washington County Librarian, Fayetteville, Arkansas; Mrs. Georgiana Greeson, Louisiana Library Commission, New Orleans; Miss Freddy Schader and Mrs. Frances Potter Neal, Arkansas Library Commission,

Little Rock; J. Mitchel Reames, Librarian, University of South Carolina, Columbia; and Donald N. MacKenzie and Miss Katherine Bridges, Northwestern State College Library, Natchitoches, Louisiana.

Much of the work was done at my home in the Ozarks town of Eureka Springs, Arkansas. Residents there due my thanks are: Mrs. Marge Lyon, long a feature writer for the *Chicago Tribune,* for information and material on the Strangites; Otto Ernest Rayburn, Ozark historian, folklorist, and editor of *Ozark Guide* Magazine for information on the free-loving Harmonial Vegetarian Community of pre-Civil War days in the neighboring Benton County, and for lending me a rare book belonging to our mutual neighbor, Everett Wheeler, the local newspaper editor, containing a fictionized account of the Vermont Pilgrims; (also, some thanks are perhaps due to Mr. Wheeler for having the book in the first place, and these are hereby given); and to Vance Randolph, the Ozark folklorist and song collector, for information on numerous messiahs and little Christs of whom he has made a long-time study.

Libraries which have been generous with material are those of Harvard, Yale, Louisiana State University, Mississippi University, New-York Historical Society, and the Illinois Historical Society. I am grateful, too, to Miss Elvira Scorgie, Harvard, Massachusetts, for bibliographical and other information on Shadrach Ireland and Fruitlands; to Mrs. Elleine H. Stones, Chief, Burton Historical Collection, Detroit Public Library, for information concerning material on "King James" Strang and "King Benjamin" Purnell; to John B. White, Librarian, and Donald Danker, Archivist, of the Nebraska State Historical Society for material on the Hutterites and Mennonites; and to George Picket for the use of a rare little volume on communities which is based in part on correspondence with some of their leaders and long-time residents. Mr. Picket's father was head of the Newllano colony in Louisiana.

My thanks go also to Mary Noel, curator of the Abernethy Library of American Literature, Middlebury College, Middlebury, Vermont, for a true copy of the Sophia Eastman letter, written from Brook Farm, which that college owns; to officials of the New York Public Library and of the Library of Congress for assistance at various times; to the Hon. and Mrs. J. W. Trimble for help on matters at the Library of Congress on several occasions; to G. P. Putnam's Sons, Inc., for permission to quote several lines from *A Yankee Saint* (the Oneida story), copyright 1935 by Robert Allerton Parker; and to The Columbia University Press for permission to quote several lines from *A Prophet and a Pilgrim,* by Herbert W. Schneider and George Lawton (the Thomas Lake Harris story).

A gratifying acknowledgment to make is that owed to Dr. C. E. Dugdale, head of the Languages Department at Northwestern State College, Natchitoches, Louisiana, for arranging my teaching schedule here to conform to the necessities of a routine of research and writing.

Finally, and in many ways chiefly, I am indebted to my wife, Olga, who has collaborated with me on various books and magazine stories and articles.

E. W.

CONTENTS

AUTHOR'S NOTE AND ACKNOWLEDGMENTS   ix

CHAPTER

1 *The Dream and the Village*   3

2 *Shadrach, Mother Ann, and the
   Contented of the God-loving Soul*   31

3 *The Shaker Discipline*   55

4 *The Jemimakins and the Universal Friend*   75

5 *Pantisocrats and Wood Scrapers*   89

6 *Father Rapp's Children*   100

7 *Frances Wright and the Emancipation of Woman*   116

8 *Nashoba and the Wolves*   126

9 *Robert Owen and the Yankee Highbinders*   135

10 *The Unharmonious End of New Harmony*   151

11 *Equity, Fourier, Brook Farm, and the Phalanxes*   165

xiii

12   *Fruitlands—Alcott's New Eden*   201

13   *Icaria*   223

14   *King Jimmy and His Saints*   239

15   *Amana, Where the Lord Usually Said No*   274

16   *Adonai-Shomo and Celesta*   299

17   *The Man Who Became God*   319

18   *God's Children and Some Other Elect Ones*   344

19   *Oneida and the Perfect Race*   361

20   *The Song Is Done*   410

Bibliography   421

Index   437

ILLUSTRATIONS

BETWEEN PAGES
206 and 207

Communal buildings at Ephrata, Pa.
The church at Economie, near Ambridge, Pa.

Father Rapp, from a painting, c. 1830
The Rappite church and hall of Harmonie, Ind.

A. Bronson Alcott
Mrs. Bronson Alcott
Fruitlands, near Harvard, Mass.

The Shaker "Whirling Dance"
"Sacred Dance on the Holy Hill of Zion"

Portrait of a Shaker Eldress
Robert Owen
Design for an Owenite ideal village

Frances Wright
The Inspirationist village of Amana, Iowa

Charles Fourier
Etienne Cabet
Design for a Fourierist phalanstery

John Humphrey Noyes
The Old Mansion House at Oneida, N.Y.

Escape to Utopia

"Ah Love! could you and I with Fate conspire
To grasp the sorry Scheme of Things entire,
    Would we not shatter it to bits—and then
Remould it nearer to the Heart's Desire?"

—OMAR KHAYYAM

CHAPTER ONE

THE DREAM
AND THE VILLAGE

MESSIAHS, PROPHETS, AND SNAKE-OIL MEN

To each they offer gifts after his will,
Bread, kingdoms, stars, and sky that holds them all.

—EMERSON

What is man born for but to be a reformer, a re-maker
of what man has made, a renouncer of lies; a
restorer of truth and good. . . ?

—EMERSON

i

IT WAS a warm afternoon in the summer of 1873 in central
New York State. Through the long shadows, two hundred
people sauntered toward the excursion train which was to
take them home. Already a number of their hosts—men,
women, and children of the Kingdom of Heaven—were moving out upon the lawns around the big brick Mansion
House to pick up cigar butts and trash left by the careless
picnickers. The men of the colony looked like any group of
unpretentious, comfortably well-off villagers. The women,
however, wore bobbed hair, curled or straight as they preferred, and short dresses with bloomers to their ankles.
These somewhat daring costumes were considered practical,
comfortable, and attractive.

A not ungenerously built female excursionist lin-

3

gered. For her, the burning point of interest in the Kingdom was that there was so much marriage and giving in marriage that all the men were considered as husbands to all the women. Indeed, it was this facet of life in the colony which drew the weekly stream of excursionists. The big woman shook her head in wonder. God, it seemed to her, had acted most unwisely in permitting this den of polyandrists to prosper in their share-the-wealth enterprise with its fornications which went by the name of "complex marriage."

The evidence of financial prosperity was really the most shocking thing she had observed—for certainly there was nothing openly sinful to be seen on the part of the people. Of course, one had no doubts concerning the orgies which went on when no visitors were near, though outwardly there was merely a comfortable establishment of three hundred or so people who were pleasantly ready to show visitors about, to serve them a meal if necessary, and to answer their questions.

The woman girded up her courage and approached a pretty girl who was playing with a little boy, obviously her own.

"Tell me," she begged, "how will your child know who its father is?"

This was no new question at the Kingdom. Cheerfully, blandly, the girl made the standard retort: "Why, just the same way yours will. He'll have to take his mother's word for it."

The inmates of this strangest of the many strange "village communities" then in the United States were convinced that their religious, social, and economic systems, their method of scientific mating to produce the best children were the culmination of the Christian's long search for the proper way to get along with himself, his fellow man—and woman—and his God, the pattern, in fact, for the reorganization of society which all people of common sense would eventually desire to follow.

Things had not always gone so well with them as in 1873, nor yet with their forerunners, rivals, and colleagues in the communitarian movement, the leaders of which had begun bubbling up in this country two centuries before. Some of the communes were based on social and economic principles, even to the extent of definitely trying to replace religious dogmas with ethical codes. Perhaps Frances Wright, a Scots heiress who established a "free love" commune near Memphis, dedicated to wiping out the slavery of women to their husbands and that of Negroes to anybody, and the Owens of the great New Harmony, Indiana, commune were the most noted for this in their day. Great furor was raised in the national press over their discounting of revealed religions and "priestcraft," their advocacy of basing opinions on facts, and their impatience with orthodox marriage.

But Frances was championed, for her human-rights views, by Quakers, abolitionists, and fledgeling labor organizations of the 1820's. Broad thinkers flocked to the Owens—village atheists, free thinkers, humanitarians, and women's righters, not to mention free loaders. Robert Owen's thinking was broad enough that he could countenance one group in his borders who insisted on orthodox religion, and another who blasphemously named their leaders the Father, Son, and Holy Ghost.

Other leaders ignored the matter of religion, or perhaps merely demanded a profession of some sort of Christianity. Basically, what all of them professed to be trying to do was to relieve the human race of paying tribute to those who had no moral call on their pocketbooks, those they considered the useless and parasitical, the nonproducing, who were usually listed as the middleman, the stock-market speculator, and the capitalist of whatever kind. Naturally, each leader drew people who, for whatever reason, were in agreement with him, and the reasons ranged from sheer laziness and opportunism, to hope for betterment of personal misery, to burning conviction.

Other communes were religiously based. Some of the leaders had received revelations that they were deities. Others, on similarly excellent authority, were not exactly deities, but were recipients of divine gifts rather above the humdrum. Immortality in the flesh was perhaps the most popular of these gifts, particularly since the prophet was usually empowered to confer similar immortality upon those believing in him. That sort of thing has led to the impulse to classify the spiritual prophets out of hand as quack-religious.

But the whole history of religion, from the most ancient times, is soaked with the blood of those who could not agree on a definition of terms, and what is one man's quackery has often been another man's salvation. Was Shakerism quackery because Ann Lee was "the female member of the Godhead" and because she disliked romping in bed? She was bitterly hated in her day on both counts, true, and her aversion to sex perhaps made celibacy easy for her though she made a great virtue of such abstemiousness; but she led a hard life for the sake of the simple religion, however noisy it may have been, which she followed as rigorously as she required her unread people to do.

On the other hand, King Benjamin Purnell of the House of David, and Koresh who had us living inside the earth, and Thomas Lake Harris who became God and grew very rich enforced celibacy upon their followers while secretly evincing perhaps more than a mere platonic interest in the comelier female disciples. At best, one must judge that they but imperfectly understood the revelations on which they based all their dictums and actions. Certainly, while crying hypocrisy, one must remember that the actions of a paranoid always appear perfectly reasonable to him in his ideas of the special grandeur heaven has bestowed upon him. All in all, quackpot, rather than quack, often seems the fairer term.

The religious prophets drew mostly the great unwashed to them, but sometimes they attracted the educated, the accomplished, and the moneyed, to the hideous embarrassment and anger of the relatives. Harris—"The Primate of the Earth," before he was deified—was especially good at that. He reduced his followers, in their loving submission to him, not only mentally but physically to the status of serfs— and like other prophets, he held all the property of the communal enterprise in his own name.

But some of the religious communes were reasonably democratic—as, for instance, Oneida—and the leaders of other theocracies, as in the case of Ann Lee or "Father" Rapp or Dr. Keil, were little or no better off than the led. John Noyes, of Oneida, for instance, gave himself few privileges not accorded the laity, and then only—as in connection with the commune's stirpiculture project—because of his superior spirituality.

The real power of all these leaders came not merely from an ability to scare the daylights out of some who chanced to hear their discourses, but from a responding of the spirit which excited a deep love, spiritual or otherwise, in the prospective disciple for the prophet and a consequent desire to be submissive to him. This is seen repeatedly, all through the religious branch of communalism.

Religious or secular, the prophets had the basic idea of providing for the pooling of labor and goods and of living from a common supply. But just there the resemblance was likely to dwindle sharply among the innumerable starry-eyed versions of the communal scheme, each of which guaranteed its devotees salvation here or hereafter or both. Messiahs of every imaginable persuasion, religious, economic, or philosophic, cried in the wilderness in the tradition of messiahs since the first confidant or manipulator of the Unseen put on his buffalo skull and rattled the keys to his conception of the Kingdom.

As it has ever been with the prophets, these latter-day

ones were sometimes ignored, sometimes revered, sometimes scourged and scorned as the snake-oil men of religion,
economics, and humanitarianism. Some observers saw the attempts to raise humanity to a world-wide brotherhood of
share-the-wealth communes as but the tail of the great
dragon of change which was crushing Europe with religious
and non-religious wars and with the social and economic upheavals of the Industrial Revolution—all of which, day
unto day, were pouring hordes of the bruised and hungry
into America at every port.

The communitarians, with a larger and larger sense
of their own importance as public interest increased, were
inclined, then, to feel that the tail was wagging the dragon,
for they firmly believed themselves at the head of an inescapable world-wide change. Scorners said that the whole
thing was more nearly but the scaly appendage of that old
serpent called Satan who was tramping to and fro, seeking
out whom he might devour with schemes of communal
money juggling, sharing of wives, and amalgamation of the
races—all obviously wrong, else God would have created
everyone rich, of the same color, and equipped with a suitable stable of mates.

And what was it that ailed this world which the
prophets yearned to save? In general, it was sin—but the religious prophets worried about those sins which might damage the souls of their prospective converts, while the secular
leaders condemned those of society which put men, women,
and children in sweatshop and factory for fourteen hours or
more a day, with hunger and the debtor's prison—and
bonded servitude for whites as well as blacks—casting long
shadows over all.

The secular prophet declared that in his commune
men would be prosperous on two or three hours labor a day
since there would be no employer, landlord, middleman,
banker, or speculator to live in luxury while the worker
shivered in a black hut with a crust or, quite likely, without

one. The workers in fact would have money and leisure for culture and travel.

But it was not economic misery, as such, which made people respond to the religious prophets, at least at first. For it was primarily salvation—usually from the wrath of God in the immediate end of the world—that these leaders vended; plus, unconsciously, the opportunity to belong to a mutual-admiration society.

Accordingly, it was to the spiritually and socially inept that they most greatly appealed, for both their verse and chorus were on millennialism and it is to the psychologically oppressed, the bitterly vengeful who want the sinful to get their comeuppance, the socially unaccepted that the millenary cry proves the siren song. Those in comfortable slots are ordinarily able to convince themselves that the good machine will run itself for their time. Nevertheless, the naive, the ignorant, and the emotionally immature of all classes are susceptible to any logic if it be repeated often enough, and "Millennium Now!" inroads were made into all cultural groups.

Probably in every generation for 1800 years, scholar, theologian, or solemn rustic had proclaimed the immediate end. And as had been particularly true in England and Central Europe for several centuries, droves of sturdy prognosticators, some of whom could read and write, prowled the countryside. They were blessed with multitudes of humorless, literal-minded people to work among.

Not only were these self-anointed prophets unable to obtain hearings without the millenary doctrine, just as a tonic would not sell in the South unless swamp fever be included in the list of doomed diseases on the label, it was their own chiefest theological interest. Preachers are naturally subject to the same pressures as the laymen of their cultural strata, and, as will abundantly appear—sometimes in a sadly amusing way, as in the case of Prophet William Miller—they were progressively alarmed by their own cries of the end. But sometimes the alarm seemed to become a bit mechani-

cal. One sounder of the tocsin in the current century long
published a monthly paper, *The Final Warning*, with the
finality renewed each thirty days.

Generally, each Second Comer was certain that all the
wicked—that is, all people not of his sect—would be destroyed, with the earth left to "the righteous," or that the
righteous would be caught up into heaven, or that a comparable combination of millennial catastrophe and joy
would occur. Signs and portents of the end were seen in
floods, drouths, bank panics, bloody moons, wars, and rumors of wars. Comets, as they had been for centuries past,
were esteemed as particularly excellent millenary omens:
most probably they were the Star of Bethlehem returning to
announce the Second Coming much as it had announced the
First.

People believed, and abundant proof for their stand
might be found in the Bible, but if more was desired a new
prophet would be along in a few moments with the ultimate
pronouncement. Many a man was certain that to himself
had been revealed the unknowable day and hour. Others
were certain only that it was likely to be before morning and
that people should prepare for it while they might—specifically by subscribing to the beliefs of the revelator in question and making a suitable contribution to help carry salvation farther just in case tomorrow by some miracle should arrive. These people were earnest and self-sacrificing in their
efforts in many cases, and none more so than Prophet
Miller and Mother Lee whose missionaries terrified thousands from New England to Ohio and Kentucky and led
them into congregations, and, particularly in the case of
Ann Lee's Shakers, into communes.

As had happened with small sects during the terrible
post-Reformation religous wars in Europe, the converts drew
together into tight communities, or fled to far wildernesses,
to escape the blows or mockery of the world and to preserve
their creed. Sometimes they had the plan of living communally. In other cases, it was merely natural that they

should in such circumstances work and share together. Remarkably enough, in some of the sects which adopted the
communal tenet by accident, as it were, it became of basic
importance and was clung to as necessary for salvation after
some of the original precepts, perhaps those over which blood
had been spilled, had been quietly forgotten.

But a fair question is, why did men choose to flee into
communes to save the world, rather than to stay in the world
and slug out the issues on the world's ancient no-quarter
terms? As to the leaders, some did fight for years in legislative lobbies, before being driven by frustration to a secluded
village where, they were certain, they would be vindicated,
approved, and given adulation by their disciples. And in the
process they would show the world the way to happiness.

The difficulty often was that they were not men of vi
sion, but of visions, blind to the most elemental needs for
the success of a commune. They have been called escapists,
in flight from the hurly-burly of the world, and this probably
was true of some of the leaders. But others—like the Owens,
and Cabet of Icaria—asked only that they be allowed to step
aside for a few moments to organize their pilot communes,
after which they would be glad to carry the world along with
them to prosperity. To them, their escapism was only of the
mind, yet it amounted to a flight from reality. But then, have
not all the world's advances been made in flights from reality, by men who were unaware that they were doing the impossible?

As for the followers, they were in good part of another kettle of fish. In the Dark Ages, the general attitude
toward monks and nuns was the ribald one celebrated by
Boccaccio, although, no doubt, many sincere people did retire to pray for the sins of the world. How much of this was
from a deeper desire to escape family responsibility or the
horrors of war, famine, and pestilence, no one can say. By
the same token, some dedicated religionists and philosophers
must have entered the communal villages for noble reasons.
Others, just as certainly, wanted somebody to tell them what

to do, to serve as brain and conscience and guardian. Some were simply gregarious and without much to do, and they fell in with a persuasive prophet at the right moment.

Others obviously thought themselves shrewd in getting into an organization which promised to make them comfortable, secure for life with little labor. These included the drifters, the fiddle-footed opportunists who had nothing to lose and who were so eager to share the wealth—just anybody's—that they became professional joiners, drifting to a new colony as soon as the current one collapsed. The highly successful Shakers had a name for these gentry—Winter Shakers. They were likely to appear in the score of Shaker villages in the fall with pious mouthings, sit by the fire all winter, and backslide in the spring when the heavy work began.

Religious or secular, the first necessity of a prophet was for disciples to bow down and hang upon his wisdom. Preferable, of course, were those with means for getting the Utopia started. If one possessed a farm, God was not unlikely to designate it as the chosen spot for the New Zion. Then there would be room for the worthy poor who might praise the prophet's name—and delve and spin and hew and plow.

The foundings follow that general pattern, with, usually, an ensuing nip and tuck struggle for survival. And there must have been many a sinking of heart, while everyone presented a cheerful countenance to his fellows, as calamity and ruin ever grinned at their heels. This is inversely reflected, one almost feels, in the elaborate claptrap of codes and constitutions which they drew up, like gaudy uniforms to cover the ragged shirts and the poverty of flesh beneath. The more of these codes a colony possessed—and some drew them up afresh every week to take care of fresh ideas and dissensions—the more certain the whole thing was shortly to tumble into the dust.

When survival came, it was invariably because of a

religious creed which commanded hard work and abstemious ways; or because of a secular creed, as among the Icarians to whom communism was a religion, which involved the whole personality so that men were willing to suffer persecution, ridicule, and hunger. In chariots drawn by dragons, the dedicated could not turn back. They had to save themselves and the world. But hordes, only pixy-led, faltered and soon vanished.

Even as the foundings and the survivals followed patterns, so did the failures. Lack of money was often given as a cause of disaster. But a great sufficiency of money, at the start, was no assurance of success, while communes beginning on a hand-to-mouth basis often did survive.

But, oddly, the most notably successful communes carried the seeds of eventual death and dissolution in their most basic tenets, as by some mad, cosmic logic of the gods. For instance, the prophets, religious or secular, had a penchant for meddling with marriage or the family organization. Some confused sex with religion, or discomfort with sanctity, or license with duty. Some saw celibacy as the highest good. Others wondered if selfishness in general was not the blight of man. Then let there be the limit of unselfishness: If you would borrow the daughter of one of the brethren, let him lend you his wife also. This sort of thing caused a great deal of commotion both among the membership of such communes and the reading public who avidly consumed the news stories on nests of free lovers and in pious horror heard the sermons preached against them.

Some leaders thought a middle ground the best solution to the vexing inclination of men and women toward each other. That is, it were obviously better that children be produced somewhat in the manner of potatoes; but since there were certain obstacles to that, it seemed the clear will of God that the elect take just enough of the devil's broth to prevent extinction of the chosen, as among the German Zoarites in Ohio—and even less of it might be taken, it occurred to some of the sterner groups, if the elders selected the mates for the young ones. This made the young most unhappy—a circumstance which was noted, too, among the free lovers and among the complexly married Oneidans when the elders selected the pairings whether for "social" or "propagative" cohabitation.

Villages which survived into the second generation were likely to founder from lack of strong new leadership, or from the weariness and exasperation of the young who had not gone through the white fire of conversion as had their parents. The youngsters disliked the queer garments often prescribed, or doing without the pleasures of the encroaching world; of having all their sittings down and risings up, their choice of work, their matings or prohibition of all mating, at the beck of elders, though assured daily that the authority of these was from God.

Celibacy destroyed some highly prosperous communes, both because of the failure of the members to reproduce and through an increasing inability, with the passage of time, to attract outside recruits. The country had undergone a gradual change in religious outlook and experienced an increase of general sophistication.

So perished the Shakers and the Rappites who once were worth scores of millions. Others, as the Zoarites, also a million-dollar group, and the Modern Timers, were finished by inability to compete with worldly manufacturers, and the Amanists of Iowa very nearly followed—for the world intruded, inevitably, upon those who did business with it, and those who failed to advance in business methods were simply pushed out of the market.

Further, as working conditions in the world improved, people were not so eager as once they had been to surrender their freedom into the hands of prophets, elders, and committees in exchange for a full belly, a warm back, and perhaps the assurance of heaven. And it should be noted that some of those improvements in industry and in social legislation had been brought about by agitations early participated in by such communitarian leaders as the Owens,

Frances Wright, and Frederick Evans who was long chief elder of the Shakers.

Despite the failures, in a century's time a hundred thirty or more villages, housing a hundred thousand people from first to last, endured long enough to get into the record. In the 1840's, when more than forty Fourieristic "phalanxes" were established in which each person was to do just the kind of work he liked best, "Association" created so much heat from cracker barrel to Congress that it became a national issue.

Brisbane, the prophet of Fourierism—although he abjured certain points, such as free love, of the master's philosophy—claimed two hundred thousand disciples. Many were joined into clubs which hoped in time to establish themselves in communitarian villages. But money was necessary for the purpose, and money was scarce since the terrible drouth, cold, and financial depression of the late 30's. Indeed, the hardship of those years may well have led to the great interest in Fourierism after a dozen years of disillusion in lay communalism following the debacle of the New Harmony experiment. The forty villages withered away and at last in bitterness Brisbane disowned all connection with them as being only pseudo-Fourieristic. Like Brisbane, other leaders at times claimed wide national followings.

Besides the recorded villages, no one may reckon the scores of communes which must have bloomed in isolation and died unsung with the first frost, in poverty of goods or spirit. For instance, in 1870, one just begun had "at present" two men and three women. It is not heard of again. *Frank Leslie's Illustrated Newspaper* for December 12, 1857, remarks that "The Free Love Society near Sandusky, Ohio, has been broken up." What free love society? Broken up by whom? Why? The answers must have been important to someone but no record seems to have been left.

There were indeed as many reasons given for community failures as there were participants and armchair analyzers. But one overriding failure was that of the leaders to understand that the world is too vast a place to be taken apart and reassembled to the taste of any man, and another was their failure to understand human nature. They showed this most blatantly in merely indicating that they did understand it and were only about to change it.

ii

Where did it all really start? Often the bloodbaths following the Lutheran Reformation are seen as the beginning of the movement—but men had cried for a sharing of the wealth just as they had killed each other for the love of God and just as they had tried reformations long before Luther blundered into the combination of historical circumstance which, with his particular appeals, made his rebellion the unexpectedly big one.

The dream of Utopia is found in all cultures in visions of happy hunting grounds, of the heavens of desert peoples who equip these abodes with trees and cool waters, or with such refinements as trains of sloe-eyed houris. The Eskimo places his in the warm earth while his hell—the anti-Utopia —is in the cold sky. The Garden of Eden is a Utopia of the past, of the golden age of innocence, and the Millennial Age of the Second Coming is one yet to appear.

Plato envisioned his Republic for this earth with slaves to comfort the upper classes. A "royal lie," endlessly repeated, would control the minds of citizens from childhood onward. There would be state love festivals for the controlled propagation of at least the better strains of people, and with no foolishness of falling in love.

But later, if medieval man had any dreams of Utopia on earth, he were wise to keep them to himself. Christian civilization with its learning, its science, its arts, had been crushed by successive inroads of barbarians who were scarcely restrained by the papal dictums which somewhat held down the slaughter of Christians by each other. The final crushing of Rome in the fifth century marked the beginning of the Dark Ages which are so called because of the black mental stagnation of particularly the first half of the thousand years.

Men were busy trying to keep alive—but part of the stagnation came from the destruction of libraries and other evidences and sources of civilization so that such scholars as there might have been more or less had to start from scratch. Too, the Church pretty much quashed the arts and forbade the literature of the classical ages for the most part. Scientists proved points—which simple observation would have disproved—by "Aristotle saith." Money had pretty much disappeared so that alchemy flourished in its search for gold. Philosophers sought not for the cause but for the purpose of things—*e.g.*, the sun was there to warm the earth, and eclipses were to show the power of God and to warn of His awfulness. Free inquiry was likely to end in heresy.

The official philosophy of the age, as it advanced, was that European society was a perfected one, with pope and priests as "the head of the body," king and nobles as "the warring arms," and the serf as the toiling feet on which the whole dead weight complacently rested. Nor may the monasteries of the day be considered the beginnings of communalism, as America was to know it, for while the inmates of the cloisters did eat from a common store and obey a superior, they rested upon the slavery of the serfs who moiled in the broad abbey lands. The status quo of these serfs, and of other classes, was promoted by the preachment that each man was in a niche especially selected for him by God. Hence, it were deep-dyed sin for him to peep over the rim of his private hell at the joys of his betters, much less long to escape it. Besides, had Jehovah not commanded that he not covet?

But finally in the ninth and tenth centuries, hordes of barbarians who had continued to terrorize great populations settled in provinces they had seized—as the Norsemen in England and France and the Magyars in Hungary—and adopted Christianity. The faith was also taken into Poland and Russia, and with the Moors reasonably quiescent in Spain after their threat to seize all Christendom, a general peace settled upon Europe so that an often-crushed commerce and a recovery of learning might begin.

Thus men began forgetting they lived in a perfected society, and Europe was ready to be completely revolutionized in a series of interrelated events sparked by the Crusades. Hordes of simple, pious people had the pious thought that they could wrench the Sepulcher from their cultural superiors, the Saracens, and the illiterate lords of Europe, excited by the luxuries brought out of the Saracen lands by traders, raised murderous armies which sallied forth for the purpose, brutally robbing and being robbed on the way, and now and again allying with the enemy in the Holy Land against each other in order to gain the dukedoms and kingdoms which individuals hoped for there.

In their preparations, however, to make the journey, large amounts of money were needed, and the Church shamefully permitted men to make all sorts of bargains, without the permission of their feudal lords, to raise that money, and it further permitted existing contracts to be broken that men might head for the Holy Land. Money lending had fallen to the Jews because excommunication— a living death, with all mouths and doors closed to the culprit—was the penalty for a Christian's charging interest to a Christian.

However, it developed that churchmen everywhere had whole trunkfuls of corroding groats and silver pennies and gold pieces, garnered up through their excellent fiscal systems, and following the example of the papacy they opened these to the Crusaders. Not that they charged interest—but there were little matters of twenty to forty per cent of the principal for the trouble of drawing up the papers on which the lord made his mark. Lands were taken in hock on similar polite fictions, and as Christian bones whitened Eastern deserts, the Church lands broadened—

in England, for instance, to hold perhaps a sixth of the realm, with more to be added.

Of enormous importance was the freeing of vassal towns in return for heavy sums. This gave rise to a free middle class of people owing allegiance directly to the crown. Loot pouring in from the Holy Land, plus peace and general trade, spurred the economy and lords encouraged even their serfs to pay feudal dues in cash rather than labor. England's greatness was based on wool—as the wool-sack of the Lord Chancellor still testifies—and to produce this wool for the looms of the Continent, lords fenced in farming and grazing lands used by their serfs for centuries, and many of these demoralized creatures were crowded off the manors to squat on whatever bit of land someone would permit at murderous rental. Those with skills fled to the towns and offered their labor in such quantity as to break the stranglehold of the trade guilds.

Gunpowder was blowing the gaudy, brutal, unchivalrous age of chivalry out of existence. Subterfuge on the charging of interest was dropped and international banking developed. Rich middle-class merchants and money men built palaces and fought their way up into the brilliant new culture by patronizing artists and putting their sons to tutors and sword masters and their daughters to dreary hours at the lute, like so many duchesses—and smoldering, displaced barons, held at bay by the middle-class armies of the kings, swallowed their pride and married bourgeois millions.

So bubbled the medieval stew, with now and then a rumbling, deadly plop in the middle. Hungry priests in England ministered to hungry peasants. Agitators preached sharing and rebellion and the constant saw of the levelers was

> *When Adam delved and Eve span*
> *Who was then the gentleman?*

After the Black Death of the 1300's, the Crown froze the wages of peasants and free laborers so that for years they sank into increasingly greater misery while all else advanced. Wycliffe agitated not only for Church reform—extermination, for instance, of those creatures so savagely represented by Chaucer's Pardoner—but for nationalization of land for the benefit of the poor. However, he would have no part of rebellions and he held aloof from the atrocities of peasant riotings. The culmination was the march on London where the peasants were pacified and sent home with fine promises—and there, scattered, were fallen upon by lord and abbot in grisly retribution. Like the peasants in the bloodier uprisings in France, they had gained nothing.

Wycliffe had to flee to the Continent to save his life, but many of the poor priests—eager for the Bible he had promised which they, as well as the plowboy, might read—remained to champion his "Lollard" movement and were burned for their pains. Lollardism, with its other priests who scarcely understood the Latin they parroted, went underground, but it was not extinguished.

In 1415 the fire Wycliffe had lit had spread across Europe to flame in Johannes Hus and to kindle the faggots around him. A century afterward, the stench of his martyred flesh was still strong in the nostrils of a hundred thousand Hussites on the borders of Germany when Luther threw his ink bottle at the devil.

Luther was saved from burning largely by the greed of the German princes who sensed a broad desire for change in their lands and who saw opportunity to stop the flow of money to Rome and to confiscate abbeys and lands and ecclesiastical palaces if they repudiated the authority of Rome. That is, these were the lay princes. Many others of the three hundred were also churchmen and they wanted no part of Luther, unless it be his head.

Yet, no sooner was Luther victorious—and unexpectedly at the head of a new church rather than a mere reformation—than he began losing great segments of people who had been eager to join him. But he was completely unable

to compromise on the theological differences between twee-
dledee and tweedledum, or to have truck with those who
differed from him in any particular. He lost the Humanists
of the New Learning. He lost the Hussites—but then he
loathed Bohemians, anyway, on principle, as became a good
German. He lost scores of intellectual and theological cults
whose names are now meaningless. Perhaps most importantly, he lost the eager mass of the German peasantry who
at first supposed Luther might be the reincarnated Frederick
Barbarossa whom they long had expected in a second coming
to lead them out of bondage.

The German peasants had of course been aware of
the Hussite upheaval. There were numerous saint cults and
mystical sects among them, even while they remained Catholic. Men among them were in direct communication with
heaven—men like Hans Bohm who before the turn of the
century had wandered about tootling up crowds on the
dudelsack, whereupon he would strip, sit in running water,
and tell of receiving messages from the Virgin that the end
of the world was at hand. The Holy Office had been remarkably lenient with such people, but in their exasperation
they finally had to have him burned.

But Luther would not be Barbarossa. Indeed, he told
the petitioning peasants that they had no right to appeal to
"natural right" in their demands for more tolerable conditions. Rather, he said, as Christians they must expect injustices until reform be brought about through the piety of
the masters.

In the bloody Peasants War which followed, leadership was seized by the Anabaptist Thomas Munzer whose
sect practiced some communal sharing and sexual irregular-
ities. Under him atrocities flamed across a third of the
Germanies. Castles were burned and scores of rich religious
houses, expropriated by the princes, destroyed. Luther
feared the upper classes would be wiped out. He cried for
the princes to "stab, crush, and strangle," promising heaven
to any who might die in the salutary work. They stabbed

and strangled with a will. In the end, the maimed and gasp-
ing remnant of the peasantry was driven back to its old
dunghills, worse off than before.

Now, repudiating both Catholicism and Lutheran-
ism entirely, the peasants turned increasingly to the mystical
cults. Some became antinomian—that is, above the law,
meaning the law of the Bible which most regarded as the
only spiritual authority. The Antinomians, saying they were
in a state of grace, held that they could not commit sin
and needed no law. This usually led to scandalous and dis-
ruptive excesses. And perhaps to a man, the mystics were
Anabaptists. That is, they demanded adult baptism, and
thus required that those baptized as babies be baptized
again, which is the exact meaning of Anabaptist. This was
anathema, a capital offense to both the established churches,
for it mocked their power to give valid baptism.

By the time of the Thirty Years' War, the peasants had
lost the fury of those of Luther's day. Taking a literal view
of the command not to kill, they had usually added pacifism
to their tenets, and they had been through long persecution because of their refusal to give military service. Then
most of Europe came in to fight on German soil, always
with the impeccable excuse of proving who loved God the
more and the consequent ritual by which this were best
shown. The peasant sects were regarded as fair game by
both sides. Men killed those who would not defend themselves. They were filled with wonder and ribald amusement
to see men stand by in anguished prayer while their wives
and daughters, sometimes mere children, were raped by
platoons of soldiery. Principalities were reduced to grave-
yards. Württemberg, for instance, fell from four hundred
thousand to fifty thousand people. Land went back to nature
while the driven mystics fled hither and yonder before the
storm, eating grass and corpses and praying for Jesus to
come on and confound their foes.

This millennial expectation undoubtedly made the

sufferings more bearable. Naturally the brethren drew together for the comfort of numbers, for the stronger to help the weaker and for the keeping up of religious practices, and quite naturally there was common effort in labor when some brief refuge was found and common sharing when provisions materialized. And as naturally, comfort was taken that the band was emulating the congregation at Jerusalem, as told of in the Book of Acts, in which the people sold their property and shared the proceeds equally, no man calling anything he owned his own.

Some of these groups escaped to other countries, and indeed a few, including antinomian groups, performed the almost impossible feat of escaping to America where their communalism made a solid foundation for the beginnings of the movement here.

Meanwhile, nonreligious Utopianism was astir in England. In the early 1500's, probably well aware of Wycliffe's levelling agitations of more than a century before, Sir Thomas More wrote a follow-up to Plato's *Republic*— his *Utopia,* which was to supply the generic name for the scores of such never-never-land books, including the inevitable and usually boring spoofs, and for the communitarian movement itself.

But *Utopia* was not the book it appeared to be. It was really a plea for the alleviation of the brutalized condition of the English laborer and peasant—a plea which More dared not thrust in plain verbiage into the teeth of the Bluff King Hal who was busy disposing of the early echelons of the seventy thousand Englishmen, some of them criminals of nine and ten, whom he was to hang during his reign. Indeed, as if to avoid affront to Henry by distribution of the book among the masses, More published it in Latin.

It is concerned with the views of a seaman who is amazed at England, as compared with the mythical Utopia —"Nowhere."

In Utopia, it seems, men were not brutally executed for mild "crimes." Rather, they were given work so that they might avoid those crimes. Nor in Utopia were there hordes of nonproducing lords and gentlemen—men who in England "not only live in idleness themselves, but also carry about with them at their tails a great flock or train of idle and loitering serving men, which never learned any craft whereby to get their livings. These men, as soon as their master is dead, or be sick themselves, be incontinent thrust out of doors."

Nor in Utopia have sheep taken the place of men, while in England "They consume, destroy, and devour whole fields, houses, cities. For look in what parts of the realm doth grow the finest and therefore the dearest woole, there noblemen and gentlemen, yea and certain abbots, holy men no doubt, not contenting themselves with the yearly revenues and profits, that were wont to grow to their fore-fathers and predecessors of their land, nor being content that they live in rest and pleasure nothing profiting, yea much annoying the weal public, leave no ground for tillage, they inclose all into pastures; they throw down houses; they pluck down towns, and leave nothing standing, but only the church to be made a sheep house. And as though you lost no small quantity of ground by forests, chases, lawns and parks, those good holy men turned all dwelling-houses and all glebeland into desolation and wilderness. Therefore that one covetous and insatiable cormorant and very plague of his native country may compass about and inclose many thousands acres of ground together within one pale or hedge."

In Utopia, everyone had a craft, lived simply, and shared in common with his fellows. Marriages were eugen-ically arranged. All religions, from moon worship to Chris-tianity, were tolerated.

Henry VIII, of course, whacked off Sir Thomas's head, but not because of the book. His answer to it was to permit the lucky recipients of the confiscated Church lands to enclose further for the raising of sheep, and to pass poor laws, chief provisions of which were that paupers must starve quietly and decently in their home parishes and be whipped back to them at a cart's tail if caught trying to abscond to a more prosperous area.

Elizabeth strengthened those laws, helping breed up the atmosphere which made it possible for Cromwell to behead the divine-right Charles I in 1649. Cromwell, the successful revolutionist, took a chary view of other upsetters of the peace, such as peasant groups demanding division of the national wealth; "Fifth Monarchy Men" carrying religious banners and demanding that Buckingham Palace be turned over to them as a residence for "King Jesus" whom they expected to arrive at any moment; and "Diggers" and "True Levelers" demanding abolition of social classes and seditiously plowing up public lands and planting them in advocacy of redistribution of the soil. There were antinomians. There were Ranters who disturbed church services. There were sects who joined the Fifth Monarchy Men in demanding that Cromwell establish a government based on the books of Revelation and Daniel. There were the Seekers who formed the "Family of Love," and there were the Quakers who hailed Jacob Naylor as the Christ at Bristol in 1656. Cromwell squelched them all, with blood if necessary.

Too, the classic "state of nature" philosophy, picturing a golden age in which all men lived as brothers, was polished off as having existed in England until the Normans arrived. Now, said the petitioners, the descendants of the Normans held all the land, and it was demanded that these be driven out and everything given back "to the people" in common. Other proposals would have enfranchised the propertyless—and all of them got exactly as far as might have been anticipated since it was the sons of the Normans who acted on the petitions.

Indeed, the landholders declared that "the natural and best base for a strong and prosperous nation is an ignorant, well-disciplined laboring class," and the lower orders were assured by the Anglican hierarchy that those orders had been established by God for good reasons. The Round-heads agreed, echoing Bishop Latimer who had added that God had not intended that men should own things in common since, if they did, they could not steal, the property already being theirs; and accordingly the commandment bearing on that would not have been handed down. This excellent logic was everywhere applauded except perhaps by the poor.

Hobbes and Locke took the old Sophist "social compact" philosophy in working out a justification for private property and social classes. Anciently, in the "state of nature," Hobbes said, men lived communally, with each seizing what he could by strength or cunning from the common supply. Life was "solitary, poor, nasty, brutish, and short." Then, to better things, men contracted with strong leaders who would create order and safety, in return for which obedience and labor would be given. Locke said that on the contrary there must have been private property during the "state of nature," but with little means for its protection by weak and ordinary people. Accordingly, they made the social contract.

In any case, it seems that this contract was so sacred it might not be broken, regardless of the rise of tyranny. For more than a century, this "contract" philosophy was important. The noble savage in America was used constantly as an example of the golden, natural state of man in the early stages of the contract, despite the fact that he was on every hand at the throats of his fellow noble savages when he wasn't lying in the shade smoking and scratching while his women got the crop in.

In time, Rousseau adapted the philosophy to fire up the French masses for their revolution. In his view, government was originally by the consent of the governed and must ever be by that same consent. Unfortunately, when the bumbling Bourbons had been disposed of, the people had nothing they had fought for. They had merely found a new set of masters.

Meanwhile, the Industrial Revolution had begun in England some thirty years before, just as His Majesty George, the Third of the drones from the Hanover hive, took the throne. It was made possible by the discovery of how to make iron with coal instead of wood, and just in time to save the last of England's trees; by inventions for the textile industry; and by improvements on the steam engine. Hungry people poured into the mill towns from the fresh inclosures that were to feed the new spindles and looms, and all the horrors of the slums were soon manifest in these places. Constant improvements in the machines put men out of work faster than the swelling economy might reabsorb them. Children could do nearly half the work and women much of the rest. Hence, children, many of them rented from orphanages and workhouses, often had jobs while adults were idle. Fourteen hours was the standard day.

All this led to rioting and destruction of machines, and that to the retaliation of owners and the king's troops. As laws harshened, the death penalty was inflicted for destroying machinery. Slow starvation seemed to be the penalty for operating it. But some of the mill hands did escape to America by selling themselves into terms of bondage here —usually seven years—in return for passage.

Others were thinking of coming here, too—philosophers, both French and English. Before 1800, disillusioned by the development of the French Revolution toward which many Englishmen were sympathetic, men were drawing up plans for communes in America where it was declared that anything was possible—and where, certainly, some religious communes were already operating successfully. For suddenly it had become possible, the new philosophy said, to have overnight what the people of Europe had struggled uselessly for more than five centuries to obtain—social and economic revolution. And it was possible to have it without

war, which was a good thing in view of the fact that there
was no help either from war or legislation. In communal
villages, men would have their private, personal revolutions.

Such, then, was the atmosphere in which communalism was wafted to America. The atmosphere which made it
possible for an Alcott not to be condemned for dragging his
"Little Women" to a run-down farm and starving them in
the name of saving humanity. Or for John Noyes, the ex-
ponent of complex marriage, to win attention with his "Essay
on Scientific Propagation" in which he asked, "Who can say
how much the present race of men in Connecticut owe to the
numberless adulteries and fornications of Pierrepont Edwards?" And, he observed, "Corrupt as he was, he must have
distributed a good deal of the blood of his noble father,
Jonathan Edwards."

The atmosphere which made it seem logical to thousands that they sell or give away their property and prepare
to "go up" from a burning world on a certain night—and,
after that did not work out, on another certain one. And
for Peter Armstrong to drag his family back into some of the
roughest country in Pennsylvania and labor for years to
prepare a place to which the 144,000 to-be-saved-of-Revela-
tion might flee for refuge. Or for "the Invisible Presence" to
beget children by the numerous virgins—apparently honor-
ary and otherwise—in his colony in backwoods Illinois. Or so
legend has it.

But all these and most other prophets, bizarre or
workaday, ended in disillusionment. Horace Greeley, who
was neck-deep in the fevers of Fourierism, but never entirely over his head, explained, sheepishly but cogently, and
perhaps better than any of the others, what the trouble was:

Along with many noble and lofty souls, whose impulses are purely philanthropic, and who are willing to
labor and suffer reproach for any cause that promises to
benefit mankind, there throng scores of whom the world

is quite worthy—the conceited, the unappreciated, the played-out, the idle, and the good-for-nothing generally; who, finding themselves utterly out of place and at a discount in the world as it is, rashly conclude that they are exactly fitted for the world as it ought to be.

The communal impulse is not yet entirely dead but its heyday was last century when the names of Shadrach Ireland and Bronson Alcott, of John Noyes and Jemima Wilkinson and Fourier and his fellow Frenchman, Cabet, and all their kind were heard in the land. They left a fascinating record in living, in searching, and often, as they were certain, in finding.

By a poisonous fleshly nature
This dark world has long been led;
There can be no passion greater—
This must be the serpent's head:
On our coast he would be cruising,
If by truth he were not bound:
But his head has had a bruising,
And he's got a deadly wound.

And his wounds can not be healed,
Light and truth do now forbid,
Since the Gospel hast revealed
Where his filthy head was hid:
With a fig-leaf it was cover'd
Till we brought his deeds to light;
By his works he is discover'd,
And his head is plain in sight.

—Shaker hymn in celebration of celibacy

CHAPTER TWO

SHADRACH, MOTHER ANN, AND THE CONTENTED OF THE GOD-LOVING SOUL

THE WOMAN IN THE WILDERNESS HAD TWO WINGS

THE work-and-share arrangements of such groups as the Jamestown and Plymouth people were not intentionally Utopian (though the people no doubt looked upon America as a sort of Utopia) and certainly were not part of the communitarian movement. They were merely expeditious and were dropped as soon as ever they might be. Indeed, the Puritans here brought from England a cold disapproval of all attempts of the lower elements to level wealth and society.

But oddly, the first intentionally Utopian project in America—an extremely ambitious if not entirely communal one—was that of a Puritan missionary to the Massachusetts Indian, one John Eliot. A dedicated man, Eliot had already translated various pious works into Algonquin, which

31

indeed the tribesmen might have read as well as any other language, when, in the 1650's, it occurred to him that his Indian friends did not have what he felt to be a proper form of government.

In fact, he could think of no government anywhere which exactly suited him. He hoped to remedy that for all Christendom by establishing "Christian commonwealths." And it seemed fitting that his pilot system should give its blessings to his aboriginal charges, for the Bible, with its minutiae of rules for daily conduct in the Levitical code, was to be the Magna Charta; and, further, in Eliot's bright lexicon of ethnography, the Indians were descendants of the lost Israelite tribes which had first benefited from those divinely appointed rules. Therefore, the Indians should be the first to rebenefit from them. Eliot, of course, was not alone in the Indian-origin theory. It still attracts people and is indeed an article of faith in the several branches of the Mormon church.

In Eliot's commonwealth, the people would be in subjection to the most godly men who would read and meditate upon the Bible "all the daise of their life." Nor would any pestiferous Quakers nor anyone of "the dirty Romish religion" be tolerated. Eliot expounded all this in a volume which he circulated in England along with the suggestion that the Protectorate be ended and Christ, "the only right heir to the Crown," be made king.

All this somehow less than pleased the insurgent Charles II who was just then coming to the throne of his murdered father, and, moreover, coming by divine right as God's earthly representative who could do no wrong. The book was promptly declared heretical and was banned, since it in effect denied the sacredness of the prerogative of the fun-loving Stuart-Bourbon-Medici Charles to milk the tight little island of a super-royal living. Further, in Massachusetts, all who might "have any of the said Bookes in their Custody shall on theire perrills within fowerteene dayes" destroy or deliver them up to the magistrates.

So perished the Christian Commonwealth.

In 1663, just two years after that book-burning, there did arrive a bona fide group of Dutch Mennonite communitarians under Peter Cornelius, or Pieter Corneliszoon Plockhoy, as the English called him, to settle near New Amsterdam. Plockhoy had long been a social theorist and had concluded that governments might make the poor happy by gathering them into small communal groups. He never really had opportunity to find out if his ideas would work: The invading English who took New Amsterdam coolly reported that they had despoiled "the Quaking Society of Plockhoy to a very naile."

Shortly after that, Germans fleeing the bitter situation at home began arriving. Most notably they were attracted to Pennsylvania by the religious toleration and the medieval outlook, government-wise, of the Quakers, which at the same time permitted ultra-modern and coolly-calculated business methods.

Business, however, was the least of the interests of some of these communities. Indeed, they are best remembered now for the names they gave their communes, as, "The Society of Irenia or the True Church of Philadelphia or Brotherly Love, or Brethren in America." "The Society of the Woman in the Wilderness, or the Contented of the God-Loving Soul" was so named because of the statement in Revelation, where the Church is symbolized as a woman, that "there were given to the woman the two wings of the great eagle, that she might fly into the wilderness unto her place, where she is nourished for a time, and times, and a half time, from the face of the serpent."

The members of this group were devout and stern religionists. They were also mystics, astrologers, and alchemists, and Rosicrucians. One of them discovered the philosopher's stone, it seems, but he somehow failed to disclose it to the public, nor was there any great outpouring of gold which he had transmuted from base metals. The Contented searched the heavens with a telescope day and night, watching for the coming of Jesus which was to occur in 1694, and there are improbable stories of their being deceived by pranksters who arrived dressed in flowing robes. 1695 arrived, still without the Second Coming, but the Contented adjusted their minds to the situation, declared they were still immortal in the flesh, and went on searching the heavens. Still, though, as some of them sickened and died in the usual manner, there was serious weakening and falling away.

Some of the migrating societies were antinomian. Ordinarily they did away with the Bible, the sacraments, prayer, church services, and conventional marriage, sometimes to the point of establishing a community of women. In short, their comfortable doctrine of once saved, always saved, permitted them to do anything they wished, while at the same time allowing them to remain unsullied Christians.

Antinomianism usually or always led to sex scandals, and such groups were often driven out of communities by their worldly neighbors—unless they sooner fell apart from the internal pressure of quarrels and jealousies which, despite the great and permanent outpourings of grace, somehow rose among the freely-sampling brethren. An example is the "Newborns," or Baumanites, who achieved "new birth" through mystic rites in their colony at Oley, in eastern Pennsylvania. Bauman, their untutored leader, held them with his visions and prophecies, but their sex excesses led to their destruction by their neighbors.

The longest-lasting of the early German-American Pennsylvania communes was Ephrata, in Lancaster County. It began in 1732, and might be said to have lasted until 1937 when a remnant of the uncloistered order of the society joined a Seventh Day Baptist group. However, effective organization ceased in 1905.

At first there was a lesser order of married peasantry who lived on the land and an inner circle of ascetic monks and nuns who lived together in a cloistered existence, with any married couples among them freely giving up their sexual privileges. The order survived extensive dalliances of the leader, Beissel, with some of the prettier young female celibates and with the wife of his closest friend. Perfection of body, soul, spirit, and of daily activity was the goal, and it was sought under rigorous discipline. There were foot washings, love feasts, healings by laying on of hands, and three immersions were necessary in baptism. Saturday was their Sabbath. They refused to take oaths, to bear arms, or to associate with the world politically or socially. At their height, there were three hundred in the cloister.

Guides of German descent still show visitors through the stone buildings with their low, narrow doors—"strait is the gate and narrow the way"—and tell of the inmates who were "spiritual wirgins, midout wows," held to their celibacy not by oaths but by conviction. Following the example of the builders of Solomon's temple, they erected their structures without nails, and there was no sound of a hammer heard in them, nor any iron allowed. Even the altar cloths were pressed with a "smoothing iron" of wood.

Benjamin Franklin has left an intriguing glimpse of the Moravians who for some years, through expediency, were communistic in their numerous thriving villages. Indians massacred some of them and Franklin unwillingly accepted a commission from the royal governor to fortify the frontier to protect the remainder—pacifists with whom he was impatient for their refusal to protect themselves.

He was much surprised to find them in military array, for they had obtained an act of Parliament relieving them from bearing arms. Well, said Bishop Spangenberg lamely, they had thought themselves "conscientiously scrupulous" of fighting—but suddenly to their own surprise they found this idea adopted by but few among them. "Common sense," observed Franklin, "aided by present danger, will sometimes be too strong for whimsical opinions."

He "inquir'd a little" into their practices. He found they worked and ate together and slept in large dormitories in groups according to age and sex. They worshiped in such groups. Mingling of the sexes was seen as a chief root of mischief. Franklin asked whether it was true that mar-

riages were by lot and was told lots were used "only in particular cases." A young man desiring a wife would speak to
the elders who, if they were satisfied with him as suitable
marriage fodder, would report him to the eldresses. These
would select him a wife. If the ladies found several girls
equally suitable for him, lots were resorted to.

Franklin objected that if the matches were not made
by mutual choice some of them might chance to be very unhappy. " 'And so they may,' answer'd my informer, 'if you let
the parties chuse for themselves.' " Adds Franklin, who was
in good position to speak on that score: "Which indeed I
could not deny."

Because of differences in accounts, one may say only
that it was sometime—perhaps several months, perhaps several years—before 1769 that the people around the backwoods hamlet of Harvard, Massachusetts, some fifteen
leagues or so over the hills from Boston, noticed that a half
dozen farming families near the Willard and Cooper places
were slipping into each other's houses at night and, to judge
from the sounds, holding religious meetings. Glimpses of a
strange, pretty young woman were had by prying neighbors,
but nothing more could be learned about her than that
her name was Abigail Lougee. Some people thought she acted
like a married woman. Others did not.

From the insinuation of meaning into the chance remarks of the Willards and their friends and children, it
gradually became a settled thing in the community that
these people were concealing a male prophet who had
brought the woman there—a man who, as it eventually developed, was never to die but to live forever in the flesh.
Those who believed in him were to share his glory in the
Millennium which it seemed was to begin soon.

The people of Harvard were not greatly surprised,
for some of the rising sect had been in trouble in time past
with the local authorities for religious offenses, including

that of "encouraging Lay-preachers and Exhorters to preach and Exhort in their Houses, whome we are satisfied are not called nor sent of God to such Business."

A similar satisfaction would doubtless have been felt concerning the self-ordained Reverend Shadrach Ireland whom in fact the Coopers and their friends were concealing. Nor would these officials probably have been impressed had they known that Ireland was in the way of becoming America's first home-grown communitarian prophet. But it is unlikely that even he knew that.

Shadrach—or Shadrack, as some spelled his name— was a tall, gangling man with a lantern jaw and a shock of reddish hair, and a fine roving eye, one may judge, for a well-turned ankle. He was possessed of several gifts of God, including those of speaking in tongues, laying on of hands, and receiving revelations from heaven. He was by trade a woodworker and a maker of clay pipes in his home at Charlestown, hard by Bunker Hill, but he apparently dropped those prosaic callings when the divine mantle fell upon him at a New Light revival meeting.

People were amused at his pronouncement concerning his immortality and his divine commission and these heresies were ignored even by the magistrates—but then he denounced the established Congregational church as stagnant and the entrenched clergy as "slothful and self-indulgent." The outraged fathers promptly had him indicted as a heretic.

Shadrach did not remain to be tried. Vanishing between two suns, he appeared before daylight one morning at the Cooper place. Since he was promptly taken in and hidden, he may well have been one of the lay preachers who had previously got them into trouble. Among other things, he announced to the Coopers that he had been "called of the Lord to forsake wife and family," which was to say, his six children. If that was a hardship for him, no doubt he bore up as best he might for the sake of the young woman, Abigail Lougee, whom he had fetched along as his "spiritual wife." Whatever that term may have meant, the prophet and Abbie slept together.

In later years, some backsliders wondered if Shadrach's mania for hiding was not inspired by a fear of pursuit by law officers or by the male relatives of his wife or Abigail, but at the time he made it a matter of divine command. His growing circle of followers always spoke of him, even among themselves, as "the man" to lessen the chance of inadvertently betraying his presence to outsiders. Nevertheless, his presence and his very name and his bestowal of immortality upon his people became public knowledge. But still he remained hidden.

Then in the fall of 1769 the countryside was startled by a night-long hammering and clattering at the Willard place. Next day, spies discovered that a large house was abuilding there. Questioning brought short answers. The work continued, mostly at night, with a dozen or more men making quick progress by lantern and moonlight.

Soon several of the New Lighters moved in, including Abigail Lougee, as well as "another Abigail whose [family] name was Cooper," and, as no one doubted, the invisible prophet himself. Such New Lighters as did not leave their own places to live in the new "Square House" or in the old Willard house came to work on the farm and to contribute provisions for the prophet's household.

Shadrach had formed them into a society, and so persuasive was he and so great their feeling for him that they put themselves and much of their goods into his hands. Willard in fact gave him a deed to the farm for the use of the society. Some of the woodwork in the Square House, which still stands, is reputedly Shadrach's production. But there was one feature of the edifice which no chance caller ever saw in the prophet's day, and which came as a surprise to the occupants who in 1845 uncovered a secret stairway leading from the cellar to the cupola, with a wire running up it to a little bell.

The purpose was clear. Shadrach had spent much time in his cupola "watching for Jesus"—or, as detractors had long before remarked, for those men who he thought might be on his trail. The warning system could apprise him of chance callers so that he might keep quiet.

Shadrach's prophecy of his immortality worked out one hundred per cent perfectly until one night in the summer of 1780 when a flaw appeared in it. He rose from bed, taken with a violent illness, and walked the floor "groaning with deep groans" and declaring he felt the wrath of God. Abigail cried for help. Abigail Cooper finally got a light kindled but by the time she hastened in with it Shadrach had fallen.

He gasped that if he appeared to die they must not bury him, since he would rise again on the third day.

"And if I don't rise then," he whispered, "I will rise on the ninth one."

He did appear to die. The disciples believed his words. At least they told each other they believed. They had to believe in order to keep up their belief in their own sharing of his glory. As the body lay upon the high bed they fasted and prayed. Some worked the next day as usual so that the neighbors might not suspect that something unusual was afoot and perhaps even invade the place and learn that the leader was not exactly himself at the moment.

The third day came, but by then the changes in the body were so pronounced that the most convinced could no longer maintain the vigil. Two of the strongest stomach got the remains into a coffin which they worried down to the cellar beneath the house where they bricked it up. Months later, they removed it to a cornfield in the night and placed growing stalks back over the grave. In time, in some unknown way, the death was commonly talked of—and indeed the ridicule was so great that some of the disgusted disciples backslid from the faith.

This scene was frequently to be reenacted in communitarian annals—nor indeed is it unique to America.

Much the same thing occurs concerning the saint's body in *The Brothers Karamazov,* and the idea of resurrection itself is widely found from ancient times, with supporting examples.

Strangely enough—though by no means uniquely—Shadrach's organization survived him, and, absorbed by the Shakers, it may in a sense be said to have lasted longer than any other bona fide communitarian establishment, coming down as it does well into the present century. Too, it was probably the communitarian arrangements of the New Lighters, deliberately adopted by them, which gave the idea for permanent common sharing to the Shakers, the first great communitarian sect.

Abigail Lougee, the spiritual wife, is heard of no more after her soul mate's death. Perhaps she returned to her family. At any rate, Shadrach had been dead just about a year when Abigail Cooper, still living at the Square House, saw in her dooryard a plumpish, round-faced, not unpretty little woman of almost fifty, followed by several other women and a half dozen men.

The latter wore knee-length coats, broad flat hats, and had their bangs square-cut like freshly-trimmed mules. The women were in sunbonnets and drab dresses with handkerchiefs pinned across their bosoms—this to smooth out the enticement of the lines, as Abigail later learned.

She coolly stood them off at the door. One of the men equably introduced the leader: "This is Ann the Word. Christ is making the Second Appearing in her. We have come to bring you the Gospel."

"I have the Gospel," Abigail assured him.

Certainly she wanted no gospel from these people. She had heard their noisy meetings for several nights past at the house of Isaac Willard and she loathed their dancing and yelling and singing. Further, for months she had read of them in the papers. She knew that the leader, Ann Lee, was an illiterate factory hand from Manchester, England, and in this country had been jailed as a British spy—for the Revolution was in full fury.

Released, Ann and her coterie had incited anger and persecutions toward themselves. They were Quakers who did not say thee or thou—their only peculiarity of speech was yea and nay, as commanded in the Bible—but who shook and jumped so much in worship that they were derisively called Shaking Quakers, or Shakers.

They were forever being beaten and driven out of towns for casting devils from the sick by means of witchcraft and for preaching that it was sinful for men and women to lie together, to be one flesh as commanded in Abigail's Bible. New Englanders were not notably celibate at that time, and mobs of them had risen in fury at the disruption of homes and of betrothals by Shaker conversions.

Despite Abigail's determination, the Shakers insinuated themselves into the house with the help of one of the New Lighters who had attended their meetings. They calmly informed Abigail that they were going to make her love them "just a little."

"I don't love you at all!" she assured them bluntly.

Elder William Lee only smiled. His sister, Mother Ann, was not listening.

"Why," she exclaimed, "this place is appointed unto me!" She looked wonderingly about. "I saw this very room in a vision in England."

While Abigail's irritation grew, her friend brought food. Elder William's long, ascetic face quivered and tears came to his eyes. "I often weep in thanksgiving at the goodness of God in giving us food," he explained.

Abigail forebore the obvious comment, and her anger and alarm increased as Mother Ann remarked that she and her people had an engagement in an adjoining town, but would return.

"We'll tarry with you a while and hold a meeting," she assured Abigail.

Elder William left an apple on the mantel, abjuring

their hostess to think of the Believers when she looked at it. Her impulse, when they were gone, was to throw it away, but somehow she did not. Rather, in the following days, she found herself more and more often picking it up and considering those who had left it. And all this was to bring down upon her the scourgings and scornings which for years had been heaped upon Mother Ann and her earlier disciples.

From the age of six, Ann had been put to work in hat factory or cotton mill by her blacksmith father. Around her was poverty, sickness and degradation. The poor were born in hunger, they lived in it, and died in it. Sex and gin—and sometimes religion—were the solace of the poor. Hogarth would have needed to look no farther than Manchester for the material for his Gin Lane series.

It is unlikely there was anything in the way of human activity that Ann did not see in the alleys, tenements and doorways where the poor and the tipsy sought shelter. Indeed, she saw so much that she developed even as a child "a horror of marriage and a conviction of the uncleanness and depravity of sexual intercourse." Her mother promised her she need never wed, but when Mrs. Lee died Ann's father married her to another smith, Abraham Stanley. The deaths of her successive children in infancy convinced her the more strongly of the wrongness of marriage and sex. She viewed those tragedies as punishment for the transgressions that brought the children into the world, which of course was to take the solid Mosaic view that the sins of the parents should be visited on their children.

Her solace was years-long attendance at an endless Quaker revival. In agony of spirit, "sometimes sweating actual blood," she might pray all night there. The congregation, like any Quaker group, was seized with extended spells of trembling—an expression of "God's indignation against sin." But this particular group also went into the transports of wild dancing and shaking that led to their being mocked as the Shaking Quakers.

It must be confessed that they made rather a nuisance of themselves, exhorting their neighbors, accosting people on the streets, and invading public houses to preach. At first there was amusement, but despite the constant humbling of themselves in their exhortations, they were judged to have an inherent holier-than-thou attitude and amusement changed to anger and outrage. The Shakers suffered mockery, insults, and beatings. When these did not stop them, they were pestered with repeated jailings on the blanket charge of profaning the Sabbath.

It was while she was in Manchester jail in 1770, Ann testified, that God gave her a vision of the Garden of Eden and showed her the first act of human transgression—the plucking of the forbidden fruit of pleasure from their bodies by the man and woman. In that act, God told her, was the root of man's fall and the consequent answer to the question of what he must do to be saved.

God also told her the True Church was to be established through her—for she was the new incarnation of Christ who had first been incarnated in Jesus of Nazareth. She was the Capstone of the Temple as Jesus had been the Corner. As soon as she was released, she preached to her friends and most of them accepted her testimony. They adopted her doctrine of celibacy and took the name of the Millennial Church, or United Society of Believers—sometimes adding "in Christ's Second Appearing," the appearance of course being in Ann who was thenceforth called Mother, Ann the Word, and Ann Christ. She was not worshipped, however, being seen as "the Elder Sister" just as Jesus was "the Elder Brother." Yet, she was considered "the female member of the Godhead."

All this moved the public to greater anger and ribaldry than before. Once Ann was dragged down several flights of stairs by the feet and through a gutter. Her younger brother (not William, who apparently permanently deserted his family to go to America with her) beat her about the face and head with a broom handle for her preachments at him. She said she felt nothing—that God imposed His hand between her and the stick. Nevertheless, she bore the scars to her grave.

There were other miracles: A nobleman felt a mysterious urge to ride to a certain place. There he saw Ann, a stranger to him, being beaten by a mob. He rescued her. Orthodox religionists dragged her before a ministerial board which it was expected would condemn her to have her tongue bored through with a red hot iron. The board washed its hands of the matter and the mob took the Shakers out to stone them to death. Miraculously, the stones would not strike the Shakers—except for one man who was somewhat injured. He was obviously weak in the faith, for "afterwards he fell away."

Ann was next locked in solitary confinement in an insane asylum and left to starve to death. However, a Shaker boy slipped in each day, thrust a pipestem through the keyhole, and gave her milk and wine. After a fortnight her tormentors were confounded to discover her in excellent health. Even they then recognized that she was the subject of miracles. Perhaps they were partly moved by the unnerving report that appalling curses in body and purse were befalling her previous bedevilers.

Ann was released and "from that day allowed to live in peace." Her chroniclers seem to notice no connection between that halcyon existence and the fact that simultaneously, under inspiration, she "withdrew her Testimony from the world"—that is, she quit preaching at nonbelievers.

In 1774, after two years of this quiescence, when she was thirty-eight, she was told in another vision to go to America where at last the True Church would be established through her. With her unhappily celibate husband and her brother William, her niece and six other men and women, she took ship for New York. The captain of the

Mariah became increasingly incensed over the progressively more fervent dancing and shouting orgies on his deck. He bluntly informed the Shakers that a repetition would result in their being thrown overboard. Mother Ann answered that another service would be held if God so directed them.

God soon so directed, and in the midst of a great storm, at that. The captain ordered the crew to jettison the worshipers—but, says the official Shaker account, a great wave struck the ship just then, springing a plank so that water roared into the vessel. The frightened captain saw all on board as doomed.

But not so! "Mother" told him "to be of good cheer as not a hair of their heads should come to harm." She had just seen "two bright angels by the mast" who assured her of this. The Shakers fell to and helped with the pumps and the drawing out of water, but matters worsened by the minute. Then a monstrous wave sprang the errant plank back into place. The captain gave Mother full credit for the salvation of the vessel, for unexplained reasons, and allowed the Shakers to dance as much as they pleased all the way into New York Harbor.

It was an uneasy country in which they landed. A country where children learned to recite "Baneful tea, be-gone!" and where treasonous persons called "patriots" had dumped that staple to the tune of eighteen thousand guin-eas' worth into Boston Harbor, which port was closed in retaliation by the king's men so that the people suffered for necessities. They were also moved to flout the smuggling laws more thoroughly than had been the usual custom. Too, up and down the seaboard men were readying their necks for a noose by becoming delegates to something called the Continental Congress. In New York, Tories were in the saddle, but the city was restless.

Mother Ann had no interest in politics. The thing at the moment was to exist and wait on the voice of God. Her husband found work as a blacksmith and she as housekeeper for the wife of his employer. The other Shakers went up the

Hudson to Albany where John Hocknell, the moneyed man of the Society, purchased land. No immediate move was made to live on it. While his companions found jobs in the town, Hocknell returned to England for his family and friends.

Ann seems not to have announced in New York that with her the millennium had begun, nor that she was the female member of the Godhead. Presently Abraham fell ill. Apparently she gave up her job to nurse him and by the end of his near-fatal siege they were destitute. He showed his appreciation for her care by falling into association with "the wicked at public houses," and by "opposing Mother in a most ungodly manner," and urging her "to live in sexual cohabitation like the rest of the world." She could make but one answer to that.

At last the frustrated Abraham "brought a lewd woman into the house" and told Ann that unless she changed her ways he was going to marry the creature. And so he may have. Here we unhappily lose all sight of him.

Ann's second Christmas in America found her in despair. She had no fuel, no light, no food—nothing but a cruse of vinegar. All her followers were still in Albany, and in her poverty and illiteracy she was out of touch with them. In the darkness, the scars of her old beatings aching in the cold, she wept and sipped her vinegar.

But succor was at hand. Hocknell and his party were just arriving from England. They rescued her and soon in the wilderness of Watervliet near Albany trees were crashing and cabins rising. With no thought of their eventual system of "Christian communism," the people as an expedient worked together and shared what they produced, always looking for better times ahead and for the establishment of the Church.

Four Revolutionary years passed without the founding of the Church, and Ann's followers were impatient. Then the change began. A revival was in progress a few miles away at New Lebanon. The worshipers were millennialists, convinced by "the signs of the times"—the war—that the great change of Dispensation was at hand. They had heard of the religionists at Watervliet. A party of the revivalists visited there, seeking light.

Although the Shaker millennium had just begun, Mother Ann seems to have thought the end of the world might follow at any moment. This undoubtedly made it the easier to persuade the visitors that it was a small thing to give up the pleasures of marriage, even though Shakers freely confessed that they suffered great pangs in doing so. Nevertheless, the sacrifice was one which had the virtue of frequently reminding them they were making a sacrifice.

But, besides the drama of this point and the excitement of talking constantly about sex, there was a rousing revival atmosphere with the added attractions of the abandoned Shaker shouting, clapping, dancing, and lively singing —for great store was set by vocal music among Mother's people. They produced reams of doggerel which they rigorously preserved in their hymnals. Indeed, in a later day, a Shaker of typically closed mind boasted to Emerson—in the philosopher's dry recounting—that "All their hymns and songs of every description are manufactured in the Society."

A popular subject in Mother's day was the horrors of sex. As:

> The First Adam being dead, yet speaketh, in a dialogue with his children.
>
> CHILDREN: *First Father Adam, where art thou?*
> *With all thy numerous fallen race*
> *We must demand an answer now*
> *For time hath stripped our hiding place.*
> *Wast thou in nature made upright—*
> *Fashioned and plac'd in open light?*

Adam admits that he was made upright, and after several stanzas he gets around to explaining how the Fall came about, his testimony jibing excellently well with

Mother Ann's vision in Manchester jail, and adding a few
delectable details:

> *When I was plac'd on Eden's soil*
> *I lived by keeping God's commands—*
> *To keep the garden all the while,*
> *And labor, working with my hands.*
> *I need not toil beyond my pow'r*
> *Yet never waste one precious hour.*
>
> *But in a careless, idle frame,*
> *I gazed about on what was made:*
> *And idle hands will gather shame,*
> *And wand'ring eyes confuse the head:*
> *I dropped my hoe and pruning knife*
> *To view the beauties of my wife.*
>
> *An idle beast of highest rank*
> *Came creeping up just at that time,*
> *And showed to Eve a curious prank,*
> *Affirming that it was no crime:—*
> *"Ye shall not die as God hath said—*
> *'Tis all a sham, be not afraid."*
>
> *All this was pleasant to the eye,*
> *And Eve affirmed the fruit was good;*
> *So I gave up to gratify*
> *The meanest passion in my blood.*
> *O horrid guilt! I was afraid:*
> *I was condemned, yea I was dead.*

The children object that this does not agree with
sacred writ. Adam then explains that there is a bit of a gap
in the recorded Mosaic version. That, killed by his contact
with Eve as God had promised would be the case, he was
replaced with "the beast of highest rank," the serpent,
who assumed Adam's face and form and became the father

of "the Adamic race." It was he, the Serpent, or Satan-Adam, and not the original image-of-God Adam, whom Jehovah commanded "to multiply his wretched seed."

The Shakers blandly passed this inspired medieval doctrine off as their own theology, but for some reason were not led to adopt the parallel Lilith cycle by which Hebrews and some Christian and other groups have supplied Adam with a "first wife" who was replaced by Eve.

At any rate, the "true church" of the Shakers proved highly attractive to the New Lebanonites. People sympathetic to Ann's "testimony" were somehow enormously affected by her. She was self-effacing: "It is not me but God that you are confessing your sins to. All I can do is ask God to forgive you." She had homely advice for seekers: "Keep your children clean, do not scold them for small faults and unintentional mistakes, and work hard—it is not the devil that tempts idle people, but idle people that tempt the devil." She was blunt in pointing out faults—but, "The harshness of a friend is better than the kiss of an enemy." She was humbly kind, making others comfortable first, waiting on the table, and eating afterwards—and taking a special pleasure if only scraps were left for her repast. And constantly she reminded her followers that she was only one with them, and got her strength from the Father.

And so she made her first American converts. The visitors accepted her as their savior, and celibacy and the doctrine of physical labor for every Believer as tenets. It was their noisily enthusiastic worship, and their refusal to give military service, which attracted sudden public attention to the sect. People were enraged at Ann's intimations of Christhood, her casting out of devils and laying on of hands to heal the sick, her advocacy of the celibate life, her pacifism, and they were further irritated by the general hubbub of the meetings.

When the ordinary persecutions did not avail to crush the Shakers, their pacifism was seized upon as evidence that they were British spies, and Ann and some others were jailed on charges of treason. An attempt was made to exchange them with the English for American prisoners. The English were puzzled and uninterested, and after a dreary half year the prisoners were released by their disgusted jailers. Ann declared that she was no spy, but was in fact for the freedom of the Colonies and for the very good reason that the Bible predicted freedom for them. She saw her jailing as an attempt to break up her religion.

Free, she decided to call upon the brethren at New Lebanon. After a revival meeting there, she began a two-year preaching tour across Massachusetts and Connecticut. Fury followed her. She was jailed as a witch—"She casteth out devils by Beelzebub"—and things became so bad that she and her followers began moving by night.

And so at last she came to the Square House. Her troubles—and her triumph—in America were about to begin in earnest.

Mother Ann had promised Abigail Cooper she would "tarry" a while at the Square House to hold a meeting, and tarry she did, for months, despite the evil presence of the spirit of Shadrach Ireland. He was, in fact, "one of the meanest spirits that ever I did sense," she declared after wrestling with him one night, exhorting him to salvation. For in Shaker theology the dead might yet be converted. Hundreds of thousands who had passed on—including eventually such stalwarts as Napoleon—became Shakers in good standing, conversions ordinarily being effected by Shakers who had died and made the obligatory three-days' descent into hell to preach to the lost before ascending to the seven heavens. These apparently were arranged in concentric spheres and the saved hoped to progress through them until the ultimate and presumably most inward one was attained. As for poor Shadrach, he was stiff-necked and immovable and had to be abandoned to Satan.

Yet Mother was impressed with some of his works, and it may well be that here her successors absorbed the idea for the Christian necessity of communal sharing. The millennial fever was high around Harvard. People abandoned their work and gathered to the Square House, and for half a year as many as two hundred might be praying, singing, dancing, and exhorting in informal shifts around the clock, with individuals stealing off at intervals for naps in the barns or to prepare necessary food for the throng.

The worshipers brought what supplies they could, but they were largely sustained by a stream of provender wagoned in from New Lebanon and other congregations Ann had left in her wake. The frenzy was so great that with a few score dancing in the Square House at the same time it threatened to fall, and the cellar beams had to be shored up with timbers. Nor was all the worship indoors. Shakers recorded that they

> went forth with great zeal and worshipped God with singing, dancing, leaping, shouting, clapping of hands, and such other exercises as they were led into by the Spirit. But the sound of this . . . though joyful to the Believers, was terrible to the wicked; for the sound thereof was heard at the distance of several miles.

One of the less scurrilous of the non-Shaker accounts agrees that it was all just as terrible as the Shakers thought —but in not exactly the same sense of the word:

> When they meet together for their worship, they fall a groaning and trembling, and every one acts alone for himself; one will fall prostrate on the floor, another on his knees and his head on his hands, on the floor; another will be muttering articulate sounds which neither they nor any body else can understand. Some will be singing; . . . others jumping up and down; . . . others will be shooing and hissing evil spirits out of the house. . . . One of their postures which increases among them is, turning round very swift for an hour and some-

times two hours at a time, till they are all wet with sweat;
this they say is to shew the great power of God. . . .
They run about in the woods and elsewhere hooting and
tooting like owls.

Judging from the fully sympathetic accounts there is
no reason to doubt any of this. Much of the same thing
occurred later in the camp meeting revivals of both the
United States and England. Public irritation, anger, and
alarm increased by the day as husbands or wives were converted out of family circles and betrothals broken up to the
grief of one of the parties.

The British spy charges were revived and a mob with
the local militia tore the New Light farm apart looking for
cached weapons. None were found. Frequently, mobs
swooped down and cursed and hooted and threw stones
through the windows at the nonresistant dancers. Once
Ann's brother was beaten and left for dead, but the prayers
of the others brought him to his senses. Again, Ann was
hauled on a sled into Harvard in her nightclothes in zero
weather and left there.

Finally, one day when Mother Ann and several of
her intimates were at an adjoining town, all the other
Shakers were rounded up and driven afoot ten miles. The
strong interposed themselves to take the lashings intended
for the weak—and indeed some were beaten bloodily. The
Shakers sang and prayed. At last the mob halted, warning
the Shakers to keep moving and not to return to Harvard.
All were back before night.

Responsible townsmen then informed Ann that kill-
ings were to commence if she and all outsiders did not depart. The promise was made, however, that if all transients
should leave, including Ann, local Shakers would not be mo-
lested further. Having no protection in the law, Mother
agreed—declaring, however, that if the Lord should so direct
she would return.

A leisurely retreat took her to New Lebanon on the

New York border where her first American converts lived. The Shaker celebration in her honor so roused the countryside that a mob gathered and broke into the house. Believers hid Mother in a closet. Women were beaten and thrown from doors and windows along with the men. One, possibly an unduly stubborn fellow, was thrown from an upstairs doorway three times.

At last the mob found Mother and dragged her downstairs by the feet, her head bouncing on the treads, and threw her into her buggy. The harness was cut up, but perhaps not past all use for the horse seems to have drawn the rig to the home of one Eleazar Grant, a magistrate and a bitter enemy of the Shakers. He warned Ann to leave the area. The mob, Eleazar participating, followed and at a bridge attempted to dump the buggy and Mother off into the water. For once, the Shakers made physical resistance and got their leader safely over the stream.

The mob followed all the way to the Albany ferry. Bruised, caked with dried blood, Mother was still able to say, "It is your day now, but it will be mine by and by, Eleazar Grant. I'll put you in a cockleshell yet." Grant told her to go on to Watervliet and to stay there if she valued her life.

In later years, when the Shakers were permitted a peaceful existence, they expressed surprise if one died short of eighty, and ages in the advanced nineties were not considered unusual. Daybooks bear such notations as, "Departed this life yesterday, Sister Emma Jenks, 78—why so soon, Emma?"

But those times were not yet. Within the year of the Square House beating in which he was left for dead, Ann's brother William died at forty-four. The prophetess soon knew that the hand of fate was upon herself. She was in pain and failing health from her own beatings, but she remained cheerful. She liked to rock in a chair and sing, and to look to the southwest where she said God was going to do great

things—words which were remembered in the days of the
Kentucky Revival.

She continued giving her people day-to-day advice
and a few months after William's death, not yet fifty, she
told them the time had come to name Elder James Whittaker her successor—"as she had often prophesied" would
be the case. He was thenceforth to be known as Father
James. Then, despite the prayers of the unbelieving faithful, one September night in 1784 "she breathed her last
without a struggle or groan."

Just before she expired, she said, "I see brother
William coming in a glorious chariot to take me home."
Elder John Hocknell, who was greatly gifted in visions,
testified that when the breath left her body, he saw in
vision a golden chariot, drawn by four white horses,
which received and wafted her soul out of his sight.

The chronicler remarks that the cynical may scoff at
this and the many similar visions of Shakers, and gives the
reminder that it was perfectly logical for the chariot and
horses to take Mother away, for, after all "Elijah went up in
a fiery chariot, and a cloud received Jesus out of sight."

Some of Mother's bereft followers wished to die, too,
and one woman lay down and was attempting to expire, although in perfect health, when she saw Ann as a little girl
of three with a wing held in either hand. Ann waved these,
murmuring, "Hush, hush!" The woman took this as instruction to go on living and was comforted.

CHAPTER THREE

THE SHAKER DISCIPLINE

RIGHT FOOT FIRST, LEFT FOOT THEN

Come, let us all be marching on,
Into the New Jerusalem;
The call is now to ev'ry one
To be alive and moving.
This precious call we will obey—
We love to march the heav'nly way,
And in it we can dance and play,
And feel our spirits living.

—Shaker dancing song

IF EVER a religious society was to dwindle and die upon
the death of its prophet, it should have been this scattered
one with the many pressures of the world and the flesh upon
it. But presently, through the expiring Father James two
Americans were made the "leads," one of them a very good-
looking woman of twenty-seven, Lucy Wright, the daughter
of a prosperous non-Shaker family.

"Mother" Lucy was presently the ruling spirit. She
gave Shakerism shape and form and its final character. By
1792, she had caused Shakers to sell their property and
gather to Watervliet, Harvard, or "Mount Lebanon," the
model Shaker village which was established near New Leb-

anon on the farm where Mother Ann was so severely beaten. In these villages, great "unitary dwellings" were erected that everyone might live under the same roof—except that the ministry of two men and two women had a little house of their own for the four.

"All things common" was established as the divine order, and this was preached by the missionaries who went out to found new villages, some of them to Kentucky where the great revival was getting under way. The Shakers were quite at home in the fevered millennial atmosphere of the camp meetings where whole battalions of tobacco-spitting frontiersmen and their wives and children went into trances or fits of jerks or gobblings or head-poundings, all of which were gravely pronounced to be manifestations of the indwelling of the Holy Spirit in the subjects.

They made converts, and the villages they established underwent hardship and hunger. Persecution by "the world" was rife, and there were some defections, such as that of the preacher who "sucked up our light as eagerly as ever ox drank water," and then went away to defame them. But the villages survived and soon Mother Lucy had a score of them from Maine almost to the Mississippi.

While there might be minor local variation, a village ordinarily had three "families," each in one or more large unitary houses of its own. These were the novitiate or "gathering" family, the junior to which those finally accepted then moved, and the senior or Church group. The juniors still had ties with the world which they could not sufficiently break that they might legally give their property to the Shakers. The Church group was the completely dedicated one.

There was also a house for boys and another for girls. Young saw old only at religious meetings and were ever under the eye and thumb of elder and eldress. Nor might the various adult families visit each other's houses. Each indeed had its own shops, livestock, barns, and fields. Confirmed Shakers of any order were not allowed to see worldly relatives unless it was thought this would lead to conversion of the latter.

Life ossified into a system of rules. In the solidly-made houses of lumber, brick, or stone, men lived several to the room on one side of the upper floors, the women in groups across the halls. Dining and assembly rooms for the one to three hundred housemates were on the first floor, with the village meeting house separate.

Everyone rose "at the first trump"—usually a bell— at four thirty in summer, five in winter. The situation, like every other, was covered by the rules: "Put your right foot out of the bed first. Place your right knee where your foot first touched the floor in kneeling to pray. Do not speak but if absolutely necessary whisper to the room leader."

Backs were turned to the center of the room for privacy in dressing. Beds were stripped for airing, covers folded over chairs. Windows were raised and each man "if he was a real Shaker" observed that there was no fire hazard before tiptoeing out "in marching order" to chore or ready the day's deal of work at a shop.

Women waited until "the second trump" before opening their doors that the men might be gone with their chamber pots, which were suggestive of sex—for in the inescapably salacious atmosphere of celibacy it would not do to allow occasions for sniggering to arise. The gentler sex were commanded to "go on the toes, left arm folded across the stomach, right hand at the side, tips of the fingers touching the thumb." Later in the day, the women whose turn it was made all the beds, but apparently the men swept their own floors. Each woman had a "brother" whose clothes she looked after and for whom she did small sisterly chores, and sometimes this brother might be the husband she had had when out "in the world" before their conversion to Shakerism.

A third "trump" summoned to breakfast. Occasionally the senior family might be allowed a bit of conversation in the halls before entering the "eating room," but or-

dinarily there was silence. Men and women had separate
bare, long, scrubbed tables with no glassware or fancy cutlery. Separate dishes of food were placed for each four
diners that no passing might be required. Condiments,
sauces, and syrup were in trays hung two feet or so above
the table from the ceiling, an arrangement which made
much more room on the table and which gives an oddly
decorative appearance in the old Shaker prints.

At a signal, all knelt in silent prayer. At a signal,
all rose and sat. A Shaker poem, scoring a generic "Old
Slug" for his laziness and nap-catching and other bad habits,
tells that, to parade his piety, he might kneel again in the
middle of a meal to pray a while, and then linger behind—
after another bell had called for benedictive prayer and
prompt departure—to stuff himself. No "winking or blink-
ing" was allowed at table. Meat, tea, and coffee were
frowned upon but not absolutely forbidden, and a few
men who could not get ahead of the tobacco habit were permitted occasional indulgence.

Visitors were not encouraged and such as had to be
put up found a card in their separate eating room admonish-
ing them in many-stanzaed doggerel to "eat hearty and clean
out the plate" and not to leave a mixture of wasted food.
Visiting husbands and wives seem not always to have been
separated—for cards were in the visitors' bedrooms asking
that marital privileges be foregone under the Shaker roof.

Every Shaker worked, whether novitiate, child of
six, or minister. A summer rush might take all hands to the
fields, but ordinarily the Shaker woman did not work as
hard as the average farm wife. Men did the heavy chores and
all the labor-saving devices of the era were bought or built
for both sexes—washing machines, reapers, parers, shop
equipment. Shaker women were credited with inventing
the flat broom, which replaced the club-like round one, and
the circular saw. They made preserves for sale and packeted
seeds which found a national market because honestly advertised.

Men had shops for furniture making, iron mongery, and such other light industry. Children performed piecework for the adults, but in their own quarters. If a man needed something from a woman's shop he was supposed to speak to his foreman who in turn journeyed over to speak to the forewoman—but laxities were inclined to develop until some "incident" brought a clamping down.

Innumerable minor rules were followed until they became second nature: Put on the right shoe, right glove, right breeches leg first, step out with the right foot first in walking or dancing, harness the right-hand horse first—all from some Biblical allusion. Animals or people must not be unnecessarily touched, nor animals be given people's names. Men and women had separate stairs. They were not allowed to pass on a stairway nor to speak to each other unless "a third party above the age of ten" be present. If a "world's person" offered his hand it was to be shaken "for civility," but if of the opposite sex the Shaker was required to report the contact to elder or eldress "before attending meeting." If a brother were seen erring in any particular, he was to be admonished—and if he failed then to report his sin to the elder, the witness was required to.

Newspapers were read to the family by an elder who omitted "unsuitable items," such as crime, scandal, and war. No pictures were allowed on the walls—all else aside, the frames would catch dust. There were almost no books permitted, and no musical instruments whatever. After some years, to relieve the terrible boredom engendered by the system—"to lessen rowdiness in field and kitchen," it was put —a policy of Sunday afternoon visiting was instituted.

All was carefully regimented, of course. The women of a room were assigned to visit a certain room of men. Sitting in facing rows, handkerchiefs on laps to protect clothing from hands, they indulged in an hour of small talk, riddles, joke telling, and singing. One man recorded that the meetings were dull because there was nothing to talk about, particularly since the women had little understanding of the affairs attended to by men! One brother, it was reported, sometimes eulogized a sister whom he thought to be the best cook and who could make the best johnny cake. At another meeting "there was a lively conversation about what we had for dinner; and by this means, it might be said, we enjoyed our dinner twice over."

If it was observed that some couple too much enjoyed seeing each other, this sparking, as it was called, was broken up by the lady's being placed on another list. But despite all precautions, couples contrived to make their feelings known to each other so that the daily journals kept by the official chroniclers record much "worming out" and "fleshing off" into the world.

On occasion, couples were pursued and brought back before damage was done. Once in Kentucky, angered settlers came down upon a Shaker village and demanded that a pair of elopers who had been caught before they might get to bed be freed. The newlyweds had already been reasoned out of their error and they sheepishly sent their by-then-exasperated rescuers away.

Some who fleshed off were the children of members. Others were apprentices or bound children who exhibited a distressing lack of sympathy with celibacy as they grew up. Although "it would not be home without children," this in time led most villages to refuse to take youngsters except with their parents.

But ambition, as well as the simple fact that male and female created He them, may have led some youngsters away. Theoretically, the children were given a common school education, but beyond that learning was scorned, perhaps even feared, by the administration—for "of what use is literary education to those who will have no opportunity to use it?" The official pronouncement does say that were some literary or other genius unearthed in the common school, he would be given opportunity for development, but there is no record of such discovery. Probably the machinery for both the unearthing and the cultivation was lacking.

Emerson noted that this smug anti-intellectualism made it impossible to recruit any appreciable number of educated people. Harriet Martineau, in her travels in the 1830's, found the Shakers "ignorant, conceited, inert," with "intellectual torpor" and "mental grossness." As for the women, "Their soulless stare was almost as afflicting as that of the lowest order of slaves."

Certainly the meager schooling included nothing on sex. Indeed, in keeping with the hymns on the subject, there is a legend that two Shaker girls were required to whip each other "for watching the amour of two flies in a window." But the legend has a counterfeit ring: what Shaker knew the word "amour"? As for play, it undoubtedly differed with time and place. Some protest too much that the children were allowed to play, while outsiders comment on the cowed look of the silent Shaker youngsters—but this cowedness was found among other communitarians, religious and secular. One dissident in the 1840's recorded that at his village the boys were permitted one Sabbath afternoon to "roll trucks," whatever those may have been, for sport, but there was so much hilarity that such doings were thenceforth banned.

One by one Shakers who had seen Mother Ann in the flesh passed on. Many others, however, saw her in spirit, and this became a common thing in the 1840's—a most engaging decade in Shakerism.

Partly this was from the impetus which spiritualism received among the Shakers from the national fever generated from the toe-snapping Fox sisters and the "Rochester rappings." Among the spiritual descendants of Mother Ann, subjects were entered by ghostly Indian chiefs, pharaohs, and kings who spoke through their mouths in "ancient tongues." Returning from trances, the subjects told of seeing Mother, the saints, and "the 1st fathers."

At one Shaker meeting—fortunately out of doors— no fewer than forty thousand spirits were noticed to be in

attendance, including the Virgin Mary. For weeks on end at
the height of the fever all but the most necessary work might
be suspended for incessant day and night séances in which
messages, angel songs in unknown tongues, and the music for
them were received.

One Shaker chronicler tells that he and a friend
privately were doubtful of the genuineness of all this. The
friend's scoffing was seen by the elect when he pretended to
have a trance. The medium made swift motions as if binding the fellow. Apparently a sharp hypnosis was produced
for the man struggled helplessly until some hours later when
the medium "unbound" him. The chronicler was of the
opinion that "false spirits" were back of the mass phenom-
ena, but he was impressed in spite of himself by the way
hordes of children would become senseless and rigid, or
rush back and forth in group seizures, "eyes closed but not
hitting anything."

Songs were "brought by angels from Jehovah," and at
least one had an accompaniment of "a most beautiful tune
of two airs":

> *I shall march through Mount Zion with my angelic band;*
> *I shall pass through the city with my fan in my hand;*
> *And around thee, O Jerusalem, my armies will encamp,*
> *While I search my Holy Temple with my bright burning*
> *   lamp.*

Sometimes an "unknown tongue" was mixed with English:

> *Lo all vo, hark ye, dear children, and listen to me,*
> *For I am that holy Se lone se ka ra an ve;*
> *My work upon earth is holy, holy and pure,*
> *That work which will ever, forever endure.*

Luckily, interpreters were usually appointed by divine means to translate such things into usable form.

During this time, Shakerism was enlivened by the
rise of one Philemon Stewart at Mount Lebanon. He was

visited in the night, he said, by no less a personage than "Al sign te re Jah do, the Prophesying Angel, who had been commissioned by God in a full assemblage of angels and seraphs" to deliver a message to Philemon. Al sign arrived at New Lebanon with the Angel of Mercy before him and the Angel of Power fetching up the rear, and some or all of them—the pronouns are ambiguous—wore red robes and had eyes "like flames of fire."

Philemon was not unimpressed by all this but he was not stampeded. The chief angel said to him, "Arise, O thou little one, and appear before the Lord, on the Holy Mount."

Now, the Holy Mount, usually called the Holy Hill by Shakers, was the result of a previous revelation to Brother Philemon. Under a divine command delivered to him, each Shaker village had been required to clear off the most suitable hilltop near its meeting house and to smooth the area and seed it with grass. In the center a small hexagonal space was commanded to be fenced, somewhat in the shape of the wide-shouldered coffins of the era. And in each village, from the center of this little space, flowed The Fountain of Life. Nor was it a spiritual or symbolic fountain. It actually flowed, although only Believers could see it—and some of them, in after-times, confessed that it took them quite a while, after the establishment of their Holy Mount, to be able to discern this aquatic activity. God had also ordered that a stone be placed there, Philemon said, and that it be thus engraved:

Written and placed here
By the Command of our Lord and Saviour Jesus Christ
THE LORD'S STONE

Erected upon the Holy Hill of Zion

[Date. Name of Society]

The term "our Lord and Saviour Jesus Christ" was either a rhetorical carry-over, or else it shows an evolution of thought in the fifty years since Mother Ann's death, inasmuch as early Shakers were particular in declaring that they worshiped "neither Ann Christ nor Jesus Christ" but respected them only as elders in the Church.

On the other side of the stone was a long screed, divinely dictated, concerning the fountain and warning of God's power against doubters. Erected around the fountain, on each Holy Mount, was an ornate city peopled with angels and spirits, together with such biblical personages as "Elijah and the prophets." But only Shakers could see these cities and their occupants. The Holy Mounts became centers of outdoor worship for the Shakers, but they were soon closed to a ribald public which was apt at drawing comparisons concerning the invisible wardrobe of the king which only the pure in heart might see and admire.

Anyway, Al sign told Philemon to arise and go to the Holy Mount. "And as thou goest, kneel seven times and bow low, seven times to earth; for the Lord hath words for thee to write; and thou shalt kneel, or sit low, by the side of His Holy Fountain, and the words shall be revealed unto thee, in flames of fire."

The conflagration continued until Philemon had the manuscript of a sizable book. God then gave orders—through Philemon—that it be published by the chief ministry, the holder of the purse strings, who complied. It was titled "The Holy, Sacred, and Divine Roll and Book, from the Lord God of Heaven to the Inhabitants of the Earth." It contained testimonials from those who believed it genuine, some of them received by Philemon through inspiration from such personages as Noah, Elisha, Ezekiel, Malachi, Isaiah, St. Peter, St. John (both using their posthumous canonical style, it will be observed), Holy and Eternal Mother Wisdom, and "a holy and mighty angel of God, Ma'ne Me'rah Vak'na Si'na Jah." These had all of course long since been converted to Shakerism, but many living if lesser-known members of the Church were also prevailed upon to sign the testimonial of belief.

Part of the book was made up of revelations to other Shakers. One woman wrote that "it was in the evening of the twenty-second of January, eighteen hundred and forty-two, while I was busily employed putting all things in readiness for the close of the week, that I distinctly heard my name called very loudly, and with much earnestness." But on going to the adjoining doorway, she could see no one. Then in the middle of the next room she saw "four very large and bright lights, or balls of fire" which soon joined in "a pillar of fire. At this moment I heard a loud voice, which uttered many words with such mighty force that I feared to stay in the room, and attempted to go out; but found that I had no power to move my feet."

Presently the meaningless words took on sense: " 'And lo, I say a time, and a time, and a half-time shall not pass before my voice shall be heard, and my word sounded forth to the nations abroad.' " There was a long harangue in this general vein. Finally the pillar of fire "dispersed and I saw a mighty angel coming from the east, and I heard these words: 'Woe, woe, and many woes shall be upon the mortal that shall see and will not stop to behold.' "

Philemon realized that this was in reference to the book that he was to read in the flames. God ordered that five hundred copies of this valuable work be printed—nor was Philemon left to the mercy of his publishers on details. For, God said in the revelation, "it is my requirement that they be printed before the 22d of next September. To be bound in yellow paper, with red backs; edges yellow also." A copy was to be sent to "every ruler in the world." These were duly dispatched, and the king of Sweden was urbane enough to acknowledge receipt of his.

A copy was posted in a case outside each Shaker meeting house where God had placed "four of my holy angels to guard my sacred work." Hosts of other angels were assigned to mark the doorposts of all who believed so that when those who doubted should presently receive their desserts, the faithful might be the more conveniently passed over by the destroying angel. For "sore destruction and desolating judgments" were to come upon those who made light of the Holy Roll or who said, "These are the words of Mortals and not of God." So Philemon said he was told by the Lord, Who had perhaps noticed a certain amount of scoffing—even after the grammar was cleaned up in successive editions— toward the Book of Mormon which had earlier been disclosed by an angel to Joseph Smith, Jr., another York State citizen, and in similar King James language.

Sadly, there were scoffings even among Shakers toward the Holy Roll, as it was commonly called, and in after years the book was quietly removed from display and but little regarded. Meanwhile, on the heels of its publication, Sister Paulina Bates at Watervliet announced that God had dictated a work to her. The elders threshed it over to make it intelligible, but they assured the reader that "the substance and spirit of the work have been conscientiously preserved in full throughout the whole," which was modestly held to 718 pages.

Whole battalions of angels then began dictating similar tomes to other Shakers, but by then even the chief ministry dared defy the thunderings of Jehovah therein and refused to publish them. Further, they clamped the lid on the receipt of similar revelations by Shakers, and another lid on the more blatant spiritualists who were enjoying too much limelight with their trances and séances. This was in accordance with basic Shaker principle by which individuality in any member was frowned on.

Nevertheless, Philemon continued to receive some most excellent revelations. From one was instituted an annual "warring on evil spirits," in which committees of elders visited each room in their village and with suitable posturings and incantations drove out lurking demons. Apparently this proved to be dull, for soon most or all the ministries dropped the performance.

However, Philemon had by then received directions

for what did prove to be a long-lasting and popular exercise. That is, before any seeds of the usual kinds were planted, fields were to be sown over with others which were symbolic, or at least invisible—if not to the Shaker eye, then to that of worldly man:

> Friday. Oct. 21. About a hundred thirty of us today sewed the West farm with the seed of Blessing. Sewed also the Holy Mount. Sewed also Protection, Love, Grace, Spirituality. At the Holy Hill had a very pretty time. Sung, danced, shouted.

It was at New Lebanon—perhaps again from revelation to Brother Philemon—that a new style of dancing was developed. Instead of having a whirling group of women at one end of the meeting house and a group of men at the other, each dancing as inspiration directed, the whole thing was stylized into a rhythmic march in which the men followed close upon the women in rank and file. Like the old dances, this was called "laboring," perhaps to conceal the fact from themselves that the laborers were having the nearest thing to fun that a Shaker might have.

But an order from Mount Lebanon could not quash the old order of dancing entirely. A "winter Shaker" who spent several months at Watervliet in 1842-43 reported that

> At half-past seven P.M. on the dancing days [that is, on alternate evenings], all the members retired to their separate rooms, where they sat in solemn silence, just gazing at the stove, until the silver tones of a small tea-bell gave the signal for them to assemble in the large hall. Thither they proceeded in perfect order and solemn silence. After all were in their proper places the chief Elder stepped into the center of the space, and gave an exhortation for about five minutes, concluding with an invitation to them all to "go forth, old men, young men

and maidens, and worship God with all their might, in
the dance."

They then marched "in double-quick time" until
warmed, while several stood singing in the middle. Then
they began dancing, and after a time stopped and formed a
circle to see if anyone might "receive a gift." Two sisters
did: they whirled for fifteen minutes while everyone else
stared dispassionately. They then resumed their places "as
steady as if they had never stirred."

Sometimes when a sister had stopped her whirling,
she would say, "I have a communication to make." The head
eldress would receive the communication in a whisper and
then transmit it to the congregation:

> The first message I heard was as follows: "Mother
> Ann has sent two angels to inform us that a tribe of In-
> dians has been around here two days and want the broth-
> ers and sisters to take them in. They are outside the
> building there, looking in at the windows." I shall never
> forget how I looked round at the windows, expecting to
> see the yellow faces, when this announcement was made;
> but I believe some of the old folks who eyed me, bit
> their lips and smiled. It caused no alarm to the rest, but
> the first Elder exhorted the brothers "to take in the poor
> spirits and assist them to get salvation." He afterward
> repeated more of what the angels had said, viz., that the
> Indians were a savage tribe who had all died before Co-
> lumbus discovered America, and had been wandering
> about, ever since. Mother Ann wanted them to be re-
> ceived into the meeting tomorrow night. . . .
> The next dancing night we again assembled [and
> after the dancing] the hall doors were opened, and the
> Elder invited the Indians to come in. The doors were
> soon shut again, and one of the sisters (the same who re-
> ceived the original communication) informed us that she

saw Indians all around and among the brothers and sisters. The elder then urged upon the members the duty of "taking them in." Whereupon eight or nine sisters became possessed of the spirits of the squaws, and about six of the brethren became Indians. Then ensued a regular pow-wow, with whooping and yelling and strange antics, such as would require a Dickens a [sic] describe. The sisters and brothers squatted down on the floor together, Indian fashion, and the Elders and Eldresses endeavored to keep them asunder, telling the men they must be separated from the squaws, and otherwise instructing them in the rules of Shakerdom. Some of the Indians then wanted some "succotash" which was soon brought them . . . when they commenced eating it with their fingers. These performances continued till about ten o'clock; then the chief elder requested the Indians to go away, telling them they would find some one waiting to conduct them to the Shakers in the heavenly world. At this announcement the possessed men and women became themselves again, and all retired to rest.

The writer later learned that George Washington and some other other-world Shakers had gone on missionary tour and stirred up these particular Indians. At another meeting a whirling sister announced that Mother Ann was there—in heaven, where everyone lived "in community order" she and Jesus were the head eldress and elder—and had brought baskets of spiritual fruit. Everyone stepped forth and made motions of taking and eating. Mother had also brought spiritual golden spectacles and chains and jewelry which the elder placed on the people, besides a casket of love which was thrown out by the handful upon the people. There were also spiritual band instruments, and as the people marched out to the fountain they played on them, "making sounds with the mouth." At the holy mount, they dashed into the fountain and bathed away their sins.

All this was the more remarkable in that Shakers were forbidden musical instruments and jewelry.

The last great leader of the Shakers was Elder Frederick Evans who flourished in the 1860's and 70's, after entering Shakerdom in the early 30's. He had previously come into the public eye in the labor and land reform movements, and as an associate of Frances Wright in New York—Frances, "the Priestess of Beelzebub," who founded the Nashoba "free love" commune near Memphis.

He had previously scorned Shakerism and cynically doubted the celibacy of its members—anti-Shaker propaganda was still strong in the 1820's, although physical persecution had ceased—but then he was attracted to communalism and his investigation of the religious societies turned Saul to Paul. He quickly was given responsibilities.

He was plain-spoken. A visitor asked if the Shakers, building again, might not aim for some beauty in the "human hives" in which they lived. Evans did not parrot the usual formula that all the designs had been transmitted from heaven and that the Shakers were living as in Mother Ann's day. "No," he said simply. "The beautiful, as you call it, is absurd and abnormal. The divine man has no right to waste money in his house or his daily life while there are people in misery."

Yet, today, the smooth clean lines of Shaker furniture are looked upon as beautiful, and a similar beauty is seen in some of their architecture—particularly withindoors, as in staircase or door frame, in which they were deliberately shying from the conventional ornateness of the times.

But Evans dared not attempt to exert the autocratic power of the early leads. His people had grown "rich and lazy." Their looms decayed, for they found it simpler to buy sleazy, bright cloth than to continue making their own sturdy fabric. Evans also deplored their hiring of outside help, and the fact that a hired man was bluntly expected to turn out a greater day's work than a Shaker.

Too, in some villages there were open grumblings for books, newspapers, and musical instruments. Some ministries capitulated and supplied these things in hope of holding the children. Debating societies and literary clubs were begun, but apparently no village gave countenance to the women who wished to lay aside the eternal bonnets and even the indoor caps or to let the short-cropped hair grow.

The old order clearly was passing. No longer could conversions be made. Now and then even some old person after decades in a community could bear the life no longer and suddenly departed. Despite this gradual decline, and the tragedies of uninsured fires, of bank losses, of the ravagings of the Civil War which cost South Union village in Kentucky a hundred thousand dollars, and such things as the peculations of an occasional light-fingered elder, prosperity continued.

Still, the great houses grew empty, elders ordered dwindling families consolidated, and income was increased by the rental of unneeded dwellings and farmlands to "world's people." Negro Shakers eventually moved in with their white brethren from their previously segregated quarters, and the "nurse shops," but little used in the past, were utilized for the bedfast. However, despite the great ages reached by the Shakers, there were undoubtedly fewer such cases than among equal numbers of world's people.

But individuality cropped out. The faith, in fact, was becoming a matter of celibacy and village living, with personal interpretation of almost all other points of religion. Even the total communal sharing was somewhat whittled away as individuals began selling things and using money for private purchases. In the past, the ministry had handled all money, to the last penny. However, with changing times some villages had no ministry, or ignored such as they might have. Some individuals remained as frugal and as strait-laced as always. Others bought fripperies, took train trips for sheer pleasure, and even purchased horseless carriages and then thought up constant excuses for using them.

Ann Lee had looked with horror on ordinary church buildings—"the devil's steeple houses!" But by 1900 Shakers were faring forth from their villages on Sunday to attend services in "steeple churches" in nearby towns. They even opened their creeks to worldly baptizings. Some permitted their photographs to be taken—but others, thinking it a matter of vanity, were still refusing that decades later. The Holy Mounts were neglected. The Eternal Fountains around them presumably dried up, and the Holy Cities vanished. World's people were welcomed on Sunday afternoons to hear the newfangled talking machines the wealthy communitarians could afford.

In the old days there had been no to-do at funerals. The body was not ordinarily brought into the meeting house, where a brief memorial service was held, but it was usual that the departed send a spirit message through someone. In the latter days, world's preachers came to preach conventional funeral ceremonies. Perhaps even the Shakers would have been embarrassed at one of these gatherings had one of their number risen, as in the 1870's, to deliver a spirit message from the departed.

From time to time it would become apparent that the inmates of some village could no longer sustain themselves because of age. Then came the officials from the still-strong mother society at New Lebanon to auction off the property and move the members to some stronger village. Kentucky's South Union, for instance, brought a quarter million dollars in 1923, with the money going to the mother society. However, such members as wished were allowed to accept a cash settlement of ten thousand dollars and remain in the neighborhood where they had friends. One old man and woman, after accepting their twenty thousand, were married that they might continue their companionship. A spinster and her mother became prominent Baptist workers. But the majority, weeping, climbed aboard the train and went away to Mount Lebanon.

They predicted that in time to come the dying flame

of Shakerism would burn again on the surface, instead of invisibly beneath, as it had come to do, and that when God willed this it would "consume the chaff before it."

And so still say the several old ladies now remaining of the once-strong sect—unless indeed by this moment they too are gone.

From evil practices abstain, and every other sin.
From drinking whiskey, brandy, rum likewise and Holland gin.
For it will make a rich man poor, an honest man a knave.
It will lay the rider in the ditch
The drunkard in his grave.

Intemperance often shows itself
In dress as well as drink.
Young ladies this you know is true
And from it you should shrink.

Old woman next to you I call
Now take a friend's advise
Lay by your snuff case one and all
And throw away your pipes.

Your upper lip is always dubed
Your nose is tinged with red
You take a pinch in either hand
Then go to mixing bread.

But lacing tight is worse than all
Beware of such a curse
It injures health, produces death
Oh what can there be worse.

—*A revival song of the meetings of the Jemimakins, as recorded by
one of Jemima Wilkinson's followers just after the Revolution.*

CHAPTER FOUR

THE JEMIMAKINS AND THE UNIVERSAL FRIEND

JEMIMA NEVER MADE THE MUDDLE OF TRYING TO WALK UPON A PUDDLE

ONE of the most controversial of all the communal prophets was Jemima Wilkinson, whom Mother Ann's followers accused of merely trying to ape their leader. Jemima's own disciples considered her a divinity. Onlookers called her everything from a well-meaning and earnest doer of good works to a strumpet and charlatan and thief. Apologists today go to great lengths to defend her, perhaps because her spiritual descendants keep her memory alive and, in a sense, make her still contemporary. Her followers were dubbed the Jemimakins by angry, derisive, or merely cheerful New England and New York bystanders.

It was during the Revolution that Mother Ann, on her preaching tour which ended at the Square House,

learned she had a competitor who was making an evangelical hegira through Connecticut and Massachusetts—another
Woman Christ, who, like herself, was most profoundly horrified by the unhappy flaw in the divine plan which permitted
half the world to be male; at least, Jemima was so when it
suited her purpose to be. When it was pointed out to her that
otherwise there would be no children, she said some other
means might have been devised, as in the case of the birth
of Jesus of Nazareth.

She was further unusual in that she did not claim—
at least publicly—to be divine, but she was most vehement in
saying that she was not Jemima. Rather, she was a heavenly
personage sent down to live in Jemima's resurrected body
after Jemima's death and revival. She seems to have been
unusual among female prophets in another way, too—that of
possessing a high degree of femininity and physical beauty,
if disinterested and even hostile observers, who indeed used
these qualities against her, may be believed. Certainly there is
ample evidence that with her "lustrous black hair and deep,
glowing black eyes" and fine figure she was attractive to men.
Yet, she never married. Not exactly, at least.

The precocious child of a Quaker mother and a religiously indifferent father, the eighth in a brood of ten—or
twelve, as some who knew the family said—the last of which
cost Mrs. Wilkinson's life, the winsome Jemima was spoiled
and permitted to evade her share of household chores. She
indulged—or perhaps was indulged in—a taste for "frivolous
reading," and her lack of application caused her to be returned to her father by the woman to whom she was sent to
learn "the trade of tailoress."

At sixteen, a half dozen years before the Revolution,
she was converted in a George Whitefield revival which
scourged her native Providence County, Rhode Island. Nothing special came of this. Then when she was twenty-two,
three autumns from the fateful age of "a seven years'
maiden" and spinsterhood, she was seized with a grievous
illness. By her own account, a

. . . fatal Fever, call'd in the Year 1776, The Columbus fever: Since call'd the Typhus, or malignant fever:— The Ship Called Columbus . . . brought with her Prisoners [of war], This Awful, and allarming disease, Of which many of the inhabitance in providence died: And on the fourth of the 10th Month it reached the house of [her father] Jeremi Wilki'son, ten Miles from Providence. . . .

Jemima was stricken. She saw "Archangels descending from the east, with golden Crowns upon their heads, clothed in long white Robes, down to the feet." They put "their trumpets to their mouth" and "proclaimed saying, Room, Room, Room, in the many mansions of eternal Glory for Thee."

She went to occupy one of the Mansions—or appeared to do so. But before the body could be prepared for burial, she "rose from the—BED," as one of her detractors put it with heavy wit, weary of hearing that she had risen from the dead. Her physician said she had not died at all but was under a delusion from fever which had been "translated to her head." Some people declared that she had not even been sick, but had pretended during the entire episode.

Jemima said that indeed she had died, that her soul had gone to heaven where it yet remained at the right hand of God, and that the soul which animated her risen body was not just any old soul, but that it—in fact, that she herself now—was The Spirit of Life from God. She had "descended to the earth to warn a lost and guilty, gossiping, dying World to flee from the wrath which is to come; to give an invitation to the lost sheep of the House of Israel [i.e., to the people of Christendom] to come home." She had merely assumed "the Body which God had prepared."

From that day she dropped the mundane name of Jemima Wilkinson and became the Publick Universal Friend. Usually she referred to herself in the third person merely as The Friend. Dressing as a man to ride astride, wearing a flowing cape and a beaver slouch hat, she began a tour of Massachusetts and Connecticut on a white horse. When she halted to preach she wore a modest gown, flowing in Grecian lines without a marking of the waist, and with the full sleeves all but covering her hands.

Some of her brothers and sisters, quite awed at the marvelous and effulgent being their once-frivolous sister had become, were with her, and she soon had other close disciples who were announced as her "Apocalyptic Witnesses" to answer questions about her. They quietly let it be known that she was the risen Saviour "operating in the female line."

The prophetess on down into this century has been lauded for apparently never claiming divinity for herself. Less is said about the fact that she often refused to deny that she was the Messiah. She answered questioners enigmatically, sometimes with such scriptural quotations as, "I have yet many things to say unto you, but ye cannot bear them now," and, "Who do you say that I am?"

Several congregations which she organized demonstrated man's capacity for belief by building churches for Jemima and accepting her as their circuit-riding Saviour—a lesser word will scarcely do. The unwanted Revolution into which America had just contrived to crowd itself showed that the millennium was at hand. People were asking the burning question of the Middle Ages: "What must I do to be saved?" Jemima, the Spirit of Life, the Publick Friend, confidently answered, "Follow me."

Somehow, her quiet, persuasive, blunt preaching won converts to her, complete with their purses—but it must be said that observers who had no reason to distort the matter aver that she was not greedy concerning money. On the other hand, detractors accuse her even of pilfering the private belongings of parishioners, where she lodged, for cash, and indeed say that once she escaped prosecution only by returning some hundreds of dollars once acquired in this way.

At any rate, she roundly scored those people who were building solid New England fortunes on the rum trade with the Indians and the slave trade with Africa; and her listeners, who had no more (even less, as it turned out) to expect from those rich, pious deacons and churchwardens than did she, warmed the more to her.

Not that everything went smoothly for Jemima, for she incited her followers to the putting of their religion ahead of parents, wives, and children—and, perhaps encouraged by her confidante, one Sarah Richards, a lorn victim of husband trouble, she harshly deplored those activities which were likely to be evidenced by the bearing of children. New mothers were excoriated. She suggested that one baby be named Abomination.

For some reason, her apologists today become vehement in contending that she did not preach celibacy—which makes it passing strange that while she lived she was everywhere accused of doing so, and that people complained bitterly of losing the intimate attentions of spouses in families that were split by her. Other family quarrels resulted from converts giving her extravagant offerings and putting her in their wills.

Scandal rightly or wrongly wreaths about her and a British army officer with whom she and her sister Marcy and another girl and one William Aldrich were to go to England on a preaching tour. But something happened and they did not go. Either the officer did or didn't get her pregnant, and did or didn't jilt her—and she did or didn't go into seclusion and have or fail to have the baby. Certainly her detractors never produced a child they claimed to be hers.

But anyway, she and Marcy quarreled over the latter's romance with Aldrich, although after the match was broken up the lovers finally married anyway and Jemima seems to have forgiven them. Meanwhile, it developed, through divine revelation to Jemima, that Sarah Richards was in reality "the Prophet Daniel operating in these latter days in the female line." One of Jemima's sisters turned out to be "Enoch the Prophet of Old," and another to be "John the Beloved Disciple." One Squire Parker—definitely not of the female line, which in time was to cause much scandal concerning the Friend—was revealed to be "Prophet Elijah." He fashioned himself a costume of bedsheets on the order of those he saw pictured in an illustrated Bible, and became the object of a certain amount of attention as he accompanied Jemima—perhaps pursued is the nearer word—and busied himself with assurances to the public that she was in reality the Christ. Indeed, with such an entourage, what lesser personage might she have considered herself?

Remarkably enough, perhaps, not all the money which came to her was from the unread and unwashed. Governor Stephen Hopkins of Rhode Island and four or five other men of equal standing gave her money and advice. Supposedly, this was not merely to get rid of her—but it may be significant that they did not join her society of Universal Friends. Her most important bona fide disciple was undoubtedly one William Potter, a wealthy politician, a long-established feeder from the public trough, of South Kingstown, also of Rhode Island.

There was a Mrs. Potter, and that lady may have been willing for her husband to build the new wing he attached to their mansion for the housing of Jemima and her retinue—or again she may not, for when he finally resigned his well-worn judge's bench to trail after the Friend to the "Jerusalem" she established, Mrs. P. bluntly remained at home, waiting, apparently, for him to get over whatever it was that he sought in the way of salvation.

After the new wing was built, things began going wrong for Jemima. For some reason, women began seeing her as a serpent in their midst, and, even as Mother Lee, she was accused of casting out devils by aid of Beelzebub, and of trying to raise the dead and to heal by laying on hands.

Mobs drove her, for whatever combination of reasons, out of several towns. She sought refuge in Philadelphia where, despite stonings, she preached, flanked by Potter, Squire Parker, and the various prophets operating in the female line. The Marquis de Barbé-Marbois, of the French War Commission, went with his entourage to hear her, and his chagrin at not being noticed as he took a seat near the pulpit shines through his account.

He mentions that her sect "has been added to the five or six hundred others in which so many imprudent lambs have lost their way," and that "This soul from heaven has chosen rather a beautiful body for its dwelling place, and many living ladies would not object to animate these dead remains. Jemima Wilkinson, or rather the woman whom we call by that name, is about twenty-two years old;[1] she has beautiful features, a fine mouth, and animated eyes; her hair is parted in the middle and falls loosely on her shoulders. She washes it every day with cold water and never powders it; travel has browned her a little. She has an air of pensive melancholy; she has no acquired grace, but has all those which Nature gives. . . ."

Later, Jemima was stoned from the future neighborhood of Brook Farm, apparently because her followers claimed that she was Christ. Or perhaps people had heard her pray, or preach, and noticed that she never mentioned Jesus or the Christ, but only God and the Holy Spirit. Facing her tormentors, she threatened them enigmatically: "He that wills the sitting of every cloud may be somewhere with the thunderbolt!" But they drove her on out, and no thunderbolts struck them.

Broodingly, she considered withdrawing her people into a community of their own, and apparently some sort of communal organization was built for this, with people selling their property as they could and placing the money in a common fund, for there were troubles and fallings out concerning some such fund. But at last, in 1788, while Jemima remained behind, some two dozen of her followers moved westward into what had been hostile Indian lands, but where peace was now established. Marcy's husband died of

[1] She was about twenty-six or twenty-seven.

fever on the journey. The others halted near Dresden in the Genesee country. They established a mill and threw up some board shacks which seem not to have been substantial, for "of God's air there was plenty." It was bad air, too. Malaria and dysentery struck. But the people hung on and after two years Sarah Richards recorded:

> In the year 1790—
> 13th of the 3 Mo.
> From W. Pen [western Pennsylvania?]

The Friend set out for the Genecca Country in company with a number of friend.

The number of friends is not mentioned—later, she had "several hundred" in her village—but it may well have been that others had followed the waybreakers before she journeyed on. And she went in style in a carriage with a crescent-shaped body and fancy hangings and with the letters UF emblazoned here and there. The advent of the Universal Friends helped inflate the price of land, and Jemima quarreled with some of her people who wanted to sell the first land at a profit, and with outsiders who tried to gouge her people on the price of land. After two years, she bought more land near Canandaigua, paying down two black oxen, some of her bedding, and three silver spoons, and there, in her colony of Jerusalem, she settled the faithful. The six square miles of land were apparently in the names of some trustees of the society. Judge Potter bought more land for the society and still more in his own name.

By this time Jemima had found it impractical to keep the people in a tight communal village. She let them scatter to suitable spots upon the communal acres, but certainly there was still communal sharing and mutual assistance. By inference at least, married couples were to remain celibate. There is really a bit of a puzzle here. At times, the prophetess undoubtedly excoriated those who bore children, but she seems not to have expelled them. One may suppose, rather, that she adjured them to go and sin no more, and perhaps afflicted them with the childish and whimsical punishments which she dealt out to malefactors, such as putting them on "silent fasts"—periods of several days in which they might not speak. She punished one of her sisters, Deborah, who defied her by marrying a boy named Botsford, by saying that she would never speak to Botsford again. She allowed the pair to live at Jerusalem but she kept her oath, nor ever went to their house until the husband lay dying, but she did not speak to him even then nor use his name.

The unmarried were free to form celibate households or to dwell with Jemima in the excellent house she built for herself. It was here that the globe-trotting Duke de la Rochefoucauld found her several years later living in handsomer style than any family "for fifty miles around," attended by six or seven girls "all young and handsome."

Her people had a child-like, loving trust in her, visiting her with all their problems and meeting at her house for religious services and to see that she wanted for nothing. Stories are told that she commandeered what she wanted, saying, "The Friend hath need of these things," but account books still exist showing that she paid for things—which indicates that the communalism, except for some community households such as her own, consisted mostly of owning the land in common. There seem also to have been working bees and much lending of livestock, and the like.

Sarah Richards was more and more Jemima's other self. She even began having trances and visions in which she received news and admonitions for the people from heaven, all with the blessing of the Friend. Sarah recounted some of her visions graphically. This one has obvious symbolic meaning:

> . . . Something groaned out with a horrid sound. Then I looked and behold his crown was fallen from his head and he was wringing and twisting about and in his struggles I discovered one of his feet and knew it to be the

devil, at which I rejoiced that his throne and his seat was destroyed and himself disenabled. The Friend, I left seated on an eminence, and on The Friend's countenance, a smile. . . .

Then internal dissension arose. Jemima began requiring the frequent presence of Squire Parker, and all that Judge Potter and other questioners could learn from the handmaidens was that the two were in private "blessing each other." The judge quarreled with Jemima and, departing, brought suit to regain what he had given her—a matter eventually settled against him by the courts in a decision which stood later messiahs in good stead as a precedent when disgruntled disciples desired back their goods and chattels.

Jemima took offense at Squire Parker in time, however. He began receiving unauthorized revelations from heaven, and seeing women and girls of the colony in private to advise with them on such celestial messages as had to do with them. In the upshot, Jemima drove him from the colony, and he who had so loudly preached her divinity had her indicted for blasphemy on the charge that she claimed to be Deity!

At the trial she would neither confess nor deny that she was the Christ. But mocking questions about another story which had gained prominence so irritated her that she did deny that incident. The tale was that she once announced that she could walk on water, and would demonstrate this Galilean miracle at Lake Seneca. On the appointed day all the Jemimakins gathered to see the performance. Their mistress was brought down in a litter in the style of a queen. At the water's brink she addressed the crowd:

"My friends, does anyone here doubt that I can perform this miracle?" All shouted no. "Then," said Jemima, "there is no need of my performing it." And she had herself borne back to her dwelling.

She not only denied the whole thing as false, but further declared she had never tried to raise the dead, as she was accused of doing, nor to heal the sick except through prayer. But, still refusing to say whether she was Christ, she was dismissed.

No one else dared or cared to cross her in major matters. Her people who offended her were treated as naughty children. A man who heard sounds of revelry on the second floor of her house climbed a tree and saw Jemima and Sarah Richards and others in some harmless, sportive play. Discovered, he was forced to wear a bell to warn of his presence thereafter. Others were required to wear odd garments or dunce caps for their sins.

Relations between Jemima and some of her people deteriorated over land quarrels. She found it hard to bear ingratitude from those who could have salvation through her, as unbelievers could not. Sickness came upon her. Her beautiful body, which had drawn comment from numerous journalists and diary-keepers in her younger days, was ugly with dropsy. But the scandalous stories of the Squire Parker sort died down, and the land quarrels were held in abeyance—though the latter would keep the courts busy for years after her death.

Fearful signs and portents were seen in the sky, as noted by her new confidante, Rachel Malin, successor to Sarah Richards, who had died:

A strange smoky took place in the are on the 6 of the 11 Mo 181[?] which hid the fase of the sun for untill about the 12 of the same Mo some times it seemed as if it was a going to be quite dark, it had a brasey apearence.

the 10 of the 9 mo 1815 the Friend dreamed that there was a great women head brought to the Friend and it taulked with the Friend and sed that it was agoen to have its body again.

The 26 of the 10 Mo 1816 The Friend dreamed that everything was cut short, that the hair was cut short and that the time for Sinners to Repent was cut short, and that the time was no longer than from mid night to mid day.

What flurries of preparation for the end these things may have brought about, we are not told. But at any rate things were smoother between Jemima and her people than at times they had been. The old reverence for her was renewed and at high pitch when after forty-three years of godhood she sank toward death, to the grief and shock of those who had supposed she would live forever.

Jemima had not supposed this. She had dictated a will —but refusing to admit that she was Jemima Wilkinson, rather than the Spirit of Life, she refused to sign it. Finally, to legalize the document, she made her mark, in the manner of her most unread disciple—but beneath it she wrote, "or Universal Friend."

Full accounts of the deaths of the disciples had been recorded, always with the expression, "Left time." But on the morning of July 1, 1819, her companion and heir, Rachel Malin, noted but a single heartbroken line concerning Jemima:

Twenty-five minutes past two on The Clock, the Friend went from here.

It was Jemima's hope that God would spirit her body away, as in the case of Moses, and bury it in a spot known only to Him. Her followers believed, rather, that she would rise on the third day—"as she had twice before"—that is, as Jesus of Nazareth in Galilee, and again as a young woman near Providence.

But the body neither rose nor was spirited away, and some of the disciples buried it in the cellar, apparently in hope of concealing the death from worldly neighbors to whom they had boasted that she would live forever. Later, two of the men took the body to a secret grave in the night.

Such celibacy as had existed among Jemima's followers was gradually abandoned. The people continued on their communal acres for a long time before court decisions allowed them to divide the property among themselves. But many stayed faithful to Jemima, revering her as something more than human, as did their children and grandchildren. Something of this feeling still seems to exist around the Lake Keuka haunts that she knew, and where the secret of her grave is still supposed to be passed down from father to son so that from two to four men always know where it is. Certainly her spiritual heirs still remember her story with affection and respect. They carefully preserve such relics as her bizarre carriage with its crescent-shaped body, and some of the personal articles which bear a cross and the letters U and F.

The Duke de la Rochefoucauld reckoned her to be a shrewd, calculating, selfish woman who broke up families and alienated heirs in order to inherit undeserved property herself. Others made harsher accusations—but one man who gave her much money wrote, "A Most illustrious lady, Chimme Wilkinson." He believed she was the Messiah—as did one William Turpin who did not die until fourteen years after Jemima, when he said ". . . I now resign my soul to rest in the divine love of God, and Christ my Savior and universal Friend . . ."

Pantisocracy

No more my visionary soul shall dwell
On joys that were; no more endure to weigh
The shame and anguish of the evil day,
Wisely forgetful! O'er the ocean swell
Sublime of Hope, I seek the cottag'd dell
Where Virtue calm with careless step may stray,
And dancing to the moonlight roundelay,
The wizard Passions weave an holy spell.
Eyes that have ach'd with sorrow! Ye shall weep
Tears of doubt-mingled joy, like theirs who start
From precipices of distempered sleep,
On which the fierce-eyed fiends their revels keep,
And see the rising sun, and feel it dart
New rays of pleasance trembling to the heart.

—SAMUEL TAYLOR COLERIDGE, *in 1794, when he was aflame with
the idea of founding his envisioned commune with a new social
system, called a pantisocracy, in America.*

On the Prospect of Establishing a Pantisocracy in America

Whilst pale Anxiety, corrosive Care,
The tear of Woe, the gloom of sad Despair,
    And deepen'd Anguish generous bosoms rend;—
Whilst patriot souls their country's fate lament;
Whilst mad with rage demoniac, foul intent,
    Embattled legions Despots vainly send
To arrest the immortal mind's expanding ray
    Of everlasting Truth;—I other climes
Where dawns, with hope serene, a brighter day
Than e'er saw Albion in her happiest times,
With mental eye exulting now explore,
    And soon with kindred minds shall haste to enjoy
(Free from the ills which here our peace destroy)
Content and Bliss on Transatlantic shore.

—*Proof is wanting that Coleridge wrote this, but it appears in his
works as his.*

CHAPTER FIVE

PANTISOCRATS AND
WOOD SCRAPERS

AN INFANT IS ALMOST ALWAYS SLEEPING

B Y THE time the Friend died—and, in that same year, 1819, Mother Lucy, who had established the Shakers in their permanent village order—communalism was a going subject, with public interest increasing by the year. This interest was apparent even among people who hadn't the vaguest idea of joining a village, but who thought it might be the answer to the troubles of the poor. Perhaps some of the bystanders cherished a sneaking intention of profiting from the movement eventually if that should seem advantageous.

There had in fact been for several years in New York a "Society for Promoting Communities." While conducted by a predominately Quaker group, its interest was not narrowly religious. Rather, it stood ready to help any deserving lay group. Previous to that, well before the turn of the century, possibly but not necessarily inspired in some part by the Jemimakins and the Shakers, the community fever had been rising on both sides of the Atlantic. Men spoke of settling groups of the poor in villages of three hundred—the figure used in Cromwell's day by such planners.

In fact, even when Jemima's waybreakers were heading west to establish Jerusalem in 1788, the Frenchman de Warville, of later Girondist connection, was arriving in America to investigate the idea of establishing a model republic, but the republic did not materialize. It seems a safe guess that by the time the French Revolution was over, many unsung Frenchmen, besides the well-known Saint-Simon and Fourier, were elaborating Utopias on paper.

Certainly in England, in the mid-1790's, Utopia was in the air. Coleridge, Southey, and Lovell, romantics all, not locally unknown but yet to make their fame, laid plans to establish a village on the Susquehanna in America—a wonderful place where, a land agent assured Coleridge, "the Mosquitoes are not as bad as our gnats." Nor were there any Indians, and "no Bisons." Best of all, one man could clear eight or nine hundred acres of forest in a year.

The stories of the debacle differ in detail, but at any rate Coleridge and his friends were liberals, afire with great causes, though far from wanting to be considered "atheistical democrats" or advocates of universal suffrage. Democracy was a sorry business, with everyone pulled low to the level of "mean and jealous men." Coleridge, however, would raise up a society composed of a race elevated to aristocracy. "Pantisocracy" was the word he coined for that. In this society, property would be held in common—and he coined a word for that, "aspheterized," from the Greek for nonappropriated.

Thomas Paine and George Washington were heroes to him and to Southey. They went to the trials of liberals who were outspoken about the French Revolution, to the damage of kings, and—an extremely dangerous thing—Coleridge spoke against the nonassembly and similar ukases laid down, with death as penalty, following the attempted assassination of the English monarch in 1794. He was shadowed for quite some time by government spies, and all the while he was busily writing about Robespierre and dabbling in other possible seditions.

It was he who conceived the idea of the colony in America, but he seems to have left no hint as to where he got it, unless possibly from his cogitations over Godwin's work. Southey was enthusiastic. There should be twelve young men and twelve congenial—and respectable—young women, such as Mary Evans, with whom Coleridge was distractedly in love. Should the couples marry? If so, should they practice monogamy, or exchange freely within the circle? Apparently Mary was not consulted at all, nor, indeed, did Coleridge quite picture her as going, which may have helped lead his thoughts into the broadened possibilities of the conjugal state.

Carried away with their plans, he and Southey went on a walking tour in Wales. Even where the proud Welsh pretended not to know the English of the hated master race, Coleridge made speeches about the wonders of pantisocracy and aspheterism. They saw villages of half-starved women and children whose men had been taken away to fight the French. They heard tales of bailiffs roughed up for dispossessing people of their hovels for lack of rent. Coleridge was favorably impressed—perhaps given some ideas for the pantisocracy in America—by the sight of mixed groups in bathing naked. Concealment, he decided, was really more lust-provoking than was nudity. But Southey was disgusted and horrified.

The pair finally arrived in Bristol, on the way home, to visit their friend Lovell. He was married to one of the five vivacious Fricker sisters. Their mother was widowed.

They moved in literary circles. One was an actress. Another taught school. A third was a milliner. Coleridge forgot for the moment that he was in love with Mary Evans and began courting Sarah Fricker, and Southey became engaged to her sister Edith, who seems to have liked the idea of the pantisocracy not much more than did Southey's aunt who had brought him up and who now turned him out of doors for his foolish ideas. But Lovell was enthusiastic. A book seller, Cottle, paid the young men generously for some of their work to help them raise a fund. They lectured. They wrote madly. They made a number of converts and even found some congenial souls who had the £125 considered necessary for each person. Donations were made by sympathizers.

Back in college, Coleridge continued to dream and plan. But a disagreement rose. Coleridge wanted to take one of the Southey family's servants, by name Shadrach, and his family, and treat him as a brother. Southey would take him, but not as a brother. But Coleridge was doubtful of taking Southey's mother, and Mrs. Fricker, the mother of Mrs. Lovell and the two fiancées, Edith and Sarah. He wrote Southey:

> If Mrs. S. and Mrs. F. go with us, they can at least prepare the food of simplicity for us. Let the married women do only what is absolutely convenient for pregnant women or nurses. Let the husband do all the rest, and what will that be? Washing with a machine and cleaning the house. One hour's addition to our daily labour [it had been proved, by logic, that one hour daily per person would keep them in luxury], and *pantisocracy* in its most perfect sense is practicable. That the great part of our female companions should have the task of maternal exertion at the same time is very *improbable,* but, though it were to happen, an infant is almost always sleeping, and during its slumbers the mother may in the same room perform the little offices of ironing clothes or making

shirts. But the hearts of the women are not *all* with us. I do believe that Edith and Sarah are exceptions. . . .
But Southey there are *Children* going with us. . . . (Query; . . . In the present state of their minds, whether it is not probable that the *Mothers* will tinge the minds of the infants with prejudication?) These children—the little Frickers, for instance, and your brothers, —are they not already deeply tinged with the prejudices and errors of society? Have they not learned from their schoolfellows *Fear* and *Selfishness,* of which the necessary offsprings are Deceit and desultory Hatred? How are we to prevent them from infecting the minds of *our* children? . . . How can we ensure their silence concerning God, etc. . . . *That* Mrs. Fricker! We shall have her teaching the infants *Christianity*—I mean, that mongrel whelp that goes under its name—teaching them by stealth in some ague fit of superstition. . . . I have told you, Southey, that I will accompany you on an *imperfect* system. But must our system be thus necessarily imperfect?

There was then a sharp falling out when, with war with America threatening, some of the pantisocrats, led by Southey, decided to buy a farm in Wales—a thing which Coleridge bitterly protested, for in Wales land would be high nor could they make log cabins but needs must buy a house. Apparently Southey had come into some money, but he was not going to aspheterize it, or any of the extra land he expected to purchase near the communal farm. But no farm was bought and pantisocracy dwindled away in desultory talk. Coleridge, in bitterness, laid the debacle at Southey's door. After making a futile appeal to Mary Evans, who said she would be a sister to him, he did turn his attention to Sarah Fricker who pretended that if he did not marry her she would have to marry a man she did not love. Their marriage was a mistake—or at least it proved to be so after Coleridge met Dorothy Wordsworth, the sister of the poet.

But good or bad, it and Southey's marriage to Edith were the tangible, perhaps the only results of the pantisocratic fever.

There must have been innumerable plans in this country, too, at that time, for communes, judging from the several in New York, Massachusetts, and Vermont which fortunately were caught by chroniclers.

For instance, in the late 1790's a one-time English army officer, one Dorril, announced at Guilford, Vermont, that he was the prophet and mouthpiece of God. He found disciples, including some across the line in Massachusetts. He established them, possibly in two associated villages, under his own iron theocratic rule, with community of property and reputedly of women. No meat nor leather was allowed. Pleasant bacchanals were held which roiled a clergyman, Joseph Lathrop, who lived as far away as Springfield, Massachusetts, and who brought the sect to prominence by his castigations:

> In the northern part of this State, I am well informed, there has lately appeared, and still exists, under a licentious leader, a company of beings, who discard the principles of religion, and obligations of morality, trample on the bonds of matrimony, the separate rights of property, and the laws of civil society, spend the Sabbath in labor or diversion, as fancy dictates, and the nights in riotous excess and promiscuous concubinage, as lust impels. Their number consists of about forty, some of whom are people of respectable abilities and once of decent characters. A society of this description would disgrace the natives of Caffraria.

What he forgot was that these people believed themselves under the direct rule of God. One Captain Ezekiel Foster was as forgetful. He attended a sermon in which Dorril remarked that "no arm can hurt my flesh." He knocked

Dorril down several times, refusing to desist until the whimpering prophet confessed that he did feel pain. Dorril was much downcast over this, and perhaps it was that, added to the internal pressures brought about by the social arrangements, which soon broke up the sect. Other religious enthusiasms were later rife in the area.

A year or so after the demise of the Dorrilites, it became evident that Providence was not content to manifest the glories of heaven merely through two woman Christs and an ex-army officer. This was at least implicit in the announcement in 1799 of Nathaniel Wood of Middletown, Vermont, that a newly-arrived stranger in town, one Winchell, was not exactly what he appeared to be.

Wood was quite correct. Winchell appeared to be an itinerant water-witch and lost-money finder. In reality he was a counterfeiter, at the moment taking a vacation from his work which had grown uncomfortably hot in Orange County where he was badly wanted for prosecution. At that time, water-witches were plentiful so that there was hardly a living in the science for a professional. Further, whenever he took his rod to locate a vein of gold or some buried treasure something went wrong. He ordinarily explained his failures in terms of broken mystic spells occasioned by lack of faith on the part of those who hired him.

Somehow Nathaniel Wood smelled a fellow soul in Winchell—or at least a usable one. Wood had been in brawling contentions over religion in Massachusetts and Vermont for years and finally had formed a sect around his own large family. Apparently he lacked the resolution to become a prophet in his own right, so he became a John the Baptist for "the one to come after"—Winchell, who, he announced, was touched with divinity. The divining rod, he said, was magical. Winchell obligingly put on airs and made revelations and pronouncements and drew a cult of increasingly excited religionists around him.

Their meetings continued all through 1800, with increasingly wild manifestations of dancing and reveling as the revelations centered around a soon-coming destruction of the world. The local "Gentiles"—the non-believers—were scornful or amused, and Winchell, perhaps by then impressed with himself, made frightful predictions of their fate, but they somehow did not reform or believe in him. The orgies of the Winchellites supposedly were of a sort to set the style for the celebrated excesses of the great Kentucky revival, soon to come, of which it was freely said that "more souls were made than saved" in the brushy meetings.

For instance, in the event that anyone should feel the devil in his clothing, Winchell's magic rod might direct that the garments be removed, and in one case two young ladies, without their garments, cavorted about and fled up a snowy mountain. Such disrobings had become common, from early Quaker-Puritan times in America, but the flight up the mountain—not recorded until many years later—may have become confused in local legend with a similar and well-authenticated bit of drama in a Perfectionist spiritual-mating group.

But certainly the Winchellites had a roaring good revival for the space of a year or more. Finally, Winchell was so carried away with his own awesome powers that he announced the end of the world for the night of January 14, 1801. God, he stated, would send an earthquake, accompanied by the Destroying Angel who would kill all non-believers.

Leading Winchellites, such as Wood and his neighbor Cowdry—or Cowdery, as the name became famous later in Mormon annals—went about marking the doorposts of the elect so that the angel, in his well-established method which goes back at least to Egypt in 1200 B.C., would know which dwellings to skip.

There was laughing, however uneasy, on the part of the prospective victims. In the afternoon of the fateful day the town authorities called out the militia and ostentatiously posted it to patrol the streets. The fear was that as the heat of the evening's meeting rose, the Winchellites might mistake themselves for destroying angels and that the rod might direct them to the slaughter of some of their more persistent taunters.

As has been not unusual in such cases, the world survived the night and the jeering Middletowners dubbed the affair "the Wood Scrape." The sect fell apart and Winchell and Oliver Cowdry, son of the Cowdry family, drifted to Palmyra, New York, where they became acquainted with another water-witch, Joseph Smith, Jr., who was also from Vermont and who was to have more luck than had Winchell in becoming established as "the mouthpiece of God." It is of course quite possible that Smith found a certain amount of inspiration in Winchell's briefly blazing career as a prophet. It is of interest that he, too, referred to those who doubted him as "Gentiles."

In 1817 a small group of people calling themselves Pilgrims gathered in Lower Canada around a prophet named Bullard who preached common ownership of property and living by the Bible. Since the Bible did not command them to wash, they did not wash. Since it said that the dead should bury the dead, the Pilgrims left bodies lying. And since it commanded them to fast and pray, they fasted and prayed.

Irritated neighbors were glad to see them depart when Bullard announced that they had been commanded to journey southwestward to "the New Jerusalem." They drifted into Vermont, some of them wearing skins and leather, some, queer striped garments, the men affecting beards but with upper lips shaven. Somehow, converts were attracted to them, and presumably several thousand dollars were given Bullard by the joiners. More than a hundred Vermonters followed him out of the state. Prying questioners were roundly cursed by the prophet.

They finally settled on an island in the Mississippi near New Madrid, Missouri, where their starved condition brought them much attention. Those who spied upon them saw them eating mush out of troughs, like animals, and sucking up the liquid through joints of cane. Finally the sheriff and a posse took food to the island and were met by the gaunt prophet who wildly shouted for them to leave. Crying, "Fast and pray! Fast and Pray!" Bullard ordered his people not to eat, but the adults were cowed by the officers and some of the frightened children were at last persuaded to take food.

Bullard may have been among those who died on the island. At any rate, the sect, for the most part at least, broke up and families scattered, some of them plunging into the Ozark hills, as if to escape anyone who knew of their fanatical past, and their descendants live there yet.

Even as such people were mocked and derided, so the Shakers still were too, up into the 1820's, although the outright physical persecution of them was over. They had been much against the War of 1812—and though whole countrysides in America were likewise against it on economic grounds, the Shaker objection was on religious grounds and that caused hard feeling toward them. Gradually, though, they came to be looked upon only as queer if harmless fanatics, and it was freely said that people who joined them were looking mostly for something to eat and were willing to undergo the discipline of "a few barbarous customs" to obtain it.

Then, in the 20's, as the communitarian fever grew, they were more and more looked upon with a respectful eye as dedicated religionists, and for their financial success. The Shakers themselves became heady with all this to the point that they saw themselves as waybreakers in a movement that was going to sweep the earth, forgetting that they had fallen into it by sheer accident. They were in fact so important, and not merely in the two-headed-calf category of curiosity, that no foreign dignitary considered his tour of America as complete without a visit to a Shaker village.

All this contributed to the atmosphere which made

possible the first of the great lay communes, the extravaganza of New Harmony, founded by the Owen family of England, and the lesser commune of Nashoba, established at almost the same time by Frances Wright who—for a while—was the great and good friend of the Owens. Indeed, as "the Priestess of Beelzebub," the "Whore of Babylon"—for she had the temerity to speak out in favor of free love—she was accused by the press of being too good a friend.

Also contributing to the atmosphere of communalism was the German-language village of the Rappites—but it contributed more than atmosphere to New Harmony. It furnished, at a song, a ready-made town for the Owens in which they might work their wonders.

CHAPTER SIX

FATHER RAPP'S CHILDREN

THEY DIDN'T CARE FOR WHAT NATURE MOST NATURALLY ENCOURAGES

Think how your fathers left their native land—
Dear German-land! O sacred hearths and homes!—
And, where the wild beast roams
In patience planned
New forest-homes beyond the mighty sea,
There undisturbed and free
To live as brothers of one family.

—J. G. WHITTIER: *from the Latin of Pastorius*

ACCORDING to whether detractor or apologist was talking, George Rapp, whose followers called him "Father," was variously a saint and a holder of serfs; a godly man and a dabbler in magic and Satanism; a celibate and a man who kept a young woman in his alchemical laboratory altogether too much; a loving father, and a patriarch who ordered the death of his son for rebellious behavior.

Whatever else he may have been later, in Germany, before coming to America, he was a peasant, an educated one, a big man of commanding presence. And with his followers he was to be taken—in some accounts by conventional means, in others, miraculously through the air—to Palestine with his followers to greet the returning Jesus.

100

Several hundred families warmly adhered to him, and their doctrine wonderfully irritated their Lutheran neighbors who, it seemed, were to be under Rappite rule during the Thousand Years.

The authorized Lutheran priesthood openly encouraged the usual persecutions of the laity against these heretics, who were scattered helplessly in their individual homes. At the same time the Rappites refused to send their children to the state schools or to give military service, and thus they were repeatedly fined for both their religious and secular offenses.

Their solace, in the midst of stonings, jailings, and finings, was their assurance that they were the Chosen and would one day rule their tormentors. Nevertheless, they were so near the point of ruin that they rejoiced when Rapp opportunely received a divine command that they move to America. In the next year, 1805, several shiploads of them settled in Beaver County, Pennsylvania, a dozen miles from the Ohio River, on individual farms scattered over several thousand acres. No thought of communal living was in their minds.

Then a prophet named Haller led away a large segment, leaving Rapp with some three hundred people among whom were a disproportionate number of sick, young, and aged. How these were to have been supported in the original plan does not appear, but now it was said that the only way to take care of these people, to save the colonizing project and Rappism itself, was to unite in communal order. Besides, with time so short, what difference did it make who owned what? Further, Haller's duplicity had really served to free the wheat from the chaff, and was it not fitting that the truly Chosen live as did the first Christians?

What they did not consider, they and all the others who congratulated themselves on this point, was that those Christians at Jerusalem had been driven into a tight little group by the same pressures which would be operating

1800 years later—and that they prodigally spent their resources, in the belief that Jesus would return just any day and make them victorious over their persecutors. The upshot was that the six other churches of Christendom had to raise money eventually to bail them out of their difficulties.

But if property meant nothing, Rapp's American backwoods neighbors freely asked, why was the prophet so eager to get all that of his people into his own hands, as he did in the covenant of "The Community of Equality and Society of Harmony"?—a covenant which also bound the signers to obey him without question and to hear the voices of his appointed overseers as his own. The Rappites perhaps were unaware that the Americans considered them Rapp's serfs. Rapp said calmly that his people loved him and did not feel like serfs. Certainly they gave cheerful obedience.

Buildings were raised and machinery built or purchased. More Rappites came from Germany so that soon four hundred were turning out not only large quantities of farm produce, but cloth, lumber, flour, saddles, wagons, harness, woodwork and, most profitably, whisky, for an America where everyone took his dram and where tippling was not a matter of morality.

The Rappites were, however, primarily religionists and not social experimenters. In their religious reflections, many became troubled—for had not Jesus been celibate? And observe "the original Adam": "So God created man in his own image, in the image of God created he him; male and female created he them." The plural pronoun, said the Rappites, indicated that Adam was male-female before the removal of Eve from him. That he might have brought forth young from his double self. But he was unhappy, so Jehovah humored him by separating Eve from him—this being the Fall.

The point was that the original Adam was celibate. He was also in the image of God, which proved that God was celibate. *Ergo,* the Rappites should be celibate. What they neglected to remember was that they were not Deity but German peasants.

In a revival atmosphere, agitation increased for celibacy. The point is made that the widowed Rapp cautioned slowness—but some said that this was a calculated opposition designed to whip up the fever. Certainly there could have been no rule of celibacy against his wishes. The new order was voted in. Those against it promptly left, but supposedly many of the most enthusiastic were the young. No measures were taken to insure enforcement. Personal willingness was deemed the only safeguard, and transgression, to be punished by expulsion, was expected to discover itself. The married continued in their homes, couples still occupying the same beds if they wished to. After a century, it was declared that "there never was a case of unfaithfulness to the rule."

For some reason—apparently because women were denied it—tobacco was given up at the same time as sex. However, band music, song fests, and fetes were continued. A chief disappointment was that grapes did not do well. The wine-bibbing Rappites did not care for whisky. They wanted vineyards. Too, it was expensive and annoying that they had settled so far from water and must haul freight by wagon.

Thus it was that after the War of 1812 they moved into the pacified Indian lands on the Wabash, selling the Pennsylvania colony for a hundred thousand dollars— scarcely the value of the buildings on the six thousand acres. Worldly neighbors declared that Rapp wished to move only because his people, in prosperous leisure, had time to reflect upon his one-man rule, and that he desired the hardships of a new wilderness to occupy them.

Nevertheless, the people seem eagerly to have gone. In the new land the only rumblings were in the nature of an occasional elopement—and until these became a nuisance, means of a new start was always given the erring, expelled couples. Meanwhile, the malaria of the new land for several seasons sent a steady procession of the unacclimated Rappites to the unmarked graves the Society favored. Despite this, so remarkable was the reputation of Harmonie in Europe, and so strong its millennial appeal, that it continued to grow by influx from Germany until it reached eight hundred.

The Rappites had quickly become prosperous in Indiana in the manufacture of items needed on the frontier. Stone buildings soon transformed the original log hamlet. Rappite stores were opened in non-Rappite communities and merchants over a wide area fomented trouble for the price-cutting Germans by pointing out that in the sparsely settled territory it was possible for them to swing an election. Rustic statesmen agreed, and held up the celibacy of the colony as an insulting rebuke to the God-fearing fornicators, adulterers, and holy-matrimonialists of the frontier. So great became the uproar that the Rappites were fearful of armed attack and they prepared for a siege in their stone buildings which they loopholed for sturdy defense.

In the face of their resolution, the threat passed. Father Rapp turned his attention to his church, the plan of which he had been given in a dream to be executed by his adopted son Friedrich—for his own son had died. Rappite enemies declared that Rapp had had the boy murdered for attempting to re-espouse the wife he had taken just before the establishment of celibacy, but dissidents breaking away from the community and with nothing to gain declared as vehemently that the death was a natural one.

Rapp's church—no longer standing, though many of his buildings are—was a remarkable one. In the form of a Greek cross, it lay a hundred twenty feet in each direction with pillars of various divinely specified woods standing twenty-five feet high on the ground floor. An English traveler, William Hebert, wrote that he could scarcely believe himself in the wilds of Indiana "while passing through the long and resounding aisles and surveying the colonnades of this church."

He was similarly astounded by the prosperity of the German peasants—for they were still exactly that. An American backwoodsman from a typical three-sided hovel confessed that his kind were as amazed as was Hebert: "I studies it and I studies it," he declared.

The scandalous Lord Byron thought he knew why prosperity was so rife at Harmonie. He gave his view in the fifteenth canto of Don Juan:

> *When Rapp the Harmonist embargoed marriage*
> *In his harmonious settlement—(which flourishes*
> *Strangely enough as yet without miscarriage,*
> *Because it breeds no more mouths than it nourishes,*
> *Without those sad expenses which disparage*
> *What Nature naturally most encourages)—*
> *Why called he "Harmony" a state sans wedlock?*
> *Now here I've got the preacher at a deadlock. . . .*

Life was pleasant at Harmonie as the fever died and the endless procession to the graves ceased. Rapp amused himself with laying out a vast and tortuous hedge labyrinth representing the puzzling and thorny journey to salvation. Too, he liked to exhibit a rock with huge human-like footprints, which he probably bought from flatboatmen who had taken it from formations along the Mississippi. Rapp always said it was where the angel Gabriel had alighted when fetching a message from heaven to the Harmonists. Travelers whose mental sights were not set for whimsy solemnly recorded that he was overawing his followers with superstitions.

They also said he fancied the idea of tunnels connecting the buildings that he might rise up "as if out of the earth" to mystify the ignorant workers. Probably these were not much mystified, since they had dug the tunnels—most likely during the threat of armed attack. Still, perhaps

Rapp did use the passages for spying on the workers, and he seemed to enjoy appearing suddenly from nowhere at the pulpit before the congregation.

After ten years, looking by then like a biblical patriarch, Rapp decided to move the people back to Pennsylvania, but on the river. Again, detractors said he wished to give the people the rigors of a wilderness to keep them from thinking—and there did develop some evidence later of disloyal thoughts. Harmonie was offered for sale but there were no takers for such a vast plant. However, Providence was providing.

A few miles away in Illinois lived a colony of Englishmen who endeared themselves to Rapp by taking up some of his principles for cooperative living, although they were not communitarians, and by consideration of plans to turn their enterprise into a project for the emancipation of Negroes. Rapp was bitterly scored by calumniators for supposedly driving hard bargains with white redemptioners on the ships at Philadelphia, immigrants who sought prospective masters to pay their passage to America. True or not, he was certainly for black emancipation, and this created a warm friendship between him and one of the Englishmen, Richard Flower, father of George Flower, one of the founders of the Illinois colony. Richard was about to take his son to England to prevent threatened assassination of the younger man by Illinois farmers whose Bibles commanded them to have slaves.

Rapp had received letters years before from Owen, asking for information and advice of a communitarian nature. He now offered Flower a fee of five thousand dollars if he could sell Harmonie to Owen for a hundred thirty-five thousand dollars. This was ridiculously below its real value, but the sum was known to be half of Owen's ready money and perhaps that is how the figure was reached. They expected him to jump at the offer for they knew he estimated a half million would be required for establishment of a commune suitable for testing his ideas in his own country.

And jump he did, and accordingly the Germans were presently establishing their third town of—not another Harmonie. For a subtle change had come into their thinking. Communal sharing, into which they had come by accident, was now an important tenet of their religion. But money making was their exhilaration, and they were interested in the economic theories which declared communalism to be the coming system. The new village was called Economie.

By this time, the speech barrier had faded a little. Perhaps that was in part responsible for the fact that for the first time relations were passably good with the worldly neighbors. On week days the band marched to the fields and oompah-oompahed to make time pass more swiftly for the laboring peasants. On Sunday afternoons it gave concerts which were attended by Rappites and world's people, and the Germans, who had five meals daily—including the two "bites" at midmorning and midafternoon—were likely to bring out refreshments. Much contact was had with the world, too, in the keeping of a public hotel for travelers.

For the moment, it would seem, the neighbors looked on Rapp with the same kind eye as did the globe-trotting Duke of Saxe-Weimar-Eisenach who was present when sixty or seventy girls gathered in one of the factory rooms and with "their venerated founder" seated in their midst sang "spiritual and other songs."

"With real emotion did I witness this interesting scene. Their factories and work-shops were warmed during the winter by means of pipes connected with the steam-engine; and all the workmen had very healthy complexions, and moved me deeply by the warm-hearted friendliness with which they saluted the elder Rapp. I was also much gratified to see vessels containing fresh, sweet-scented flowers standing on all the machines. The neatness which universally reigned was in every respect worthy of praise."

But minds were not entirely upon the income from the great four-story wool, cotton, and silk mills, and the Golden Rule Distillery. Not at all: all night long, on the hour, the night-watch cried, "A day is past, and a step made nearer our end—our time runs away, and the joys of heaven are our reward."

Then in the winter of 1831-32 there was an almost fatal diversion—one which amply took Father Rapp's mind off his alchemical laboratory and the young lady who allegedly was much engaged in assisting him in his search for the philosopher's stone which would coin gold even more rapidly than the "Economites," as outsiders called them, were doing.

The diversion centered in one Bernhard Mueller or Müller who called himself modestly, in this country, Count Leon. In Germany he had anointed himself duke—the Duke of Jerusalem. He intimated that he was a sadly romantic figure in that (as he said) he had been changed in the cradle, after being born into the House of Este "which on the paternal side descended from Judah and on the maternal from Joseph." A prophecy was that a great world political and religious reformer was to be born to the house—that is, Count Leon said there was such prophecy— and when little Maximilian materialized, it being known by signs and portents that he was the fated troublemaker, he was entrusted to a German woman named Müller for upbringing, while his "twin sister" was nurtured for her destiny as number three in the covey of wives of Kaiser Franz of Austria. Scoring the talk that he was really the son of Goodwife Müller, Count Leon was wont to remark that she was a widow at the time of his birth. Other people had noticed the same thing, but they had other stories to account for her possession of a new baby than that he was a royal foundling.

All that was in 1788, just as Mother Lucy Wright was establishing the Shakers in communal order at Mount

Lebanon. It was in 1810 that the future count first brought himself to public attention by writing a direful letter to Napoleon, warning the emperor of disaster if he did not bow down and repent. He failed to get a hearing—perhaps because he didn't remember to include the as-yet-unpublicized news that his twin sister was the little corporal's step-mother-in-law.

Two years later, in the Napoleonic debacle, he was, in the light of his letter, in position to remark on his ability as a prophet—a spotlight shared only by some millions of others who had uncannily foreseen that the Corsican might expect indigestion from his territorial gorgings.

A little later, as Messenger of the Archshepherd, he stirred up millennial fevers; and doubters, it seems, were struck by the fatal illnesses of body and purse which customarily plagued people of that era who failed to go along with prophets. But some were impressed, and among these was one Catherine Gunther, a sixteen-year-old who traveled with Müller that he might (as he said) instruct her in religion. He also gave her protection because of her previous betrayal by a soldier. Despite the danger of irritating the prophet, authorities sent the girl to her home village where she became the butt of crushing mockery.

Müller's preaching finally landed him in prison, but he had become a Freemason—cannily, some said—and his adherents brought him to the attention of Landgrave Karl of Hessen, Grandmaster of the German lodge. This shrewd scion of that fine old family, which fattened by selling Hessian soldiers to the highest bidder, was wonderfully impressed by the Messenger, or Organ, who, modestly disclaiming divinity, described himself only as the one sent to announce the soon-coming of Jesus in "the Seventh Period." Time was short: at the moment, the world was in period six!

Perhaps there is only Jovian irony in the Grandmaster's being caught with this moldy hay. However, Müller's persuasiveness may have been based by then on a conviction of his rightness, for the occupational hazard of prophets is that if given encouragement they fall into the common stew with their adherents. But it seems a little sad that Father Rapp should have been victimized, too.

Yet, Rapp was in a measure victim of his own prophecies, revelations, and interpretations. He preached that the Twelve Tribes of Israel were to be re-established and the Temple rebuilt and the old Jewish sacrifices therein reinstituted. Too, in the Seventh Period all property would be held in common by everybody. And, wonderfully, the secret of the philosopher's stone—and Rapp was hot on its trail—would in that period be discovered and alchemy brought to perfection. Gold thus would be had for the asking and toil would become unnecessary, although it is not exactly clear what was to be eaten after the ceasing of productive labor.

Müller announced all these things as independent revelations, and Rapp was perhaps even more charmed than was the pixillated Landgrave Karl, though the prophet in America seems not to have commented on Müller's further revelation that men would marry at thirty, leave their wives at ninety, serve God another thirty years, then lie down and quietly die—all in the Seventh Period.

The fact of course was that people were seeking salvation and that Müller, an earnest-acting, intense man, brought hope to a certain element of them just as priests and prophets appeal, each to his own kind, to various elements today. Rapp discoursed to his people of the Messenger across the sea whose prophecies corroborated Rappite dogma and revelation, and there is no hint that he wondered if perhaps the Messenger had borrowed from Rappism, or had tailored his utterances deliberately to those of Rapp. As for Landgrave Karl, he squeezed a collection from his wealthy friends and established an estate for his prophet. But then Müller became carried away with himself and began preaching unpopular doctrines so that he was driven from the Germanies. Father Rapp promptly invited him to make his home at Economie. The "count" graciously accepted.

It was in the late fall of 1831 that Müller sent one of his officials of state from Pittsburg to announce to Rapp that His Effulgence was waiting in that town until proper steps for his reception were assured. He came on then with his entourage of forty or more people, including "the Countess Leon" and a daughter. His Minister of War was beside him and one or both—as in the case of the angels who visited at Mount Lebanon, the pronouns are difficult—were "in resplendent uniform, sword at side."

Father Rapp happily escorted "the Ambassador and Anointed of God, of the stem of Judah, of the Root of David" to the church, where the band on the tower played in welcome. The Anointed then spoke, modestly characterizing the event as the most important since the creation, and announced that henceforth all the troubles and sorrows of "the Lord's people" were to cease. He also read to the eager Rappites from his "Golden Book" in which he had embalmed his jewels of wisdom.

If Father Rapp and his hard-core disciples were "the Lord's people," as they were certain they were, their troubles had, on the contrary, just begun. The Count quietly began preaching the joys of matrimony to likely listeners, and soon Rapp supposedly saw that the fellow was making headway. The great mystery is why he did not kick him out. Rapp's apologists say that the patriarch was too tender hearted, with winter coming on, to do so. Another view is that he really did not perceive a rift, or did not doubt his own power to hold his people. Still another is that the Count to an extent overawed him.

Leon also talked about the shameful way in which the Economites were regimented by the prophet and the overseers—and it must be remembered that he was working much among the second generation, people who had grown up in Rappism, brought in willy-nilly, as children, but now

of marriagable age. Suddenly, complete disruption of the
commune was threatened, and the prophet was forced to
risk a showdown, since the time was past when he dared
try to drive Leon out lest he be driven out himself, with no
redress but in the courts, with juries of men who long had
thought him a victimizer of his people. A third of his
people voted to make Count Leon head of the Society. The
remainder held with the old prophet. Rapp was ready with
a comment from Revelation: "And the tail of the serpent
drew the third part of the stars of heaven, and did cast
them to earth."

Rapp was wise enough to know that the dissidents
must be got completely out of the village, with no division
of communal acres or property to keep them even adjoining it. He agreed to pay them $105,000 on condition of
their leaving at once with only their clothing and household goods. In the end, only one hundred seventy-six moved
with Leon and his foreign disciples to a farm of eight hundred acres ten miles down the river. They established communal life with marriage permitted. The Count quickly ran
through the money, or pretended that he did. With his followers, he raised a riot at Economie in effort to obtain more
cash and Rapp called for militia to restore order.

Failing to extort additional money from Rapp in
court, Leon took some of his followers down the Ohio
and Mississippi and up the Red, finally halting on the
bluffs near the ancient town of Natchitoches, Louisiana—a
spot he chose because of its having the same latitude as Jerusalem which he said made it a likely spot for Jesus to
choose for the Second Coming. Too, someone told him
gold was to be found in the area.

The Count was snatched off almost at once to his
eternal reward in a bout with cholera. After two years of
tribulation the remnant of his people moved sixty-five miles
northward to establish Germantown near Minden where
some cabins, reputedly theirs, still stand. Legendarily, their

new site was granted to "the Countess von Leon" by President Andrew Jackson, but no record of such grant exists. The Countess soon had enough and went to Hot Springs, Arkansas, to live with her married daughter. The colony struggled along for some thirty-five years before it dissolved.

The Count had left many one-time Economites in poverty on their eight hundred acres on the Ohio—nor was drama over for them. They were fated for involvement with the remarkable quack, Dr. Keil, who also for a time seems to have been a messiah. But that is a cycle of communitarianism unto itself, one which moves from Pennsylvania to Missouri and across hostile Indian country to the Pacific Northwest.

As for the Rappites proper, not long after the Leon episode, there was talk that Rapp had procured the murder of his foster son Friedrich. The Rappites declared Friedrich was accidentally killed by a falling tree and that the public had simply dug up the same ugly story they had told on the death of Rapp's own son. Evidence which satisfied the officials was presented, and no arrest was made.

Slowly these troubles faded into memory. All settled to quietness in a static, dying society. In 1847, twenty-three years after selling Harmonie on the Wabash to Robert Owen, Rapp at the age of ninety took to his bed. From the window of his sickroom he preached to his sorrowing people. Finally he murmured, "If I did not know that the dear Lord meant I should present you all to him, I should think my last moments come."

He thought aright; but with the dedicated blindness of true disciples, the Rappites failed to consider that he might have been as wrong on other things as on how long he should live. Henceforth, they took orders from those who had been in leading positions under Rapp. As among the Shakers, religion was gradually de-emphasized with the

dying of the original Rappites. However, communitarianism, obedience to leaders, and celibacy remained basic tenets as did the belief still that Jesus would come "soon."

Through the decades, more and more Economites died off. The town of Ambridge crept up to Economie and began engulfing it like an amoeba. Rappite factories gathered dust. Tannery vats dried. Looms decayed.
Paint fell off the sign of the Golden Rule distillery. But
money continued piling up in the banks, for capital had
been invested elsewhere after it was seen that the local factories required an undesirable amount of outside help. The
Rappites owned many sorts of factories, besides mines and
oil wells, but no one was more surprised than themselves
when a lawsuit caused an estimate in court of their worth as
a possible thirty millions.

By the 1870's only a few score hale old people were
left to move spryly about the village in their distinctively
styled knee-coats, broad hats, and wide white bonnets of
earlier days. They lived together in little households of
congenial men and women, and ate together at their inn
which seems to have fed more tramps—for it was on the list
of hundreds—than it did paying guests.

Things began slipping badly in the 90's. The old
people were no longer capable of handling their great enterprise. They had been treated as children under a system
which did not develop new leaders—and at any rate, senility
was upon them. The wolves closed in. Such savage losses
were taken that it appeared they would all end as wards of
the state.

However, a manager was sent for—a boy they had
raised, by then grown to be a successful businessman who
had quit his career for music. Out of the wreckage he paid
all claims and salvaged several hundred thousand dollars—
a sorry enough showing for holdings that had once
amounted to fifty or more millions, but enough to keep the
old people in comfort.

It was 1905 when he settled the last claim—exactly

a century after the first Harmonie was established a few miles away. One more year and the enterprise was over. All the Society had joined their prophet and friends in the nameless graves of the cemetery where all were equal in death.

This was one commune which but for the rocks of celibacy on which it was wrecked might have lasted until now, at least in the form of a great stock company. As it was, private individuals soon acquired all the property except the "Great House," and that is preserved by the state of Pennsylvania as a museum—a physical monument to Father Rapp and those who were sure he would take them to Palestine to meet the Lord.

Meanwhile, long since, Nashoba and New Harmony, the first of the ambitious lay communes, which in part were inspired by the early successes of the Rappites, had had their brief hour in the sun.

CHAPTER SEVEN

FRANCES WRIGHT AND THE EMANCIPATION OF WOMAN

But where the sorrow and the treachery are
May easily be made appear:
In bridal scenes, and banquets, and in bowers!
Mid revelry and variegated flowers
Is where your mother Eve first felt their powers.

—ANON.

THOUGH the first of June, 1827, fell on a Friday, the inhabitants of Frances Wright's "Nashoba," in the wilderness a dozen miles from Memphis, were so exercised as to meet in full conclave. They usually met only on Sundays. The cause of the excitement is detailed in the daybook kept by James Richardson, a "resident trustee." (General Lafayette, for example, was also a trustee but he was in France and probably never saw the place.)

The gathering was because "Isabel had laid a complaint against Redrick for coming during the night of Wednesday to her bedroom, uninvited, and endeavoring, without her consent, to take liberties with her person." Red-

116

rick most likely asked at that point, in the reading of the charge, if this was not a free-love as well as a share-the-wealth commune.

Frances Wright was in Europe just then with her friend Lafayette, but her younger sister Camilla again "stated our views on the sexual relation." She said that as the conduct of Redrick

> which he did not deny, was a gross infringement of that view, a repetition of such conduct by him or by any other of the men ought in her opinion to be punished by flogging.
> She repeated that we consider the proper basis of the sexual intercourse to be the unconstrained and unrestrained choice of *both* parties. Nelly having requested a lock for the door of the room in which she and Isabel sleep, with the view of preventing the future uninvited entrance of any man, the lock was refused as being in its proposed use inconsistent with the doctrine just explained; a doctrine which we are determined to enforce, and which will give to every woman much greater security than any lock can possibly do.

There wasn't much Nelly or Isabel could do about it. They were slaves bought by the commune to prove the expediency of allowing the Southern Negro to work out his freedom—a project which had the interest and moral support of such high-placed men as Jefferson, Madison, and Jackson. The free-love angle was a new enthusiasm picked up in recent months by Frances Wright as part of her campaign for the emancipation of women.

However, she would not have been foolish enough to give her views on the subject to the papers at this critical stage of the colony's development—but the irresponsible Richardson did exactly that, Camilla and the white overseer, one Whitby, blithely concurring. They sent the above and other extracts from the daybook to an interested editor, and the scandal took the happily shocked country by the ears.

Children of a liberal Scot, and orphaned in babyhood, Camilla and Frances had been brought up by relatives—Frances by their maternal grandfather in England, General Duncan Campbell, while Camilla appears to have been kept in Dundee. Frances was a lonely, precocious child who read in her grandfather's library, and who angered her teachers by "unruliness"—which is to say, she exposed their ignorance by her own wide knowledge, and by asking "dangerous questions."

"Is the truth dangerous?" she asked one.

All he dared say was, "It is thought to be so." This was in the first decade of the 1800's—she had been born in 1795—and it was irritating that a girl should inquire into politics, the divorce of George IV, the French Revolution, and the shooting of English laborers who wrecked factory machines.

Parts of history were perhaps more distasteful than dangerous to the household of a British general—so distasteful that there was no mention in Campbell's library of the American Revolution. Frances was eighteen before she became aware there had been such a war, and that there was a democracy where men were said to be free and equal. Her interest in human freedom was so strong that she already had written a tragedy on the struggle of Switzerland to escape Austria, with overtones of the contemporary grindings of the Austrian iron heel on Greece.

Despite the alarmed and incessant arguments of relatives, she and Camilla at once shipped for America, where Frances was carried away with the freedom of speech, of the press, and of elections. The universal friendliness, even of strangers on the streets, astounded and pleased her. She took a rosy view of everything except slavery which so distressed her that she did not visit the South. The crowning satisfaction was the acceptance of her play for production in New

York. In published form it brought a letter from Jefferson for its expressions on human freedom. Today it makes dreary reading.

On returning to England, she had her letters and impressions of America published. They were widely translated. She was taken up by the leading minds of England and lived for a time in the home of Jeremy Bentham—he whose skeleton, says Melville in *Moby Dick*, "hangs for candelabra in the library of one of his executors," and "conveys the idea of a burly-browed utilitarian old gentleman. . . ."

It would be regrettable to know that this is not true. However, what purports to be Bentham's mummified remains have for a century and a quarter, since his death, sat in dignity in a common room of London's University College. The head is now made of wax, and nothing that was really Bentham may be there. But if it is, it is by his own request. He thought it wasteful to destroy bodies and advocated that people preserve their ancestors, properly dressed and nicely lacquered to keep out the rain, and station them about their lawns as being more interesting and informative than most decorations. In other words, in Bentham Frances found a delightfully whimsical mind, that of a man who was also a philosopher and a thinker, to whet her own against.

Presently she and Camilla journeyed to France where they were feted as in England. And there began her strange association with the aging Lafayette who was deep in the plans for an antimonarchist coup. Too, he had freed some or all of his slaves at his plantations in French Guiana—an added tie of sympathy.

When apart for a day, they wrote letters. "My beloved and honored friend," she began one, "I look round for you, listen for your foot and your voice twenty times a day. I am alone without you. I do not ask if you sometimes think of me. I know you do—very often. I am only half alive when away from you. You must continue to love me in spite of my little worthiness for in truth I love you very, very much. I have nothing as you see to tell you except this, and as you knew it before was it worth the writing? I know you will answer yes. I put my arms around the neck of my paternal friend and ask his blessing."

Lafayette's grown children were humiliated. They told their widowed father that he was making himself ridiculous. No doubt they had fears for their inheritance. They bitterly detested the English woman who put her arms around his neck. His revolutionary coup failed through bad management but he cleverly avoided sharing the scaffold with some of his associates. Presently the U. S. Congress and the President invited him to make a triumphal tour celebrating the fiftieth anniversary of the Declaration of Independence.

His family rose in open outrage that he desired Frances and Camilla to accompany him. He fell into a sulking decline and said he would not go. They reversed their field—for after all some quarter million in gifts awaited him —and begged the girls to make the voyage. On a separate ship, that is, for appearances' sake. Frances indignantly refused on the ground that this would be admission of something wrong in her relationship with the general. Lafayette stoutly agreed.

By the time the family capitulated on this point it was too late for the girls to obtain passage on his ship, but, mollified, they came on another. Arriving first, he delayed the official reception so they might see his gaudy triumph. Proudly he showed Frances off in New York and Philadelphia. She was not quite pretty, having a slight masculine cast of feature, but she had a good figure and short curly hair, and she knew how to dress.

It was while on the tour of the country—a continual fete—that she seems to have suggested that he adopt her. For whatever reason, he refused and they quarreled and parted. Just then a chief subject of conversation in the East was Fanny's countryman, Robert Owen, who had come to

America and bought the prosperous village of Harmonie on the Wabash from the Rappites. Besides the town to house and employ eight hundred, there were thirty thousand acres of ground.

Frances shared Owen's well-known religious radicalism, his humanitarian ideals for workers, and his belief in equal rights for women, and she visited him in Washington. He did not intend to go to his town just yet, but since she was journeying down the Ohio River, he invited her to turn aside and inspect it. And so she did.

Frances was astonished at the general prosperity and well-being of the one-time peasants who had conquered the machine which in other places was conquering the workers. She also visited the English colony at Albion, in Illinois, and became acquainted with the Flowers who had been instrumental in selling Harmonie to Owen. They agreed with her that in communal association might be found the means of bringing about nation-wide abolition. Indeed, they had toyed with a plan of buying Negroes and allowing them to work out their own freedom, with the income to be invested in more slaves and land, while the freed slaves would be colonized outside the States—in Texas, for instance—to meet the Southern fear of a class of free Negroes.

Frances seized upon the plan at once—or perhaps she had conceived it independently. She would establish a commune in which whites and blacks would work and share together as equals, with the slaves' share of the profits to go toward their freedom, except for a percentage which would go into a fund for purchasing more slaves. As soon as she should have demonstrated the truth of her conviction that slaves could operate factories, with a little training, as well as had Rapp's peasants, she believed that many philanthropists would set up similar colonies so that the snowballing effect would shortly wipe out slavery. An added advantage of her plan, she wrote ingenuously in one of the prospectuses such as she loved to compose, was that without slaves the bored leisure class of the South would learn to be happily useful.

Meanwhile, she had dragged the weary Camilla down the Mississippi for a reunion with Lafayette at New Orleans, a reconciliation having been effected by mail. Romantic tradition is that on the journey upriver he stopped with Frances to view the future Nashoba—a place she had not yet dreamed of—and sober history is that when he finally took ship for home, with a present of two hundred thousand dollars from Congress plus the deed to a land grant, she did not even see him off.

However, there seems to have been no rift—and certainly he called her plan to the attention of several notable men. If Frances was lonely for her paternal friend, she made up for it in some measure by rushing about interviewing Southern leaders and issuing propaganda.

At first her Negroes would farm. Trades would gradually be taught them, and manufactures added. There would be schooling for both black and white children. As she perfected this plan, Owen opened his village and returned to England for his family. Thus she missed seeing him when she went to New Harmony for white recruits for her commune.

But she contrived to win only George Flower. Leaving Camilla with Flower's family, apparently not in Illinois but at New Harmony, Frances set out with him for Nashville by water to interview General Jackson about founding her village there. While Jackson's Negroes fed them, the general said that he too held tender sentiments about freeing America's slaves and he wished her much luck while cannily shunting her off to Memphis where she speculated vastly in ground of which he had helped despoil the Five Civilized Tribes. She took with her a few slaves purchased at Nashville and, bubbling over with her humanity, bought a tract of two thousand acres of upland on Wolf River. She named the place Nashoba—the Chickasaw word for wolf. Two cabins were raised—"one for slaves and one for whites." But Frances and Flower of course were the only white people.

Frances spent much of the winter at Memphis. On clear days she rode out to Nashoba and helped clear land. In the spring, Camilla and the Flowers came down, bringing an erstwhile Shaker, Richeson Whitby. A white man gave Frances a family of slaves, making the Negro population a baker's dozen. There was also James Richardson, a footloose communal theorist who had scraped acquaintance with Frances in Memphis.

She exhausted herself at manual labor, succumbed to malaria, and almost died. Doctors sent her to New Harmony for the better air when she failed to regain her strength. By then, Owen had returned from England with his wife and other three sons, and his project was growing more bizarre by the hour, with deadbeats victimizing him shamefully.

But Frances loved the place. She and one of the sons, Robert Dale Owen, half a dozen years her junior, hit things off excellently well getting out copy for the community paper. Almost a thousand people were at New Harmony, including a good percentage of radicals, feminists, marriage reformers, would-be if not practicing free lovers, and birth-control theorists—and birth control was a dirty word which touched off sermons in orthodox churches on child murder and onanism, and which sent its blatant advocates to jail.

Discussion ran high on all such subjects at New Harmony. The elder Owen was particularly outspoken on the inequities of conventional marriage in which the wife had no legal control over her person or children, or the property she might inherit or acquire. All this made a great impression upon Frances and she began a series of articles in the paper on free love as the ideal of human association.

The national press had a field day. Editors were certain that "the younger part of the females" at New Harmony were required "to admit to their embraces the young men as long as they should be pleased with them, or not." Owen had previously been scored as an atheist. Now he was also a free lover, a wrecker of marriages.

One of his associates, William Maclure, then internationally known as a geologist, declared New Harmony to be as far "removed from every species of vice" as any place he was ever in, and that he had never been in one "where the married are so faithful, or the young so chaste." That was a broad testimonial, but it made little difference what anyone might say in Owen's defense, for in his own words he was railing against a "Trinity of the most monstrous evils that could be combined to inflict mental and physical evil" on mankind, to wit: private property, "absurd and irrational systems of Religion—and Marriage, founded on individual property, combined with some of these irrational systems of religion."

It was foregone that anyone who would attack those three institutions was guilty of any moral crime one might imagine. The *Indianapolis Journal* settled the whole thing: New Harmony was one great brothel, peopled with whores and whoremongers—this was assured because of "the licentious principles of their founder. . . ."

Owen didn't help the situation by his further suggestion of an easy divorce law so that the incompatible need not be kept tied together. He said that when the New Harmony system of equality and sharing should become universal it would be unnecessary any longer to consider the children in divorce, since the state would be bringing these up anyway, thus leaving adults at liberty to change spouses rather at will. It could scarcely be denied that this would foster a species of free love. Nevertheless, he said that for the time being the New Harmonists would live under the laws of Indiana and the United States.

Whether Frances was a free lover or not, as she was widely accused of being with the Owen men, she did absorb intellectual conviction in favor of the theory. But her health was not improving and she was advised to go to Europe. Robert Dale Owen went as far as Nashoba with her, intending to live "a life of lettered leisure" there while she, his most dear friend, went on for a sojourn at Lafayette's estate in France. Expressing great shock, then, at the ugly poverty of her colony, Robert said he believed he would go on to Europe with her.

She had a sufficient detachment from reality to believe that the "full communism" of New Harmony was working out, although the place was in a tottering condition, as anyone might have seen. But in emulation of the Owens, she resigned her sole ownership of the property and slaves at Nashoba, and drew up a charter and deed of trust designating Lafayette, Camilla, the white men at Nashoba, the Owens, and others to the number of ten as trustees. Those at Nashoba at any time were to constitute a quorum. The Negroes were supposed to be partners, too, but in blunt fact they were still slaves and were to be held as such until their freedom was worked out.

But she made stringent rules for the admission of new members. Free Negroes might join by giving labor or property. Whites would give all their property, or if they had none would pledge labor. This would make a system in which the poor worked and the moneyed took their ease— but all would be brightened by the new ideal of free love.

Nor would Frances draw the color line there. In time she foresaw a creamy-skinned race "more suited to the Southern climate than the pure European." Deciding he had had enough, George Flower took his family away. This was unfortunate for Nashoba since it left no one there of any ability or common sense.

Yet Frances blithely departed with Robert Dale Owen. From New Orleans she sent up some new members— Mamselle Lolotte, a free quadroon with several children fairer than herself, including a nubile daughter, Mamselle Joséphine. It wasn't long until Richardson was making time with the younger mamselle.

CHAPTER EIGHT

NASHOBA AND THE WOLVES

COOPERATION HAS NIGH KILLED US ALL

Land of the West, we come to thee,
Far o'er the desert of the sea!
Under the white-winged canopy,
Land of the West, we fly to thee;
Sick of the Old World's sophistry;
Haste then across the dark, blue sea,
Land of the West, we rush to thee!
Home of the brave: soil of the free,—
Huzza! She rises o'er the sea.

—Owenite song

WHITBY played overseer at Nashoba but his easy-going ways produced no crops. The Negroes were adept at soldiering and the bright star of manumission was so distant-dim that they did not care if nothing was accomplished.

The three whites lectured them on the ideal of emancipation of slaves and of womankind, on the common ownership of property, and on the righeousness of sexual freedom. Then Camilla and Whitby fell in love—or thought they did. Possibly it occurred to her there would be no overwhelming emancipation for a spinster in being presented with offspring, for they trotted off to the preacher and were married as conventionally as if they had not been philosophers.

126

Soon there were unconscionable squabbles between Negroes and between Negroes and whites. The slaves resented the presence of free Negroes. There was trouble concerning the children. And, knowing they would not be whipped, the slaves gave full vent to their feelings. Richardson recorded in the daybook:

Sunday Evening, May 20, 1827

Camilla Wright and James Richardson, resident trustees, met the slaves—Camilla Wright repeated to them how the work was to proceed in Mr. Whitby's absence. She also informed them that tomorrow the children, Delila, Lucy, Julia, and Alfred, will be taken altogether from under the management of the parents, and will be placed, until our school is organized, under the management of Mamselle Lolotte; that all communication between the parents and children shall, in future, be prevented, except as may take place by permission, and in the presence of the manager of the children.

The slaves bitterly resented that—for nowhere were the color lines and the lines of pride more harshly drawn than between those of varying degrees of Negro blood. A week later Richardson wrote:

Saturday Evening, May 26, 1827

Agreed, that the slaves shall not be allowed to receive money, clothing, food, or indeed anything whatever from any person resident at, or visiting this place, whether trustee, coadjutor, probationer, or stranger; and that any article so received, shall be returned to the giver in the presence of the slaves and trustees. If the giver be absent, the article shall be destroyed by the receiver, in the presence of the trustees and the slaves.

Agreed, that the slaves shall not be permitted to eat elsewhere than at the public meals, excepting in case of sickness.

Sunday Evening, May 27, 1827

Met the slaves—Camilla Wright informed them of the regulations agreed to yesterday evening.

Dilly having given utterance a day or two ago to some grumbling at having so many mistresses James Richardson stated to them that it is true they have many mistresses as well as many masters, and that in all probability they soon will have many more of both; as every free person who shall reside here, whether black or white or brown will be, in some sort, their master or mistress; that this is just the difference between a free person and a slave; and that they can get rid of these masters and mistresses in no other way than by working out their freedom, when they will be transformed into masters and mistresses themselves, but that in the meantime, they will gradually find out that this multiplicity of superiors, so far from being a hardship, is of palpable advantage to them, in preventing them from being at the mercy of the temper of any one individual, and in rendering the concurrence of at least a majority of the resident trustees, an indispensable preliminary to the infliction of even the slightest possible punishment, for the greatest possible offense.

It was just a few nights after this that the slave, Redrick, invaded Isabel's bedroom "uninvited, and endeavoring, without her consent, to take liberties with her person." Camilla declared she thought a flogging should follow any such business in the future, but the three-cornered contest continued between whites, fair Negroes, and dark ones:

Sunday Evening, June 3, 1827

Met the slaves—Willis having, a few days ago, complained to Camilla Wright, of Mamselle Lolotte's children beating his children; thinking it was allowed because hers were a little the fairest. James Richardson took the opportunity of endeavoring to explain to the slaves our views on the subject of color. He told them that in our estimation all colors are equal in rank, and that whatever distinctions may be established on this place, color shall form the basis of none of them.

Sunday Evening, June 10, 1827

Met the slaves—Stated to them that as some of them have on two occasions broken the swing by using it in a riotous manner, they shall no longer be permitted to use it at all—we added that they cannot be allowed to partake with us of any such amusement until their habits shall become more refined than at present.

Wednesday, June 13, 1827

Willis having reported to us that Henry declined coultering to-day on the plea of a pain in his knee joint, to which he is subject—we met the slaves at breakfast time, and told them that though we didn't doubt that Henry's knee gave him more or less pain, we had not sufficient confidence in his veracity to trust in his statement regarding the degree of ailment; that we would therefore take their votes respecting the capacity of Henry to follow the oxen to-day. From this vote we stated that we would exclude Willis because he now acts as director of their work, and Maria because she now cohabits with Henry. There were ten votes, five each way. We gave our opinion as the casting vote, in support of Henry's capacity to [plow]. He was therefore ordered to attend to it.

Sunday evening, June 17, 1827

Met the slaves—James Richardson informed them that, last night, Mamselle Joséphine and he began to live together; and he took this occasion of repeating to them our views on color, and on the sexual relation.

Just after that, with the concurrence of Whitby and Camilla, who were now married, Richardson bundled up

some extracts from the daybook and sent them off to Frances's
friend, Ben Lundy, a leading emancipationist who was interested in Nashoba. Lundy promptly published them in his
paper, the *Genius of Universal Emancipation.* They were
everywhere reprinted.

Everything had been said already that could be
thought of about Owenism and free love. Now it was said all
over again about Frances, the Prophetess of Beelzebub, the
Whore of Babylon. Frances had many friends and acquaintances up and down the seaboard and they were shocked and
incredulous, but Camilla settled the doubts of which they
wrote her.

Although herself married, she declared that she utterly
disapproved of the irrational business of two people's promising to love and live together all their lives when they could
not guarantee to control their feelings even for one hour.
She added that to her mind marriage was "one of the most
subtle inventions of priestcraft for poisoning the purest
source of human felicity. . . . The conduct of my friend Mr.
Richardson in forming a connection in the manner" had the
approval of all at Nashoba.

English and Continental papers took up the tale. Poor
Frances prepared a circular letter to her friends, not deny-
ing her convictions but confessing that her ideas, while she
believed them good, were no doubt suitable for an age
which would be more advanced than the narrow one of
1827. She left the impression that she did not want to be
thought ill of. And she upbraided Richardson by letter for
foolishly raising opposition against the commune while it
was still weak.

She brought no converts back from England—not
even Mary Wollstonecraft Shelley, the poet's widow, who at
first had intended coming. But she did bring her friend Mrs.
Trollope. That ultra-respectable, middle-aged lady was the
mother of a sizable family and had no interest in free love,
nor did she believe any of the tongue-clatter about Frances,

though the latter while relaxing at the Trollope home did wear Turkish trousers and ride astride.

Mr. Trollope's irrascibility and headaches had lost him his law practice while he plunged into debt by building a mansion to be paid for when he should come into an expected inheritance. Unfeelingly, the uncle who was to leave it took instead a wife who promptly had issue. Driven out of the mansion, Trollope was on the verge of bankruptcy. The solution: Someone had convinced the family that Mrs. T. could make a fortune by opening a really good store in Western America, say at Cincinnati, which was declared to be in the center of a prosperous area, and most advanced. She did not know the advancement consisted in such refinements as the legal requirement that garbage be placed in the middle of streets rather than on walks so that foraging hogs might not disturb pedestrians.

In short, having had no more experience with commerce than with the backwoods, Mrs. Trollope was enthralled. Frances was certain the idea was excellent. They sailed, with Mrs. Trollope planning to stay her first few months in America at Nashoba.

They arrived in the Christmas season. Mrs. T. was utterly horrified—and the more so to observe that the gently-reared Frances was undistressed by the squalor of their surroundings and in complete enjoyment at being back. Rain poured. Roofs leaked. Wind came through the floor. Clay softened and fell out of the chimneys so that the wood frames caught fire. Heroic exertions were required against holocaust.

"Desolation was the only feeling—the only word that presented itself; but it was not spoken," Mrs. Trollope wrote. "I think, however, that Miss Wright was aware of the painful impression the sight of her forest home produced on me, and I doubt not that the conviction reached us both at the same moment, that we had erred in thinking a few months passed together at this spot could be productive of

pleasure to either. But to do her justice, I believe her mind
was so exclusively occupied by the object she then had in
view, that all things else were worthless, or indifferent to her.
I never heard or read of any enthusiasm approaching hers,
except in some few instances, in ages past, of religious fanati-
cism."

Too, the wretched Camilla frightened Mrs. Trollope
with an admission that her own color and lassitude were
more from malaria than from her pregnancy. Whitby was
discouraged and concerned by Camilla's condition. When
Mrs. T. decided to journey on, he left with his wife for New
Harmony. Having completed his amour with the mamselle,
Richardson also departed.

Frances and the Negroes were left in the wilderness.
"Cooperation has nigh killed us all," she wrote broodingly.
But she would not quit. She drew up the charter for a new
"Preliminary Social Community" in which Negroes would
labor and others would pay board. It does not appear what
the advantages were to be for the board payers in living in a
fever-ridden backwoods in shacks open to weather and
scorpions. She got out a new booklet explaining that
happiness makes for virtue and personal freedom makes for
happiness, and freedom comes from crushing not only the
glaring injustices but the "tyrannies of custom and convention and pride."

Still later, Frances came to be of the opinion that in
a commune all should labor, or none should, but that the
two classes of members could not successfully mingle. It
really did not matter what the rules were for there were no
new members, no boarders, no investors in the stock she was
so ready to issue in her copperplate hand. She hired another
white overseer—who was destined never to send her a penny
of the expected farm profits in the two years remaining for
Nashoba—and left for New Harmony.

The devil heard that a number of people were going
To live on the Wabash with great Mr. Owen:
    He said to himself, "I must now have a care,
    Circumstances require that myself should be there.

"Since Adam first fell by my powerful hand,
I have wandered for victims through every known land,
    But in all my migrations ne'er hit on a plan
    That would give me the rule so completely o'er man.

"I have set sects to fighting and shedding of blood,
And have whispered to bigots they're all doing good,
    But never on earth through my whole course of evil
    Until now could I say, 'Here's a plan beats the devil.' "

—ANON. Philadelphia Gazette, *January, 1826, scoring Owen's
opposition to revealed religions.*

CHAPTER NINE

ROBERT OWEN AND THE YANKEE HIGHBINDERS

IDLERS OR BUNGLERS OR BOTH, THEY WERE WILLING
TO FORK OUT A COPPER AND POCKET A SHILLING

NOT long after Robert Owen met Frances Wright in Washington and suggested that she might care to visit Harmonie on the Wabash, he issued an invitation through the newspapers for all who were interested in joining his commune to meet him at the site. He had come a long way since his birth in Wales fifty-four years previously as the son of a saddler who was to send him to school only until he was nine.

After that he was apprenticed to a draper. In his teens he got into a small business of making superior spinning machinery, partly of his own invention. Then he went into a textile mill. Continually improving the techniques and machines there, at nineteen he was producing the best cloth in England.

At thirty he was juggling money, most of it his partners', by the hundreds of thousands in new textile combines. On a business trip he met the daughter of David Dale, a Scots mill owner. He had heard of Dale's plants at New Lanark and of the man's humanitarian treatment of his workers—a thing that jibed with his own beliefs. Miss Dale fell in love with Owen. Perhaps he fell in love with her, at least as much as he ever fell in love with any woman.

His combine bought the vast Dale plant. Made a one-ninth partner, Owen was paid a thousand pounds yearly as manager—and part of the deal with Dale appears to have been a businesslike marriage between Owen and the industrialist's daughter. Their children rated it a happy union.

Owen at last had the means and authority to try some of his humanitarian theories among the plant's sixteen hundred mill families and the five hundred pauper children it rented from work houses. He sold goods to workers at cost at the company store, paid a living wage, carried the idle workers at full pay during the terrible American cotton embargo, and established unheard-of schools for the pauper children and for those of the workers.

"Infant schools" were included—the first kindergartens in the British Isles. He believed people to be almost entirely the product of environment, and he thought training accordingly should begin early. The mill hands were grateful for these various benefits. However, they took but poorly his attempts to do away with their two chief amusements—drunkenness and sexual debauchery.

Despite the unusual profits which his system was returning, all that his partners could see was that there would be still greater profit without his philanthropies—a thing he denied, and was not in any case willing to give up. The partners attempted to squeeze him out. He formed a new combine which was eager to have his services and bought the old one out at an advance of many thousands of pounds on what they had given. Soon the new partners put him through the same thing, and it all happened a third and a fourth time, with even a set of Quaker owners uneasy lest his methods be not good business.

Owen was working out a new social system on paper and putting as much of it as he might into practice at New Lanark. Happiness of mankind was the touchstone and in his belief was the proper object of government. He failed in getting legal reforms through Parliament, such as prohibiting the working of children under ten and limiting those under eighteen to the day shift, and to only twelve and a half hours at that. The atmosphere was such that at the other extreme men were attempting to pass bills to make the destruction of stocking machinery a capital offense—for organized mobs, backed by public sympathy, were wrecking the machines all over England. These followers of an apparently mythical "King Ludd" refrained from bloodshed until severe retaliations were taken against them. Eventually, the movement died under the impact of prosperity and executions.

What Owen did at New Lanark comprised only reformation. What he wanted was transformation. In another age communitarianism might not have entered his mind, but it was in the very air of his day and he breathed it in.

The religious communes in America had shown the way to success. Owen desired to demonstrate that religion was not the necessary basis for a successful commune. Basically, he wished to divide mankind into villages of twelve hundred or so, each to be self-sufficient in manufacture and agriculture. With the elimination of middle men and their mark-ups of twenty to a thousand per cent, and without proprietors and landlords to absorb the profits of labor, only three hours of work daily would be necessary for any individual.

At one year, or at least by two, children would be taken from parents and put into infant schools for raising by the state. By twenty they would have learned several trades, besides having acquired an education suitable to the scientific age in which they lived. At thirty they would instruct and superintend, and at forty govern and advise. At fifty they would retire for travel, hobbies, and roles as elder statesmen. Private property would become unnecessary, and wars would eliminate themselves.

Owen was an amazingly compelling speaker and a prolific writer, and again and again it appeared to him that so many moneyed people were interested in his work that he could scarcely avoid being given enough with which to establish a pilot commune. But no money was actually given— and then he dealt himself a great setback by speaking against revealed religion and the pouring of money into a state church, or any other church. Unwanted crackpots flocked to him, worsening his reputation by their advocacy of his ideas —but he always hugged to himself anyone who appeared to love his theories and so it was with these.

Owen always had a childlike optimism that things must come out well for whatever he wanted, even when there was no rational ground for optimism. Where others would have despaired he continued to believe in Father Christmas —and suddenly one day the Flowers, father and son, from Illinois walked in and offered him Rapp's town.

He pretended to hedge—but he promptly took ship, equipped with a huge painting of one of the quadrangular palaces, built around an open square, in which he expected to house his people in his ideal commune. All the way over he held court, and it was freely announced by the passengers on landing in New York that he was buying Harmonie.

The Quakers of the Society for Promoting Communities met him, and though they were swiftly disillusioned at hearing his religious and other non-communitarian ideas, they were so polite that he assured the press they were for him—a mistake he was constantly making about people. Some Quakers did establish an Owenite commune, but without his agnosticism, and it was the longest-lived of all Owenite villages.

Presently, to the surprise of no one, he did buy the village from Rapp.

Owen had brought a younger son, William, a boy in his early twenties, to America with him, and while the father spent the winter glorifying himself with speeches in the East and to Congress and in hobnobbings with the President, William had to face an inflow of eager communitarians at Harmonie, where he was in charge. His frantic letters brought no helpful advice from the elder Owen—who instead placed the notice in the paper inviting all white persons interested in his commune to meet him there.

He supposed several years would be required for obtaining a full quota. When he arrived, people swarmed out of every house to meet him and he was somewhat pushed and shoved in the eager crush. He was happy to see them all for he was not yet aware that they were what his older son, Robert Dale was to call a "heterogeneous collection of radicals, enthusiastic devotees to principle, honest latitudinarians, and lazy theorists, with a sprinkling of unprincipled sharpers thrown in."

Some wanted to know when they would receive their deeds to their share of the land. Others wanted beef. Others were eager for the schools to take their children off their hands. One man wanted Owen to get someone to make him a shirt. And some even wanted to know what they had been trying to learn from William all winter—just what sort of community did Mr. Owen have in mind? All his writings seemed wonderfully good, but when one started to put his finger down upon something specific and concrete, it just wasn't there.

Owen was a man of moderate stature, thin of body from his abstemious habits and he was taking a drubbing from the shoving weight of his disciples. But they were only showing their enthusiasm, he realized. His business was to give them the environment which would change them. At New Harmony there was to be developed the pattern of trying one of three general solutions for most problems: pour in more money, draw up a new constitution, or make a speech.

He began his first day by making a speech—but the plain fact was that he had not had time to consider just what sort of communal arrangements he would have at first. Still, he didn't have to decide yet, for while he seemed to hold out articles of partnership as the promise of the future, right now there would be the Preliminary Community, to last three years. He read the constitution he had drawn up. Communitarians almost universally loved drawing constitutions and this one was the usual collection of rhetoric, philosophy, and humanitarianism.

But specifically, it provided that Owen would be in control through an executive board of his own appointment the first year, since after all he was best acquainted with his own aims and theories. The second year the people would elect the board. All that was very well, but he had already made what has often been called the fatal blunder of admitting scores of unfit people into his fellowship and of not seeing to such an elementary thing as selecting workers who might operate the industrial plants which had made the Rappites wealthy.

Owenite clubs had been formed in several states and for the most part Owen had received an excellent press, much of it in connection with his prospective school. Despite the damning of New Harmony in some quarters as a nest of atheism, applications were coming in from far places from prospective boarding school pupils. Owen's great concerns were getting the school started, and returning to England for the rest of his family—but the immediate necessity was getting the community off on the proper foot. Evening meetings were held for lectures, dancing, socializing, or for concerts under Josiah Warren, one of the several authentic geniuses of the town.

Owen spoke on such topics as the true nature of man, the evils of capitalism, the necessity that all at New Harmony should hold themselves socially equal with each other. One of his strong points was that man is never the proper subject of praise or blame, any more than a baby is a proper subject of praise for cutting teeth, since outside forces are the shapers of people. Nor may one control the impressions he receives, such as that a thing is pretty or ugly. They merely come. Further, "every man speaks according to the impressions which dictate his words." Thus it was foolish for the thoughtful, knowing the psychology of all this, to take insult from rude words.

The indoctrination succeeded so well that after seven weeks Owen declared New Harmony a success and went to England for his family; and there, instead of searching out key personnel to send to the Wabash, as he was supposed to do, he made speeches and engaged the services of one Stedman Whitwell, an architect, to erect a six-foot-square model of one of the multi-storied, quadrangular palaces such as he was going to erect in a few months in Indiana.

While urging him by mail to the business of the commune, the directors at the same time sent him optimistic reports of the progress of affairs. True, the board admitted, there was a considerable debt rising at the store where everyone had credit. But by and large things were going well—considering the lack of workers for some of the enterprises.

For instance, there were no millers to operate the mill which at excellent profit had produced sixty barrels of flour daily under Father Rapp. The big sawmill was in precisely the same difficulty, not to mention the pottery shop with its two large kilns, the saddle and harness shop, the tannery, comb and brush factory, some of the smithing works, the glazier's shop, and so on. Thus everything had to be bought to the enrichment of middle men whom Owen deplored and this was impoverishing the community purse—which was to say Owen's—at the rate of several hundred dollars a day. Further, what were they to do about housing for the people Owen was going to send? He had failed to give directions, and already the American members were crowded into barns and attics.

And by the way—Owen's friend Frances Wright was at New Harmony, looking for likely people for her proposed colony in Tennessee.

It appeared of course to Frances that the good machine of New Harmony was running itself. She had the fine faculty of being able to see only good where her friends or her heart were concerned. She could not or would not see the blunders against which the veriest unwashed backwoodsman might have warned Owen. The eight hundred happy free riders—and contentment in this free atmosphere did exist at that period—puttered in field or timber or in a desultory way in some of the small manufactures. The council was sure that master workmen would somewhere drop their steady jobs and rush to Indiana to throw in with demonstrated dreamers and radicals in time to pull them out of the doldrums.

Frances took George Flower and went off to begin her winter's work of getting up the cabins at Nashoba, and a little later, in November, Owen returned to the States.

The American press had been showing a natural reaction to remarks in the English papers concerning Owen's experiences with "American savages," who, the Britons granted, were probably the best material on which he might work. Owen of course had made no such remarks and no one blamed him—but then on landing here with his family he released one of his blasts at religion to the press and indulged in speeches in which questions from the floor finally wormed from him the flat statement that he did not believe the Bible to be the special word of God.

After that, it was a case of the devil's long spoon, and attention was turned almost entirely away from the sociological and economic aspects of his work. He received a bad press during the next two or three months while, though very badly needed at New Harmony, he preened his ego by making speeches which no one needed in the East.

While the papers advised him to return to England

where there were plenty of paupers who might be better subjects for his experiments than would the free, noble, full-bellied citizens of America, he journeyed to Washington with the model of his ideal village which he presented to President Adams, after which he felt free to take friends into the White House at odd hours to show it to them. And instead of devising means of getting rid of some of the hangers-on at New Harmony, or of providing quarters for the expected skilled artisans he needed, he simply advertised in the papers for the latter, and wrote enthusiastic letters to his son William of the forty teachers and scientists and specialists he was bringing into the fold.

In turn, William was pleading with him by mail to cease making announcements about building one of his vast palaces on the Wabash the next summer since they could not spare hands from the fields to quarry the necessary stone and since they had not the labor, much less the skill, to erect such a building.

Finally Owen did start downriver to New Harmony, taking with him teachers, books, and scientific equipment for the school. He had first interested a Scot, William Maclure, who not only was a famous teacher but "the father of American geology," an eminence he had reached through making a geological survey of the country. In turn, Maclure and Maclure's associate, Madame Fretageot, who was enormously interested in the New Harmony project, had recruited several other scientists and naturalists. Indeed, Maclure had become involved financially in the New Harmony scheme, a matter which was to cost him probably more than fifty thousand dollars before he freed himself.

In New Harmony annals, this freightage was referred to as "the boat load of knowledge." But the boat froze up in the ice below Pittsburgh, and the party broke into small groups and made an apparently joyous and free-hearted trip on downriver, now hiring conveyances ashore, again going by water, making the inevitable talks and recruitings on the way.

It was mid-January when Owen arrived at New Harmony ahead of the others, but even before getting there he announced in towns on the way that the Preliminary Community, which was to have lasted three years, was so enormously successful that he intended to arrange for full communalism at once.

But the important thing was the school, and that was placed in the hands of Maclure. Maclure in fact had once established a large trade school in Spain. It had been wrecked by Spanish politics and the interference of secret police. In the school at New Harmony there was to be no cultural folderol. It was a trade school—the first of its sort in America. Was it necessary that a boy know that the Romans called a fox *vulpes?* Maclure and the Owens thought not.

Taxidermy was taught, along with printing and engraving, drawing, carpentry, wheelwrighting, wood-turning, smithing, cabinetmaking, hat making, shoemaking, and millinery—and there were also common school subjects. Military exercises broke the monotony. These were in charge of Joseph Neef, a proclaimed atheist who as an officer under Napoleon had been able to make himself "distinctly heard by ten thousand men." Later he had taken up pedagogy in Pestalozzi's school in Switzerland, opened a school in America only to see it collapse under the weight of his atheism, and finally had come out of retirement to New Harmony.

The girls in Community House Number Two "had a little song we used to sing," as one of them recorded in later years:

> *Number 2 pigs locked up in a pen,*
> *When they get out, it's now and then;*
> *When they get out, they sneak about,*
> *For fear old Neef will find them out.*

This girl, in the boarding school, saw her parents twice in two years. Parents who insisted on coming to see their children were simply told to take their offspring home with them. Visiting of students by resident parents was also bleakly discouraged. In summer, said the girl of the ditty, coarse linen costumes were worn, with coarse plaid for Sunday. In winter there was heavy wool. Students milked cows before breakfast and the diet consisted largely of the milk with mush:

> We had bread but once a week—on Saturdays. I thought if I ever got out, I would kill myself eating sugar and cake. I remember that there were blackboards covering one side of the schoolroom, and that we had wires, with balls on them, by which we learned to count. We also had singing exercises by which we familiarized ourselves with lessons in various branches. At dinner we generally had soup, at supper mush and milk again.
>
> We went to bed at sundown in little bunks suspended in rows by cords from the ceiling. [This was so that they might be raised out of the way by day.] Sometimes one of the children at the end of the row would swing back her cradle, and, when it collided on the return bound with the next bunk, it set the whole row bumping together. This was a favorite diversion, and caused the teachers much distress. At regular intervals we used to be marched to the community apothecary shop, where a dose that tasted like sulphur was impartially dealt out to each pupil, just as in Squeers' Dotheboys school.

As Owen had said even before arriving at New Harmony, he was ready to cancel the remaining two years of the Preliminary Society. Under the new order, each member would contribute all he had—but somehow Owen did avoid the blunder of turning the estate completely and irrevocably over to the group. He retained control over much or all of the real property, and there was the final provision that should any member withdraw he might take with him what he had brought. There was a cry in some quarters at this—

for it meant that at any time Owen might take back his property. Maclure left such details to Owen. He was busy organizing the schools on the Spartan plan, certain that they would produce enough goods to support themselves. He was soon off to Mexico, leaving them to Neef and others. In reality they were never to return a penny.

There was a series of constitutional meetings, with happiness as the great goal of the new document for the Community of Equality. But alas, some members were immediately unhappy. Feelings had been wounded: "I have not been accorded the confidence [*i.e.,* the office and honors] looked for in the community," stated one man in the village *Gazette*.

Then the first of "the ten lost tribes of communism" pulled off with the removal of a hundred thirty religious dissidents who founded Macluria a few miles away. They "bought" land from Owen but paid nothing down. Their constitution excluded women from the vote.

Within a few days of the signing of the new constitution in the parent community, quarrels exploded over interpretation and carrying out of provisions. The board begged Owen to take over as dictator. He did so. The energy of all hands was then spent holding fresh meetings, and after a week Owen announced that conditions presaged wonderful success. Promptly another group of almost one hundred broke away for the remarkable reason that Owen was cool toward changing the name of New Harmony to Ipba Veinul.

The philosopher of the new dissidents, Stedman Whitwell, who had made the model of the Owenite "palace," had worked out a system for naming towns in accordance with their latitude and longitude. Hence, no two towns would ever have the same name. Further, anyone knowing the system could—with a course in celestial navigation and a few instruments, one supposes—find any town by knowing its name. Most people preferred the old system of buying a ticket and allowing captain or driver to worry about the rest.

But not Whitwell. His colony—founded on Owen's land, on credit, of course—became Feiba Peveli which showed it to be at 38.11 north latitude and 81.53 west longitude. New York, on his map, was Otke Neivul and London, Lafa Vovutu.

Optimism was officially high at New Harmony. The *Gazette* announced that idlers and brawlers were no longer to be seen on the streets and that here and there over the United States Owenite Societies were forming. It appeared probable that the entire country would soon be organized into Communities of Equality. Announcement of sweetness and light may have been a little premature. A week later Owen posted notice that the quarreling, abusing, and yelling to enforce orders was really not a good thing. Apparently he had forgotten that his thousand equals were victims of the impressions and faculties over which they had no control. Also, he said, backbiting was all too prevalent, and some people were exhibiting improper pride, holding themselves above others. People thenceforth must cease the habit of stalking about the dining hall to talk to others during meals, and from there on children must be kept out of the dining room while grown folks were eating. After all, the community was raising the children and they should stay with their keepers. A deplorable thing was the filthy habits of some members. And Owen had a final warning for the critical: "No anger ought to be felt against the female members upon their aversion to the work of cooperation; or when they brawl, quarrel, or indulge in loud talk."

The brawls led to the splintering off of one group after another to form little communes within the town itself. There was trouble over liquor. Prohibition was decreed, but everywhere people were drunk, supplied by sly bootlegging members. Some didn't like the costume which had been decreed. The Duke of Saxe-Weimar visited New Harmony on his American tour and noted that the dress "for the man consists of white pantaloons, buttoned over a boy's jacket, made of light material, without a collar; that of the woman of a coat reaching to the knee, and pantaloons such as little girls wear among us. These dresses are not universally adopted, but they have a good appearance."

Other dissension was over the penchant of some for eating and not working, over the giving of rough manual labor to professional people whose talents were not otherwise needed, and over the attempts to enforce democracy. These attempts reached the point of the drawing of numbers for the dances, but cultured girls still would not dance with dirty and uncouth clodhoppers. There was great freedom among the young people and no overbearing chaperonage in walks along the river, but Robert Dale Owen said that except for "a few ill-advised love matches," no harm appeared to come of it.

Saxe-Weimar found Owen still convinced that the entire world was to be reformed from this nucleus of New Harmony, and prisons, punishments, and wars abolished with the philosophy of his New Moral World which he was evolving. However, there was not another person in the place, among those who would talk to the duke in confidence, but who had decided Owen was deluded and that everything was doomed to failure. The duke also observed "the much vaunted equality" at a lecture where, while Owen spoke, some ruffians and ragamuffins lay around on the rostrum almost under his feet reading newspapers.

The literal-mindedness of some of the inmates was shown by an old gentleman named Greenwood who paraded slowly through the twenty-four streets of the town during a storm carrying a lightning rod. He confessed that he was ailing and tired of life but on principle could not commit suicide. However, he had hoped that the Lord would see fit to spare an extra lightning bolt for him, and he had, however futilely, given Him full opportunity.

But things were to be brightened a little, at least for Robert Dale Owen, for Frances Wright, having left Nashoba to the Negroes and the new overseer, was arriving to join Camilla.

Ode to Frances Wright

Thou wonder of the age, from whom
Religion waits her final doom,
Her quiet death, her euthenasia,
Thou in whose eloquence and bloom
The age beholds a new Aspasia.
O 'tis a glorious sight for us,
The gaping throng, to see thee thus
The light of dawning truth dispense,
While Colonel Stone, the learned and brave,
The press's Atlas, mild but grave,
Hangs on the words that leave thy mouth,
Slaking his intellectual drouth,
In that rich stream of eloquence,
And notes thy teachings, to repeat
Their wisdom in his classic sheet.

—WILLIAM CULLEN BRYANT *in the New York* Evening
Post, *of which he was editor, Jan. 29, 1829.* [*Stone
was editor of the* Commercial Advertiser.]

CHAPTER TEN

THE UNHARMONIOUS END
OF NEW HARMONY

IF MANKIND WERE ALL MADE RICH THEY WOULD BE POOR NO MORE

THINGS were not smooth when Frances reached New Harmony. Money had been officially abolished but in every lane and alley the Harmonists privately traded and bargained and bickered over cash. There was complaint over the small amount of credit allowed at the store, and Owen was publicly excoriated for refusing to divide the estate freely and unstintedly and irrevocably among the people, instead of wanting them to be partly responsible for losses, all of which it was felt that he should bear.

Dissidents declared Owen was in fact trying to make enormous profit off the little groups to whom he sold land and houses, though sales were on credit or on leases of ten thousand years with no money down. But after all, in a communitarian project was not everyone supposed to give all he had? Whose fault was it that Owen had much and everyone else but little?

The splinterings continued with new quarrels until there were eight "major" communes, some of which splintered further as bedfellows disagreed. But apparently there was much rejoining of small groups and the "ten communities at New Harmony" consisted in part, even, of some "established" by people who wrote from a distance saying they would like one of those ten-thousand-year leases, but who never really arrived on the scene. Yet Owen blandly spoke of his ten communities—besides, of course, those in other parts of the country—though he was always careful of the verbs he used, if one notices closely, so that it might not be thrown up to him that he said the communes actually existed.

It was quite possibly one of the members, Paul Brown, a constant heckler, who taught him to be careful of his verbs—for after a loose remark by Owen concerning his ten communes Brown countered sarcastically that one of them consisted of a hut or two where four families huddled together, another of several starveling German immigrants, and others of only a family or two, not to mention some which had been abandoned entirely. Nevertheless, Owen continued addressing his communiqués to the ten communes.

He kept his patience. He was beginning to see, he said, that it was only natural that these people who had not been scientifically brought up would require a considerable amount of training and experience to make a go of the Community of Equality. It was unfortunate that they fussed over wandering hogs, the neglect of partnership gardens, the exchange of "labor notes" for each other's work, unrepaired fences, the teaching of the children, and so on—but with patience all that in time would straighten out.

One William Taylor was among those who corresponded with Owen concerning a ten-thousand-year lease— and indeed he did come on promptly. He purchased fifteen hundred acres "with all that was thereon" for an associate community. In the night he moved a large amount of community property upon the ground and then claimed it under the bargain. The easy-going Owen allowed him to get away with it. Taylor then increased the offense by opening a forbidden distillery.

The quarreling and brawling, the accusations of profiteering against Owen, increased so that he offered in a new compromise to abolish the small communes, cancel their debts, and form a big commune to be called The New Harmony Community Number One. In it would be societies of mechanics, farmers, teachers, and so on. Everyone would have to join a society or leave. Owen had concluded that there were some "eccentric and violent characters" no society would have and that he would thus be rid of them. He had felt too sorry for them just to drive them out, but under the sly new rule he really did force them to depart. The scheme is completely untypical of him.

But not all hard cases had been thus disposed of. Those who had contrived to get into societies cried dictator over the banishments and prepared a coffin to hold "a funeral of the community." Someone did away with the paraphernalia in the night and the travesty was not completed. But quarreling continued. The Educational Society was so unruly, its food and candles had to be cut off to bring it to terms. The mechanics brawled, threw out their sub-constitution, and set up a triumvirate, blasphemously dubbed the Father, Son, and Holy Ghost, to rule them.

Maclure was enormously uneasy over the losses piling up for himself and perhaps that made it easier for him and Owen to quarrel over the subject matter, pedagogy, and discipline of the schools. Owen opened a school of his own which required nothing but that the children should come and hear talks by any speakers who had experience in what they were talking about. This did not last long.

The harried Maclure went to the Rapps and bought $40,000 worth of Owen's notes for a reputed $25,000. He

then forced Owen to accept them as a $40,000 payment on
Maclure's part of the community losses. In the midst of ugly
words and vituperations, he settled his other affairs, tore up
his will which would have left his fortune to New Harmony, and departed. He did, however, retain title to some
of the land there.

Owen knew that the project was finished. After two
years nothing was left to hold things together except the
optimism of a few and the last-ditch greed of the remainder. He gave various reasons for the debacle, including
the remarkable one that Maclure had not handled the schools
correctly. Again, he said, the real trouble was that the Rappites had promised to leave a working force to keep all factories going until it might be replaced gradually by other
workers. The Rappites said this was not true and the evidence is that they were correct, for Owen's statement was entirely in the odor of afterthought.

There were in fact as many reasons given for the failure of New Harmony as there were people there. Some said
Owen did not have a workable system to begin with. Others
that matters would have worked out but for the improper
selection of people. The music master, Warren, perhaps
came nearest the difficulty—if one admits the basic system to
have been workable. Remarkably enough, he found that the
failure lay in "too much democracy—the community was
talked to death." That is, everything required a series of
meetings, when people should have been in field or factory,
and each meeting ended in a vote-taking, which offended
some clique or group, thus necessitating another series of
meetings and vote-takings.

Owen had roundly advocated—as had many, since the
days of Locke—the idea that the person may be deliberately
shaped by arranging his environment. It never occurred to
him that the environment which he did arrange was from
the first fatal to his hopes.

Nevertheless, at the end, he still thought some of the
little societies might take hold and grow. He placed an

optimistic communique in the New Harmony *Gazette* and said goodbye, promising new and great things on his next return from England.

The golden goose was dead. That was obvious. Inmates fled singly and in dozens. If they must work for a living, they preferred doing so for cash wages.

Still, Robert Jennings, a dyed-in-the-wool Owenite, brightened the *Gazette* with accounts of progress. Frances Wright and Robert Dale Owen helped fill the columns. In two months all the societies had disbanded. A few people hung on from inertia or in hope that Owen would think of something when he returned.

When even the printers had gone, it appeared the paper must suspend, but a teacher who still conducted the remnant of the school, Phiquepal d'Arusmont, a Frenchman some fifty years old, hastily learned the craft. He was later to be still more important in the Fanny Wright saga.

Frances had discovered herself to be a speaker. She decided to give a series of lectures at Cincinnati as an antidote to a revival meeting which then racked the city. Mrs. Trollope lambasted that same revival in her book of American adventures, and no doubt she had mentioned to Frances in her letters that relays of preachers nightly opened a yawning hell to their listeners, working them into orgies of shouting, hysteria, and fainting; and that preachers, exhorting girls and women at the mourner's bench, did not always keep their hands where they should.

Frances took a hall and great crowds turned out to hear "the Priestess of Beelzebub." She required no small courage to speak her mind against "priestcraft" and the excesses which were going on. She pleaded for freedom of thought, a rational view of all things, and a standard of morality consisting of a high code of action, rather than one centered upon the worship of a being which she said must ever remain unknown to humanity.

There were fulminations and angry threats of violence, but it developed that she had admirers and defenders, and the danger passed.

In fact, her lectures were so successful that she had to repeat them in Cincinnati the next month. Then she and Editor Jennings, "a thick-set and well-constituted little Scotsman," formerly a preacher, began an endless tour of the East. Said Mrs. Trollope:

> That a lady of fortune, family, and education, whose youth had been passed in the most refined circles of private life, should present herself to the people as a public lecturer, would naturally excite surprise any where, and the *nil admirari* of the old world itself would hardly be sustained before such a spectacle; but in America, where women are guarded by a seven-fold shield of habitual insignificance, it had caused an effect which can scarcely be described. "Miss Wright, of Nashoba, is going to lecture . . ." sounded from street to street, and from house to house. . . .

She lectured on freedom of thought, pleading for rationality and for free universal education of children beginning at two. She demanded that women be given some voice in the control of their children and property, rather than kept in the power of their fathers and husbands.

In some places newspapers conspired to ignore her. In others she was spoken of well enough until she attacked "priestcraft" and the folly of believing in systems of religion just because some preacher said they were true. She was agnostic, emphasizing that she was not atheistic and would believe any truth demonstrated to her. She tried to show that there was no necessary connection between morality and religion of any kind.

Her biting attacks on capitalistic and industrial monopolies and abuses turned the power of money against her. Her connection with the "one vast brothel" of New Harmony was enlarged upon and her marriage beliefs aired as she had the effrontery to advocate birth control. It was utterly beyond credibility that a woman could make such a shameless spectacle of herself. She was liberally misquoted and always to her disadvantage. Several times panics were attempted with spurious cries of fire in the lecture halls, or the puffing of smoke through them from tar barrels. She always remained calm and held her audience.

Even the women she was trying to help were hostile: "I write on my knee, my sweet love," she wrote Camilla as she went by boat from Baltimore to Philadelphia, "in a cabin crowded with ladies who perhaps feel in my company as in the presence of a new importation from the south seas, and I most certainly in theirs as some such unfortunate antipodean to whom the surrounding minds and manners are as uncongenial as the bonnets."

Soon she was on the way to New York, "the head seat at once of popular energy, sectarian and clerical wealth and power, and financial and political corruption." As soon as she began saying the things about all preachers that they freely said about each other from their pulpits, she was damned as "a bold blasphemer and a voluptuous preacher of licentiousness" with "iron equally in her head and heart; impervious to the voice of virtue and case-hardened against shame." So said the *New York Commercial Advertiser*. The *New York American* declared she had ceased to be a woman and that it would take the liberty of referring to her as "a female monster." The *Evening Post* advocated that any hall rented to her be burned down—let the owners and insurance company take note and beware. A mob tried to wreck her carriage but her calmness prevailed over them. Things were a little better when staid Quaker ladies who believed in her principles began escorting her as a guard of respectability.

"Ada" had her say in doggerel in Fanny's *Free Enquirer* as soon as it was established in New York:

THE PANIC

The dear fellows have taken a fright;
And forsooth not without a good cause;
For the lectures of Miss Frances Wright
Are received with unbounded applause.

What a fuss among bigots and priests,
What a running and groaning and praying,
And proclaiming of fasts and of feasts,
To disprove all that Fanny is saying.

She tells us we women possess
An intellect equal with them;
But this the poor souls won't confess,
And that part of her doctrine condemn.

Her adherents increased, for she advocated the abolition of imprisonment for debt, equality for women, equal civil rights for all citizens, and the abolition of requiring witnesses in court to state their religion. Her support of the Workingman's Party, which was powerful enough to elect a man to the New York legislature in 1828, caused it to be dubbed the Fanny Wright Party.

Robert Dale Owen appeared and he and Jennings and Frances established a ménage where they pursued simple living and published the *Enquirer* which gained a national circulation. Phiquepal d'Arusmont came on to print it. Camilla presently arrived with her baby but without her husband. Her marriage had been the product of loneliness and, when the baby died, it was not resumed.

Frances's worst scorner came to be the *New York Courier and Enquirer* which coined the term "Wright reason" to disparage her intellect and logic. It also lumped in, cleverly or in ignorance, the money-leveling schemes of the more radical of the Agrarian Reformers with her policies. The editor enjoyed running such witty bits as this:

At a numerous and highly respectable meeting of the friends of *Wright Reason,* held at the sign of "The World turned upside down" in the Five Points, last evening, Mr. Ichabod Ragmuffin was called to the bench and Messrs. Rag, Tag, and Bobtail appointed secretaries. The meeting being properly disorganized, the following preamble and resolutions were passed unanimously:

Whereas all men are born free and equal, and bring nothing with them into this world, it stands to reason they ought to remain so, and take nothing with them out of it. It is therefore contrary to Wright reason, and the laws of nature for talent, industry, economy, enterprise, and honesty to raise one man above another, in reputation or property. Therefore:

Resolved unanimously, That it is against the laws of nature and the principles of Wright reason, that because one man chooses to work and another do nothing, the former should get rich and the latter remain poor. . . .

Frances bore up. The business of Nashoba still hung over her, though, and she could no longer pretend it would ever be any sort of success. She and d'Arusmont took the slaves to Haiti and freed them under the auspices of the Negro Haitian President Boyer—and one may suppose that by then the beneficiaries were fairly addled over what had befallen them the preceding several years. What became of the free Mamselle Lolotte and her children? The record seems not to say. Perhaps they had already returned to New Orleans, or settled in Memphis.

Frances was scarcely back in New York when a story burst that she had accepted money from the Haitian President Boyer. The press reminded the world that Frances was a free lover and an amalgamator of races. She published receipts showing she had paid full duty on the slaves and that Boyer's money was a contribution to help settle the manumitted Negroes on his land.

This changed no minds. She became apathetic and weary. New scandals were raked up: When at Nashoba, had she not written Jennings, asking him to come teach school there and suggesting financial arrangements by which his wife and children might be kept in the East? She published the correspondence, placing everything in harmless light. It made no impression.

It seemed to her her very presence was harming the things she advocated. She announced her retirement from public life—and her engagement to d'Arusmont. This precipitated a quarrel between the pair and Robert Dale Owen. Owen declared later he had seen the man as a pretty useless fellow from the first, but the evidence is that his bitter dislike dated from the announcement of the engagement. One view has it that Owen had been using Fanny's funds with a lavish hand and that the dispute was over money. At any rate Frances and d'Arusmont and Camilla prepared to leave for France, with no wedding yet performed. The editor of the *Courier and Enquirer* outdid himself in what he called "a doleful Ditty made upon the departure of that 'mother of the Gracchii' Frances Wright, the 'petticoated politician'—from free America, after a brilliant career of regeneration, concluded by three distinct farewell addresses. To be sung in the most melancholy strain imaginable by Robert Dale Owen, Doct. Baxter, and every American Mechanic and Working Man who cannot think or act without the aid of English radicals and Jacobins and American Tories."

Tune "Oh! Put the Onion to your Eye"

> *Oh Fanny Wright—sweet Fanny Wright*
> *We ne'er shall hear her more:*
> *She's gone to take another freight*
> *To Hayti's happy shore.*
> *She used to speak so parrot-like,*
> *With gesture small and staid;*

So pretty in her vehemence—
Alas! departed maid.
Tho' we are men of age mature
How can we rule ourselves?
Unless we all wear petticoats,
We're laid upon the shelves!

She beat Jemima Wilkinson
Joana Southcote quite,
E'en Mother Lee was nothing to
Our little Fanny Wright.
For she had gold within her purse,
And brass upon her face;
And talent indescribable,
To give old thoughts new grace.
And if you want to raise the wind,
Or breed a moral storm
You must have one bold lady-man
To prate about reform.

And so on, down to:

Farewell, ye young mechanics,
Ye lusty men and true;
All—One and all—both great and small,
My heart is warm for you.
This cried she on that Tuesday night
When in her whitest gloves,
Her grey eyes, at the Bowery
Looked on her hundred loves.
Her Owen was forgotten,
And Baxter looked an ass;
Tho' one hung up her Leghorn
And the other filled her glass!
Those dignified Philosophers
Those Platos of the west,
Were nothing to the jacket-boys
Who fired her virgin breast.

Ye are the bone and sinew
The marrow of this land;
And yet ye are but blockheads
Who cannot understand:
So I have come to teach you
What Spence has taught before,
That—if mankind were all made rich
They would—be poor no more! . . .

Thus spoke this gentle maiden
Not more than six feet high.
How beautiful her curly wig!
How restless clear her eye!
She had a very little book
She seemed to look upon;
But buxom lads with peachy cheeks
Much more her notice won.

So Frances was gone, leaving her causes in the hands of Owen and the Evans brothers, George and Frederick, the latter of whom was finally to lead the Shakers. There was a long delay in the marriage. Perhaps d'Arusmont's demand for her permanent retirement was the cause, or perhaps it was her demand that she retain control of her property. Finally, as the marriage was about to occur, further delay was occasioned by the death of Camilla—a lasting shock to Frances.

After six months she and d'Arusmont were married on July 22, 1831. The ingenuous speed with which she became pregnant may have quenched any belief that she had ever practiced free love or the equally heinous birth control of Robert Dale Owen's onanistic *Moral Physiology*. Her daughter Frances Sylva was born April 16, 1832.

When the child was three years old, the d'Arusmonts left her in Paris and journeyed to America to see about literary matters and to close out the holdings at Nashoba where Whitby lived with his second family. As she was to continue doing until her death, Frances had been sending him the annuity left him by Camilla in her will.

Old emotions seized her. She took to the lecture platform and would not give it up. The papers dug out all the old scandals and warmed them over. D'Arusmont bitterly returned to France. He and Frances saw each other but little during the final fifteen years of her life. Just before her death he divorced her.

The various Owen brothers, prominent in politics or public and scientific affairs, lived at New Harmony which their father gave them in lieu of previous settlements he had made upon them. A cultural remnant of the finest minds of communal days had settled there, but the life Frances might have had with them was impossible because of her restlessness and concern with "causes," and her estrangement from at least some of the Owens.

As for Robert Owen, Sr., in 1828, when Frances was involved with the Workingman's Party in New York, he had returned for one more attempt to revive the commune. He offered to finance a new venture if the people would suggest something and agree to work at it. Under the plan evolved, sharpers bought land at such liberal terms that they never bothered to pay and he never got it back. Not waiting for eventualities, he earmarked an expected three thousand in land payments to maintain the school a while longer, hoping, he said, for a permanent, nationally-known institution to rise there. He left. The three thousand never materialized, of course, and he did not return.

The sons sent him a bit of income, eked out with their private contributions, in his old age. Money really made no difference to him, at least in small quantities. He had about fifty thousand dollars left and he enthusiastically planned a commune in Mexico, but it was not begun because of difficulties with officials concerning religion. Once more he started an endless search for a million with which to open a village in England, and indeed he was connected with several communes there.

In America, in the final phase of her career, Frances concentrated on women's rights and must be remembered as a prime mover in the legislation on their behalf. But she was a lonely and tragic figure, despite the hurly-burly and crowds. The suspicion is that as much as anything she was escaping marriage. Early in 1852 she slipped on the ice in Cincinnati and broke her hip. She lingered until Christmas, an invalid, and died at fifty-six. One of the most enduring legends about her is that she founded in 1856 "The first woman's club in America with a written constitution, the Minerva Club," which indeed was founded in that year in New Harmony.

For an additional five years Robert Owen lectured in England. He still believed someone would provide the million necessary for his ideal commune when he collapsed and died while reading a paper, "The Human Race Governed Without Punishment," before the Social Science Association of England. This was in 1857. He was eighty-seven years old.

In time, Frances's daughter Sylva married a man named Guthrie and they, or at least their descendants, settled in the United States.

CHAPTER ELEVEN

EQUITY, FOURIER, BROOK FARM, AND THE PHALANXES

THE COURT OF LOVE WAS OVERRULED

> One hears the frequent statement of the country members that one man was ploughing all day and another was looking out the window all day—perhaps drawing his picture, and they both received the same wages.
>
> —EMERSON, on Brook Farm

i. JOSIAH WARREN'S EQUITY

EVEN as cooperation had "nigh killed us all" at Nashoba, the collapse of New Harmony nigh finished off secular communalism—or so it appeared for almost fifteen years. Throughout the 1830's nothing of consequence occurred in the field of religious communalism, and in that time only one secular village was founded, Josiah Warren's Equity colony in Ohio. It was Warren who had declared that New Harmony was talked to death—and necessarily so, since people who own property together must attempt to agree on how it is to be used, a thing he viewed as impossible.

In his village, then, each man would own his own property. He would invest his time, money, and reputation to suit himself, and at his own risk. There would be no constitution and no vote-taking and no opportunity to blame others for one's failures. Why, then, have a village? The answer was that under Warren's benevolent anarchy men might exchange labor to the advantage of all. No one would be rich, but everyone would have as much of what the community produced as he was willing to work for.

But Warren was in no hurry, after the collapse of New Harmony, to establish his commune. And Ebenezer Elliot had served up the sentiment of many in rhyme in 1831:

> *What is a communist?*
> *One who hath yearnings*
> *For equal division*
> *Of unequal earnings.*
> *Idler or bungler or both*
> *He is willing*
> *To fork out his copper*
> *And pocket your shilling.*

By communist Elliot meant a dweller in a share-the-wealth village.

Warren wished first to test his system of labor exchange on a small scale, and also to learn several trades, for he felt that the more sorts of work a community leader understood the better it would be.

A classically handsome man, Warren had come to Cincinnati from the East in his early twenties and had become prosperous as a musician and as the inventor and manufacturer of a patent lamp. He was not yet thirty when his humanitarian ideas put him in Owen's train. He took his wife and their young children to New Harmony where he stayed until Owen's tacit admission of defeat.

At once, then, in Cincinnati he opened his Equity Store which was promptly dubbed the Time Store. The principle, which had been advanced in theory for more than a century, and practiced in a small way at New Harmony, was that in making a sale the merchant should charge only the wholesale price plus a trifling percentage for overhead. But then if the customer had consumed, say, twelve minutes of the clerk's time, he signed a ready-printed "labor time note," promising to work that number of minutes for the bearer on demand. These notes, as supplied by Warren, bore engravings of beehives, hour glasses, and such, and various Poor Richard sayings cautioning one to improve the shining hour.

The notes were negotiable. If the neighborhood blacksmith, for instance, should need some painting done he might go to the store and give Warren a note for ten hours of smithing and take ten hours of the merchant's accumulated painters' notes in return, and then demand the promised labor of those who had signed them. But if it was not convenient for the painters to work out their notes just then, they might redeem them with Indian corn, the value of which would be reset from year to year according to local crop conditions!

Now, Warren knew as well as any other man that the world had spent some thousands of years getting away from a barter economy—but his plea was that under a money economy the bankers and money men could and often did convulse men and nations and rule for war or peace at will by manipulating cash and credit. But, he said, the bankers could not corner human energy which in his system would replace money.

The weakness in all this, apparently unsuspected by him, was that in the end he tied the whole thing to the national speculation in basic grains, for certainly a farmer would dispose of his grain where he best might, and a non-farmer might well go out and purchase grain, if it were to his advantage, with which to redeem a note. But as for the Time Store itself, so many who came to scoff stayed to buy that prices were driven down in the neighborhood until other merchants, in desperation, accepted Warren's help in putting in his system. Convinced that he had proved his theory, he closed shop and while the merchants drifted back to their former system he began his study of printing, wheel-wrighting, and other trades. Part of his idea in this was to prove that the long apprenticeships demanded by master workmen were mostly to keep down competition.

It was not until 1835 that he established his Equity village, with labor exchange and a government of "individual sovereignty." Labor exchange functioned so well in the static little community, in Tuscarawas County, Ohio, that one man built a brick house at a cash outlay of less than ten dollars. Without a national system of labor exchange some money was necessary and various members had to go out into the world to work for cash in order to buy necessities which the village did not produce. However, this was viewed as but a temporary impediment, one which did not harm the basic system. The village school supposedly was superior to Owen's in results—and certainly Warren did not stifle liberal education nor keep children from their parents.

Malarial epidemics soon broke up the village. Satisfied that his theories had been fully proved and that those who wished to profit thereby might do so, Warren left his followers to remain in association or not—and they seem to have not—while he returned to his studies in printing. These led him to developments which revolutionized the printing industry and which affect it to this day, but at bitter disappointment to him. He received but a pittance for his inventions in stereotyping and picture reproduction. His high-speed press, the first to use paper from a roll, was sabotaged so often by workers who feared for their jobs that he finally broke it up in disgust.

He also devised a new system of musical notation, but while it was more easily read and learned, it could not replace the old one. He opened a time store at New Harmony, and though it drove down the prices of other merchants, Warren was disheartened by the rascality of drifters who signed labor notes and then vanished. In 1848, at the end of the great wave of the village-making of that decade, he founded his Utopia, as he frankly named it, in Clermont County, Ohio.

In it there were "no lectures on principles, no priests and prophets. . . . There were no collisions because there were no property rights in conflict. All matters of taste, all plans, sane or insane, were left to the individual." There were no laws, either, but one of the brethren remarked, in a newspaper interview, that "if anyone steals my property or injures me, I will take good care to make myself square with him."

Concerning women, he added that "we let them do about as they please, and they generally please to do about right. . . . Marriage? Well, folks ask no questions in regard to *that* among us. . . . There is no eaves-dropping, or prying behind the curtain. . . . The individual is sovereign and independent and all the laws tending to restrict the liberty he or she enjoy are founded in error and should not be regarded."

A land boom, with the crowding in of neighbors, made it impossible to conduct an anarchy, since the lack of laws and jails left no good way to cope with criminals, and at the same time rising prices made it profitable to sell. Warren opened a third community—the Village of Modern Times—in 1851, on Long Island where Brentwood now stands. It lasted a generation as an anarchic cooperative.

After Warren had wandered on in pursuit of other interests, Modern Times established a community-owned factory which required vote-taking; worse, the village became subject to the booms and busts of the Civil War era because of its cash dealings with the world through the factory. Being within convenient commuting distance of the city, it was chosen by several New York criminals as a home base, they no doubt finding it comfortable to relax in a place where there was no government nor means of law enforcement. These people, together with assorted crackpots and reputed polygamists who flocked in, made good copy and the place attained a newspaper reputation as being inhabited by freaks, fools, and faddists.

Warren had long been writing and publishing. Now he turned almost solely to the production of calmly-worded sociological and economic treatises which were used in colleges and universities until the turn of the century. Thus he had some influence on the thought of two or three generations of scholars and students, and on the liberalization of American thought in general.

"A remarkable American, Josiah Warren," John Stuart Mill said of him.

ii.   BROOK FARM

Warren was fleeing from the bankers, the vested interests, the bucket shops. He was fleeing from the machine to a certain extent, and from the growing industrial octopus— for in his small anarchies there was no place for any more industry than was needed by consumers on the spot. Like all of the basically sane communitarian leaders, he was an idealist, struggling in his own way to lead people into a new day and using such of the tools at hand as appealed to him.

Indeed, people everywhere shrank back in horror, or viewed in anger, or fled from the growing industrialization which was crushing a great and growing segment of the people and forcing them into a slum existence. Legislation to change things was slow or impossible because of the cry for individual freedom. The men who made the most noise about it were those same men who owned the factories, the canals, the railroads, the mines. What they wanted, of course, was freedom for themselves to continue doing as they chose.

It was perhaps inevitable just then that the planners of brave new worlds should turn once more to the communal village, with the spectacle of wealthy and apparently contented Shakers and Economites and the German Zoarists in Ohio before them. The contention, however, of the secularists was that without "savage and barbaric religions" similar groups of people might be even more contented. However, the planners and their possible followers were given pause by keen memory of the Owen debacle and, further, they seemed neither to have funds nor the drive and persuasiveness to enlist moneyed backers.

The money panic of 1837, the terrible and widespread drouth of the next summer and the hardships of the unprecedented succeeding winter, all no doubt helped make possible the flood of communes, mostly secular, which suddenly began pouring across the East and into the West. Further, there was rising a generation which knew not Joseph and did not fear failure merely because of the difficulties of a vaguely-remembered Englishman who had been hornswoggled—one might chuckle over it by then—by shrewd Yankees.

In the 1840's, communes erupted at the rate of more than one every three months for the decade. While these were mostly nonreligious, the primal lava at the same time was spewing out every sort of communal-minded Second Comer, post-Millennialist (*i.e.,* the Coming had already occurred and the Millennium was in progress, or had come and passed), and religionists with dreams of a system of "spiritual matings" which in practice did not somehow remain entirely spiritual. There were also coveys of non-religionists of the same general delighted lunatic fringe.

Even Transcendentalism, an important intellectual and spiritual force in its day—if it may be said not to exist until now—had its fringe of crackpots and the Boston-Concord area was given many a treat in the early days of "the Newness." This Newness was in part a rebellion from Calvinism and classicism. The romantic era in literature was crowding out long generations of writing which—like Milton's, for instance—was forced into certain physical patterns, often borrowed in some measure from the classical Greeks and Romans, whether violence was thus done to authors' inward ideas and feelings or not. Too, classicism dredged constantly into mythology for its figures of speech and its analogies.

The new writers, particularly since the days of Burns, were navigating by instinct—as indeed did some of the ancients—letting form fit itself to material. Further, they were interested in the individual, and in "natural" nature. That is, a forest, or a host of golden daffodils, growing wild, was more a joy to see than was a park or a formal garden. Religiously, Unitarianism, in New England and among intellectuals in Europe, was crowding the Trinitarian religions. Unitarianism indeed became the religion of perhaps most of the familiar figures of Transcendentalism. To the Transcendentalists at large, whether Unitarian or not, men ceased being the damned children of Adam and became the beloved children of God. Emerson and his kind called upon them to live in harmony with their basically divine nature. Further, he declared that the individual was superior to society, and that when man fully realized his divine nature there would be no need for governments. In all this, the age of reason was pushing down hard upon the remnants of the age of dogmatic faith.

It was the matter of individualism which appealed to many in the early days of Transcendentalism. A group might be seen wearing close-fitting garments, cut to the contours of the body. Why? "Well, we are followers of the Newness—and certainly there is no better pattern for garments than the shape of the body." Did young men let their hair grow, wear open collars, and carry on loud conversations at lectures and concerts? "Oh, we believe in the New Learning—and how can there be a philosophy of freedom if one is not free to express himself at all times?"

Allegedly, churchgoers might glimpse someone flitting about his premises in the altogether on Sunday morning: In heaven, it was reasonable to believe, even the fig leaf was discarded. After all, the original Adam, in the image of God, wore none. And so, under the Newness— And so on. Arrest him? The story says no.

And one day the Reverend Dr. Ralph Waldo Emerson was called on by a delegation of young men, one of whom greeted him with an amiable, "Good morning, damn you, sir," while another added, "We are hell-fired glad to be here."

Mr. Emerson—who loved mankind in general, but only tolerated individuals—was embarrassed and puzzled. Why the swearing?

"Well, damn you sir, we are of the Newness and we wish to demonstrate that profanity is not the use of vile language spoken calmly, but spoken to relieve harsh feelings, so we put an oath in each sentence."

The embarrassed minister took his guests indoors to get them out of earshot of the neighbors.

Emerson always disclaimed any particular connection with the New Learning, but he could not escape the role of a founding father in the public mind. Certainly he shared its high ideals of mental and spiritual freedom and believed that all an individual needed was within, that he needed no preachers to lead him to Deity.

Another tenet of Transcendentalism—or at least in the philosophy of some of the leading minds—was that all men should do some physical labor in order to lighten the burden of the working classes who might thus be somewhat freed to seek culture on their own account. And this idea helped lead to the inevitable talk of establishing a commune of "thoughtful and cultivated people" who would practice fully the principles of the Newness.

Two Unitarian ministers, Doctors Ripley and Channing, discussed starting one forthwith. "That good attempt," Emerson remarks dryly, "ended in an oyster supper with excellent wines." But soon Ripley and Channing had taken definite steps, buying an old homestead at West Roxbury, a few miles out of Boston, as the site. They called it Brook Farm. Emerson did not join. He saw nothing to be gained. While he did not say so to Ripley, he did not believe the venture would succeed—and at any rate he had already tried physical labor and had concluded it was not intended that "the writer should dig."

Ripley was an enlightened idealist who for several years had been enthusiastically visiting religious communes and studying their methods. In his own village he would show the world how to escape the tyranny of the machine, of constant drudgery in the field, and to pursue education, culture, and the pleasures of leisure, all from a proper application of one's time. Closely bound up in this was the outright humanitarian idea of producing utilitarian things so that the traditionally laboring classes might not have to sweat in sun or factory to produce them for the intellectuals. This would be comparable to a decision today of making one's own automobile so that the wage slaves of Detroit might have leisure to attend lectures. Ripley's system would have returned America to the handcrafts and small machines of Jefferson's day. Whether he actually wanted that is problematical.

At any rate, he did want "plain living and high thinking," and certainly the Brook Farmers had a good deal of both, and just as certainly they developed halos over the sacrifices they were making in doing manual labor, for they felt that the intellectual work of which they were capable was of a higher order and was more nearly its own reward than was the physical.

It is ironic that a venture with such high purpose and one which almost succeeded should best be known through the journals of Hawthorne who never really was in sympathy with its aims or philosophy and who loathed the life there.

The fact was that after fifteen years of literary labors he had only a precarious foot in the editorial doors. He had to have leisure to pursue his career, or he had to give it up. He was in love and desirous of some situation which would allow him to marry. He was drying up under the onerous duties of counting baskets of coal at customs.

Brook Farm seemed the divinely-sent answer. Perhaps his prospective sister-in-law, Elizabeth Peabody, helped him reach that conclusion for she wrote in the *Dial* of her feeling that the project was a laudable attempt to establish the kingdom of heaven on earth. There would be "leisure to live in all the faculties of the soul" under Association, with everyone pitching in to help with the tasks necessary for basic existence. There would be "leisure for production of intellectual goods." And there would be cash income from the sale of material goods to the public. The profit would be divided among the Farmers on a basis of hours worked and of shares of Brook Farm stock held.

And so Hawthorne plunked down one hundred dollars (he later pledged a thousand but surely never paid it) for one share of stock—for the founders had the wit to require financial participation by every member, to the scorn of idealists who analogized about a father charging his children to belong to the family. Hawthorne was made a director of agriculture, which, being interpreted, meant farm hand. He knew nothing of farming—but then, he knew nothing of anything which might be turned to immediate cash account by the Society. However, it was assumed that anyone could do routine labor—and of course should do some to lessen the burden of the world's downtrodden. Hawthorne agreed.

On a raw spring day in 1841, he walked out to the Farm and on April 13 he wrote his fiancée, Sophia Peabody: "Here I am in a polar Paradise. I like my brethren in affliction very well; and if you could see us sitting around our table at mealtimes before the great kitchen fire, you would call it a cheerful sight." The broom was still new at this time and Hawthorne was yet under his compulsive determination to like the idea and the place. Further, the group was still small enough for him to feel somewhat a part of it.

His pen then gouged slyly into Margaret Fuller, the feminist, a fellow member—rather, that is, a periodic visitor—for whom he did not care: the eight cows had been "increased by a transcendental heifer belonging to Miss Margaret Fuller. She is very fractious, I believe, and apt to kick over the milk-pail."

Sophia understood he was talking really about Miss Fuller who was intent upon upsetting the *status quo* concerning her "causes." Fortunately, Sophia did not edit out such things as that in preparing the letters, which form his Brook Farm journal, for the press—for there have been querulous criticisms that she altered his letters, though this was largely to eliminate the embarrassing phraseology of a man in love, a private and personal thing: "Ownest wife. [They were not, of course, yet married.] God bless thee, ownest. Thy lovingest husband."

"I intend," his letter continues, "to convert myself into a milkmaid this evening, but I pray Heaven that Mr. Ripley may be moved to assign me the kindliest cow in the herd, otherwise I shall perform my duty with fear and trembling."

Dr. Ripley, a medium-sized man, bearded, with "the kindest eyes in the world," and of monumental patience which never became ruffled, did not put him to milking at once. Rather, Hawthorne foddered cattle, carried wood, repaired fires—and next day, with Ripley, "commenced a gallant attack upon a heap of manure."

Further: "Miss Fuller's cow hooks the other cows and has made herself ruler of the herd, and behaves in a very tyrannical manner." Then to his joy the herd "rebelled against the usurpation of Miss Fuller's heifer; and whenever they are turned out of the barn, she is compelled to take refuge under our protection. She is not an amiable cow; but she has a very intelligent face, and seems to be of a reflective cast of character. I doubt not that she will soon perceive the expediency of being on good terms with the rest of the sisterhood."

There was brilliant conversation at meals, at manure hauling, and in the evenings. Hawthorne was really out of place, for he was an introspective man and the people around him were pulpit orators and extroverts of other sorts. Hawthorne's single hope was that the intended boarding school and the "small manufactures" which were to be established would pay a dividend sufficient that he might feel free to take off enough time actually to accomplish something with his writing. He was trying to buy one thing—time. Time in which to write. At least he did gain something to write about, although it was of no immediate cash value.

Ten years later, in *The Blithedale Romance,* a novel with a setting very like the Farm, he allowed himself to get in a few licks at the system, and he indicated something of the spirited and slightly racy turn of the conversations held before "the great kitchen fire." He also castigated a feminist named Zenobia, which indicates some horn-locking, in the early days of his manure hauling, with the really well-known, unhappy, unpretty Miss Fuller:

> She was made for a stump oratress. Her mind was full of weeds. She made no scruple of oversetting all human institutions, and scattering them as with a breeze from her fan. A female reformer, in her attacks upon society, has an instinctive sense of where the life lies, and is inclined to aim directly at that spot. Especially the relation between the sexes is naturally among the earliest to attract her notice.

> Finally one day: "Did you ever see a happy woman?" demanded Zenobia—*i.e.,* Miss Fuller. "I do not mean a girl on the sunny side of experience, but a grown woman. How can she be happy, after discovering that fate has assigned her but one single event, which she must contrive to make the substance of her whole life? A man has his choice of unnumerable events."

> "A woman, I suppose," answered I, "by constant repetition of her one event, may compensate for the lack of variety."

> "Indeed," sniffed Zenobia.

But Miss Fuller said flatly that she didn't believe in trying to do things in groups and she drifted away, finally enlisting herself in the cause of freedom in Italy where at last a man forgot the outward long enough to fall in love with her and make her pregnant. And indeed, finally to marry her, though she had stoically made up her mind to be happy even if that latter did not occur. She and her count and their child were drowned in sight of shore on the return to America—and Hawthorne was ungenerous enough to doubt that she was ever married. She must have cut him deeply in some of their encounters.

He had convinced himself that it was a fine thing to do part of the world's physical labor so that the farmers in the vicinity might have leisure to cultivate their minds. But

> . . . one of the first questions raised, after our separation from the greedy, struggling, self-seeking world [related to] the possibility of getting the advantage over the outside barbarians in their own field of labor. But to own the truth, I very soon became sensible that, as regarded society at large, we stood in a position of new hostility, rather than new brotherhood.

In an address to the Fourier Society in Boston, in 1844, Charles A. Dana remarked that, "Our ulterior aim is nothing less than Heaven on Earth,—the conversion of this globe, now exhaling pestilential vapors and possessed by unnatural climates, into the abode of beauty and health, and the restitution to Humanity of the Divine Image, now so long lost and forgotten. . . . Here let me say distinctly, that the practical result we first aim at is Wealth. We declare, without hesitation, that universal wealth is a necessary condition of the universal development of Humanity; without the one the other is impossible. We do not make war upon any part of human nature, but only upon its false circumstances and subversive conditions."

But this reach for wealth, as Hawthorne had said, put

the Farmers in a position of hostility to their neighbors whom they were impoverishing by taking their vegetable customers—and by the unfair method of washing their own goods, thus making them more attractive, before offering them for sale. Certainly the neighbors might thus have had more leisure with the loss of their market. Yet, such as they had apparently was spent not so much on the cultivation of their minds as in working up a sullen temper toward Brook Farm—and herein may have lain the germ of the final destruction of this cooperative of Unitarian intellectuals.

The vegetable market aside, the neighbors were of Puritan stock and outlook—the same outlook which had led their ancestors to hang noisy, contentious Quakers, male and female, on Boston Common two centuries before, and, in a nearer time, to stone Jemima Wilkinson and her followers out of their neighborhood. Further, the Brook Farmers denied the Trinity with their Unitarian deity. Infidels! And who doubted the story that went round that they had sacrificed a white ox to Jupiter? The further insult was that they had music and dancing every night and picnics on Sunday, with two afternoons off each week for having fun—while honest men bordering on the Farm had to scrabble to make ends meet.

The philosophy of the Farmers was "Here and Now! This instant is appointed to live for all you are worth." And cooperative labor at laboring time made the times of leisure possible. Dr. Ripley made a point of choring at the barns before breakfast.

The two afternoons of holiday were Hawthorne's chief opportunity for writing. He early convinced himself that he might continue the routine for a long time—that he was contented as week after week he cleaned the years' accumulations from the barn. The hands might be defiled, but not the soul. Two months changed his tune: "Of all the hateful places that is the worst and I shall never comfort myself for having spent so many days of blessed sunshine there. It is my opinion that a man's soul may be buried and perish under a dung-heap or in a furrow of the field, just as well as under a pile of money."

But, then, wasn't that what Dr. Ripley had been saying all along in his desire to give men freedom from such endless work? In another few weeks Hawthorne moaned, "O, labor is the curse of the world and nobody can meddle with it without becoming proportionately brutified! Is it a praiseworthy matter that I have spent five golden months in providing food for cows and horses? It is not so." He had only taken "the morsel out of some wretch's mouth" who might otherwise have earned it, and would never again, as he said, fall into the laudable error of thinking better of the world's improvability than it deserved.

Ripley had a reputation as a teacher. He had moved his Boston school to the Farm and children were sent to it from afar, some of them being "boarders" and others "half boarders," even as were some of the adults, these terms regulating the amount of labor done.

One of the students, Sophia Eastman, wrote home, to Franklin, New Hampshire, in part:

> It is certainly a delightful place. There are four separate buildings. The Pilgrim House, the Eyrie, Cottage, and Hive. There is an aristocracy prevailing here, although many complain of being neglected. I think there should be a distinction made, but you know it is against their principle, but they all treat me with as much kindness and respect as though I paid five dollars a week for board. You recollect the plan of this Community speaks of receiving no individuals unless capable of refinement, a great taste for literature, and possessed of superior abilities, but I assure you there are a great many of the reverse. The fact is they are rather dull and backward in their studies, and I think some will always remain so, though there are many pretty ladies and gentlemen and some mean characters I should think (I judge only from looks and appearances). There

are three horns blown in the morning, the first is sounded a little before five, the second half past five, and the third at six, to call them to breakfast. Immediately after breakfast I proceed to the ironing room, which is to the Pilgrim house (or to the washing room just as they wish me to) and there remain until the horn sounds for dinner, which is half past twelve. The work is very hard and wearing to the constitution. It is now vacation many of the teachers are absent, and we study at our rooms. Mr Ripleys sister is my teacher. She is a old maid and is one of the most presise beings I ever saw. We go to Miss Ripley's room and there remain three hours. I find I have grown pale and poor already though I feel pretty well most of the time. You will now wish to know what their religious principles are. I regret to say that many have no principles at all. But very few go to church on the Sabbath, and it is a fact they do knit and sew. On Sunday Mrs Ripley invites them to the Grove where they spend a few hours in reading gipsy stories. I have seen many things I shall not mention here. A carriage is provided in the morning for those that wish to go to church. I have walked one Sabbath and rode two The Unitarian where I attend is two miles from the community, the orthodox half mile. I dislike the principles very much indeed and I know you will not approve of this, but you know any one is not obliged to imbibe these sentiments. There are four ministers here who have renounced these sentiments and become Transcendentalists. They seldom attend Church on the Sabbath. The truth is that this institution is something like the Shakers, after a person remains here a short time they become attached to the place and are unwilling to leave and [accordingly they] join the Association. I have assisted many of the young ladies in their studies. I can see that they like me very much but it requires considerable policy to be in such a place, and to get the right side. They all appear uncommonly interested in my welfare. Why it is I cannot tell. The girls appear very fond of me because I appear so cheerful and happy. If they feel low spirited they come to my chamber. Have written one letter for a lady to her mother who was 3 or 4 years my senior. My room mate is a native of Ireland and is a orphan. She is a very good girl but rather ignorant not such a person as I should wish to have for a companion and friend. But I make a great deal of her and she appears to like me very much. She is a Catholic but I think she is a Christian. There is a dancing school tonight and it seems to be all confusion. They have balls dancing schools and all manner of amusements but I have attended none of them.

It is nothing uncommon for people to get married and then part from their husbands. There are three who board here and there husbands have left them Tell brother if he should get tired of Sara he must come and live here If any of the family should be sick or suddenly taken away you had better write to the Rev. Mr. Ripley as I might get it sooner. The mail goes out and comes in every day. Good Night.

Sophia

There was a charge of four dollars weekly for child, pupil, or college preparatory student, and this paid for "board, washing, fuel, lights, and instruction in all branches." Whether poor Sophia's long hours entirely paid her keep does not appear, but it does seem that even "full boarders" were required as a matter of principle to do some chores—which may indeed have lessened what the flat rate otherwise might have been. The pupils were not the regimented wretchlings of the New Harmony school which had convinced even Owen that children should not be treated like orphans or machines. Apparently, despite the work hours and the abundant play, the pupils at the Farm made rapid advancement.

The building program caused a steady but not

frightening deficit, despite the steady productivity of the farm and of the various "light industries." The solution was for those who had outside assets to buy a few more shares of stock and this was freely done for perhaps no one among the several hundred who were at the farm at one time or another doubted its eventual success to the very moment of collapse.

Care was taken to keep out visionaries and crackpots. The penniless and ill were refused admittance on the excuse that the Association could support no dead weight in its early stage. If a visiting visionary demanded opportunity to speak, it was given at the evening assemblage in the main building, the Hive. But the Farmers had a low and frankly exhibited boring point and made no scruple of interrupting a feminist to say that if the world's women did not like their trials all they had to do was to organize another Brook Farm where the women had perfect freedom. If any speaker did not intrigue them, they began talking, playing cards, or dancing, to the confusion of the orator.

One itinerant, for instance, advocated general adoption of the whole-grain diet on which he said he thrived. He stayed a few days as a probationary, carrying a little bag of wheat on which he had to be constantly chewing in order to get enough. When caught filching table scraps from the chickens, he was fed and banished. Another speaker who had discovered the secret of going without sleep, thus increasing his usable time to twenty-four hours daily, was presently found slumbering in his chair and sent on his way.

On the other hand, wandering musicians were always welcomed, whether violinists or bell ringers. Not that all was music, picnics, and dancing. The Farmers liked intellectual exercise. They relished saying that many of them read Dante in the original Italian, Hegel in the German, Swedenborg in Latin, and Fourier—who was soon, in his writings, to become their mentor—in the original French. Detractors always quipped, "And Margaret Fuller in the original English." Lowell, in his *Fable for Critics,* condemned a culprit to thirty days at hard labor—that is, to reading Miss Fuller's works. Hawthorne, who left the Farm for good in early winter of the first year, would have agreed.

The humanitarian principles of the Farmers extended to the protection of their animal brothers. They were against meat eating—although of course that did not mean they weren't to have some slabs of pork in the Sunday beans —and against hunting. Wild animals had a right to existence. Except for rabbits. Those were suspected of nibbling the crops and were forthwith executed and consumed at table.

iii. FOURIERISM AT BROOK FARM

After some three years, it was seen that many basic trades were not likely soon to be represented at the Farm. And there was continued worry over the steady, if small, deficit. While the line of reasoning is not at all clear, these things apparently influenced the decision to change the Association to a "Fourieristic phalanx." Certainly the Farmers were not overcome by oratory—for Albert Brisbane, the great apostle of Fourierism in this country, was not an orator. He was simply a young man who early in life, even in his teens, had felt that he had a great mission, at that time undisclosed, to perform. Later, then, he became pixillated with the sense and nonsense, the logic and the incomprehensibilities, of a Frenchman who, as it turned out, was to die a little too soon to see the flowering of his philosophy. This, of course, was Charles Fourier.

After the failure of the French Revolution, the Frenchman Saint-Simon declared that he had been wrong in his ideas of democracy and equality—that (even as Coleridge put it) this made for mediocrity. The ideal, he said, was to raise up an aristocracy based on talent, and go on to Utopia from there.

But Fourier said that Utopia would come only from

a logical recognition of the fact that people and human nature follow certain basic principles, and he put himself to the task of discovering and tabulating those laws. His idea then was to set up a commune in which people would be free to follow those natural laws so that constant coercion, rebellion, and unhappiness would be things of the past.

Fourier was born in 1772, the son of a cloth merchant, in Besançon, and oddly his talents were a mingling of the artistic and mechanical. He lost everything in the burnings and lootings of the Revolution, was imprisoned, released, and put to fighting. He had seen enough theft, dishonesty, pain, exploitation of men and waste of both men and materials to sicken him. None of it, he was certain, was according to "natural" law.

That is to say, he recognized no naturally-existing bad impulses. All such came from bad organization of society. The passions—his word for emotions—he said are not hostile to universal concord, and indeed would lead to such concord if given opportunity. They should be unbridled, rather than chained by laws.

He classified twelve of these passions. Those based upon the five ordinary senses he placed in a "luxury loving" category. He found that a second group of four stems from feelings of friendship, love, paternity-family, and "ambition or corporation." The remaining three passions, discovered by Fourier himself, are, first, "the desire for intrigue, planning, and contriving," which nature uses to make men try to excel each other; then the "papillone" or butterfly instinct which makes man desire variety and novelty; and finally the "composit" passion which makes him desire union with others—presumably in all degrees of human association. This passion also functions somehow in giving increased pleasure from interplay of the gratifications of any of the several other passions simultaneously.

Just as mass is attracted to mass in the physical world, so, said Fourier, is man subject to numerous "passionate attractions," so that all his twelve passions, were it not for the ugly forces of civilization, would unite in "harmonism" to move him to harmonize himself with everything around him. The first step toward Utopia, then, was to gratify the passion of people to work in groups—and this were best done by providing villages, or "phalanxes," in which would live eight hundred twenty people, each representing one of the eight hundred twenty basic talents. Really, he said, for efficiency there should be just twice this number in each village.

In the proposed villages, with their vast communal buildings like those of Owen's ideal, the harmonizing passions would lead each person to get along with everyone else while doing exactly as he liked and sleeping where he would. Marriage, of course, would have to be abolished in the cause of freedom, although family groups might be preserved. There would, however, be "courts of love" with an elaborate system of license to give everyone, including marital partners, complete choice. No doubt there is buried somewhere in Fourier's numerous turgid volumes the solution for one-sided love, for lack of ambition to do any of the world's work, and for any other problem which might arise, but these solutions do not show on the surface.

Nor would private property and the instinct to make a profit be abolished. Some would be wealthier than others but their wealth was to be quietly enjoyed and not flaunted, lest poor members be made to feel bad. At intervals profits would be divided, five twelfths going to labor, four to capital, and three to "talent." All work was to be accomplished under fanciful terminology and in accordance with the laws observed in nature. Since children like to play in dirt, they would, on advancing from the state of "Weaners," be organized into scavenging groups known as "Little Hordes." For their repellent work they would be honored most of all groups, would lead parades, and in fact would receive "the Salute of Esteem."

The harmonizing instinct, it appears, grows out of a law of nature, in that nature is made up of a vast "order" which regulates everything "in the law of the series." Every object is in some natural series and all things move "in serial order." Hair grows at the proper time upon an embryo, and leaves on a branch obtain moisture in the order of their growth. This makes for harmony. It is only harmony which keeps the stars flying from the orbits, and without it a man might have one hand or twenty. For highest attainment, humanity must bring itself under the "divine law of the series."

Further, labor is hampered by "waste, loss, repulsive and dangerous tasks, fruitless toil, class hostilities, warring, monopoly of gains," and so on. But—the capitals are Fourier's—"Proper Organization of Labor will evolve Attractive Industries, Harmonious Communities, and will ensure the Equitable distribution of Gains and the protection afforded by Mutual Guarantees."

The Law of Attractions would draw each individual naturally into his rightful place in the perfect society. Hence, because of the interplay of all the twelve passions, there would be no competition, no opposition, no quarreling. The phalanx would assume responsibility for the welfare of each member from birth to death. In time all mankind would be organized in 2,985,984 phalanxes with an Omniarch ruling from Constantinople which was chosen because, it seems, it is "at the center."

And Fourier was nothing if not thorough. He had discovered that even the planets are amorous, that they bear young planets, that they live through infancy, youth, and maturity, and finally die as did the moon which succumbed to a fever contracted from the earth before the Flood. In the planet's life span of eighty thousand years, the earth, in the early 1800's, was at a relatively young stage.

This condition apparently still prevails, since, when our little cosmos enters the period of Harmony, men will grow tails, it seems, equipped with eyes. We will have six bright new moons. The sea will turn into lemonade—there is some indication that this may be accomplished through technology—and men may dip up a barrel at any beach. Corpses will in those days turn into pleasant-smelling gases and drift into space. The climate will be superb. "Anti-lions" will replace the present-day fierce lions, and there will also be anti-snakes, anti-vermin of every sort, anti-sharks, and so on.

To help run things smoothly meanwhile, until the onset of the period of Harmony, Fourier stood ready to create not only Unarchs, Duarchs, Tetrarchs, and so on, to rule over one, two, three, or more phalanxes, but three Augusts, twelve Caesarinas, forty-eight Empresses, a hundred forty-four Kalifs, and five hundred seventy-six Sultans to assist the Omnarch. But being a poor man, forced to eke out an existence as bookkeeper and clerk because of his losses in the Terror, he expected suitable contributions from candidates for those high positions in order that he might get the system started with a pilot commune.

He anticipated little difficulty in this, and while he ran ads in the papers that he would receive philanthropists at his home, he advised his friends not to buy land since all land would lose its value with the advent of his system. Patiently, for the last dozen years of his life, he was at home to the philanthropists, but none came. One attempt was made by a Fourier Club to found a commune, but they gave a ball to celebrate the opening of their phalanx at the place they had taken and used all their money in entertainment and fell apart therefrom. Another group came to almost as quick an end because of the dissensions over who would sleep with whom.

Fourier, early in his philosophic career, had written Owen, apparently without receiving a reply, and as Fourier gained a bit of attention Owen declared that the Frenchman had filched from Owenism all that was practical in his scheme. Fourier countered with the reverse charge. Probably each, like many others, independently conceived such basically similar systems.

Fourier died in 1837 at sixty-five.

When the American Albert Brisbane became fired with Fourierism as the solution to the problems of humanity, he went to France and had daily interviews with the master for several years. He was perfect timber for a Fourieristic disciple, for at fifteen, while tramping through the forest, he had been filled with a "spontaneous intuition" that he "belonged to a vast army in which each individual had his place and function, and that those who left its ranks to attend to individual concerns could not advance in the great achievement to which they were destined." Further, "it is not right for the individual to work for himself," and, worse, there was the crime, committed by many, of living off the labor of the masses. Fourier's creed of rendering manual labor attractive was the thing which first drew Albert Brisbane to the Frenchman.

Returning to this country in 1834, instead of trying to organize a phalanx Brisbane began thinking and haphazardly writing about Fourier's ideas. Quietly he dropped the business about Corporations of Love and Courts of Love which had proved somewhat disastrous in the minor attempts of Frenchmen to establish phalanxes. He soft-pedaled other points which he feared Americans would think ridiculous and emphasized the glories of Attractive Industry and Laws of the Harmonies and the Series—and, amazingly, Americans took not only to the idea of attraction, but to all the fantastic terminology.

Brisbane published four volumes drawn from Fourier's philosophy, with undoubtedly some of his own intermingled. He traveled, lecturing and forming clubs, but he lacked fire and brilliance of presence. Nevertheless, so great was the interest that newspapers gave him much space and he bought room for a daily column in Horace Greeley's *Tribune*. Greeley, in fact, was much impressed by the idea of the phalanx and its promise of reconciling capital and labor. He visited several phalanxes, waxed enthusiastic, but never joined one even as a part-time or commuting member. Other editors attacked both men fiercely for their leveling ideas.

Ripley's people at Brook Farm knew of Fourierism even before organizing their own society and they more and more welcomed Brisbane when he came among them, but it really seems silly, at this distance, of the Farmers to have changed to a "phalanx." Nor does it quite appear why they did it. But certainly they fell in love with the Fourieristic phraseology. Their letters and publications are full of discussions about the harmonies, and of each man's being a microcosmic universe, full of harmonies, unto himself, but they failed to see that if they had the capabilities that would make a phalanx successful, the phalanx was not needed. That is to say, they already had a suitable Association.

One may suppose, however, that they were carried away by the idea of being the ideal community at the head of what promised (to their minds) to be a triumphant social movement. They viewed the opportunity and the responsibility with reverence, and it is obvious that they mentally removed their shoes before picking up the works of the Master to delve deeper into the great mysteries.

By this time, communalism had become the chief tenet of some religious groups, one cherished above their "other" religious principles, so that the Shakers, Rappites, and Zoarites seriously considered merging on the strength of it. Indeed, communalism had become so sacred a thing that, viewing themselves as the head of the movement, they welcomed even nonreligious Association—always with the capital. This same sort of feeling obviously infected the Farmers.

Too, Brisbane sold the Farmers the idea of their becoming the official Fourieristic publishers; and finally, there was the bait for Ripley that as head of the leading phalanx he would be made president of the national organization called The Friends of Association. And so the change was made— and the hurt was instantaneous in the losing of some badly needed members because of the childish rigmarole that was adopted. And the financial wound, from indulging in Fourieristic publishing, was deep. Otherwise, the only change

seems to have been a great deal of running around to Fourieristic meetings and a reorganization of the Farm into "serial
order." The children's orders, at least, were equipped
with flags which they were allowed to display when they had
done well.

The farming, of course, was done by people in "the
farming series," which was divided into the Garden Group,
the Orchard Group, and so on. The houses were operated by
the Domestic Series, divided into Kitchen, Laundry, Chamber, and Waiters' Groups. So with manufacturing and publishing, and even recreation which was in charge of the
Festal Series. It is incredible that grown people should have
so troubled themselves with terminology, but they did.

In practice, one might be in the Potato Digging Group
today and in the Laundry Group tomorrow—for as Emerson
remarked, "the ladies took cold on washing days and it was
ordained that the gentlemen shepherds should hang out the
clothes, which they punctually did."

All this brought in no additional money but everyone
had a fine time. There was hope that when the phalanstery—
a building to hold the entire membership of a hundred fifty
—should be completed, the income would balance the outgo.

The school was dealt a blow when Pilgrim Hall, the
chief dormitory, mysteriously burned. Then a pupil came
down with smallpox. Frightened parents took children away.
The school was so depleted, as other cases developed, that it
was "temporarily" closed. Only the classes for the youngest
ever began again.

Coupled with all this, there were mutterings, largely
among the younger members, that all business matters were
poorly handled and that things would be much better if good
business principles were followed. Rebellion was threatened,
but apparently there was never a showdown.

A second fire took the building called the Eyrie. Still,
the Farmers in general were sure they would muddle
through and see good days again—and perhaps they would

have except that early in March of 1846, five years after the
establishment of the Farm, the phalanstery, completed except
for the plastering within, burned down one night.

It might have caught from a stove which had been lit to
warm the place through for plasterers who were to go to
work next day—but people commonly believed that vindic-
tive neighbors had started the three fires. This one, together
with the smallpox, had in reality finished the Farm. A few
people hung on for a while but the moving hand had writ.
Most of the members scattered and three years later, on
April 13, 1849, eight years from the day of Hawthorne's first
entry in his Brook Farm journal, the trustees wound up all
affairs—happily with no breath of scandal, which was not the
case with the closing of many communes in that decade.

iv. THE LAST OF THE PHALANXES

During the forties there were innumerable "national
conventions" of community leaders and would-be's. This
was a time of anti-ism, and a meeting which began as anti-
slave might very well convert itself into a committee-of-the-
whole in the interests of the anti-Catholic, anti-Irish, anti-
Mason, anti-Trinity, or anti-Unitarian fevers. And somewhere along the way someone was certain to say a few words
in the interest of starting a community—or phalanx, as the
going term was then.

Emerson mentions a convention of Utopians in 1840 in
New York—The Friends of Universal Reform. He said there
were present madmen, madwomen, men with beards,
Dunkers, Muggletonians, come-outers, groaners, Agrarians,
Seventh-Day Baptists, Quakers, Abolitionists, Calvinists, Unitarians, and Philosophers. Later, one man single-handedly
organized more than a hundred "national conventions" of
those interested in communities—and turned each into an
Abolitionist meeting!

All through the forties phalanxes rose—the North
American Phalanx, the Wisconsin, the Alphadelphia, the Al-

truist Community, and others as interestingly named, until it appeared that Fourier's grand envisioned total was surely to be reached.

But two years was a long time for a phalanx to survive. The members of one mushrooming colony were often fugitives from last week's communal disaster and also of the one of the week before that. Some lived in as many as fifteen communities from first to last. The phalanxes were filled with people who had failed to make a go of things as individuals. Somehow, it did not seem to transform them into social and economic successes merely to take them, like shrimp, en masse. They did sometimes show enterprise in departing between two suns with the cashbox and other movables. The laggards who had not thought of that were likely to use the catastrophe as excuse to drift to some healthier-appearing colony. The brethren of the Social Reform Unity, composed of Brooklynites who had settled near Goose Pond in what is now Monroe County, Pennsylvania, perhaps knew what they were doing when they placed seven locks on the safe, with the keys held by seven men.

Some phalanxes did almost succeed—on paper. One day the leaders would be issuing glorious communications to the press of the additional five hundred wealthy converts who were coming to join in the fall. The next, under some catastrophe of fire, peculation, bad management, belatedly-discovered insolvency through a checking of the cash to make a payment on the land, or whatever, the whole structure would be in the dust to the tune of recriminations and harshness among the scattering members.

Life must have lacked general charm and contentment in these phalanxes, as compared with that at Brook Farm. It is questionable, however, whether the inmates were aware of such shortcomings since water is likely to rest at its own level. One A. J. Macdonald made a hobby of visiting communities to write about them—and in fact he was still enthusiastically for communitarianism, in some envisioned ideal form, after seeing scores of failures.

While the Prairie Home Community in Logan County, Ohio, did not call itself a Fourieristic phalanx, its only difference from many of the phalanxes must have been in terminology. When he went to visit it, Macdonald was told "very coldly" by a pedestrian that the community was "down the road" and he gathered that the Prairie Homers were not popular. Presently he found the place where some hundred thirty people, many of Quaker extraction, most of them farmers, lived on five hundred acres. They had a pair of two-story frame houses, a log cabin, a flour mill, and an old sawmill:

> At the door of the dwelling house there was a group of women and girls, picking wool; and as it was just noon many men came in from various parts of the farm to take their dinner. At the back of the house there was a long shed, with a rough table down the center, and planks for seats on each side, on which thirty or forty people sat. I was kindly received . . . and a good dinner it was, consisting of coarse brown bread piled up in broken lumps, dishes of large potatoes unpeeled, some potato soup, and a supply of melons for a second course.
>
> I sat beside a Dr. Hard, who noticed that I took a little salt with my potatoes, and remarked to me that if I abstained from it, I would have my taste much more perfect. There was but little salt on the table, and I saw no person touch it. There was no animal food of any kind except milk, which one or two of them used. They all appeared to eat heartily. The women waited upon the table, but the variety of dishes being small, each person so attended to himself that waiting was rendered almost unnecessary. All displayed a rude politeness.

The place was disorderly and men appeared to be without a clear idea as to what they were to do. There was no government. Anyone might join who wished—the land was there for all. The leading principle was to practice the golden rule. Some were obviously not well and those who worked did not seem to exert themselves. Several people arrived from Indiana to join the Community. They "reported quite a stir" in that state in regard to it. By and large, there were too many people for the place and too many idlers among them:

> The young women were industrious, attending to the supper table and the provisions in a very steady, business-like manner; but the young men were mostly lounging about doing nothing. At bed-time there were too many persons for each to be accommodated; so the females all went up stairs and slept as they could; and the males slept below, all spread out in rows upon the floor. This was unpleasant, and as the sequel proved, could not be long endured.

The next morning a Sunday social meeting was held in the flour mill. Farming was discussed, as was the mortgage on the property. One man said he had planned to hold his farm to fall back upon if the Community should fail, but then it came to him he could not give his heart and soul to the movement if he made such reservations so he had sold it and put all the money into Prairie Home. Others said they had done the same. Still others said they would sell their places if they could but that times were hard and buyers scarce. "At the close of the meeting some singing was attempted, but it was very poor indeed."

The next day much time was wasted holding a meeting about having a plow repaired. Idlers ate melons and threw hulls in the dooryard. But the industrious said, oh, well, those fellows would move on soon. One man became much heated that another would not contribute a box of shoe-blacking to the general use. Was not everything supposed to be owned in common, even though the brother had purchased the blacking himself? Still, in general, despite the adverse remarks, and considering the group as a whole:

> I must say I never saw a better-hearted or more industrious set of fellows. They appeared to struggle hard to effect something, yet it seemed evident that something was lacking. . . . People . . . had to eat, drink, and sleep . . . but they seemed not to reflect who was going to supply the means, or where they were to come from.

Macdonald left, after observing that "Phrenology seemed to be pretty generally understood, and I was surprised to hear rude-looking men, almost ragged, ploughing, fence-making, and in like employments, converse so freely upon Phrenology, Physiology, Magnetism, Hydropathy, &c. The *Phrenological Journal* was taken by several of them."

Just two months later Prairie Home collapsed when the mortgage holder demanded a payment. Several members lost heavily. Most had nothing to lose. Some were "ready to try the good work again. The cause of failure assigned by the Communists was their not owning the land they settled upon; but I think it very doubtful whether they could have kept together if the land had been free, for as I have said before, there was something else wanted."

But in the midst of this fever for secular communes, the religionists did not lose out entirely. One Andreas Bernardus Smolniker, for instance, established the Peace Union Settlement in Warren County, Pennsylvania, in 1844, with a group of Germans on ten thousand acres. He had been a professor of Bible Study and Criticism in Austria, but the signs of the times showed him the end was at hand and in response to messages which he received as "Ambassador Extraordinary of Christ, and Apostle of His peace" he founded his community. It broke up soon and afterwards Smolniker wandered over the country in his capacity as Ambassador of Christ.

And in 1842 was founded Hopedale in Worcester County, Massachusetts. It lasted for some fifteen years, with a hundred seventy-five people at its peak. The members had to profess Christianity, but could have any personal Christian creed they wished. No swearing was permitted, no "God contemning words and deeds," no unchastity, no alcohol, no oath taking, no compromises for slave holding, no violence against government, society, family, or individual, no office holding, voting, aiding posses, asking public interference for protection which could be given only by force—"etc.," whatever that might have included. The founder, the Reverend Adin Ballou had sought to establish "a miniature Christian republic." At the end he said the whole thing was a total failure—that his people were too depraved for building a community. What actually put the crusher on was that one enthusiastic brother, by name Draper, quietly bought up stock, squeezed Ballou out, took the property, and squeezed everybody else out. But apparently, said one observer, no one much cared except Ballou.

The canny Draper continued to call the place a community, and he listed officers for it, apparently in order to keep the taxes down.

As for poor Greeley, who had championed communitarianism with high enthusiasm, he remarked with rueful penetration:

A serious obstacle to the success of any socialistic experiment must always be confronted. I allude to the kind of persons who are naturally attracted to it. . . . These may have failed again and again, and been protested at every bank to which they have been presented; yet they are sure to jump into any new movement as if they had been born expressly to superintend and direct it, though they are morally certain to ruin whatever they lay their hands on. Destitute of means, of practical ability, of prudence, tact, and common sense, they have such a wealth of assurance and self-confidence, that they clutch the responsible positions which the capable and worthy modestly shrink from; so the responsibilities which would tax the ablest, are mistakenly devolved on the blindest and least fit. Many an experiment is thus wrecked, when, engineered by its best members, it might have succeeded.

And as for Brisbane, to the end of his long life he declared that Fourierism had never failed because it had never been tried. No community had had the requisite eight hundred members and the requisite half million dollars before opening, and all that had been accomplished was to put a needless and unfair blot upon Fourier's name.

Some Brook Farmers retorted that in their black days, but still at a time when they might have survived with help, he began talking them down in his addresses, trying to raise a hundred thousand dollars with which to begin a new and proper commune, on the excuse that Brook Farm was failing.

There is no way of knowng how near their ideals were to those of Fourier, but from time to time, on down into the 1900's, villages were founded on the general plan of those of the 1840's. Indeed, that in which Alexander Woollcott was born in New Jersey in 1887 was called The Phalanx. It was established by his grandfather, John S. Bucklin, who took it over as private property after the commune failed.

Many of these dozens of scarcely known "colonies" were cooperatives, rather than communes—cooperatives in the manner of the early Brook Farm with profits to be divided on the basis of labor and of stock owned. It was in such a cooperative that Upton Sinclair lived in New Jersey—Helicon Hall—until it burned in 1907. For quite a number of years—at least in the 20's and 30's, perhaps on into the 40's—what might as well have been called a phalanx existed at Fair Hope, Alabama. It advocated the single-tax idea.

Famous in the 1930's was the New Llano Colony of

Louisiana, formed originally in 1917, on the west coast. It at one time had perhaps a thousand members, and because of much favorable publicity during the Great Depression it received mountains of mail which brought the confident prediction that thousands of similar communes would be established "during the next year." It planned several branches of its own in the Southwest and in Colorado—but insurgents seized control and the whole thing collapsed in smoke overnight. There is still much litigation to go through, concerning property worth a dozen millions, to settle its affairs to the satisfaction of all concerned.

Oddly, various leaders of collapsed communal and cooperative projects still believe that their ideas were good and that if they had the money to try again they could establish a workable village.

Ode to Alcott

.   .   .   .

Above our squabbling business hours,
Like Phidian Jove's, his beauty lowers,
His Nature satirizes ours;
    A form and front of Attic grace
    He shames the higgling market-place,
And dwarfs our more mechanic powers.

What throbbing verse can fitly render
That face so pure, so trembling-tender?
    Sensation glimmers through its rest,
It speaks unmanacled by words,
    As full of motion as a nest
That palpitates with unfledged birds. . . .
.   .   .   .

Himself unshaken as the sky,
His words, like whirlwinds, spin on high
    Systems and creeds pellmell together;
'Tis strange as to a deaf man's eye,
While trees uprooted splinter by,
    The dumb turmoil of stormy weather;
    Less of iconoclast than shaper,
His spirit, safe behind the reach
Of the tornado and the speech,
    Burns calmly as a glowworm's taper.

—JAMES RUSSELL LOWELL

CHAPTER TWELVE

FRUITLANDS—ALCOTT'S NEW EDEN

THE LITTLE WOMEN WERE OLDER THAN THE GROWN-UP CHILDREN

A RE there no beasts of burden here?" a prospective new member of "Fruitlands" asked, watching some of the men spading up a piece of plow ground.

"Only one woman," grimly answered Mrs. Alcott, the mother of the "little women," as she dried sweat from her face and turned to the fireplace where a meal for the philosophers was cooking. Soon they would be in to eat and then to relax and with high-flown talk to "make a new heaven and a new earth."

Mrs. Alcott's heart was not in the communitarian experiment in which she was involved—and indeed she thought her husband, always impractical, had at last gone insane. Thoreau called him "the great expecter," and Carlyle mockingly dubbed him "A venerable Don Quixote. All bent on saving the world by a return to acorns and the golden age."

Bronson Alcott was indeed burning with Transcendental enthusiasm, but he had only scorn for the endless picnic, as he called it, of Brook Farm. A man less sincere than he might have welcomed the opportunity to take the starveling Alcotts to the Farm, for while he was considered by Emerson one of the great minds of the age, he was so inept that he could not support his family. By quarreling with the parents of his pupils, he destroyed the new-method schools he established, but he was an incurable optimist so that when the cupboard was bare he sat blithely back, knowing matters would somehow right themselves.

Which was to say, Emerson would come to the rescue or Mrs. Alcott would scrounge from relatives or make some other embarrassing shift to pull the family through. In 1842, at loose ends, Alcott was ill with desire to accept an invitation of English educators who were using his methods to visit them, but he had no money. Emerson treated him to the trip—Alcott went alone—and he was made much of. A school which had been named for him met his most extravagant hopes. Tots of from three years up, as he advocated, were hauled from bed in the small hours, given cold baths, regaled with breakfasts of pulse and that finest of beverages, cold water, and then put to their music, physical exercise, and books.

Charles Lane, of the English group, returned to America with him, bringing a thousand volumes which Alcott declared to be the finest collection in the States on mystical, metaphysical, and theosophical subjects. Further, he and Lane were going to establish a commune along new principles. With the pair was Lane's stripling son, William.

The Lanes were a great trial to Mrs. Alcott as long-staying guests, for food and money were scarce in her household. Louisa—then turned ten—later satirized Lane as Timon Lion in *Transcendental Wild Oats,* but others declared it was Alcott and not Lane who assumed the role of dictator of the "Con-Sociate Family" at the "New Eden" which was formally called Fruitlands because fruit was to be the chief item of diet.

Both men poured out a spate of optimism concerning their plans, making speeches and writing letters to the papers and collaring prospective members. Emerson disappointed them greatly in refusing to join a project which he felt was "without feet or hands." Lane finally found a location fourteen miles out from Concord near the Shaker village on Shadrach Ireland's old site. There was a dilapidated farmhouse with a hundred or so acres, a few cankered apple trees, and a bit of woodland. Summer was at hand, the season far gone, and no crops had been planted by the owner. The price was twenty-seven hundred dollars. Lane had only two-thirds of that sum and he refused, in a burst of practicality, to mortgage the place for the remainder. Rather, he bought the land for his eighteen hundred with the proviso that the house be lent him for a year after which he must pay the remainder or allow the owner to move the building away.

A tenet of morality at the New Eden was that animals should not be required to work for man. However, in the pinch of time the son William Lane and a man named Christy took a pony out to start things. The twelve-year-old Anna Alcott wrote in her journal early in June:

> I walked part of the way from Concord to Harvard. I felt sad at the thought of leaving but Father and Mother and my dear sisters were going with me, and that would make me happy anywhere, I think. We arrived at our new home late in the afternoon. Our first load of furniture had come before us. We found William, Christy, and Wood Abraham all here. Mother was well pleased with the house. There is no beauty in the house itself, but to look out on three sides, you can see mountains, hills, woods, and in some places the Still

River may be seen through the trees. At some distance are the Shaker Villages. On the whole, I like the house very well. After eating our supper we fixed our beds and went early to bed. Having no time to put up the bedsteads, we slept on the floor which made my back lame. Friday and Saturday in working and arranging the house in order. To-day in the morning I cleared the table and washed the dishes, being washing day. I washed with Mother and got dinner. In the afternoon I sewed and read. I did not do much this evening, for I went to bed when I had finished the dishes. The men have been planting to-day corn, and cutting wood and fixing round about the house out of doors.

Wednesday, 11

I began my school to-day. We commenced by singing, "When the day with rosy light." It seemed so pleasant to sing with my sisters. After singing I wrote my journal and the girls wrote in their books. They then studied arithmetic lesson. I then gave them recess, after which they spelt, read and Louisa recited geography. At eleven the school was dismissed. In the afternoon I sewed for my dolly and took care of Abba, then all went to walk in the woods. It was quiet and beautiful there and I felt a calmness in myself. . . . I made some oak leaf wreaths, one for father and one for mother, and stuck flowers in them. They looked very pretty indeed. Then we returned from our walk and prepared for supper. In the evening I sang with Christy, William, mother, and sisters.

Mrs. Alcott may have liked the house, but she neither then nor later gave lip service to the project which so carried her husband away: if the world desired an example of the simple and abstemious life, so far as she was concerned it might have considered the life of the Alcotts up to then. But even a more rigorous regimen than she was accustomed to was soon established—beginning on the first morning, in fact.

They were up from their pallets at daylight. The men trooped off to the brook for cold baths, while Mrs. Alcott and the girls obediently took similar ones indoors. Then she hastened to prepare a meatless, greaseless, eggless, milkless, butterless breakfast: they had cornmeal mush and cold water.

For at Fruitlands there were innumerable taboos. Molasses, cane sugar, coffee, and tea were forbidden, the beverages because they were considered unhealthful, the sweets because slave labor would have gone into their production. Similarly, cotton garments must give way to linen when the current ones should be worn out, since Negro chattels had sweated to produce the cotton. Wool would not do because its use was to rob the sheep of his God-given covering—apparently no consideration was given the great comfort of the sheep in having the fleece sheared in summer—while for silk a worm must die. Linen was the answer, the crushing miseries of Irish peasants who produced flax for absentee landlords apparently being of a different order from those of the sheep, the worm, and the undoubtedly more comfortable black slave.

All animal food was forbidden. Eggs? To eat the germ of life was "Feejee cannibalism." One's brother, the chick, had a right to be sat upon and hatched. Milk? The calf had a vested right in the milk—and, anyway, for the human hand to take it was to prostitute the cow's maternal instinct. Meat? A repulsive food, it now occurred to Bronson Alcott, one that blunted the human qualities, making an animal of man, and requiring the murder of the creature. Animal manure on the fields? Similarly repulsive, it transmitted terrible qualities, not to mention diseases, to man who ate the grain therefrom.

As for shoes, it were best, really, to walk in bare contact with the earth, but concession might be made for shoes composed of wood or fabric. Some magic, non-animal product would surely be discovered soon which would make durable and comfortable footgear. Meanwhile, the Con-Sociate

Family would regretfully wear out the leather shoes brought with them.

Such precepts were impressed upon the girls, whom the adults took turns in teaching. Anna was required to write a composition on flesh-eating. She copied it into her journal:

Composition

Life was given to the animals not to be destroyed by men, but to make them happy, and that they might enjoy life. But men are not satisfied with slaying the innocent creatures, but they eat them and so make their bodies of flesh meat. O how many happy lives have been destroyed and how many loving families [of animals] have been separated to please an unclean appetite of men! Why were the fruits, berries and vegetables given us if it was intended that we should eat flesh? I am sure it was not. We enjoy the beautiful sights and thoughts God has given us in peace. Why not let them do the same? We have souls to feel and think with, and as they have not the same power of thinking, they should be allowed to live in peace and not made to labour so hard and be beaten so much. Then to eat them! eat what has had life and feeling to make the body of the innocent animals! If treated kindly, they would be kind and tame and love men, but as they now are abused and cruelly treated they do not feel the feeling of "love" towards men. Besides flesh is not clean food, and when there is beautiful juicy fruits who can be a flesh-eater?

One may wonder how much of the new philosophy was by now the precocious, tender-hearted child's, and how much of it was put down to please her teacher who at the moment was Christy.

In the course of a few months there were to be seventeen persons at Fruitlands, living on the diet of grain, nuts,

Communal buildings at Ephrata, Pa., early German-American Christian commune established by Konrad Beissel. *Photo by Pennsylvania Historical and Museum Commission, Harrisburg.*

The church at Economie, Father George Rapp's third and last commune, near Ambridge, Pa.

Father Rapp, from a painting on wood, *c.* 1830, now at Economie. *Photo by Pennsylvania Historical and Museum Commission, Harrisburg.*

The Rappite church and hall of Harmonie, Ind., later bought by Robert Owen and renamed New Harmony.

A. Bronson Alcott   Mrs. Bronson Alcott

Fruitlands, near Harvard, Mass., site of Bronson Alcott's short-lived Transcendentalist "New Eden."

The Shaker "Whirling Dance" which often caused a trance in one of the dancers — a sign that he or she had received the gift of prophecy.

The Shaker "Sacred Dance on the Holy Hill of Zion." From the center of the enclosure flowed The Fountain of Life which only Believers could see.

Portrait of a Shaker Eldress who
died in 1908, at the age of 100.

Robert Owen. From an
early 19th-century print.

A self-sustaining ideal village, as conceived by Robert Owen,
which would house some 1200 people. From an old print.

Left: Frances Wright, champion of human rights and founder of "Nashoba" in Tennessee.

The Inspirationist village of Amana, Iowa, a German theocratic commune; no longer communistic, the Amanist Church and several villages continue to prosper.

Above: French socialist philosopher, Charles Fourier.

Right: Etienne Cabet, socialist politician and publisher, leader of the French Icarian immigration to the New World.

Below: Design for a Fourierist phalanstery. No such community was ever built, but many communes, influenced by the American Fourierist, Albert Brisbane, called themselves phalanxes.

Left: John Humphrey Noyes, founder of the Oneida Community of New York.

The Old Mansion House at Oneida, N. Y.

fruit, and potatoes—the latter not favored by all since they grew beneath the ground instead of in the sunlight—but with old members falling away after brief trials, there were never seventeen at one time.

It was just as well, in Mrs. Alcott's view: all the arrivals but two, a Miss Ford and a Miss Page, were men, and Miss Page spent her time writing poetry since she did not particularly like to cook, wash, and do housework. It was she who asked if there were no beasts of burden in the New Eden.

Her departure followed a visit to a neighboring farmstead where, unaware that one of the Alcott children who had gone with her was noticing, she ate a morsel of fish. When the philosophers heard of this they took Miss Page thunderously to task.

"But I only ate a bite of the tail!" she excused herself.

"The entire fish had to suffer and die that you might eat its tail!" Lane cried, and the weeping lady packed her trunk.

As for Miss Ford, she taught music, and Louisa did not like her. She doubled in other subjects, too, including physiology, of which Louisa reported: "Miss Ford told us about the bones in our bodies and how they get out of order. I must be careful of mine, I climb and jump and run so much."

The horse at first sent out had been let go. The Fruitlanders not only wanted no animals laboring for them but they wanted no manure even accidentally on their fields. Still, in a spirit of fair mindedness, they took some from the barn to spread, decided it was a disgusting business, and declared they would use God's way which they said was to turn under green cover crops to enrich the soil. Moreover, they had observed that at Brook Farm, and on the average farmstead, vast amounts of human energy were consumed in laboring for animals which theoretically were kept for the benefit of the owners.

Accordingly, the Con-Sociate Family tried "spade culture," which indeed was a two-continent fad of the day. Mockers contended that the Fruitlanders planted berry vines and fruit trees under the impression that these would bear the same year. They were not that far from reality and besides they had an experienced farmer among them, Joseph Palmer, already famous, or notorious, depending on the view, as "the martyr of the beard."

After a few days of spade culture the philosophers' hands were so swollen they could grasp neither the handles of their spades by day nor of their pens by night, as Lane mentioned in a letter to Thoreau whom he was attempting with delicate flattery to cajole into joining the commune—an attempt which came to nothing. The spaders decided that until the ground was looser they perhaps had better have some plowing done. Palmer hastened to his homestead of No Town near Fitchburg, almost twenty miles away, to fetch oxen and implements.

The oxen turned out to be one ox and one cow he had broken to work together. The big man declared he could not work on the Fruitlands diet, and it was winked at when he prostituted the cow's maternal instinct and consumed the product, foaming and warm, in the privacy of the barn. Still later, several teams were hired for rush work in turning under the green crops for manure.

Alcott might give in to a bit of light animal labor but he was uncompromising in his principles of human asceticism which he had so suddenly adopted. To Lane, who had led rather a monk's life in England, this asceticism still seemed "luxurious in the highest degree." Nevertheless, on account of it several prospective Con-Sociates left the New Eden almost as soon as they arrived, though they had been warned of the rough diet, cold baths, and "spade culture" in advance. Too, they found Bronson Alcott standoffish, cold, and self-centered, and quite possibly, some alleged, with too good an opinion of his physical handsomeness. However, he seems to have been quite amiable in later years when he came down from his pedestal to bask in Louisa's fame and learned to lecture on the subject his audiences loved—his "little women."

"Diogenes and his tub" were Alcott's ideal, declared the man who was to become Father Hecker and found the Paulist Fathers. Hecker, about twenty, had tried Brook Farm but there was too much pleasuring and laxity there to suit him. He suffered internal conflict at the Farm to the extent that he paced the woods, weeping and "wringing his hands." Then Thoreau visited him and the two left together—in order to ascertain, someone declared, the absolute minimum of food on which a person might live.

Really, Hecker and a girl had fallen in love but he feared he had insurmountable scruples, which he characterized as religious, against marriage. His journal, in which a "her" has been unavailingly traced over to change it to "him," is proof that he was really trying to ascertain, when he came to Fruitlands, if he could give the girl up. He soon found the New Eden not stern enough for his tastes, although it surpassed Brook Farm in that respect.

He loved the fine talk which was always deliberately indulged in just after breakfast ("This morning there was held a conversation on the Highest Aim. . . .") but the Family did not "awaken in me that sense of their high superiority which would keep me here to be bettered." Urged to speak out, he said that Alcott was too secretive and self-centered to be a successful leader, and that anyway he was too much burdened with a family to function in that capacity. Besides, there was no fruit here and fruit had been advertised as the diet. Further, there was too much of a tendency toward "literature and writing" for the ultimate prosperity of the commune. So saying, Hecker left.

Another "character" was Samuel Bower who lived on raw beans and raw grain which he pounded up to simplify mastication. He believed the fullest human realization required nudity, but there was a certain amount of objection to this even by the Family, so that he compromised by going forth at night to tramp about naked. Sometimes he went so

far as to journey out by day in a sort of toga and before the
countryside became aware of his identity the constabulary
was several times called forth to cope with "a wandering
lunatic."

As the summer wore on, the men found leisure to
assist Mrs. Alcott with some of the heavier tasks. They were
elated when the first crop—species now unknown—grew
heavy enough to be turned under. They seem to have given
no thought to saving it to eat or to trade for food. Some of
their more inspired idiocies must surely have been committed
behind Palmer's back, for he had a family at No Town
whom he occasionally had to see about.

There was more excellent conversation in the evenings.
The men had refused Mrs. Alcott the use of her lamp because a whale would have had to suffer to feed the flame.
They bought bayberry wax, but something went wrong with
the candlemaking, or perhaps the candles were used up and
the purse empty. Quietly, on a no-lamp, no-mending basis,
Mrs. Alcott lighted her wick and it was noticeable as time
went on that the philosophers found more and more excuse to draw to her corner instead of sweltering by the
remains of the supper fire at the chimneyplace to write their
letters. After all, they said, a woman was a woman and must
be indulged a little, just as Abram Wood, a most faithful
Fruitlander, must be called Wood Abram since he felt the
turning about of his name the best way to express the New
Learning.

But it was the bearded Joe Palmer who was the
copper-lined, ring-tailed old original of the crew. It chanced
that his farm was on a bit of land which was included in no
township—hence the name No Town which he had given it.
In a day of smooth chins he had let his whiskers grow into a
great mass which made him an object of curiosity and for
some reason of raillery and scorn. When he married, his
harassers declared the marriage was not legal because banns
had not been posted. But it was counted legal when he proved

he had posted notice on a tree in his "home township" of No Town, which was to say in his front yard.

When he went into nearby Fitchburg, urchins mocked him. Even a minister asked why he wanted to go around looking like the Devil. "Don't you have your personages mixed?" Palmer asked. "I have seen no representation of the Devil with a beard—but Jesus Christ had one." The nonplused preacher subsided; years later when beards came into style he grew one of his own. Meeting him, Palmer stroked the preacher's beard and murmured, "Knoweth that thy redeemer liveth?" meaning himself as a protagonist of not "scraping the face and neck from fifty-two to three hundred sixty-five times a year."

But he almost hadn't been living. Four men had attacked him one day, throwing him down to shave him. He struck out with a pocketknife, cutting them about the legs. They fled. Palmer, beard intact, was fined ten dollars for "unprovoked assault." Refusing to pay he was thrown into prison—not, however, as a culprit, but as a debtor. For upwards of a year he remained there, sometimes enduring semi-starvation, though able to pay for food which the jailer refused to bring him. When he asked for water it was as likely as not to be thrown upon him so that all he had was what he could sop up from the floor with his bread which was otherwise so hard as to be inedible. Part of the time he was refused coal, and the amounts for which he paid were always woefully skimpy when brought. For months he was in solitary confinement.

Much of this was in an effort to make him pay up and get out. He was even told he would be released if he would declare himself unable to pay the sum. Stubbornly he refused. Finally the authorities and his wife brought word that the fine had been forgiven and that he might leave. He declared he was not there of his own will and would not leave of his own will. The jailer procured help and Palmer was carried bodily out and placed upon the sidewalk.

There is difference of opinion as to how he came to be at Fruitlands. Certainly he was interested in its theories of personal freedom, but whether he joined as a member or was hired as a farmer is unclear. At any rate, he was never paid any wages. His wife and grown children were too busy or too shrewd to join the project.

Emerson visited Fruitlands soon after its founding. He concealed whatever he may have felt at the loose, drawer-like breeches and linen tunic-coats affected as the official costume—Mrs. Alcott dissenting—and declared that all looked fine and rosy "in May." But, he said, let us see how things look in December.

December was coming all too quickly. Not that the philosophers realized it. Mrs. Alcott feared for her husband's mind for she saw him working, eating, living in a way to which he was not accustomed and in a manner, some of the time, as if he really did not know what he was doing.

But there were pleasant moments—picnics, jaunts to view the Shaker way of life, shower baths for the girls who stood behind a curtain while Alcott dribbled pitchers of water over the top. Mrs. Alcott and Anna wrote letters and poems to each other. Anna recounted in her journal:

> This was Lizzie's birthday. I arose before five o'clock and went with mother, William, and Louisa to the woods where we fixed a little pine tree in the ground and hung all the presents on it. I then made a wreath for all of us of oak leaves. After breakfast we all, except Abraham, marched to the wood. Mr. Lane took his fiddle with him and we sang first. Then father read a parable, and . . . asked me what flower I should give Lizzie on her birthday. I said a rose, the emblem of Love and Purity. Father also chose a rose. Louisa said a Lily-of-the-Valley, or innocence,—Mother said she should give her a forget-me-not, or remembrance. Christy said the trailing Arbutus, the emblem of per-severance. Mr. Lane gave her a piece of moss, or

humility. Abba gave her a Wake-robin. I do not know
what that means. We then sang. Lizzie looked at her
presents and seemed much pleased. Mother gave her a
silk thread balloon, I a fan, Louisa a pin-cushion, William a book, Abba a little pitcher. . . .

Lane taught the children composition and fractions,
and had them compose "vegetarian wafers." In Louisa's diary
are some samples in which his own strong hand seems
evident:

Vegetable diet
and sweet repose.
Animal food and
nightmare.

Pluck your body
from the orchard;
do not snatch it
from the shamble.

Without flesh diet
there could be no
blood-shedding war.

Snuff is no less snuff
though accepted from
a gold box.

Apollo eats no
flesh and has no
beard; his voice is
melody itself.

A month after Elizabeth's birthday, membership had
so dwindled that Mrs. Alcott and the girls were helping in the
field, and spirits were so low on Abba's birthday that Anna
writes "we did not do anything to celebrate except that I put
some presents into her stocking last night and she found
them there this morning."

The house was so empty that Anna prepared a room
which she was to have happily to herself—but soon, as ad-
versity threatened to divide the children among relatives on
"visits" that they might have enough to eat, she and Louisa
again slept together for mutual comfort. This is learned
from Louisa's journal, for in midsummer the diary of the
older, more perceptive Anna breaks off—literally: things had

descended to a point so painful to Bronson Alcott that he tore out the latter part of her account of them. It was to be twenty years before he could bear to speak of the experiences at Fruitlands, once he had washed his hands of the venture.

But Louisa's journal remains intact: "September 1st. —I rose at five and had my bath," the ten-year-old writes. "I love cold water! Then we had our singing-lesson with Mr. Lane. After breakfast I washed dishes, and ran on the hill till nine and had some thoughts."

Later, Mr. Lane read a story about a rich girl and a poor girl:

> "I liked it very much, and I shall be kind to poor people." And, "Father asked us what was God's noblest work. Anna said *men,* but I said *babies.* Men are often bad; babies never are." "We had bread and fruit for dinner. . . . I get to sleep saying poetry,—I know a great deal."

> Thursday, 14th.—Mr. Parker Pillsbury came, and we talked about the poor slaves. . . . I ran in the wind and played be a horse. . . . In the evening they talked about travelling. I thought about Father going to England, and said this piece of poetry I found in Byron's poems:—

> *When I left thy shores, O Naxos,*
> *Not a tear in sorrow fell;*
> *Not a sigh or faltered accent*
> *Told my bosom's struggling swell.*

> It rained when I went to bed and made a pretty noise on the roof.

> Sunday, 24th.—Father and Mr. Lane have gone to N. H. to preach. . . . Anna and I got supper. In the

eve I read "Vicar of Wakefield." I was cross to-day, and I cried when I went to bed. I made good resolutions, and felt better in my heart. If I only *kept* all I make, I should be the best girl in the world. But I don't, and so am very bad.

And two weeks later: "I wish I was rich, I was good, and we were all a happy family this day."

Morality had been pounded into the child—but the men, going away on junkets, blithely boarded trains and ferries without money and when asked for fare calmly stated that they could not pay but would "give a conversation"—an informal lecture—to the passengers in return for passage.

Conductors argued futilely that this would be of no benefit to the company. There was really little choice, however, but to bear with the men, in their odd garments, as insane, or to throw them off or have them arrested at the first stop. Apparently without exception the resigned officials gave them free passage. The promised talks were made. A reporter declared those of Lane and Alcott "incomprehensible."

It chanced that the lemming-like migratory fever struck all the men of Fruitlands at once so that only Mrs. Alcott, the children, and Lane's ailing son William were left at New Eden. By further chance there was a crop of barley that the experts had not plowed under. They had even got it cut and Mrs. Alcott and the girls had helped rake it.

As weather signs increased she watched the road in increasing anxiety for the grown-up male children's return. The larder was low. The garden stuff was almost gone. Some corn had been harvested but the only thing which might see the Family through the winter was the barley.

Definite indications of rain appeared, and by great labor Mrs. Alcott and the children and the sick William Lane got some of the crop into shelter. Lane and Alcott returned somewhat discouraged at having brought no converts to share the impending winter famine. Bower, the raw-bean eater, drifted in, packed his toga, and departed, miffed that no one would journey with him to a climate where people might go naked. Wood Abram looked over the little pile of unthrashed barley and left, his name still hind-side to. The weary Mrs. Alcott somehow raised funds—probably they were sent her by relatives for the purpose—and she and the third daughter, Elizabeth, went to Boston to visit their kin. Recorded Louisa:

> I shall be very lonely without dear little Betty, and no one will be as good to me as Mother. I read in Plutarch. I made a verse about sunset:—

> *Softly doth the sun descend*
> *To his couch behind the hill,*
> *Then, oh, then, I love to sit*
> *On mossy banks beside the rill.*

> Anna thought it was very fine; but I didn't like it very well.

Anna, too, composed verse:

> *I never cast a flower away*
> *The gift of one who cared for me*
> *A little flower—a faded flower*
> *But it was done reluctantly.*

> *I never looked a last adieu*
> *To things familiar but my heart*
> *Shrank with a feeling almost pain*
> *Even from their lifelessness.*

> *I never spoke the word farewell*
> *But with an utterance faint and broken*
> *A heart with yearning for the time*
> *When it should never more be spoken.*

This from a child who "sewed for my dolly, and in the evening . . . played."

Mrs. Alcott returned and someone provided money for Anna to have a short sojourn with relatives. Finally even the die-hard Joe Palmer gave up. He took his cow and ox and went back to No Town, believing no less than ever, though, in the stated principles of the New Eden.

By then there were sharp differences, recriminations, even, between Alcott and Lane. The latter was ready to dissolve the enterprise. Alcott had alienated too many members with his lofty manner, the Englishman intimated. Besides, "there was not enough self-discipline around here." Frankly, he added, he had about decided it was the Shakers across the river who had the correct idea.

Toward the last of November Alcott conferred with his family: "Father asked us if *we* saw any reason for us to separate." That is, to part from the Lanes and break up the experiment. Louisa adds, "Mother wanted to, she is so tired. I like it, but not the school part or Mr. L."

"The school part" may refer to a brief attendance of the Alcott children at the village school in Still River. They did go there some, oddities in their brown linen bloomer outfits, each with an apple and a slice of brown bread for lunch. Other children felt sorry for them and fed them.

Finally the December Emerson had feared was literally upon the land. Lane took his son and went over the river and up the hill and joined the Shakers, or at least made arrangements for membership. Leaving his son with them, he went to Boston, pausing at Fruitlands to tell the Alcotts he intended selling the farm. They must not cut any more wood, he said, as there were but fourteen acres of it and he would need the tract to please a buyer. This small-hearted ukase smells of a final, sharp exchange of words.

Alcott considered the snug quarters and full bins of Ann Lee's disciples, and he considered his own principles. He called a family council to decide if they should not all become Shakers. Mrs. Alcott put her foot down with flat finality. She had been through a nerve-wracking summer and fall that her husband might reform the world. She had no Shaker leanings and she said so. Meekly, Alcott dropped the matter and took private stock of the situation from other angles. And Louisa wrote:

> December 10th.—I did my lessons and walked in the afternoon. Father read to us in dear "Pilgrim's Progress." Mr. L. was in Boston and we were glad. In the evening father and mother and Anna and I had a long talk. I was very unhappy, and we all cried. Anna and I cried in bed, and I prayed God to keep us all together.

In the eyes of his acquaintances, most of whom had always misunderstood him, Alcott knew that he was a fool, a ridiculous and dreaming failure. One day he went to bed and while winter howled gave himself up to the business of dying. He would neither drink nor touch the food his despairing family put beside him. They wept. There were prayers. The girls begged him to live for them and their mother. He turned to the wall and refused to answer. He wished only to expire.

This fit of depression and self-dramatization continued several days. Then in the middle of a night it came to him that his family needed him. He would live for them! He would take care of them! He fell upon the sustenance at hand in the darkness. Next morning his grieving family found him in high spirits. They helped him downstairs. There were a few withered, wormy apples, and a bit of bread remained from the last of the barley. Scraps of wood had been gathered for the hearth.

Mrs. Alcott had already sold most of the furniture for subsistence. As soon as Bronson had his feet under him that day, the rejoicing family loaded what was left upon a sled. Mrs. Alcott had rented rooms from a family down the valley, promise of help having come from her brother who had aided her before. A job of woodcutting was to be given Mr. Alcott, a proposition which he faced with his usual childlike blitheness as the family drew the sled to the new home.

It turned out that after all he was not made for wood-cutting. Mrs. Alcott found sewing to do, however—as at a later time Louisa was to work as a domestic, washing and scrubbing to keep the family in a pittance of money. Soon Emerson and others banded together to give Alcott a leg up, and once more the family was on the way back to town.

It also turned out that Lane decided his own future was not with the Shakers. It was not that he didn't care for celibacy, for he was a confirmed ascetic. The trouble was that the Shakers wanted him to do physical work and he was a philosopher who felt he could give his best to the world in a rarefied existence of "being, not doing." Actually, these prosperous Shakers worked but little in comparison to the spade-culturist Fruitlanders. Lane probably was rationalizing in the reason he gave for backing away from them after his period of thought.

He took a trip to No Town and persuaded Palmer to return to Fruitlands. After all, spring was coming and without Alcott to gum the works the New Eden might yet succeed. The pair drew up an elaborate prospectus for a new commune—with the stipulation that every member must contribute some cash. The penniless Lane wanted Palmer to hurry and contribute some, but Palmer was wary. No one else came forward to join. Lane abruptly journeyed to Emerson's house and made some sort of arrangement about the land title, of which Emerson was trustee. Then he sold Fruitlands to Palmer, apparently on credit, and went to England.

Presently he discovered that he was not quite as ascetic as he had supposed. He married a schoolteacher, and busied himself writing to Palmer for money which doubtless was for overdue payments on the farm. Later, he implored Palmer's son to pay his father's debt.

At the end of his life, Lane wrote a bitter letter to a friend and, either from settled conviction or in momentary depression, damned himself as a dreaming nincompoop and wondered what his existence had come to and what he had proved. Pretty much of what he had stood for, he said, had been off the track.

As for Fruitlands, Palmer lived on there, conducting what he called his private commune. His wife was there to help him rock on the porch in the evenings and watch the growth of the mulberry trees the philosophers had planted and to listen for the trains coming down the track of the railroad which had been run through the farm soon after the debacle.

The rest of the membership changed so rapidly, except for a few regulars who sponged off Palmer for years, that for two decades the neighbors called Fruitlands the tramps' colony. A kettle of beans or some potatoes were always ready for drifter or respectable visitor. Palmer somehow found satisfaction in this. He knew he was being victimized by some of the moving army of men "on the way to take a job." He hoped, however, that here and there he was giving some worthy person the nudge needed at the moment to save him from despair.

Finally the Palmers died. The old house stood deserted. No one else cared to live there and be a friend to man. The buildings were falling down when, moved to pity by its history, a romantic and poetic-minded friend of Mrs. Alcott bought Fruitlands. She restored the house— which is still preserved by an association—and tracked down the bits of furniture which were there in community days and bought them back again. *The Dial,* at Brook Farm, had fortunately printed the catalogue of the thousand volumes fetched from England, and these too were largely restored so that in the end the place became a monument to the hazy, golden dreams of the philosophers.

The race of man shall wisdom learn,
    And error cease to reign:
The charms of innocence return,
    And all be new again.

The fount of life shall then be quaffed
    In peace by all that come;
And every wind that blows shall waft
    Some wandering mortal home.

—Communitarian poem

Plodding on their weary march of life, Association rises before them like the *mirage* of the desert. They see in the vague distance magnificent palaces, green fields, golden harvest, sparkling fountains, abundance of rest and romance; in one word HOME—which is also HEAVEN.

—JOHN HUMPHREY NOYES of Oneida

CHAPTER THIRTEEN

ICARIA

AH, SOON WILL COME THE GLORIOUS DAY, INSCRIBED ON MERCY'S BROW

IN COMMUNITARIAN annals no other group approaches the Icarians for bullheaded persistence despite continuing failure—and not the persistence merely of a few leaders but of ordinary members who were fired by a common dream. Disaster tramped on the coattails of these Frenchmen from the day in March of 1848 when the vanguard landed in New Orleans. They desired passage up the Mississippi and Red rivers to the million acres which their prophet, Étienne Cabet, who was still in France, had bought in Texas.

Details of the transaction are muddled. But Cabet did pay an entry fee on, as he supposed, a million acres, and he may have paid something besides. Eventually he was to pay one dollar an acre for additional land that he might want for the total of a million Frenchmen whom he expected to take to Texas. At any rate, to seal ownership to the original tract, is was necessary that the Icarians—Cabet's coined term for Utopians—occupy it by July 1. There was of course plenty of time for reaching it before then, but this group of sixty-nine, all of them men, wished to get crops planted for the feeding of the fifteen hundred who would come a bit later with the leader.

Agents of the Peters Land Company, which had operated widely in Europe to find taxpayers for Sam Houston's empire, had told Cabet that his tract was washed by the Red River and was accessible by boat. The advance party learned, to its consternation, that while it might indeed go up the Mississippi and the Red to Shreveport, in western Louisiana, navigation was blocked there by "the great raft" —an inpenetrable jam of trees washed down from above during floods, and stretching intermittently for many miles upstream. Icaria still lay two hundred fifty miles away, with the worst of roads between.

It is quite probable that letters were waiting at Shreveport from Cabet's "minister," Sully, who had preceded the group. He had gone on and bought a farm a hundred miles to the west to use as a way station and was lying there sick. The Icarians took anxious counsel and stored most of their goods. The remainder they piled into a wagon which was to be drawn by several yoke of oxen they had bought.

They started across the prairies and woods and hills and swamps, courageously chanting their all-for-one-and-one-for-all songs. But the rains came. The wagon broke down. It sank into morasses. The oxen bogged. The party became lost. The expedition ran out of food. They knew nothing of hunting in such country. People fell sick. But all were more or less alive when they met the land agents at Icaria to-be.

And now, messieurs, show us our million acres that we may occupy them!

The representatives of the Peters Company studied

the plattings. There appeared to be a slight misconception. The contract seemed actually to call for one hundred thousand acres and not a million. Still, anyone might see for himself that it was wonderfully rich land, worth a million acres anywhere else—just observe that excellent stand of mesquite and scrub oak it was producing!

The Icarians could only swallow this further chicanery and leave adjustments to Cabet. They would throw up a shelter or two to mark the site of the future city and buy a few horses and plows from their scant stock of money and begin planting. A shelter there? Unfortunately, said the agents, that particular square mile was reserved to the state!

So with another choice site. It was not that all the Icarian land did not join—although, as it turned out, it joined only at the corners of the sections. Every other square mile in vast checkerboard fashion was retained by Texas in order that the value might increase with the settling of the intervening squares. Nor would the establishment of a village be considered as occupation of the hundred thousand acres. Before the first of July a cabin must be erected on each half square mile which was to be held, and an occupant placed therein. Any land not so occupied would revert to the Peters Company, and might be had only at the price of one dollar per acre. Any that was occupied would be given the Icarians. This of course was because it was expected that their settling there would bring other people.

There was no possibility that the sixty-nine tenderfeet might build even sixty-nine cabins in the time left. They wrote to Cabet and fell doggedly to work to save as much of the land as they could.

Fourier had worn his life away writing massive volumes of his addled philosophy and waiting for a millionaire who would like to become a "Kalif" or Sultan in the Fourieristic scheme. He was in no way successful until after death and then only in America and through a disciple. Ironically, through one hack novel his countryman Étienne

Cabet by accident seized all France by its communal ears and was pushed into the position of a prophet—and no one was more surprised than Cabet. He woke one morning and found himself famous.

Driven into exile in the 1830's in the on-again-off-again republic-monarchy musical-chair upheavals of France, he went to England where he met Robert Owen who was back from the debacle of New Harmony. Cabet passed some of his five years in England reading Sir Thomas More's *Utopia*. From this he dreamed up a novel, *Un Voyage en Icarie,* with a fairly commonplace never-never land as the background.

He was an experienced writer and publisher, the owner of a rabble-rousing newspaper which had got him into hot water several times before his exile. On his return home in 1840, he brought out the novel which, because of its impudence toward the standing order of things, was instantly popular. Thus it made widely known his dreamland where there were no rich, and where everyone was required to work. Taxes were fair and there were old age pensions. The products of industry were divided among the producers. Everyone was required to marry and sexual relations were orthodox. Education was extensive. Rule was by the majority, with women allowed to state their views in assembly, though not to vote. So much for the dreamworld. In moving toward it, the Icarians proved to be profitable consumers of the flood of pamphlets the master poured out. For years he resisted the pleadings that he open a commune, declaring long study of the problem by the prospective members to be necessary. Besides, he pointed out, land was so dear it would be almost impossible to get enough on which to establish an Icaria.

But it chanced that Mexico had been despoiled of her most northerly province and that the new owners, who called themselves Texans, had given up their dreams of an empire reaching to the Pacific, preferring to become one of the States. Their agent told Cabet they had a marvelous location for this proposed Icaria of his of which they had heard —they said—with admiration.

The tall, thin prophet was amazed and ecstatic at the vast amounts of land to be had in Texas for what seemed almost nothing. With ground so cheap, a commune could not fail. Robert Owen, as practical as ever, advised him to seize the chance. Cabet was approaching sixty, but the hero worship of his followers crushed his remnant of caution. He paid the fees for establishing entrée, as he supposed, into a million acres of adjoining tracts on the Red, agreeing to occupy it by July 1 which was not six months away.

So it was that he sent his commissioner, Sully, to take charge. His intention was to begin the removal of his "million" followers—he had, probably, 400,000—in the summer. However, the charge boiled in the press that he had no intention of sending anyone, but was interested only in milking his dupes of dues. Thus he was goaded into sending his "advance guard" when he did, in the dead of winter. He described their departure in *Le Populaire:*

> At length, on Thursday, February 3, at nine o'clock in the morning, there was accomplished one of the grandest acts, we believe, in the history of the human race;—the advance guard, departing on the ship "Rome," has left Havre to enter the ocean and voyage toward Icaria. . . . These courageous Icarians, placed on the stern-deck of the ship, entoned in unison the farewell chant, *"Partons pour Icarie,"* to which the spectators responded in a thousand cries of "au revoir." . . . May the winds and waves be propitious to you, soldiers of humanity! And we, Icarians, who remain, let us prepare without loss of time to rejoin our friends and brothers!

Three weeks later came the Revolution of February 24 which crushed Louis Philippe and established the Second Republic. Icarianism had helped precipitate the Revolution, but, ironically, Cabet, the old revolutionary, lost out as the government was seized by men who loathed him and all the swelling communistic philosophy then bubbling in Western Europe and England.

A Cabet-for-President boom moved the faithful to urge the prophet to recall the "advance guard" but, for whatever reason, he did not. Meanwhile, his friend Louis Blanc contrived to get into the government and to obtain the passage of "the right to labor" legislation. Against much opposition, 100,000 unemployed were put to work in national shops, but these were administered by men who made certain that the shops should become financial failures. Blanc and Cabet were discredited and Icarianism as a national movement collapsed.

On March 27, when Cabet's advance guard reached New Orleans, the citizens were firing cannon to celebrate the downfall of Louis Philippe—for another ship had crossed with the news in four weeks instead of seven. Some of the guard decided that Icarianism was done for and returned to France. The remainder, as has already been told, went on to Texas and fell to the task of trying to save some part of their land.

Things could scarcely have gone worse with them. They were artisans, not peasants. They were clumsy with axes and the hovels they threw together on the half-sections were scarcely habitable. As for turning the incredible prairie sod, their plow parted in the middle when they hooked enough oxen to it to move it. The water was bad. Illness struck. Yellow fever, their doctor called it—but they soon perceived that he was insane, rather than merely eccentric as they had supposed—and since the disease killed but three, it probably was only malaria.

The weather opened a bag of tricks, all bad. Six who were able to travel left to seek work, having reformed the world as far as they felt called upon. The others were moping around, working a little on the days when no chill was scheduled, when ten of the eagerly expected five hundred reinforcements straggled in. That was Cabet's answer to their cry for help. Nineteen had set out from France, but nine had fallen ill between New Orleans and Icaria. They would be along when they could travel. Too, more cabins would have to be built—the thirty-two which had secured some 10,240 acres of land would scarcely hold the fifteen hundred who would arrive in the winter with Cabet.

The newcomers fell to work, but the chief result of their arrival was that there were only that many more "regenerators of the human race" to fight, bleed, and die in the disenchanted cause. One of them wrote to the prophet:

Icarian Colony Sept. 2, 1848

Poor Father:—

How can I depict to you the situation in which I have found our brothers? Almost all those who survive are sick. Four are dead; the first was Guillot, the second, Collet, who was killed by lightning, the third was Guérin, and the fourth Tangé. . . . We should not be able to bring the women here by these abominable roads. Wagons could not make more than two or three leagues a day. One finds no villages, but only farm houses at long intervals, and in none of them have they beds for four persons. One does not even find bread; for the people of the country do not make bread except in small quantities at the very moment of eating. . . . All our attention is given to those who are most ill, and to preparations for departure. But what is most annoying is that we have incurred a debt of seven or eight thousand francs, and we are embarrassed for the means to liquidate it under the circumstances. If we can arrange with our creditors we will occupy ourselves exclusively with our retreat to Shreveport. . . .

Ever your devoted
Favard

For whatsoever reason—partly those of embarrassment and his desire to escape from political failure in France, no doubt—Cabet tried to keep news of the fiasco quiet, but too many people knew about it. Nevertheless, in his *Populaire* he eulogized the sacrifices and hardships of the immigrants and, far from admitting that Icaria was being deserted, he sailed on December 15.

Meanwhile, the Texas Icarians had broken up into several parties, partly through contention, partly through the idea that small groups might better find accommodations on the road, and, dividing their money and supplies, most or all of them started for New Orleans, hauling the sickest. Several died and were buried along the road. When the remnant staggered into the Crescent City in mid-winter, Cabet had arrived—but "the first fifteen hundred" who were to have been with him were not quite a third of that number.

It must always be borne in mind that these groups were made up of individual human beings, each with his loves and hopes and dreams, his ambitions, his burning desires for success and approval. There was, further, the intense, revivalistic group feeling, and the belief that a great, unselfish thing was being done for humanity. This was the year of the Communist Manifesto—and communism was a burning religion with the Icarians.

Nevertheless, the religion of many of the new group was given a setback by the condition of the "advance guard." Cabet wished to go at once to Icaria, but there was bitter, flat rebellion. Almost two hundred re-embarked for France, taking nearly $5000, a third of the total funds of the enterprise. The others scurried around, finding the cheapest of living quarters, while Cabet talked to land agents about the "ideal location" of which he dreamed.

Finally he compromised. In the tow of agents who were trying still to sell the town of Nauvoo, Illinois, four years after the death of Joseph Smith and the removal of the Brighamite Mormons to Utah, he journeyed up the

Mississippi. At Nauvoo he bought the fire-gutted shell of the temple, plus mills, shops, a communal dwelling house, many individual houses, a distillery, and the first tract of an eventual 1500 acres of land.

This would do as a stop-gap location, he said, until the envisioned ideal spot could be found. When he returned to New Orleans a few more of the brethren had followed the first dissidents to France. Several others had taken jobs and were through with Icarianism.

But Cabet was cheerful as he led the remaining two hundred eighty up to Nauvoo. He was no longer young. The year was 1849 and he had been born in 1788, just before the French Revolution. The son of a cooper, he studied law and practiced at his birthplace of Dijon until he moved to Paris in his early thirties. There he joined in the treasonous connivings of the Carbonari which also engaged the energies of Frances Wright's paternal friend, Lafayette.

Cabet was hotheaded, but a capable politician for the temper of the country and the era. Louis Philippe tried to win him over with appointments, but though he accepted the honors he did not wear the chain and this led to trouble. In parliament his tongue brought him the alternative of jail or exile and so he went to England where he wrote the fateful novel. Thus he who did not want to be a communal prophet was made one through accident, while Fourier died neglected. And so he came at last to Nauvoo.

The first thing was to establish the administration. A general assembly was elected, but daily affairs were in the hands of the chairmen of the committees for education, health and amusement, finance and provisions, clothing and lodging, and publicity. There was quite a stream of the latter, for Cabet, who as a matter of course was elected president, got out a constant spate of philosophy and information in English, German, and French. And while he attracted no American members because of the language barrier, he doubled the number of his people from France

—and this despite the fact that those who had deserted in New Orleans had charged him in the French courts with embezzlement of their funds, and indeed had seen him declared guilty *in absentia*.

Mme. Cabet had remained in France in charge of Icarian affairs and was busy collecting money and sending converts over. But she and the many family relatives in the home office absorbed so large a percentage of the funds that at Nauvoo it was voted to close it. Apparently no action was taken, however. Presently Cabet went to France and won a reversal of the embezzlement verdict, and in triumph he returned to Nauvoo.

On the surface, things looked good. Cabet was in a fortunate position for a communal leader. He had a membership held together by common purpose and devotion to him and his cause. He had good buildings—and a supply of stone in the old Mormon temple for many others, for while he had intended restoring the temple for use as a community center, a tornado took part of it down and it became, rather, a quarry. Too, he had capable artisans. The Icarians in general were reading people, broad-minded, cheerful at the great communal dining hall, and ready to entertain themselves in the manner of the Brook Farmers in the evenings.

His difficulty was that he was dreamy-minded and not sufficiently informed to detect existing weaknesses. Most importantly, he did not have enough farmers. Instead of training some, or hiring American plowboys, he fell into the practice of buying much food. This was made possible by the continuing steady contributions from societies in France— sums which kept him from seeing that his commune was operating at a dangerous deficit. Without them he might have forced the place into self-sufficiency, for certainly the potential was there. As it was, he felt prosperous and successful.

In itself this shows the general dreaminess which kept him looking beyond the horizon, unwilling to grasp the bird in hand—to say Nauvoo was Icaria and to set about taking all the city over. That might have made him the most successful of all the prophets. Still, he wanted a preconceived "ideal" place. He kept waiting for a shower of riches from heaven with which he would create wonders, and in hope of luring that sum out of someone he wrote a booklet *If I had $500,000.*

In the first place, he said, this tremendous capital would open unlimited credit to him—which was to blink the fact that debt had ruined many a communal enterprise in the past. With his cash and credit he would erect whole rows of houses, install gas, and hot and cold water systems. The finest schools would be instituted, along with opera houses and parks. Manufacture and agriculture would be on the highest level. Everyone would be happy.

In anticipation of the five hundred thousand, he traveled, looking for the ideal site. He found it in southwestern Iowa, near Corning. Three thousand acres, presently to be enlarged to four, were optimistically purchased on credit. But a debt of twenty thousand for that good soil? Pouf! It was nothing, against the expected half million.

Still, no one seemed in the mood to drop so much money into the prophet's palm. Perhaps this contributed to his crochety temper. He began making his people less than happy. He decreed that the entire output of the distillery was henceforth to be sold, for the evils of drink were to be banished from his paradise. Further, the liquorless Icarians were to abstain from tobacco.

These rules necessitated the setting of spies and it was impossible to spy on a man's drinking, chewing, or smoking tendencies without spying on his private life in general. Talebearing was accordingly at a premium. What was Agricole d'Hauterive saying about the leader, madame? Ah, what the director should *really* hear was what Madame Agricole was saying! And in school, even the children were saying—

Soon all this gossip and anger and suspicion put

things at sixes and sevens. The anti-Cabet party, composed mostly of the younger members who could obtain no places in council, snowballed in size. It elected three directors, promising at the presidential polling in six months to replace Cabet himself.

Cabet refused to seat the three, though he was clearly in the wrong. Each side hailed the other into the civil courts of Illinois. The streets of Nauvoo, which had seen no riots since the departure of the Saints, were now lively enough. People rolled and tumbled in the dust and dragged each other by the hair and wielded sticks and stones. Brawlings invaded homes and workshops, field and school. Pupils trounced the Cabetian teacher. Cabet was too infirm to fight but he watched from an upper window and lustily egged on his adherents in the street brawls.

His enemies, being in the majority, announced to him that he was expelled and must leave, and in great bitterness and agitation of spirit he capitulated. A hundred eighty supporters left with him, after six and a half years in the place—not for the prospective wilderness paradise in Iowa, however, but for St. Louis. Icaria was well rid of him, his opponents declared. Not so, he countered. Icaria was where he was, and the broilsome riffraff remaining at Nauvoo without him were nothing.

Not a week later, in St Louis, while planning the future, he died of a stroke. Grief was intense. Indeed, one disciple committed suicide in order to join him in death.

The angry Nauvooans still considered themselves the true vine—but this did not run the shops which had been crippled by the desertion of so many key workers with Cabet. Too, the societies in France considered the Icarians in St. Louis as possessors of the covenant and to them were sent the customary contributions. The Nauvooans were badgered by the agents of the Mormons for something on account, and by Illinois for taxes. Similar demands came to them from Iowa land agents and tax collectors, although the land there had been in Cabet's name and had fallen to his heirs in France.

However, financial arrangement was made with those heirs and the Nauvooans trekked to Iowa where they might hope at least to survive. Lacking timber, they built sod huts which were miserably unsatisfactory after the comparative luxury at Nauvoo—and far worse than any of them had lived in in France. Weather and luck were against them. There was illness. The logical series of general disasters occurred. Clothing was reduced to rags. Feet were shod with wood.

Discouraged Icarians drifted away, leaving fewer than two score of all ages to carry on. Meanwhile, the St Louis Icarians had found work in their various skills. They did not live communally, but rented a hall where meetings might be held. They published a little journal of the society. Some soon adjourned to the country and began a commune but through illness and business adversities it came to nothing.

Soon those at Corning were the only if not the true Icarian vine. They narrowly saved themselves from bankruptcy by giving their land back to their creditors under a scheme which permitted them to try then to redeem half the acreage. The prosperity which came with the war of 1861 made the redemption possible or they surely would have lost everything. As it was, they barely squeaked through.

Oddly, they began turning toward Cabet in their minds as they grew older until in the 1870's all bitterness was gone and they revered him as their messiah. But this reverence scarcely improved their starveling existence. They still wore wooden shoes and took pride in a democracy so extreme that "our president couldn't sell a bushel of corn without taking a vote." Sunday was a day of lazy fun, for they still had no church and no theism.

Membership dwindled almost to nothing, which gave an additional prosperity to the handful who retained the flocks and herds. This prosperity brought applications for membership and the society grew to eighty. The quarrels between factions as at Nauvoo were repeated—but this time the old heads were those who had been young rebels in Illinois. They were conservative now, and set in their ways, resentful of upstarts.

The newcomers complained that there was not even the communism of which so much was heard. True, there was a unitary kitchen and community dining hall—but observe! The vegetables for it were raised in patches behind the homes of individuals who looked on them with proprietary eyes. There should be instead a large communal garden. And some ate at home, and kept cows in their sheds, and carried the milk into their own kitchens. Well, yes, admitted the old members. It was more convenient that way—and the milk was shared. There was enough for everyone. The cow belonged to Icaria and Icaria drank her milk. What of it?

Well, it wasn't proper, said the insurgents, who talked much of Marxism, of Christian Communism, and of "Jesus, the First Communist." Further, it was not Christian to forbid membership to the many prospective members who were turned away. A big membership would certainly better things.

The conservatives, knowing how they got where they were, and recollecting that numbers had not always made for prosperity, would not listen. So in their most Christian way the "new" party went to court. The colony, they said, had registered with the state as an agricultural commune, but was engaging in manufacture, too. Thus it was the duty of the state to revoke the infracted charter.

The court agreed. The insurgents obtained a new Icarian charter for themselves. The older members cannily made a bargain which gave themselves a thousand acres of land and several houses to be moved onto it, and no debt. They called themselves the New Icarians. Soon, as they had forseen, the insurgents who had wrecked the good machine were insolvent and fleeing from their creditors. Some whined for admission into the New Icaria and were refused. A few opened an abortive commune in California.

The old originals, the New Icarians, clung to their commune almost to the turn of the century. But their children were cold to the Icarian dream. The parents were dying off or were too infirm to make the old fire burn. Sorrowfully they divided their acreage into private parcels that their heirs might be satisfied.

For the sixth and last time, counting all failures and attempts, Icaria was finished. It is another of those endings which seem the sadder because unnecessary. With a little forbearance and common sense added to the bulldog persistence, Nauvoo today might have been Icaria still.

. . . .

Then was the little harbor thronged
With fishers and their boats
Canoes and skiffs and sloops they used
'Most every craft that floats.

Then was there gathering in the dusk
And hurrying in the dawn,
From Epoufette, from Pointe aux Chênes
Where'er the news had gone.

From Manistique to Rabbit's Back,
Seule Choix and far Death's Door,
From Poverty and Summer Isles
Each sent their three or four.

From Scott's Point and from Mille Coquin
They came to Saint Helene,
"Arch Newton now must lead us on,
We'll sweep the Beavers clean."

. . . .

*—Rhyme by one of the army of frontiersmen who drove the 2500
Strangite Mormons out of the Beaver Islands in Lake Michigan
in 1856.*

CHAPTER FOURTEEN

KING JIMMY AND HIS SAINTS

AS EVE HAD LED ADAM OUT OF THE GARDEN
MAN MUST NOW LEAD WOMAN BACK TO IT

FOR several hours the two thousand people of Big Beaver Island in Lake Michigan had had a rousing good time in their unfinished temple singing hymns and listening to sermons and harangues. At last in the mounting heat—it was July eighth—the great moment came. A bulge-browed, heavily bearded little man with impelling dark eyes and wearing gorgeous robes strode into the temple and to the platform in the center. He was attended by a robed man armed with a sword, and escorted by "the Twelve" and by "the seventy elders and priests of the Church." People shouted. Women fainted. Babies squalled unnoticed. Men wept in religious ecstacy.

When things quieted there was fanciful ceremony

239

of which the little man, James J. Strang, was the center. The new revelation God had given him was repeated: that the Almighty had "chosen his servant James to be King and hath appointed him King of Zion."

At the climax, the beefy, besworded aide, an erstwhile actor named Adams, put a gold crown on the little man and shouted, "I crown thee James, king of Zion!" Adams had been expelled from Mormonism by the late Joseph Smith, Jr., for various alleged derelictions, but, declaring the charges to be merely the regulation ones under which "the prophet Joseph" got rid of those he did not like and to be "base phalshoods," Adams had become Strang's right-hand man. The charges may not have been so "phals": at the moment, Adams was keeping a Philadelphia prostitute on the island—a matter which was to lead to great trouble for Strang who thought the lady was the actor's wife. And like his private life, the prime minister's costume might not have stood inspection at close range. It most probably came out of his prop trunk, complete with his Richard III tin sword. Some said Strang's crown came from the same place.

Anyway, Strang was crowned and so began "the First Year of the King," otherwise known as 1850, in perhaps the only coronation of royalty ever held in this country except for the infantile pomposities in connection with festivals and athletic contests. Not that intimations of royalty began or ended with Strang's doubtlessly sincere conviction that God had raised him to this eminence: Joseph Smith had declared himself a king and had created princes, and in 1957 the press reported that an eminent bishop of one of our evangelical sects had announced himself as "king of all the nations of men."

With his crowning, James Jesse Strang was no longer merely "Saint James, God's one and only living Prophet, Revelator, Seer, and Mouth-piece; President of the Church of Jesus Christ of Latter Day Saints; Sole Legal Successor to Joseph Smith, Jun." He was King James I and the calendar was changed to mark the circumstance. There had been rude indications that the rest of the world, of which he declared himself Lord and Vice Regent of God, might be a bit tardy in taking up either King James or his calendar. However, on Big Beaver Island it was Anno Rex I, and July 8 was forevermore to be known as King's Day.

This first King's Day was expected to be otherwise noteworthy for a new dispensation Strang had promised to announce concerning marriage. Few had any doubts that it would sanction "plurality." It was a fairly open secret as to why Saint James had brought Miss Elvira Eliza Field, a well-stacked schoolma'am of nineteen, to the island. His wife Mary had known for some time that the crop-haired brunette, now in the short dress and bloomers of the Strangite women, was the "Charles J. Douglass" who had traveled about the country in man's clothes with Strang the preceding winter.

Strang had formerly spent much breath in denouncing polygamy and the "spiritual wifery" of the Brighamite Mormons, but it was supposed he now had discovered new and different light. Several years previously he had dug up some brass plates, under direction of an angel, with strange writing on them. The angel had also lent him the same peepstones Joseph Smith had used in translating the hieroglyphics on his gold plates, and with them Strang was translating the brass ones into *The Book of the Law of the Lord*. Not infrequently had the commandments found in these plates brought an about-face in Strangite doctrines. In was in the plates, too, that Strang had discovered that "my servant James" was to be "King of Zion."

Strang stood five feet three in his boots. As a puny baby, dragged about New York state by his parents, he had been remarkable for the size of his skull. In childhood—he was born in 1811—he was considered stupid. He said later the difficulty was that he roiled inside with questions beyond the power of those around him even to consider, much less to answer, so that he withdrew into himself.

As a frying-size boy, he developed a hot desire for fame and power, but despite a talent for backwoods forensics and a gift for contemptuous sarcasm which routed opponents, he became disillusioned. In 1832 he wrote in his journal—and this passage is in English, though much of the diary is in a code of hieroglyphics:

> March 21st Birthday I am 19 years old and am yet no more than a common farmer. It is too bad, I ought to have been a member of Assembly or a Brigadier General before this time. . . . I am eager and mankind are frail and . . . I shall act upon it for time to come for my own benefit.

The great name he desired still was not achieved by the time he was thirty. However, while scraping a living as a country editor, postmaster, and lawyer, he had acquired a wife, Mary Perce, daughter of a Baptist preacher, and they had three children. He had been expelled from church for what others called heresy, although he thought of himself only as a "cool philosopher" and freethinker. He discovered that being in a "churched" condition was not good for business and he retracted sufficiently to get back in.

All this was in Chautauqua County where Mormonism was rife. He had a poor opinion of that cult, and not a very good one of some of his in-laws who embraced it. However, when these migrated to Burlington, Wisconsin, and began making good financially, he joined them with his family and quickly became a convert.

There are two views of his adoption of Mormonism. That of the sect which he eventually founded was that he experienced religious conversion on hearing the preaching of Lyman Wight who was known as the Wild Ram of the Mountains in Saintly circles. The other is that when Wight traipsed through the Burlington country in 1844, soon after Strang's arrival, the future King James was incredulous that heaven should heap prestige and prosperity upon such a fellow, uneducated, a poor speaker, and, in Strang's view, a poor reasoner.

Strang might have entered the Mormon congregation at Burlington, but he had a better idea. Wishing to impress himself upon the mind of Joseph Smith, Jr., with what eventual plan in mind no one knows, he ignored the January cold and left immediately for Nauvoo which was all the way across Illinois on the Mississippi. (This was some four years before Etienne Cabet bought part of the remains of the ill-fated Mormon city.)

Smith saw at once that Strang had a brain which might be useful to him. He gave Strang prestige by baptizing him himself in the unfinished Nauvoo temple, in the baptistry which rested upon twelve iron oxen in accordance with revelation. A few days later Strang was created an elder by Hyrum Smith, the prophet's brother. That was remarkable advancement, and it later stood in Strang's favor in his claim of succession to the Mormon prophetship.

It was providential that he had reached Nauvoo just then, for time was running out for Smith, since in the inscrutable wisdom of an all-wise Providence the uxorious leader of the turbulent Saints was soon to be murdered in the Carthage jail. At the moment Smith was making a fresh, bold bid for power in announcing as candidate for the Presidency of the United States. What his private hopes were, no one now knows, but no one seemed able to regard him with cool detachment. People were either burningly for him or bitterly against him, and even those who were laughing at his Presidential pretensions may have felt a little uneasy lest he somehow at least horse-trade himself into the Vice-Presidential nomination, and eventually enter the White House through the death of the President.

These eventualities were viewed as possible because of the peculiar position Smith occupied in Illinois, a key political state. His town of Nauvoo, with fifteen thousand Mormons, was the largest in the state, outranking Chicago. The Illinois Whigs and Democrats were so evenly balanced that Smith's great, controlled vote meant victory for the party to which he might give it. And in turn, the Illinois vote might mean victory nationally for either party.

The Mormon vote had moved bootlicking legislators to give the prophet incredible civil and military powers. He was authorized to issue writs which no one else in the state except justices of the supreme court might issue, and he was brigadier general of the Nauvoo Legion which had been made a state militia and heavily armed with state weapons, and given an authorized strength of two thousand men, which was no small army for the day. The politicians who had raised Smith up had come to hate and fear him, and the common people, who had welcomed the Mormons into the state as Abolitionist martyrs when they were driven from Missouri, were in uproar because of the sex scandals which hourly swirled out of Nauvoo.

The fact was that Smith was in great fear that the Mormons were to be driven from Illinois. He was charged with harboring river criminals who had taken refuge in Mormon baptism. He was accused of knowing more than he should about the large amounts of counterfeit money floating in western Illinois. He had survived numerous attacks through the years by both non-Mormons and resigning Mormons, including that following the collapse of his wildcat bank in Ohio which ruined some of his more substantial followers. Indeed he was not certain that Mormonism could survive where it was against an entire state roused by sex scandal—for the gentlemen of Illinois obviously were not willing that Smith should indulge in what was denied them by their religion, their laws, their pocketbooks and their wives.

Further, they shared the universal human weakness for meddling, and suddenly it was not enough to rail against Southern slavery: polygamy was much more interesting to be against since it permitted racy sermons and lectures, and sexy talk in piously scandalized mixed company. Besides, a great many people stood in hope of reaping fortunes if the

Mormons were despoiled. Smith knew that public opinion would back anyone who might mount an offensive, with prospect of success, against the Saints.

He also had a certain amount of trouble within the ranks, for many conventionally moral people were in Mormondom and they were deeply disturbed by the talk of polygamy and spiritual wifery among their chiefs. The Utah branch of the Latter Day Saints today holds that under the revelations which they say Smith received the prophet had "about fifty polygamous or spiritual wives," but that he did not cohabit with them. Later supposedly made innocuous, spiritual wifery at that time was said by backsliding Mormons to be a comfortable system whereby men and women whom heaven intended to be spiritual mates might cohabit on earth, even though either or both happened to be married otherwise already.

Smith discussed with Strang the possibility that the Saints might be forced out of Illinois. Strang suggested that the Burlington area should provide an excellent new site. Smith sent him to make a summation of the possibilities. While Strang was doing this, Smith was inveigled into jail on a minor charge. He might have refused to answer the warrant, but felt that he could clear himself in court and that a legal victory would strengthen his position. But once he was in durance, he was charged with the capital offense of treason, the probable idea being not to convict and execute him, but to permit him to escape so that he would flee from Illinois. However, the state militia which the governor had guaranteed would protect him connived in the murder of the prophet and his brother Hyrum by a mob.

At the moment Joseph was killed, Mormon bigwigs on distant journeys in behalf of his Presidential candidacy were struck with strange sadnesses or inexplicable glooms which were not made clear to their minds until they heard of the murder. Strang was vouchsafed no piddling premonitions nor puzzling glooms. Rather, he was divinely ordered to betake himself to Florence, Michigan, where a great convention of elders was gathering from the "stakes"—the Mormon parishes—of Michigan and other states.

No great men of Nauvoo appeared. Such of those as were not on journeys—and included among the travelers were most or all of the Twelve Apostles of the church—were at Nauvoo seeking to seize control of the Great Corner Stake from each other, usually by announcing revelations that God had appointed them as Joseph's "only legal successor." Receipt of revelations was in fact a deciding thing since the head of the church was "God's mouthpiece." As they started their sad journeys back to Nauvoo, some of the Twelve also modestly let it be known that the mantle had descended upon their shoulders.

To the Florence convention Strang soon exhibited his hole card—a letter postmarked at Nauvoo nine days before Smith's death and signed by Smith's hand—or one which Strang's opponents said the little man obviously thought enough like Smith's to satisfy any reasonable person. The letter related that "borne on wings of cherubims, the sweetes [sic] strains of heavenly musick thrilled in my ear," and thus Smith was taken up for a conference with the Almighty who, among other things, said "& now behold my servant james j Strang hath come to thee from far for truth when he knew it not & hath not rejected it but had faith in thee the shepherd and stone of israel & to him shall the gathering of the people be for he shall plant a stake of Zion in Wisconsin & I will establish it & there shall my people have peace & rest & shall not be moved for it shall be established on the prairie on white river in the lands of Racine & Walworth. . . ."

Strang said this clearly showed that both God and Joseph intended that Strang be the new prophet. Some in the uproarious convention asked why he had not gone to Nauvoo to take over instead of coming to Florence. Mockers intimated that perhaps he feared someone at Nauvoo might receive a revelation to "grease and swallow" him—that is, in Nauvoo parlance, to slip him into the river with a stone on his neck. Strang answered with powerful oratory, now sarcastic, now coldly logical, now floridly inspired, and he was doing very well for his case, bidding fair to be confirmed as prophet by the convention, when someone noticed that the *j* in the June of the postmark bore a dot over it while on other correspondence of the same date from Nauvoo there was no such dot.

Clearly shaken, Strang agreed that there was undoubtedly a dot on his—but, recovering, he said there were so many ways in which a bit of ink might have got there that it was silly for people to quibble over it. The uneasy elders finally decided that all who wished might confirm Strang as prophet, while others should abstain from voting lest in voting against him they later find themselves guilty of sacrilege should he prove actually to be God's selection.

Strang sent his adherents forth to rouse sentiment for him in the stakes of Zion. Failing in an attempt to intercept the Twelve on their way to Nauvoo, he returned to Wisconsin. He did not want it publicly known that the Great Corner Stake was to be moved from Nauvoo until he had quietly acquired land—for which just then he had no funds since the Mormon treasury was out of his reach in Illinois, a place which, it is notable, he widely avoided.

Then the dissenting elders in Michigan discovered in the sacred Mormon writings that successive prophets would be anointed by an angel as Joseph had been. They wrote Strang a letter. He answered calmly that he wished they had mentioned all that sooner, since he had been walking near Burlington at the moment Smith died, at which time a heavenly host came down through a riven sky and approached him. An angel anointed him and in a discourse which proved to contain five hundred seven well-chosen words—Strang enclosed a transcription of them—told him he was the successor in the prophetic line. However, the angel did not mention Joseph's death, and Strang had assumed all the to-do to be merely in confirmation of the prophet's letter.

Why, the elders demanded, had he not sooner mentioned so fairly unusual a thing?

Strang's reply amounted to a shrugging, "Why didn't you ask me?"

Strang's envoys to Nauvoo were very roughly treated and indeed put in fear of their lives, but they succeeded in making some converts for him. Early in 1845, Strang called for the Saints, wherever they might be, to gather at the future Corner Stake of Zion on his brother-in-law's farm near Burlington. The celestial city would be called Voree which he said meant Garden of Peace. There the Saints would be in the Order of Enoch—a revival of an attempted communal living project the late Joseph had established at Independence, Missouri.

However, general response was but little greater than that exhibited by Brigham Young and some other members of the Twelve whom Strang ordered to report to Voree for trial and disciplining for their pretensions and their pronouncements against the future King James.

Yet, some plums did fall into his lap. Several disgruntled former officials from Illinois, having failed in their bids for power, arrived to acclaim him. These included Apostle John E. Page, and William Marks, President of the Stake of Nauvoo. Strang published documents showing that the entire Smith family, except the prophet's wife Emma, had accepted him. Emma had had enough of Mormonism, at least for the time being, despite her position as Elect Lady and Daughter of God—or the more elegantly worded *Electa Cyria,* as she became after a bit of scholarship crept into the church. However, before the Smiths, who had quarreled bitterly with Brigham Young over the spoils and the succession to the prophetship, might move to Voree, something went wrong and they did not come. In later times, some of them declared the written endorsements of Strangism to be forgeries.

But there was to be a sequel, although it would not

transpire until a year after the founding of Voree, that is, in 1846. Meanwhile Strang was urging his followers to join the Order of Enoch and give their property to the church. In time, he said, everyone would live in a vast single establishment, but at first, because of the pinch of circumstance, there would be individual housing. He emphasized repeatedly that there would be no "plurality" or spiritual wiving. Only property and labor and income would be pooled in the Order, not spouses.

God had first "declared" the Order to Joseph, but when Smith preached community of property in his early career in Ohio he was tarred and feathered for his pains—or at least that was the excuse the mob used. Later, then, God "declared" the Order to "my servant James." But strangely, although the Saints professed to accept the voice of their prophet-revelator (when confirmed by the church that he had heard aright!) as the voice of God, it had always been notable, as it was in Strang's day, that those who owned anything were not inclined to join in sharing the wealth.

Later, in Utah, Brigham Young forced many to join in chapters of the Order, but in all of them there was much dissent and grumbling because of the free riders. One day he upbraided an elder for refusing to unite with the Order in his district, whereupon he was asked if he belonged to one. With a twinkle, Brigham answered that he planned to join one just as soon as he found a group which could manage his property better than he himself could. The Orders did not last long.

Today, of course, the Mormon Church is deservedly famous for its welfare program which keeps all its people off public relief, and for the help of those who need assistance in any way.

As for Voree, some dozens of converts did straggle in. Part of them were eager to be Enochites, and they fell to work putting up huts of logs, bark, slabs, stone, earth—anything that was available. But the others told Strang flatly they had no intention of providing a refuge for the lazy and that they would stay only on condition that they not be required to join the Order.

Irritably, Strang took the matter under consideration —and an opportune revelation came to him that he might settle them in a "tithing order," but it was understood that it was much below the more exalted, if hungrier, Order of Enoch. But quietly, grimly, as he collected what tithes he could from them on account, he made up his mind that they should come to taw when he was a little more powerful. After all, this was a theocracy, ruled by heaven, and it was not a good thing for heaven to have to gainsay itself.

At the moment, the primary necessity was merely to survive as a prophet, and while private individuals followed their own devices he put the "Order" to scrabbling out whatever sort of living it might. But the truth was that he did not seem to be getting anywhere with everyone hanging cagily back to see, before joining, if God would give him the success which would truly mark him as the anointed. Fortunately, then, an angel, as Strang said, came to Voree and whisked him through the air some little distance and put him down in the woods. He was told to dig under the roots of a certain tree where he would find a set of inscribed metal plates, with important writings in "an ancient tongue."

How was he to read it? Simple: the angel handed him the "interpreters," the peepstones—"two stones in silver bows —and these stones, fastened to a breastplate, constituted what is called Urim and Thummim"—which had been used by the Prophet Joseph to translate the golden plates years before.

The Prophet James did not make the blunder of others who had been accused by the Mormons of humbuggery in digging up plates in the tradition of those given Smith by the "resurrected personage," Moroni. Rather, he hastened home for several witnesses who felled the tree and dug out the stump. In overpowering excitement, several feet underground they found nine brass plates bearing "picture writings" and the crude profile drawing of a man. Facsimile engravings of these writings bear to the casual eye a resemblance to the cipher Strang had long used in his journal.

However, there apparently was a difference, for without the "interpreters," which he kept hidden for his private use, Strang could not read the plates. With them, the few scratchings took on scores of pages of amazing meanings. After a private session with them, the prophet announced that the plates were "the lost books of the law," once housed in the Hebrew Ark of the Covenant.

Soon he reported to the public that eminent non-Mormon scholars—unnamed—agreed that the writings were an authentic "ancient tongue." He said that crude treatments of the plates had already been given the world—*i.e.,* the sketchy translations known as Genesis, Exodus, Leviticus, Numbers, and Deuteronomy. The originals, these "Plates of Laban," had been lost so long that their existence "had come to be doubted."

Some impolite people suggested that the plates might have been cut, and not long before, from an old brass kettle; and others that a posthole auger might have been used to bore a hole slantwise under the tree for their deposit. And even though the Plates of Laban were mentioned in the Book of Mormon, Brighamites thought it remarkable that they should have been found just where they were, although they saw nothing remarkable in the golden plates' being found near the home of the Prophet Joseph in New York. They charged Strang with fraud and cheap imitation.

Still, swarms of people came to look and some to become convinced and to join Strang and in part even to enter the Order of Enoch. By winter he had a rabble of possibly three hundred people as against the two thousand he claimed in his publicity.

There is small profit in asking why. Prophets have followers because people believe in them, and that is the only answer that can ever be given to such a question. Joseph Smith, assisted by that same Oliver Cowdery of the Wood

Scrape incident, established as a tenet of Mormonism when he organized his church in 1830 that God had not ceased revealing matters of religion to man. Further, revealment could continue indefinitely, but never through but one man on earth at a time, a man who would be God's prophet and mouthpiece. Further, Smith revealed that word of mouth revelation might at any time supersede and overrule the written scriptures. These include the Old and New Testaments "which are correct as far as they are correctly translated from the originals," the Book of Mormon, and various writings of Joseph Smith, Jr.

Smith made a few converts in New England rural sections, but by and large he met rough treatment in his home ground. He went to Ohio and very quickly won some three to four thousand people. His interpretation of the Bible, his vivid recounting of visits to him by angels, his confabulations with God, his promises for a great inheritance for his Saints, were exactly the thing that appealed to those people. But where one person fiercely loved and followed him, many loathed and mocked him as a gross, crude, ignorant, and potentially dangerous impostor.

His very death stamped him as a martyr and impressed his followers with the truth of his teachings. These teachings indicated that a new prophet must follow him to lead the church. In the midst of noisy brawlings, and repressions by secret police, Brigham Young was the capable winner, although he announced bluntly that he would not traffic in revelations. Great sections of Mormondom pulled away. Some thought Strang was the anointed prophet and they believed implicitly his accounts of talks with God and with angels. In short, they received individual revelations that he was the prophet. He filled a need that was felt by many people of the day, people conditioned by the fears and hopes of many brands of backwoods preaching, poverty-stricken people who wanted the earthly riches promised to the Saints and who believed there was no other way to heaven than through this new religion which in fact was the ancient, true

religion given back to the world through the Prophet Joseph.

Strang was an earnest, indefatigable administrator.
He had enough problems to crush a man, but something,
perhaps his burning dream of power and leadership—if one
wishes to remember the journal entry when he was nineteen
—or his own conviction of his calling as a prophet, kept him
always one jump ahead of disaster. Next to the money problem and the obtaining of converts to replace the procession of
departing brethren, the greatest trouble was a stream of sex
scandals. In the midst of his constant trying and excommunicating of offenders, Strang recorded that things were at such
pitch that he could not enter a house where there was a
woman without everyone's wondering, with knowing looks,
"why Brother Strang was going in there."

Too, there were controversies by mail with Brigham
Young and other non-Strangite leaders. The thirty or so men
who had announced as "sole legal successor" to the Prophet
Joseph were industriously excommunicating each other like
so many rival popes. Young cut Strang off and delivered him
over, in the usual Mormon formula, to be "buffeted by Satan
for a thousand years."

Strang in turn banished him and others from the
priesthood, cut them off from the church, and blasted them
generally, condemning their bones "to rot in the living tomb
of their flesh" and their bodies to be wracked with "chilling
agues and burning fevers. May peace and homes be names
forgotten to them." Also to be denied them was "the beauty
they have betrayed to infamy" in the polygamous ravishing
of girls. Indeed, all feminine beauty was to be "to their eyes
a crawling mass of putridity and battening corruption; its
auburn tresses the posthumous growth of temples of crawling worms; its fragrant breath the blast of perdition. With
desires insatiate may each gratification turn to burning bitterness and glowing shame."

Strang did however excuse Sidney Rigdon from all

this. A ruthless man as a high-riding official under Smith, Rigdon had been edged out by Brigham Young and had taken most of the wealthy Nauvooans to Pennsylvania to establish a commune near Father Rapp's Economie. Strang invited him to bring his people to Voree where, while they were cozily ensconced in the Order of Enoch, Rigdon would be number-two man. Rigdon treated the invitation with brusquerie and so he too had to be locked out of the kingdom.

The Prophet James constantly announced reception of revelations from heaven, full of "lo" and "know ye" and "do ye," with divine cajolings and threatenings by turns to move the people to industry. Despite the poverty at Voree, there was soon a revelation that God wanted "a meet dwelling" erected for the prophet—one with a special room where he might do his translating in privacy, for from time to time, the revelation promised, he was to be given other ancient records to work over.

Too, a great communal dwelling was to be erected for the Order of Enoch on the Hill of Promise, and to be called the Tower of Strength. Near this ornate building was to be raised a tabernacle—"the greatest building in the United States." The round-heeled paupers were ordered in the revelation to turn in their "gold and jewels" for the erection of these buildings, of which the central halls were to be an acre in extent and the walls yards thick, and to fetch furlongs of "flawless marble" for floors and roofs.

Now, there did not appear to be a great deal of flawless marble in those parts and particularly not at Voree. However, a dwelling of sorts was scraped together for Strang and a little desultory work done on a foundation at one corner of the vista marked out for the temple. A bit of progress was otherwise made, despite disrupting jealousies in the "College of Apostles" and among other handsomely titled dignitaries in their muddy boots and wool hats.

Strang in fact seemed to be grasping the coattails of solvency. Then he alienated most of the brains of the place by seeking out and admitting to high favor several Mormons who had been storm centers before they were "cut off" by Joseph Smith, and who were repugnant to many of his ex-Nauvooans. Chiefly, he courted Dr. John C. Bennett who professed ability to bring a number of moneyed men into Strangism, and Bennett's friend, the actor George Adams. Adams said he really had not indulged in all those fornications of which he was accused—that he was kicked out because of jealousies engendered by the flocking of so many to him "whereaver and wheneaver" he opened his mouth to speak.

As an Illinois state official, Bennett had procured vast favors for the Prophet Joseph at, it was commonly said, no loss to himself. He then became a Mormon, rose to high civil and military preferment, and finally quarreled with Joseph over Sidney Rigdon's daughter whom each desired as a spiritual wife. Since spiritual wives were stated officially not to be slept with, but were taken merely to elevate them spiritually, it might logically be asked why the rivalry—but at any rate, crossing Smith meant that Bennett had to go. Smith got him off quietly without the usual public charges of crime or fornication, for he was a prominent and possibly dangerous man.

Bennett did not maintain the silence which he had at least tacitly promised. He at once published an exposé of Mormonism, declaring that the whole train of crimes and orgies of which the Saints were constantly accusing each other were true. These same charges, reprinted in Gentile papers, had always roused the fury of the Mormon hierarchy who declared that a plot of defamation was under way. Besides, Smith defended himself, the charges, as appearing in the Mormon press, were usually not factual but were used simply to get rid of undesirable people who might not be disposed of otherwise! Probably no dictator has ever made a more remarkable defense for himself than that.

Now Bennett said to Strang that his own exposé of Mormonism was a lie, written merely because he was angry about the things which had happened to him at Nauvoo. He really thought Mormonism a fine thing, and so on. There he was, a self-proclaimed liar, a calumniator of the church and of God's Anointed, Joseph Smith, Jr.—but Strang forgave him and urged him to hasten on to Voree with his moneyed men.

Bennett answered coolly that he wanted no man-made appointment—but that he would come if Strang should chance to receive a revelation that Bennett was to be next to the prophet. And as if he had no doubt that this prestige-making revelation would be forthcoming, he gave Strang copious advice as to how they would conduct affairs, adding that steps should be taken at once to get the envisioned University of Wisconsin established at Voree.

And by the way, he said, Strang should write Joseph's brother William Smith, a nominal Strangite, to come on to Voree and to bring his mother, old Mrs. Lucy Smith, and also to bring the bodies of Joseph and Hyrum as well as "the mummies and papyrus." All these, he said, would be excellent drawing cards in bringing Mormons into Strangism.

"The mummies" have been confused with the bodies of Joseph and Hyrum, probably because of the juxtaposition in Bennett's letter, but they refer to some Egyptian mummies Smith had bought from a medicine peddler. Some Egyptian writings came with them, and Joseph, apparently without the aid of the peepstones, translated them and announced that one concerned the adventures of Abraham. He obviously had full faith in the inspiration of his translation for he published a picture of the papyri along with it and Egyptologists had a good laugh. Josephites accused them of framing against the prophet and the relics were long exhibited at Nauvoo. William Smith did come to Voree, but he had not yet brought "Miss Lucy" when he quarreled with Strang and left. As patriarch of the church, Smith was empowered to issue divine blessings, for a fee, and he became hurt when Strang seized at what proved to be an abortive opportunity to win Joseph's son whom he was going to make an additional patriarch. William wrote Strang that a "supa-fuity" of patriarchs would cheapen and spoil the office. He withdrew.

Before William's arrival Strang had received the revelation which Bennett desired, and the doctor and Adams came. Bennett was eager to explain away his calumniations of some of the old Nauvoo hands now at Voree, but several of these left, angry and disgusted with Strang, and spread harsh warnings against him while receiving revelations that they themselves were the only legal successor to Joseph Smith.

Bennett made temporizing excuses concerning the various wealthy men he had promised to bring. As General-in-Chief, he organized military displays. Soon he pleased Strang by promoting a secret Order of the Illuminati, in which there were high-sounding titles. Oaths treasonous to the United States and Wisconsin were taken to Strang by the select group of Voreeans who were admitted. When he anointed them in a dark room they saw with awe that their hair glowed strangely where the oil was rubbed.

In a few days enemies published the passwords and treasonous oaths and mocked the halos as being from phosphorous. Presently Bennett decided there was not much to be made at Voree. Possibly he had secretly tried to wrest control from Strang and had failed. He did not resist when he was expelled under the regular charges of adultery and unfaithfulness to the prophet. He departed, casually confirming the phosphorous hoax of the Illuminati.

Time and again Strangism almost foundered but the prophet always struggled back up. He could foresee great success if he might but get his followers away from the intruding world, and particularly if he might obtain a large amount of cheap, preferably free, land. That would assuredly bring converts.

His mind turned to Beaver Island, the beauty of which had struck him on a lake journey. It was sixteen miles

long, its hills well timbered, and there was plenty of land for
"an inheritance unto the Saints." The waters around it were
one of the finest fishing grounds in the world.

As if possession were already accomplished, a celebration was decreed. Included would be a baptizing for the
unsaved dead. However, baptizings must be held in the
temple, and scarcely more than a barn had grown up at a
corner of the spot where "the greatest building in the
United States" was to stand. And everyone would want to
participate in the baptizing, for which there simply was not
room.

But the situation was saved. Strang announced that
the Prophet Elijah had visited him and told him that until
there was time to complete the temple, White River was
"sanctified and made holy" from "the bathing pool unto the
water wheel." The rites thus might be held there. Elijah
also had ordered that a recorder of baptisms for the dead be
ordained. A duplicate would be kept "in the archives of
heaven." And accordingly it came to be put down that
George Adams, the ex-actor, was baptized for John Adams.
He was baptized twice more for John Quincy and Sam
Adams. Strang and others were baptized for various dead
relatives and for such notables as Lord Byron and Cromwell.

Even though he had become Saint James, instead of
merely the Prophet James, Strang in the upshot had difficulty persuading Mormons to move to the Beaver Islands
and squat on land which they might lose, since the government allowed no homesteading there. Those Saints who did
go to Beaver quarreled with each other and split into groups
which promptly "cut off" each other from the church.

Too, there was a group of "gentiles" at one end of the
island, fishermen who had already chosen spots for future
homesteads on which they intended to file whenever the government should open the land. They were alarmed at seeing
the vanguard of the Mormons, a sect which had been the
center of much brawling from New York to Ohio to Mis-

souri and back to Illinois. Mormons ordinarily interpreted their sacred writings as justifying them in taking anything they could from gentiles, and they had a reputation, justified or not, for "wanting what jined them." Further, they were hated for their recent doctrine of "plurality," and the gentiles made no distinction between the Brighamite Mormons who were for this plurality of wives and the Strangites who were not. Nor was the situation helped by the announcement of one of the invaders that he was the lion "come up from his thicket, and the destroyer of the Gentiles."

Strang was busier, poorer, shabbier than ever. As head of the church he made long, exhausting preaching journeys, with trips to Beaver thrown in. He wrote impudent letters to high government officials and politicked in Washington, demanding that the Beavers be given to the Strangites as a refuge. At the same time he quietly tried to claim the islands by right of occupancy, appealing to Mormons everywhere to go there and to take a year's provisions in order to be independent of the gentile trading post on Paradise Bay.

The gentile fishermen had come to think it great sport to knock down the pacifist Strangites when these came for their mail. Strang had long before received a revelation commanding nonresistance, but now he discovered in the Plates of Laban that that was not the proper way. Consequently, the growing congregation of Saints on the island thrashed some of the bullies and there was a sullen truce.

In the spring of 1849 Saint James returned to Voree to see his wife and to attend to affairs at the commune. It chanced that a Saint named Field was there with a view to settling. His daughter Elvira, who was about seventeen, expected to teach at the Voree school. However, they decided to return to Michigan—but not before Saint James had become pleasantly acquainted with the girl. In fact, when she was gone he could not get her out of his mind.

Back at Beaver he called in Adams and swore him to

secrecy. How, he asked, would Adams like to go to the mainland and sound out Miss Field on a proposal of marriage from Saint James—who would soon make her a queen? The astounded actor reminded the prophet of his preachings against plurality.

Well, yes, Strang agreed. But he had been digging a little deeper into the Plates of Laban and it turned out that polygamy was after all the proper order. He did not explain how it was that God had happened to tell him at various times that, on the contrary, it was wrong. Rather, he said he wondered that it had not occurred to him sooner that it was right, for after all when one considered that Abraham and David and Joseph Smith were polygamists and were in heaven, one could only realize that plurality was of the heavenly order. Too, were not these the latter days of the world? And in the latter days would not seven women cling to one man?

Adams was silent before this admirable logic. He hastened off in his office as procurer. Strang consummated the celestial seduction at some unknown place with the willing Elvira and the girl went to New York with him without telling her family anything about it—for she had been warned by Adams to complete silence. Her people were in distraction as they searched over Michigan for her all winter, not knowing whether she was alive or dead.

Under the name of Charles J. Douglass she spent the winter with Strang, her black hair cut off. In public she was his nephew in her black broadcloth suit. In private, as they skipped about in his campaign to win converts, she was the pretty girl of eighteen who had thrown her cap over the windmill for him. At times they were uneasy, for people had a habit of staring at the round bosom of her vest, despite her bindings. Frightening rumors reached Mrs. Strang at her parents' home in western New York where she was visiting. Once in debate Strang was accused of polygamy. Elvira was on the stage with him and they thought exposure had come but it turned out to be only a stock accusation. When on occasion it was suggested the nephew might be a girl, Strang answered with scurrilous invective.

Adams wrote from Boston that he had a thousand converts for Beaver. The anti-Mormon press carried stories of Adams's drinking bouts and of his ham acting when he had a go on the boards in his old profession. Strang reminded aggrieved New York Saints that King David danced naked before the daughters of Israel. There was nothing wrong, per se, in acting. And anyway, he said, the papers probably were lying. He would not forsake his loyalty to Adams.

In the spring he sent Elvira to Beaver on one boat and took his family on another. On the way he told Mary of the new revelation concerning plurality. She did not publicly rebel. There is no record of what she may have said privately.

At the island there were things to take Strang's mind from romance. There had been storms and blizzards and disease and hunger and death. The gentiles had conspired to refuse to trade with the Saints during the winter and the colony was reduced to hunger, with many lying ill. Some had survived only because a few tender-hearted gentiles had slipped food to them. Many Saints had left and there had been depredations by the "Lamanites"—Indians. These "Lamanites" were descendants of the "ancient Jews," it seemed, and in the Book of Mormon had been equipped with horses in the pre-Spanish days in America. Under Mormon tutelage they were "to blossom like the rose" and become "a fair and delightsome people."

Strang settled their hash by showing the iron fist, accompanied by the blunt language his growing number of converts made possible. Too, he reminded them of the school for Indian children the Saints conducted, and shamed them for their ingratitude. From then on his relations with nearby Lamanites were excellent. Not so with the gentiles. By force of arms he took a cow an Irish family was accused of stealing from a Saint. A cry resounded up and down all the Michilimackinac country: The Mormons were in open brigandage!

But there was new hope in the colony. Strang had brought money and converts and more of each were on the way. Adams would bring his thousand. The missionaries in England would send a shipload or two. Since the majority of foreign converts were always women, this would help out in the forthcoming polygamous dispensation.

Strang took Miss Field into his home for the time being. Whatever the arrangements may have been in the *ménage à trois,* he did not squire her in public, where she appeared from the first in woman's dress. Saint James had a hundred things to see about—his paper, *The Northern Islander,* the setting of type for *The Book of the Law of the Lord* from the brass plates, and the handing out of numerous daily revelations on every minute trifle of daily living. And work went forward on the shell of the temple.

God had commanded the eternal establishment of communal ownership for everyone at Beaver and not for just a few as at Voree. However, it occurred to Strang that if he had two wives every man would want two under communalism, and there were just not that many females available. Then he discovered a passage in the Plates of Laban which indicated that the true economic and social order was a system of individual ownership and private labor, with tithes and taxes coming to the church—*i.e.,* to Strang. Then those who could not afford extra women could blame no one but themselves.

Yet, as a sop to the "eternal establishment" of the Order of Enoch, the plates recommended that groups associate under leaders who were to be called princes in the coming monarchy. These groups would live in the princes' houses in communal order. Somehow, the idea never proved popular.

There was disappointment when First President Adams arrived at Beaver, not with the promised thousand but with a woman who he said was his wife who had formerly stayed in the East. And there was further disappointment: Strang's missionaries in England were failing to win converts. The drab spinsters of the mills, much needed in a polygamous program, continued to embark for Utah instead of heading for Beaver. The trouble was that the Brighamite missionaries were only too well acquainted with the priests Strang had been so unlucky as to choose to represent him. For in past years, in an upheaval at Nauvoo, it chanced that Strang's missionaries had each testified of certain thefts, fornications, and general scalawaggeries of which he knew the other to be guilty, and Brigham's men had the printed record.

Now here the boys were in England, happy Strangites together, and there was small point in their saying that those thefts, fornications, and scalawaggeries had never occurred, but that the testimony had been fabricated at the demand of higher-ups. The fact remained that the guilt was as they had said, or that they had perjured themselves. The Brighamite missionaries laughed them down.

Mrs. Strang told her husband there was something suspicious about the woman with Adams but Strang did not listen. Everything was running better than usual. Even a few people whom Saint James considered educated and well-to-do were coming in to settle along what would be known as the King's Highway after the coronation. He announced that in obedience to revelation he would be crowned on July 8.

Mockery flamed among the gentiles who dubbed him King Jimmy, a mockery touched off by anger stimulated against him by the Newton brothers and other traders, particularly those on Mackinac Island some fifty miles to the east. Mackinac had long been the center of civilization on the Michigan frontier. Strang was taking its business, selling wood to steamboats, dealing with trappers, and absorbing the fishing trade. He interfered in the sale of whisky to Indians, and he illegally held large sections of mainland as well as various islands by scattering a few settlers there.

The fishermen and traders of the region agreed to celebrate the Fourth of July with a massacre of the Saints and a general rape of the women.

News of the project reached Strang. He imported cannon and small arms. On July 3rd, boat after boat of gentiles drifted into Paradise Bay and a mob began carousing on the far shore. The Saints prepared for attack that night, but the gentiles celebrated themselves into stupor. At daylight Strang waked them with a blast from his cannon.

A few sleepyheads stared across the water. Strang plunked a ball into the edge of the bay before the astounded scoundrels at the tavern. The host bawled an indignant and querulous objection. Strang bawled back that the Saints were only celebrating the Fourth but that if there was any trouble the tavern would be blown instantly apart, as would the larger fishing smacks over there.

The raiders stood around trying to work up their courage. They ended by falling into quarreling cliques, accusing each other of spilling the plot. But their failure only increased the determination to destroy Strang.

Four days later all was fiesta among the Saints. At Font Lake, in the interior, a heifer was ritually butchered and set to roasting, along with other meats. People were to bring roasted fowls, symbolic of the ancient Hebrew burnt offerings. While the barbecue was cooking for noon, everyone crowded into the roofless temple for the coronation.

When his people were calm enough, King Strang spoke. Mrs. Strang listened without outward show to the pronouncements on plurality while her new "sister," Elvira, modestly looked at the ground. The Lord had been reasonable in the revelations, though, as things turned out. It was recommended strongly that the Twelve Apostles take extra wives, but it would be a matter of choice with others. If a wife objected to another woman for good cause, the husband was to look a little farther. If her objections were merely whimsical and captious, they were to be ignored.

Practical reasons for plurality, it seemed, were that

multitudes of unborn souls were waiting for "tabernacles" —bodies—in which to dwell. Under plurality, many unattractive women who would remain single under ordinary conditions would receive husbands since it would be man's duty to take those women, too—for while an unmarried woman might enter one of the three heavens she might not attain "elation" therein. A man's glory in heaven would depend much on how many children he had, and a woman's glory would be in proportion to her husband's. Consequently, "plural" families, the husband and all his wives, would achieve greatest glory in the afterlife. "As Eve had led Adam out of the Garden, man must now lead woman back to it."

Nor would women be shut out entirely from the taking of plural mates. Under the new law a man was required as in Old Testament times to take a dead brother's childless widow and raise up children by her. These would receive the late brother's name and glorify him. On the other hand, a widow left childless might select any succession of male Saints she wished and under the Law, regardless of their marital status, they would be required to warm her bed until she proved pregnant. The children resulting from these unions would be considered her dead husband's offspring to glorify him in heaven.

Plurality and spiritual wiving had long been bitter subjects among Mormons and there was no member of the various sects of Mormonism who had not taken a stand. A few Strangites left the island and founded a commune in Michigan but there was no widespread rebellion. Indeed, Strang's sect grew more rapidly than ever.

However, very few people took extra mates—no more than twenty-five men all told. Legends survive in the area of anguished wives superseded by young women, but only one man besides Strang ever had more than two wives—and that was Lorenzo Dow Hickey who had accused the prophet of polygamy in New York. Further irony was that it was Mrs. Hickey who had written Lorenzo from Beaver that there was too much talk to be ignored that Saint James had a woman in the East.

Strang ignored the clamor in the gentile press that the new oaths the people had taken to him were treasonous. Then for some reason he quarreled with George Adams and drove him from Beaver. The excuse was that, as Mrs. Strang had suspected, the woman with him was not his wife—and adultery and fornication stood high in the Strangite list of crimes.

Ashore, quivering with pious indignation, Adams told awesome stories of the immoralities and treasons of Strang. He also brought suit for heavy damages to his character and his nonexistent purse. Strang went ashore for trial to avoid invasion of Beaver by worldly officers and was sentenced to two life terms in prison by an Irish justice of the peace. A higher court took the view that the justice had overestimated his powers and freed Strang. Petty legal and illegal harassments followed. Strangites migrating to Beaver were carried past the island by bribed steamer captains and put ashore on barren places. Gerrymandering was resorted to to disenfranchise the Mormons.

But Strang's star was still rising. He was a saint, a king, and now it was revealed that he was a divinity. The theology already provided that all his people might in time become gods, minor deities somewhere between angels and the Godhead, but that would be after death. The king's elevation had come sooner. He viewed Joseph Smith as his John the Baptist—the "Forerunner" whom "man should kill." Strang was the mighty one who should "dwell thereafter." Pinned down on occasion when hauled into gentile courts, the Strangites freely stated they believed him to be "supernatural." This, then, would show why they clung to him even while not following him into plural marriage.

The next gentile move was to prefer federal charges against Strang of treason, piracy, counterfeiting, and trespass on the public domain. In great good humor, to the surprise of the officers of the gunboat *Michigan* who had expected a fight when they went for him, he surrendered for trial. The frontier was jubilant. The Newton brothers, island traders, and their friends were confident that if Strang did not hang for treason he would be in prison so long his commune would break up.

But some of the rougher element of the gentiles on their end of Beaver did not wait for it to break up. They mounted an attack upon the Strangites and one of the gentiles, a man named Bennett, was killed. A coroner's jury of six Mormons and six gentiles decided he got what was coming to him—but then three of the gentiles refused to sign the verdict on the ground that they had no evidence the Mormon coroner was a qualified officer.

This tactic was designed to leave opportunity for a murder charge. Gentile reinforcements arrived at the trading post and buckets of tears and printing ink were expended on Bennett in the Michilimackinac country. The Mormons buried Bennett and covered the grave with stones as a mark of shame, telling their children to toss another rock on the grave as a curse when they passed. The gentiles on the island simmered but did not risk another fight.

In Detroit Strang convinced a jury that as God's vice-regent and Lord of the Earth he considered himself only the spiritual ruler of the world and not the temporal ruler. He pointed out that in his newspaper he was referred to as Mr. Strang, and that it was dated in the usual manner and not in the new chronology. Freed, he secretly decided to enter politics. The gerrymander law required Beaver Island votes to be delivered an impossible distance by a certain hour. By rousing everyone at midnight to vote—unless the tally had been made up sooner—and starting a man at once, Strang astounded the officials by delivering on time. Further, since the Mormons were in majority in the sprawling, misshapen county which had been set up, he had elected almost a full slate of Mormons as officials.

Aware that the angry people of Mackinac would waylay him on his journey to take his place in the state legislature and would hold him until it adjourned, he traveled a devious course. But he was detected and officers chased him into the legislative chambers after a wild journey, expecting to drag him out before he might take oath. The dignity of the body would not permit this and the officers were expelled.

Strang created considerable respect for his abilities before the session was over. Many of his colleagues of course were not from the enfevered frontier and, while he had more learning and probably a better mind than most of them, he got along well with them. Indeed, he had proved himself a clever politician, and the legislators, courting his favor and his controlled vote, passed his bill to make Beaver Island the chief part of the since-vanished Manitue County. This made him supreme in his stronghold under both the laws of Michigan and *The Book of the Law of the Lord.*

He made the most of it. He dragged the gentiles of Beaver into his courts and convicted them of something, administering confiscatory fines wherever possible. For instance, state law provided ruinous penalties for selling whisky to the Indians. And the concoctions of alcohol, creek water, and tobacco juice which were peddled at enriching rates to these "Lamanites" were considered whisky.

Still, some gentiles simply refused to do anything which might be construed as violation of the law. Finally in exasperation Strang issued a ukase: Any outsider remaining on the island after another twenty-four hours would be baptized into Strangism and charged the customary tithes and taxes. All left, complaining loudly to the state governor who ignored them. Both parties wanted Strang's support at the Presidential conventions, for as Strang went so probably would go Michigan and Michigan might decide the national election. Strang enjoyed the situation as greatly as Joseph Smith had enjoyed the similar one in Illinois. He fully expected to be allowed to nominate the next President. For the moment, he set his own eye modestly on Congress.

The Michilimackinac people were more interested in the things at hand. There were armed encounters on un- inhabited islands between fishing parties. The county sheriff —one of Strang's men—and his Beaver Island posse were badly shot up in a fishing village on the mainland and then were chased for hours—object, murder—across the lake, bul- lets of the pursuers falling just short of the boat and its wounded crew. The gentile villagers abandoned their homes before retaliation might come. Strangites occupied the place and held it at gunpoint against unwitting strangers to whom it had been sold.

Success bred courage. Strang boycotted all trade with Mackinac Island and Detroit. He breathed threats against other trading centers. Three thousand adherents now poured money into his church and the wealthy leader built a house befitting his station for his two wives and their children, for Eliza was fruitful. However, though honored with office and title, Mrs. Strang suddenly took her children and went to Voree where her parents were living—evidently as Strangites, although her father had been a Baptist preacher. Afterward Mrs. Strang occasionally visited the City of James and Strang sometimes went to Voree where he was entertained in her parents' home.

Eliza was much taken aback when he married a spin- ster, "Aunt" Betsy McNutt, as an example that the less- favored women should not be ignored. Betsy promptly con- ceived. She and Elvira Eliza had three children each when King James cast his eye on a pair of seventeen-year-olds, Sarah Wright and her cousin Phoebe. Despite their parents' objections the girls said they were in love with him. Tradi- tionally, he married them in the same ceremony, although in later times the girls denied this. Soon both were pregnant, as were Elvira and Betsy. Strang added to his house, provid- ing quarters for each wife. He visited them in turn but required them to eat together and to join in family prayers.

A clique of well-to-do members increasingly resented Strang's interferences in the prosperous businesses they had developed. These were a Dr. Atkyn, the Johnsons, Bedfords, and Wentworths, all led by Dr. H. D. McCullouch, an ex-Army surgeon. They were blatantly anti-polygamist. The women refused to wear the pantalette costumes. Further, the men were of obvious resolution—but Strang had developed the conviction that he was invulnerable to earthly harm.

Elvira begged him either to drive the dissidents out with an unexpected, concerted show of force, or to get along with them. Strang declared that all he was interested in was their tithes and taxes and that he intended these should be paid. Then the anti-polygamist Bedford was caught in the most *flagrante delicto* with the wife of Strang's friend, Apostle David Brown. Brown complained loudly to King James. Strang hinted that Bedford deserved death but Brown misunderstood, or was not willing to go that far, and with the help of friends only gave the fellow—who happened to be his former fishing-business partner—a severe hiding. Bedford lay in wait to ambush Strang but, failing to get opportunity, fled to the mainland with McCullouch and others of the clique who feared a general retaliation, for in some way they knew that Strang had been apprised of the intended murder.

Captain McBlair of the gunboat *Michigan* illegally took these men back to Beaver, concealing them from view as they steamed into the bay. Two hid in the boat which went ashore with a message that requested Strang to visit the steamer for a talk with McBlair. Elvira said a king should command the captain to come ashore. Strang said a refusal would show fear, and that he feared no man.

As he reached the pier, Wentworth and Bedford leaped up and began shooting him. Despite three wounds, he grappled with Bedford and hung on until beaten loose with a pistol. The assassins fled back to the ship. McBlair refused to surrender them to the island sheriff—who was the county sheriff—saying he would deliver them instead to the officers at Mackinac.

He did so. They walked into the jail and out again to the cheers of a happily berserk mob and were never tried.

Although a bullet was in Strang's spine, he was miraculously alive. In the June dusk men carried him to his house. Ten days later the *Michigan* came loaded to the guards with an army of roughs. They were met with such an attitude of ferocity that they steamed away without trying to land. Strang knew the respite was temporary. He saw that the end had come for himself and for Beaver. He commanded that all retire to Voree.

A steamer took him and Betsy McNutt and Phoebe Wright and some other Saints down to the Wisconsin shore. His other wives, Elvira and Sarah, stayed behind, expecting to sell their property to gentiles. At Voree, Strang's wife Mary helped nurse him. At Beaver, most of those who had the means of leaving did not wait to try to sell their property, and it chanced that those who had such means also happened to be the chief men, the priests, elders, and apostles. Scarcely a person of consequence remained. Later they excused themselves by saying they left in accordance with Strang's command. Still, something seems wrong with the business.

They left barely in time to save themselves. The raiders returned many hundreds strong in a flotilla of commandeered steamers. The unorganized and leaderless island farmers dared not resist. Sick and well, they and their wives and children were driven furiously aboard the boats, little time being wasted by the invaders except for the rape of the more comely women and girls. The boats took them wherever it was most convenient for the individual captains— some to Chicago, some to Mackinac, some to the nearest bay ashore. Some of the unfortunates were scattered by new mobs. Others were aided by gentiles.

Strang was not told of the pillaging and plundering,

the destruction of the temple and whipping post and press, nor of the mistreatment of women, nor that the Saints were forced to carry away one at a time the rocks from Bennett's grave. He was told only that the people were scattering and that in the sky over Beaver some of his departing people had seen a golden cloud which promised good things for the future as it swirled into letters to spell the legend

ZION — J S

On King's Day—July 8—he wept when asked if he would name a successor. Despite the troubles which had developed because Joseph Smith had died too suddenly to name one, he expired next day without making a designation. He was buried in an unmarked grave. A few Strangites gathered at Voree, but the village dwindled and expired. After the place went back to nature and became a cow pasture, some of Strang's children removed his remains to a cemetery in Burlington. Until he was forgotten, miracles of the throw-away-the-crutches variety were common at his grave.

Groups of Strangites drifted from one stake to another. While Elvira remained at Voree, the other three plural wives went with a congregation to the wilderness of Jackson County, Wisconsin, and formed a settlement. Each except the legal wife, Mary, bore the prophet a posthumous child. Never marrying, Phoebe Wright lived in the Jackson County settlement almost sixty years, dying in 1914. Betsy McNutt moved away and finally abandoned the faith of her husband though she seems to have remained Mormon. Sarah Wright married a Mormon doctor, learned the healing craft from him in Utah, and left him and Mormonism when he felt the call to take an extra wife. She said she did not believe in polygamy.

Elvira finally gave up the hard struggle at Voree, moved to Michigan, and at the point of death gave her four children away. Recovering, she managed to get them all back except one who had been adopted. Marrying a gentile, she bore more children and died in 1910, at eighty, in Courtland, Michigan, a firm anti-Strangite, anti-Mormon. Mary Strang never married again.

From time to time Strang's sons were approached with the plea that one assume the prophetic mantle and call the flock together. None would have anything to do with the prophetship, nor even the sect, although some of their children reputedly became Mormons. A succession of old men here and there have passed the assumed Strangite mantle to each other, even to this day, and a scattering of Mormons still consider themselves of that faith. They say that Strang was "the only legal successor" to Joseph Smith, and that that makes their church the true one.

Strang has become a money-making tourist legend on the island where once he was a prophet, saint, king, revelator, divine mouthpiece, vice-regent of God and Lord of the Earth, and divinity. But no one knows what became of the peepstones. Perhaps the angel came and took them away.

CHAPTER FIFTEEN

AMANA, WHERE THE LORD
USUALLY SAID NO

FLY FROM WOMEN-KIND, AS A VERY
DANGEROUS MAGNET AND MAGICAL FIRE

Ebenezer you shall call it—
"Hitherto our Lord has helped us"—
He was with us on our journey
And from many perils saved us.
His path and way are wonderful
And the end makes clear the start.

—SONG GIVEN CHRISTIAN METZ *by the Lord, Dec. 7, 1842, concerning the name of the first home of the True Inspirationists in America.*

THE collapse of forty Fourierist phalanxes, from the North American in the East to Silkville in Kansas, was to strengthen the saying that only religious communes might survive. Some of these successes, indeed, were begun during the Fourierist decade. Several morals might be drawn from the career of that at Bishop Hill in Illinois, beyond the obvious one of starveling Swedish immigrants putting home-based social reformers to shame.

A slight parallel may be seen between Luther's own account of his being frightened into the religious life by a thunder storm, and Eric Janson's conversion to crusading. He was plowing one day at his home near Bishop Hill in Sweden when he fell unconscious in a physical seizure. Coming to, he heard the audible voice of God: "Ask anything in my name, I will do it, saith the Lord."

Janson and one Jonas Olson, on the strength of that promise, began a stormy pietistic campaign, stirring up the peasants against the established Lutheran church. Church and state dealt with the dissidents in the usual severe manner. Finally a dead-or-alive reward was posted for delivery of Janson to the authorities. Easily recognizable because of protruding front teeth, he fled the country, and but cautiously returned to it during his efforts to bring his followers to America to establish them in a communal village.

The authorities backed and filled, making promises and breaking them, and it was only by direct intervention of the king that the first batch of immigrants was allowed to depart. Others swiftly followed. Some hundreds of them supposedly walked from New York to Illinois. Others traveled by canal and lake, and walked the final hundred miles from Chicago to Red Oak Grove near which the American Bishop Hill was established with the people living in dugouts, mud huts, and soddies. Soon eight hundred were crowded into damp, dark quarters. Food was scarce.

Cholera struck. Such remedies as other people might have—chiefly calomel—were lacking to the Swedes. But death was considered no calamity among the Jansonites. Janson himself would cease tending the ill, when someone, well that morning, was sinking into eternity in the afternoon, to say cheerfully, "Go—die in peace!" More than a hundred did die, in peace or otherwise.

Janson had promptly sent out missionaries to convert Americans to his beliefs. Traditionally, they brought not one. Certainly there was nothing but hard work and short rations and the promise of heaven to attract them, and the Americans seemed to feel they could have those things at home. Amusingly enough, Janson's fellow prophet, Jonas Olson, was converted to Shakerism when he stopped to win souls at a Shakertown.

He returned to Bishop Hill, but for the moment at

least he was unable to force the Shaker tenets—which, practically, is to say celibacy—upon the Swedes. About this same
time, some debts were collected back in Sweden. A few
buildings were begun—and in extremity, what resources
could be scraped up were used to send Jonas Olson, the
Shakerite, and some young men to hunt gold in California.

Then trouble erupted through a young man who
had married Janson's cousin. The understanding was that
the girl was not to be taken from Bishop Hill—but several
times she was taken, and each time some of Janson's people
went and stole her back, once dramatically using relays of
horses which they posted on the way. Americans threatened
mob action against the Swedes—and the whole thing was
brought to a climax when the husband shot Janson in the
courtroom to which the affair was taken by a lawsuit.

The widow and others confidently awaited Janson's
resurrection on the third day. At last, in grief, they held the
funeral. Mrs. Janson declared that her little boy was to be
leader—but she gave the leadership to an elder named Berg-
lund until the child should grow up. Presently, however,
Olson returned from the gold fields—with no gold—and
took command, whereupon Mrs. Janson left and became a
Shaker.

During the next three or four years, miracles were
worked. The original forty acres on which they had huddled
the first winter grew to many hundreds. Bricks were constantly burning and houses and buildings going up from
them. All sorts of shops were erected. Flax was raised and
linen sold. Broom corn was produced on contract. Cattle
were improved. Men hired out in droves to build a railroad.
A dining hall, to seat a thousand members, was erected. By
1859, they owned ten thousand acres which they worked in
common—no great amount for almost a thousand people,
but they felt prosperous. Families lived separately, but
drew supplies from the common store. Life was simple.
Education was held to the rudiments and no amusements

allowed. There were daily religious services under those who felt called to preach. Olson tried to force celibacy upon the colony, apparently with no great success, but dissension was roused.

Worse yet, the trustees managed affairs to suit themselves, with no control by the group. One Olof Johnson went out and mortgaged the entire enterprise. The anti-Olsonites, comprising about a third of the group, rose up at this and demanded that they be given a third of the property. Assets of a hundred thousand dollars were set aside to pay off claims and the demanded division of the remaining $750,000 was made. Which was to say, that the Jansonists, as the dissidents called themselves, received about a quarter million dollars in property which they promptly divided among themselves in houses and small farms, for they had had enough of communal living.

Within two years—by 1862—the Olson group had splintered and resplintered several times, and, in bitterness and recrimination, it too divided its property. Meanwhile, when the hundred thousand had failed to cover the debts, a plague of lawsuits came down. Finally, part of the debt was saddled upon the property of each family, and for the next fifteen years the lawsuits continued. Pietism had long been crumbling. Some of the men had fought in the Civil War. Methodism and Adventism were taken up.

Nordhoff, in the 1870's, found Bishop Hill "slowly falling into decay. The houses are still most inhabited; there are several shops; but the larger buildings are out of repair; and business has centered at Galva, five or six miles distant. . . . On the whole, it is a melancholy story." And one, he was sure, which would have ended more happily had there been a strong central authority to keep affairs in order, and some leniency in keeping the young people satisfied. And he remarks shrewdly that had there been no debt, so that everything might have been instantly divided at any time, there might have been little or no demand for division.

But it was the Germans who were conspicuously successful as communitarians. In the 1840's the Rappites were rich and vigorous. The alternately celibate and uxorious Zoarites in Ohio, whom Father Rapp had helped to settle, were making money at manufacturing in their drab, paintless town. Elsewhere various groups of Hutterites, Mennonites, and Moravians were living in one degree or another of communalism or cooperation. The Ephratans were a solid landmark in Pennsylvania. And the public mind easily confused capitalistic German groups, such as the Amish, with the communitarians because of their peculiar dress and stern ways.

In the 40's, there were important additions. Dr. William Keil, for instance, a doctor and faith healer, and by scurrilous report a magician and proclaimed messiah, came into the backwoods of Pennsylvania and ministered in the area of the one-time Rappites who had been lured from Economie by Count Leon and then abandoned. Keil was a big Prussian of commanding appearance, a bit over thirty. He had been a tailor in New York until he received the call to heal and preach. His people denied that he claimed divine status, or even that, as some reports had it, he claimed to be one of the two witnesses of Revelation.

True or not, on such excuse mobs broke up his meetings until he finally took several hundred people to Shelby County, Missouri, in 1844, and established them in communal order, all work and all goods in common, which he believed true Christianity demanded. He was a benevolent if fanatical dictator, and his people, who for the most part seemed to love him, made his whim their law. He soon had a thousand people in his drab town of Bethel, farming or making woolens, shoes, wagons, wheels, whisky, and the like for the market. Each family lived to itself—he did not tamper with marriage or homelife—and took from the community store whatever it needed. No record was kept. It was felt that public opinion would keep down hoggishness.

But after eleven years Keil became restless and de-

cided to go to the Pacific Northwest—and while for fear of
Indians some of the several score who migrated with him
went by ship, taking the Isthmus route, he declared that the
Indians would not hurt him and he went across the plains.
He had promised his son Willie that the boy might go, but
Willie died before the beginning of the journey. Sealing
the body in a lead coffin of whisky, he put it in an open-sided
hearse and it led the little caravan.

At every fort and hamlet—for 1855 was a bad year for
Indian massacres—attempt was made to turn the Keilites
back. But Dr. Keil always merely signaled to the band and
as it played the people boomed out a fresh hymn in German
and they went on. Wagon trains were massacred before and
behind them. Once a whooping mass of braves came down
upon the Keilites. Instead of making useless attempt at
defense, the Germans began singing to the blaring of the
band. The startled Indians drew up, listened to the music,
stared at the coffin in the hearse, and finally left, consider-
ably baffled. A few days later some Indians they had fed
returned several cattle which some other Indians had stolen.

In Oregon, near Portland, they established the town
of Aurora where they became known to travelers on the
main road, which led through the place, as the "Dutch-
towners." They became famous for their cookery and hotel
and for their vast apple orchards. They provided a place of
refuge for young men from their town of Bethel, back in
Missouri, who wished to avoid the Union draft. Though
pacifists, the Aurorans nevertheless organized a spiffy militia "for show."

But with his declining years, "King Keil," as some
of his people began calling him, failed—indeed, refused
flatly, when begged—to train a new leader to follow him.
When he died in 1877, what should have survived at least
as a great stock company simply fell apart in the quarrels
engendered by the attempts of various men to take over.
The enterprise in Missouri was dissolved, too. Unfortunately, the Keilites despised learning—as Dr. Keil bellig-

erently made clear to reporters. They wrote little and published nothing so that all the records concerning them are external.

Far more remarkable than the Keilites are the Amanists. A striking thing about them in their early days was their system of government, which was through a *"Werkzeug,"* an Instrument—an instrument of the Lord, that is. When the *Werkzeug* spoke in official capacity, the people believed he was giving them words directly from God, that God had "seized his tongue"—or hers, as in the case of a famous Instrument who was known among the Amanists as the Old Sister.

In a typical scene, she was speaking one day in the bare church where the men sat on the backless benches on one side of the building and the women on the other. She trembled as she always did in her trances when the Lord had taken over her body and voice. Words came loudly from her mouth: "I, the God of Jacob and of Isaac, have seen that Elder Stuck is proud in his own conceits."

At her shoulder the scribe who constantly followed her, in church or out, to take down any inspired utterances, busily scratched at his tablet. At the end of the year the Great Council would have all her words printed for the ponderings and enlightenment of future generations. It must be remembered that Elder Stuck was convinced that this was God talking:

"Elder Stuck is allowed forty-two dollars yearly for his expenses at the store. Now he wants forty-five because George Froebel has forty-five. Elder Stuck should be ashamed. The conditions are different. I decree he shall be cut to forty—and take warning lest I cut him still more."

Elder Stuck humbly bowed before the *Werkzeug*. Her name was Barbara Heinemann Landmann. Shaking under the trance of Inspiration, eyes closed, she began a hymn. Everyone joined in. Trailed by the scribe, she moved jerkily down the aisle and around the seats to the other aisle where she halted before a young man, eyes still closed.

The singing ceased. She cried, "Friedrich! Friedrich! O, Friedrich!" Indeed it was Friedrich, as the *Werkzeug* had known, for she had eyes other than her physical ones.

Friedrich forced himself to his feet. He was pale. He spoke meekly: "*Ja?*" And he stole a frightened glance toward the other side of the big room toward the girl Minchen. In her black dress and black hood she looked at her hands gripped together in her lap. She was coffin-white.

"I, Jehovah God," cried the *Werkzeug*, "have seen My son Friedrich look longingly at Minchen. And I have seen the minx blush and glance at him with calf eyes when they meet on the path or in the eating room. I say that she was not meant for him nor he for her. Marriage is a bad thing for anyone, for that matter. I command that they two shall get their minds from the lusts of the flesh and attend to My holy business. And moreover Minchen is to be sent to West Amana until I say otherwise. And I say that they shall pray diligently to get the other out of mind and heart. I the Lord God have spoken!"

Friedrich bowed. His lips moved. Finally a croak of submission sounded. He was trembling almost as much as the *Werkzeug* as he sat down. The Old Sister moved around to the women's side:

"Bertha Scheuner, I, Jehovah God, command that you shall be allowed to attend meeting no more until you tear down the vain vine of flowers from your porch. If you want a vine, plant a useful one, like gourds or grapes." . . .

The Amanists were in the stolid, fervent, pietistic tradition. There was no foolishness of democracy. They were a theocracy and for the best of reasons: God had ordered it that way. The wisdom of God was shown in this by the way New Harmony and Icaria and other places had talked themselves to death or hobbled their energies with democracy and vote-taking.

Their eight villages in Iowa lay in an oval from one to three miles apart, but the inhabitants were kept so near home that dialectical differences developed from one settlement to the next in the course of a half century. Only the leaders circulated, and then only for necessary business.

Was a decision necessary for the welfare of the fifteen to eighteen hundred communists? The Great Council of Brethren might make it if it were on a minor, routine point—unless the *Werkzeug* should come along with an inspired veto. On important matters they sent for her at first and waited on the Lord.

The words from her trances were held to have the same degree of authority as the Scriptures, for with logic it was said God would not speak with one validity in 4000 B.C. in the Garden and with another in 1875 in Iowa. The only safe attitude was instant agreement with the *Werkzeug,* and diligent prayer that the heart be brought into line with the pronouncements while the hands were obeying.

The Amanists, "The Community of True Inspiration," the Community being the Church, were come-outers from the Lutheran church which they originally had wished to reform. They were the poverty-stricken fringe which in all congregations, being unable to afford dances and cards and horses, has cried that the rich leaders have seized control and are abandoning the teachings of "the fathers." Thus in turn the Methodists came out of the Anglicans, the Nazarenes out of the Methodist denomination, and now that the Nazarenes have become comfortably well off, the unhappy fringe is pulling out of them to meet in little mission houses which in time will grow steeples and give birth, fifty years from now, to still more mission groups.

And so the contemptible, because poverty-stricken, Inspirationists followed off after leaders named Gruber and Rock in the early 1700's. Attracting an ever-enlarging brotherhood, they made things difficult for themselves by invading Lutheran services and reviling the priests.

Their writings were burned by the executioner in

Zurich. The Inspirationists, male and female, were locked in stocks and pelted by the rabble who, it is recorded, were urged on by the clergy with lusty hoots. Then the sufferers were paraded through the streets, followed by official torturers who riddled their backs with sixty-two lashes each so that the cobbles were splattered with blood.

The sect flourished under martyrdom. Time and persecution cut down the two leaders. A piece of curious calculation survives, showing a preoccupation with mystical sevens and threes:

Gruber had served the Lord "2 times 7 years" when he died. Then "3 times 7" years later Rock died. "The time of his pilgrimage on earth was 10 times 7 or 70 years, 3 months, 3 days. In the year 1707 when he was 4 times 7 years old, he emigrated with Bro. E. L. Gruber from his native [principality]. In the year 1714, when he counted 5 times 7 years, there came to him the gift of the Spirit and of Prophecy and he made until 1742, in 4 times 7 years, over 100 lesser and great journeys in this service. In the year 1728, when he was 7 times 7 years old he lost his faithful brother, E. L. Gruber, and in 1742, when he counted 9 times 7, or 63 years, he ceased to travel into distant countries and spent the remaining 7 years largely at home."

With the death of Rock and with no persecutions to keep the faith hot, a "lukewarmness" set in. The elders, though they were not Instruments, were firmly entrenched. They perpetuated themselves in the selection of successors of their own cast of mind. After seventy years, one Michael Krausert announced that God had appointed him as *Werkzeug*. The jealous elders were slow to accept him but part of the congregations did and schism ensued. Soon one Christian Metz announced that he too had divine inspiration. Krausert said he had received a message that this was true.

Then Barbara Heinemann, a "humble and unlearned servant maid," declared herself gifted with the holy in-breathing. She is remindful of Ann Lee: She was illiterate, she had been put into a spinning mill at eight, she later became a house servant. As a child she was blessed with dreams and visions. In 1818, as she received her inspiration, God indeed "told Brother Krausert He desired to use Barbara as His handmaid."

The elders hedged while permitting her to learn to read and write a little. Then despite Krausert and Metz, a clique of them declared her a false Instrument. Krausert weakened under opposition and fell from the faith under torture by civil officials. The revelations to Metz at last established himself and Barbara as true *Werkzeuge*—Instruments.

However, it chanced that Barbara had an eye for the boys. The communicants were pretty certain that an Instrument should not marry, and that assuredly a female one should not. Nevertheless "Satan tempted her to marry a schoolteacher named George Landmann." The ensuing uproar, plus the promptings of the Lord, grew so strong in the ears of the lovers that they "repented" and did not marry. That is, they didn't until the next year, 1823, when Satan definitely got the upper hand.

Barbara then became a blunt Instrument indeed. God made it clear to her own mind that she was summarily dropped as His *Werkzeug*. What she did not know was that heaven was only keeping her in reserve. Meanwhile, Christian Metz was supreme.

Not that he lacked competition. From time to time charlatans were brazen enough to rise in meeting in the various towns where Metz was accepted and give out messages as Instruments. But Metz was always warned from on high. He promptly denounced such pretenders and got them quashed.

The upsurge of new inspiration moved the people to bring all the old persecutions down upon themselves.

The tolerant prince of Hessen offered them an old nunnery where they might gather into isolation. Metz recollected God had placed that nunnery under a curse when the Moravians lived there. He prayed about it. God said it would be all right for the Inspirationists to move in. Through Metz's mouth He added, "I will be with you under the present circumstances, know and learn ye that my hand can make something out of nothing and nothing out of something. I can bless and curse; I can change a curse into a blessing and a blessing into a curse." He also sent the prince a kind message through Metz. Hesse could not see Metz just then but he returned polite thanks through his valet.

Merchants, artisans, peasants, and factory hands gathered in, eventually forming four associated congregations. They did not yet live from a common purse but there was communal give and take, with differences of former positions in life smoothed out by Christian fellowship. Metz remained the leader. Once he was "laboring"—*i.e.,* was in a trance—for thirteen hours, God speaking through him in a steady torrent of words which came out in rhyme. Anyone who took his hand received a personal stanza of admonishment, approval, or hope.

Military upheavals among the principalities brought demands for armed service and all the old troubles began again. The sufferings of the Inspirationists finally moved God to inspire them to migrate to the United States where during the 1840's they gradually acquired eight thousand acres of the Seneca Indian reservation near Buffalo.

Religious history was repeated: the difficulties of individuals showed the Inspirationists that only by pooling resources and strength might they provide for everyone and preserve their unity and religion. However, they emphasized that they had no social theories to prove—only religious ones.

Outsiders could find it only wonderfully tedious to read of the constant activity of God in the theocracy: "God named the settlements Upper, Middle, and Lower Eben-

Ezer, meaning 'Hitherto God hath helped us.' " Everything was done by the Lord. The Lord did thus and the Lord did so.

The "Ebenezers," as the Inspirationists were promptly nicknamed by their neighbors, became known as good businessmen, fair in their dealings and uncommonly sagacious. And although the 1840's were the decade of rising and dying communes, the Ebenezers established a sound prosperity. Converts across the river in Canada formed a village there of their own.

But all was not smooth. The Indians refused to leave the reservation as they had agreed. By the time the Federal government persuaded them to, the booming town of Buffalo loomed at the community border, and ruffians pestered the religionists. Further, more land would soon be needed and the prosperity of the region, in good part caused by the eight hundred Inspirationists, was making the cost prohibitive.

Christian Metz was happy when a revelation came that they should move west to cheap land. Dissension rose. Some desired to divide everything and cease communism. The Lord then issued an ultimatum, on March 19, 1854, following "a very important revelation" of the previous fall in which He had "expressed His grief and displeasure" over the quarrel. Now He said "it was not His holy will and never should be that communism should be abolished." He added, "As truly as I live, neither through artful devises or skill and diplomacy nor cunning or power of men" should there be such change. This perpetual ultimatum was to cause a deal of inconvenience later.

The grumblers gave in and consumed their excess energies in arguing about removal. The impatient Metz poured forth revelations that Eben-Ezer should be removed to the West. Then the Great Council used up valuable time discussing ways and means. But now Metz had help: After twenty-six years of testing, Barbara Heinemann Landmann had received from God "a little ray of light" and was in a word, despite her marriage, back in grace. Like Metz, she was the Instrument for revelations. Once she and Metz were "in labor" at the same time, giving forth antiphonal pronouncements, turn and turn about, word by word or sentence by sentence. In their exultation, though their eyes were closed they could move about the meeting house without bumping into anything and stop here and there and speak to any person by name.

At least at first, this double authority seems to have led to no great friction. Later, Barbara's interceptive mechanism picked up such a disproportionate amount of restrictive and painful legislation that the people groaned to Metz and he had to take her privately in hand on various occasions. Apparently she deferred to him when there seemed a confusion of revelation.

Now "Metz and three others" were named in a peremptory revelation to follow the human tide to "bleeding Kansas" which the year before had been opened for settlement in a disgraceful Congressional horse trade. A small-scale civil war, prelude to the national conflict, was under way there, Kansas being occupied in deciding under "squatter sovereignty" if the territory should be slave or free.

The committee quickly retreated from there to the more peaceful Iowa where, after some consultation with the folks back home, they bought their first tract of almost twenty thousand acres on the Iowa River, twenty miles southwest of Cedar Rapids, purchasing all the ground between their proposed village sites regardless of the price set by the elated sellers. Nor did they dump their Buffalo villages upon the market in the manner of the Rappites. They sold them gradually as interested buyers were found for an acreage, a woolen mill, soap factory, or large communal dwelling, and trekked to the new location in small groups.

The new home was to be called Bleibe treu—Remain Faithful: "This had been laid into the heart of the Werkzeug, Chr. Metz, who later poured it forth in a song beginning thus:

"Bleibtreu soll der Name sein
Dort in Iowa der Gemein.

"But since it was difficult to express this word or
name in English, it was proposed instead to write the Biblical name Amana, which signifies glaub treu—believe faith-
fully—and had thus a very similar meaning. To this the
Lord gave his approval in an important song which was
poured forth through Christian Metz on September 23,
1855."

There were in fact eighteen stanzas of this important
song. And it should be said that Amana, apparently the
name of a hill in The Song of Solomon, was accented by the
Inspirationists not in the manner to be used by radio an-
nouncers a century later in peddling the food freezers the
Community was to develop, but on the first part: AMana.

Remarkably, no splintering or schism developed during the ten years required for the move, though the people
were separated by half a continent. During this time a young
man in love with "the wrong girl" might very well be sent
back to Eben-Ezer to forget her. But oddly, though marriage
was thought not a good thing, just about everyone did marry
—including Christian Metz as well as Mrs. Landmann. For if
older and wiser heads could not persuade a young couple to
decide on celibacy, marriage was permitted between those
of whom God did not disapprove.

However, the engaged were but little allowed to see
their prospective spouses. The wedding might come at the
end of a year's betrothal if the young man by then happened
to be at least twenty-four. Otherwise they had to wait until
he attained that age, and this led to elopements and consequent expulsions from the Community and the village. In
time the pair might be readmitted. Girls were never permitted to marry outsiders. If a man married a world's person he was expelled for a year and then readmitted if his
wife showed conversion.

Marriage ceremonies were solemn, with the Instruments and elders exhorting the couple "for a long time" concerning their obligations and duties. There followed a modest repast at one of the eating houses, after which the pair visited the home of the bridegroom and then that of the bride. The elders assigned them an apartment, a large sitting room and a bedroom in some home—usually that of one of the parents—with single beds which it was hoped would prevent the mind from straying too far from religious contemplations. The Amanists did not skimp on quarters. Most remarkably for communitarians, they believed that everyone should have opportunity for privacy. Accordingly, as families grew, separate homes were built for them.

Meanwhile, the new couple was regarded as having fallen from a proper spiritual state because of their marriage. They were accordingly "set back" to the children's order in church. Only by piety, devotion, submission to the elders, and general fervency might they work back up. But if they produced a child, this was regarded as fair evidence that they had not been as spiritual as they might have and they were promptly put into the children's room at church again.

Finally all the Inspirationists were in Iowa where they formed the villages of Amana, East Amana, Middle Amana, West Amana, and Amana-under-the-Hill, which is now High Amana. These lie north of the river, and a mile and a half to two miles apart. South of the river are Lower South and Upper South villages. Almost at once a railroad came to the village of Homestead at the edge of the Amana lands. It was apparent that there were too many "hostile spirits" in that town. There was a feeling the Amanists should buy the place and move the worldly inhabitants out. Barbara Landmann sought inspiration "and the Lord in his mercy gave His affirmation." Accordingly, Homestead was acquired.

With the Civil War, the Inspirationists were beset by the Union draft. In Germany they had rebelled from military service. Here, to show their sympathy with the North, they took advantage of the law which allowed them to hire substitutes. Later, there was general feeling that they had done wrong in participating even indirectly. There were also internal troubles because some of the young men voted in county and state elections. "But then we quit because we didn't like the turn politics have taken"—which seems rather a novel reason for not voting. The elders wanted no worldly politics, though, to cause disunity among the Chosen.

Metz died but he had had the satisfaction of seeing his people well settled under God, the Instruments, and the elders. All the rest had but to obey. Each village had its farmlands, shops and mills. Amana products were in demand. Neighboring farmers found a good market for raw materials at the villages. The Germans paid cash and never dealt again with a man who cheated them.

Gradually, on the fringes of each village, houses were built for hired families—and it seems strange that worldly people should have been permitted to live so near. Yet the elders were sure of their power over the young—and help was necessary because the Amanists had to interrupt their work several mornings each week for the prescribed religious meetings. Anyway, the hired men produced more since the average Amanist, as one wryly remarked, took care to do no more than his neighbors.

Always declaring themselves a religious rather than a business enterprise—which made it wonderful on the taxes then and later—the Amanists were chary of accepting new members. Yet, people who heard of their prosperity were always arriving to demand membership. Often these had to be given the means of returning home. A few were admitted at the inspiration of the *Werkzeug,* usually on probation, but sometimes she pronounced one fit for instant membership.

The Amanists prospered, each reminded often by his catechism and the Old Sister that he was "but a maggot." There were periodic upheavals when everyone was forced to confess his sins. The young people were inclined to reticence in this but there was no let-up until the elders were satisfied there was nothing more to be wrung out of them. The printed record of one of these colony-wide bouts, and of the feast called the Lord's Supper at the end of the days-long upheaval, fills almost three hundred pages.

Children went to school the year round. They recited aloud in chorus. During work periods little boys and girls learned to knit and big ones went to jobs to learn trades. Formal study was limited largely to the three R's. It was said that advanced learning would but make the young restless. The Community had no need for learned people. What one needed was to be able to study his Bible and his catechism and to do a little figuring.

A bit of broadening was tried in permitting newspapers and magazines to come in, but when the grace of God was withdrawn from the Community, as evidenced in hardship, the Old Sister received a revelation that it was because of the worldly reading. She put the people back to their Bibles, except that trade journals were still allowed to come. Oddly, anyone who felt the urge to write a hymn or poem, even on a mundane matter, so long as there be a pious moral, was encouraged to do so. If considered good, it might be placed in the next published Amana book.

Boys and girls were discouraged from talking with the other sex on the way to school. Young men were warned away from young women as "a highly dangerous magnet and magical fire." In the same tradition, the sexes ate apart in the community kitchen-eating halls which were scattered through the villages, with from fifteen to thirty persons eating at each, and with the women taking turns at kitchen work. At mealtime, women hastened about with baskets for the sick and for mothers of babies under two who ate at home. At meeting, each sex had its own entrance "to prevent silly conversation and trifling conduct."

As was usual in German communes, there was a five-meal-a-day schedule, including snacks at nine and three. Tobacco was freely used as were meat and coffee, but each person had his "wine ticket," a man being allowed a quart a week from the cellars under the meeting house and women and children half as much. There were general stores where each family received from twenty-five to fifty dollars credit yearly, purchases being entered in a little book carried by the customer. At the end of the year one might do rather as he chose with any of the credit he had "saved." However, there was little to do with it and sometimes great boxes of charity goods were made up from the savings and sent to the needy in American cities.

There must have been private longings for fripperies, with the added fear that the Instrument would know of the covetings. One woman confessed in after years that as a girl she somehow came by some earrings which she wore in a rather empty and wicked pleasure when she could hide in her room.

Children learned to read music and to chant the tuneless hymns in the manner of a former age, but musical instruments theoretically were not allowed. Yet, it was winked at if someone made a simple one, such as a flute. Men dressed at first in "fall front" breeches and collarless coats, but those who had to meet "the world" at the stores, railroad depot, or grain elevator dressed more and more in the world's garments. If a young man bloomed out in such, he was less and less rebuked, for it was noticed that by the time he was thirty he would likely be wearing "colony trousers" of his own desire. Beards were grown. Mustaches were a sign of vanity and were ruled out.

The women dressed in loose, drab garments, with "shoulder shawls" to smooth out the form. The smallest girls had the same style, and all females wore a little hood on the back of the head. For church, the same sort of clothing was worn, but for best taste it was black from hood to shoe. Unlike the neighboring "hook and eye" Amish people, commonly called "the Hooks," with whom they were confused in the popular mind, the Amanists did not abjure buttons.

Church services were ordinarily simple—a little singing, a little praying, some reading from the Bible or the voluminous printed saying of the Instruments, a quiet talk from an elder, perhaps an inspired utterance from the *Werkzeug*. There were no preachers, or if any felt called they were still expected to labor through the week in field or shop. The women did the chief reading and praying one day, the men the next.

Sunday afternoon was the high tide of the week for any restive young. There was respite from school, church, and work. Walks were permitted. Girls went in one direction, boys in another. "Perhaps they meet in the course of the walk," an elder admitted, "but it is not allowed." Thus in 1874, while the Old Sister yet had nine years of her rule remaining.

The majority of the young people who left the colony returned in time, seeking readmission; and this was usually granted, at least after Barbara Landmann died. They found the world no simple place in which to survive. Besides, as one declared, there was "nothing fit to eat in the world." Amana was not such a bad place, after all. There, there was friendship, security in old age, and no bothersome business of having to think. The elders did that. All the common man had to do was his duty—"to have heartfelt love and devotion" toward the brethren, and "child-like obedience toward God and the elders," as the catechism said.

Further: "Do not esteem yourself wise. Suppress your supposed wit and cleverness. Gladly give up your plans and submit to the advice of others. You are dust and shall again become dust and food for worms. Do not love beauty nor dainty dress." Good Inspirationists were to be quiet, uncritical of others, to "desire nothing," nor covet. They were to remember that God was watching each act of each moment. They were to transact no business of any sort—particularly with worldly people. They were to avoid "dinners, weddings, feasts, entirely; at the best there is sin."

Still, there were simple pleasures. Visitors remarked upon a generally happy outlook, nor did the children seem sad and cowed as in many communes. Youngsters were taught manners at school and would crowd up to shake hands with a friendly stranger until so many outsiders came to stare and goggle as to constitute a nuisance. At Christmas, children received small presents, though no trees were allowed, and on Easter Monday they were given colored eggs.

At last the Old Sister died. Without an Instrument, it fell to the First Brethren and the Great Council to preserve the old ways. Nevertheless, things were changed by littles until by the turn of the century most of the men dressed in worldly garments—though the women and even the tiniest girls were kept in their little black hoods and sad dresses. Young men organized "study clubs," but formal education was held to low level. Some boys dared form an orchestra and as long as they played quietly they were overlooked, but they were not allowed to give public performances. Social life still consisted in attending church eleven times weekly. Exclusion from meeting was thus a potent punishment which kept down possible incipient rebellion.

Came the automobile, and in it thousands of tourists in the season when the lotus bloomed along the six-mile length of the canal which had been led from the river. In other seasons, they came to stare just at the Inspirationists. In their odd clothing, the young Germans were more and more embarrassed—for it chanced that they were staring back and could not help noticing and liking what all the world but themselves was doing. The radio was developed— and while some elders had purchased automobiles for business use when the chief motive power of the villages was still the ox, there was no excuse for anyone to have a radio.

Things changed still more in the booming '20's. People who might not feel exactly like working, and who must have their meals brought from the eating house month in and out, still might feel like making a quaint apron or whittling out a toy to sell half openly to a tourist. Old heads complained that when anyone did that and put the coin into his own pocket, communism had ceased.

Some Amanists even contrived to find excuse to go to worldly towns and put money into the world's banks. Money from the sale of fruit from a tree in the back yard. Money saved from a cash allowance for maintaining one's drab, unpainted house. Here and there someone found courage to buy a radio, or other worldly goods, and the rebuking elders could find no practical way to stop such heresies when exclusion from meeting would not do it. A young woman might dare appear in something besides the strict Amana garb—or leave off her "shoulder shawl" and let the world learn the startling fact that she possessed a bosom. She might adorn herself with a string of beads—and nothing was done about it as long as she still put on the costume of 1720 to go to church.

Nevertheless, Amana was still strongly Amana in appearance and spirit. Women lullabied their babies and grandbabies in German. Sturdy urchins and black-capped little maidens still played their round-games to German doggerel. Sleepy merchants still saw the Community stores run deeply into the red every year—but the deficit of those and of other departments could always somehow be made up from the profits of the woolen mills—or if those did not return a profit this year, then perhaps the national sale of smoked hams or cure-all patent medicines would.

With the depression of the thirties, a deficit piled up so rapidly in the over-all operations that bankruptcy and dissolution threatened to come in a matter of months. Back at Buffalo, God had given an unalterable order that communism must never cease among the Inspirationists. However, a strong clique began agitating for re-forming into a stock company which they argued would enable Amana to survive. Sentiment grew in that direction for the new generation did not remember Christian Metz, nor the Old Sister who had been dead forty-nine years. They saw a greater measure of freedom in the proposed plan. There was in short a vast disenchantment with the infallibility of the

elders and a weariness with the dronings from the recorded
words of the Instruments which one had to hear eternally in
church.

Lacking an Instrument—though aware that God
might raise up a new one at any moment—each person
sought for personal inspiration and voted his convictions in
the election which was held to determine whether God had
repented of His order that they should never drop communism and if they should reorganize. And so "the Great
Change" was voted in.

With shrewd wisdom, the community put an outsider
in charge of industry and business with dictatorial powers.
The business became "The Amana Society." Organized separately was "The Amana Church Society." Church and
state had divided. Theocracy was gone. Everyone received
shares in the business enterprises—a voting share, plus common stock in proportion to his years of service. The old and
feeble were provided for but others who wanted to eat
Amana food were required to work in field or factory or to
purchase, under liberal terms, one of the many small businesses. People who had not felt like working were inspected
by the manager. Those who to him seemed able were given
the choice of producing or going hungry—for the storekeep-
ers, whose losses would now come from their own pockets,
were not giving credit to people of no prospects.

But soon the grudgingness was forgotten and people
generally sought to earn all they could for a heady new
power had been discovered—the power of cash, backed by
that of the down payment. And money was plentiful, for
with the discharge of hired help there was a saving of $5000
each month in the payroll. Houses bloomed with paint.
Ornamental plantings appeared. Comfortable furniture was
bought.

Sidewalks and streets proper for cars were demanded,
and had. Schools were affiliated with those of the state, and
athletic and debating teams organized. Plays were produced
—the first ever seen by the Inspirationists. The styles of the

world were brought in. Soon most girls and women looked like those anywhere, though for a time even the most modish still dressed for church in the old costume.

Another great discovery was made in the closing of the "eating houses"—with home cooking it was learned that what had been supposed an economical way of dining had been much more costly than when women began cannily pinching pennies in their own kitchens.

Such was the Great Change and it is perhaps the significant point in the story of Amana. Men discovered that they liked to be kings in their own yards and houses, with no paternal elder to interfere. They received their wages and looked forward to their dividends from their stock. Production increased and old markets were held with the competition which might be offered under the new efficiency. Indeed, one business became so large—that of refrigerating equipment—that the Society decided it were best to sell it, and this was done.

Still a quaintness survives with ornamental if utilitarian plantings of grapevines around the houses as in the Old Sister's day. Still conscientious care is given to making things, whether the fine and lovely woolens, or the toys of some old German artisan, or the widely-sold bread.

Amana the Villages will be here a long time, though communalism is gone from them. The Community of True Inspiration, which is Amana the Church, will also be here a long time. As it was two and a half centuries ago, it is the custodian of the individual and village consciences.

The great Archangel's trump shall sound
(While twice ten thousand thunders roar),
Tear up the graves, and cleave the ground,
And make the greedy sea restore.

The greedy sea shall yield her dead,
The earth no more her slain conceal;
Sinners shall lift their guilty heads,
And shrink to see a yawning hell.

We, while the stars from heaven shall fall,
And mountains are on mountains hurled,
Shall stand unmoved amidst them all,
And smile to see a burning world.

The earth and all the works therein
Dissolve, by raging flames destroyed;
While we survey the awful scene
And mount above the fiery void.

—Millerite Hymn Book, 1843

CHAPTER SIXTEEN

ADONAI—SHOMO AND
CELESTA

SEVENTH MONTH, TENTH DAY, YEAR OF JUBILEE!

PERHAPS the most incredible spectacle of the incredible '40's was the Millerite fever. The intellectuals were having their binge in Transcendentalism, Universalism, Unitarianism, the ascendancy of scientific outlook, and nullification of the Bible. Spiritualism seized the minds of hordes of all social strata, from the Shakers on up and down. Fourierism had its day. In religious communitarianism, John Humphrey Noyes deliciously horrified the country with his Perfectionists and their "community of wives."

For the rest of New England, and indeed for hordes as far west as Ohio, Millerism roused what was perhaps the most widespread millennial hysteria of the Western world since the year 1000 when the end had been expected

299

throughout Christendom by a broad segment of the people, from serf to philosopher.

Even as is true today, prophets in Miller's era arrived at the date of holocaust by developing a chronology based upon the figures mentioned in the books of Daniel, Ezekiel, John's Gospel, Matthew, Revelation, or even Leviticus. They always ended neatly with a date just a short time ahead.

The method involves taking some number of days mentioned in a prophetic passage—such as the 2300 days of Daniel—and, holding that each day represents a year, adding and subtracting various other numbers of years. These years may be some of Daniel's other numbers, or such a likely one as the age of Jesus at the time of the Crucifixion. They seem invariably, too, to include the date of some "great event," such as the fall of Rome, or a crucial date from the life of a captain or king, religious or secular, whom Daniel or John clearly had in mind in speaking of "the ten-horned beast," or "the beast rising out of the sea, having seven heads," or "the exceeding Great Horn." If Napoleon be "the exceeding Great Horn," and if the date of Waterloo won't quite work out, then possibly Napoleon's birth or death date, or the debacle in Moscow is the indicated one. If none will work, then the Little Corporal obviously is not the exceeding Great Horn, and some other—perhaps Marlborough?—must be lit upon.

In such manner, many dates have been arrived at as the year of doom. Jehovah's Witnesses just now have settled upon 1984 as the deadline for the Battle of Armageddon. A prophet wandering through the Ozarks during the last Great War had charts which, worked out in various ways, invariably came to 1945, and with Hitler rather than Nebuchadnezzar —who was prominent in Miller's charts—as the personage actually meant by the reference in Daniel. Unsubstantiated —but undoubted—information now is that this prophet's date has been moved up to 1959.

Edward Everett Hale dryly remarked that "the mathematical instincts of New England" especially approved of all this neat business with biblical numbers in the early 1800's. The great general interest of the day is reflected in the mention of two female millennial prophets in Whittier's "Snow-Bound." One of these was Lady Hester Stanhope. The wealthy granddaughter of Lord Chatham, and niece of William Pitt, she went to the Holy Land, built herself a villa on Mount Lebanon, smoked a four-foot-long pipe, and procured two white Arab horses which she planned would be ridden into Jerusalem by Jesus and herself after the descent. She expected that to occur at her estate.

The other, Miss Harriet Livermore, was of similarly impeccable tribal connections, her father being a Massachusetts judge and Congressman. She went about the States preaching of the Soon-Coming, and wandered restlessly abroad. Whittier, who knew her with mixed emotions for many years, conveniently has her stranded in "Snow-Bound" with his family during the blizzard. He mentions her penchant for travel, and her visit to Lady Hester:

> *Unmarked by time, and yet not young,*
> *The honeyed music of her tongue*
> *And words of meekness scarcely told*
> *A nature passionate and bold. . . .*
> *She sat among us, at the best,*
> *A not unfeared, half-welcome guest. . . .*
> *And under low brows, black with night*
> *Rayed out at times a dangerous light;*
> *The sharp heat-lightnings of her face*
> *Presaging ill to him whom Fate*
> *Condemned to share her love or hate. . . .*
> *She blended in a like degree*
> *The vixen and the devotee. . . .*
> *Brows saintly calm and lips devout*
> *Knew every change of scowl and pout;*
> *And the sweet voice had notes more high*
> *And shrill for social battle-cry. . . .*
> *Through Smyrna's plague-hushed thoroughfares,*

Up sea-set Malta's rocky stairs,
Gray olive slopes of hills that hem
  Thy tombs and shrines, Jerusalem,
Or startling on her desert throne
The crazy Queen of Lebanon
With claims fantastic as her own . . .
She watches under Eastern skies
  With hope each day renewed and fresh,
  The Lord's quick coming in the flesh
Whereof she dreams and prophesies! . . .

Miss Livermore settled upon the date of 1847 for the
end, despite the Millerite fever for 1843. On various occasions she spoke in the House of Representatives, reputedly
with Cabinet members and the President in the large audiences which turned out.

In fact, she wished Congress to round up all the
American Indians and send them to Palestine, for they, she
said, were descendants of the lost tribes of Israel and it
seemed but fair that they should enjoy at first hand the benefits of the millennial reign.

Something seems to have gone wrong with the project. Miss Livermore went to Palestine in behalf of it, and reported to Whittier that she and Lady Hester Stanhope fell
into a quarrel when the latter would not agree to her riding
one of the white horses in the event that Jesus should arrive
during her sojourn. Others say she imagined the incident, as
she did not meet Lady Hester.

Other prophets were crying the end for still other
years in the '40's—but it was Millerism which seized the popular imagination. William Miller, born in 1782 in Vermont,
is ordinarily referred to as an "unassuming," uneducated
farmer of Low Hampton, New York, where indeed he lived
out his adult life. Married in 1803, he produced a large family, drifted from piety into free thought, served in the War
of 1812, and abruptly and with some embarrassment returned to piety and orthodox evangelical Protestantism. Al-

ways bookish and philosophic, when he fell afoul of the biblical prophecies it was headlong.

From the Bible he dug the doctrine that upon the arrival of Jesus the world would burn "as a scroll" with all the wicked; that then Jesus would return to it with the "saints" who had been caught up out of the holocaust and would reign gloriously in "the new earth" for a thousand years. Then Satan and the wicked would be released from where they had been shut up, would be defeated in a great war, and would go down to the lake of fire—and from it the smoke of the tormented wicked would rise forever.

Clearly there was nothing without purpose in the Bible—including the prophecies, the hints, the numbers. Finally Miller discovered that many combinations of figures would work out to the date of 1843. For instance, in Leviticus xxvi, 23-24, the Lord speaks of punishing Israel for its sins "yet seven times." A "time" (said Miller) is a year. For some reason, perhaps one having to do with Jewish chronology, he calculated years at 360 days each. And each day in each year stands for a year. Therefore:

7 x 360		2520 years
Counting from Birth of Christ	A.D.	0
This gives the year	A.D.	$\overline{2520}$
Subtract the date of the first captivity in Babylon, at which time the punishment was to commence	B.C.	677
End of the world	A.D.	$\overline{1843}$

Beginning about 1818, Miller spent five years working on this sort of thing, conning the Bible endlessly. He was enormously disturbed as one chronology after another produced the same date. (There is no record of the hundreds of chronologies he may have toyed with which ended with other dates.) He was concerned for the world, but he was highly diffident about mentioning his discovery to others, partly from natural modesty, partly because he feared mockery for his religious turnabouts.

However, the Lord troubled him until, through clear omens, he knew he was called to speak. He was so full of his subject, so thoroughly acquainted with the Bible, so able to counter every objection and to mention and refute other logical ones his audience had not thought of, that the little congregation he addressed one Sunday was electrified and carried away. Invitations came to him from other churches, usually Methodist or Baptist, and as his fame spread he spent all his time traveling about with his gospel while his sons, who seem not to have been among his converts, cared for his farm. Such collections of money as may have been made for him—and he preferred to pay his own frugal way as far as possible—appear to have been negligible.

Various doom-prophets had postponed the burning of the world until the end of the Thousand Years, or had canceled it entirely. But part of Miller's great appeal was in the engulfment of the world, and that fairly soon, in fire, with only the Millerites being caught up ahead of the flames to a "marriage supper in the skies." All who doubted the clear prophecy and failed to make the indicated preparation would be lost. But Millerites were guaranteed, because they did believe, that they would live until Jesus should come and thus never experience death.

"Whole congregations" were converted. Several preachers took up the cause and traveled in Miller's name. By 1832 the prophet, whose quiet, unprepossessing manner always disappointed new congregations until he began speaking, had acquired quite a prose style:

> I am satisfied that the end of the world is at hand. The evidence flows in from every quarter.—"The earth is reeling to and fro like a drunkard." Is the harvest over and past? If so, soon, very soon, God will arise in his anger, and the vine of the earth will be reaped. *See! See!*—the angel with his sharp sickle is about to take the field! See yonder trembling victim fall before his pestilential breath! High and low, rich and poor,

trembling and falling before the appalling grave, the dreadful cholera.

Hark!—hear those dreadful bellowings of the angry nations! It is the presage of horrid and terrific war. Look!—look again! See crowns, and kings, and kingdoms trembling to the dust! See lords and nobles, captains and mighty men, all arming for the bloody, demon fight! See the carniverous fowls fly screaming through the air! *See*—see these signs! Behold, the heavens grow black with clouds; the sun has veiled himself; the moon, pale and forsaken, hangs in middle air; the hail descends; the seven thunders utter loud their voices; the lightnings send their vivid gleams of sulphurous flames abroad; and the great city of the nations falls to rise no more forever and forever! At this dread moment, look! The clouds have burst asunder; the heavens appear; the great white throne is in sight! Amazement fills the Universe with awe! He comes! He comes! Behold the Savior comes!—lift up your heads, ye saints—He comes! He comes! He comes! He comes!

Millerism received an enormous impetus when, before dawn of November 13, 1833, there came a "rain of fire" over much of New England—what surely has been one of the greatest of all meteorite displays of recorded times. For an hour or more "the stars fell out of the heavens" in such continuous torrent as to waken people and to light up rooms so that watches might be read.

Surely this was a sign of the end! But despite even other heavenly wonders, Millerism remained a rural thing for the next six or seven years, and one which created no overwhelming fanfare. After all, 1843 was still quite a little time away and it was difficult to maintain fever of effective degree for so long. But then there came the terrible drouths of the late '30's, with the worst the country had known doing massive damage in 1838. It was followed by the worst winter until then recorded, the effects accentuated by empty streams

and dry wells and drouth-stricken granaries. The hand of
the Lord was further seen in the devastating money panics
which crushed whole countrysides.

All this Miller took to his fire as potent fuel—but still
there can be little doubt that the movement would never
have become the vast thing that it did without the Reverend
Joshua V. Himes who got hold of it in 1839 and, while acknowledging Miller as the anointed prophet, very nearly
took Adventism away from him. Under Himes, Millerism
went to town, both literally and figuratively.

Soon Boston and Philadelphia were having wild pro-
tracted Millerite meetings, and temples were built. Other
staid cultural centers of New England were invaded. Adventist literature was showered upon the world. Enormous
sums of money were collected—but there seems to be no
truth in the tales of the enrichment of Himes and other
"elders," for, also, enormous sums were spent and none of
the elders ended in affluence. Nevertheless, Himes's reputation for high living became such that a newspaper cartoon
showed the Boston temple "going up," as the expression
had come to be, with Miller seated atop it and hordes of
happy saints looking out of the windows, while from amid
the flames below Himes extended supplicating hands. But
Satan held his coattails, and the caption was "You must stay
with me, Joshua V."

The spiritual descendants of the Millerites—the various Adventist groups who view Saturday as a holy day—have
for a solid century expended a great deal of ink and vocal
and emotional energy declaring that neither Miller nor
Himes nor the other elders set an exact date for the burning
—only the year. It is as if they protest too much, for certainly
they did not raise any objection to the date. But the whole
thing is a trivial point when compared with the admitted
profundities of the prophet which have for a century been
swallowed without chewing.

Certainly from some source and by some chemistry
the Millerites came into universal agreement that the joyous

time was to be April 23. Adventist activity increased as the day neared. Millerite campaigners increased their exertions. Staid New England congregations of Unitarians and Episcopalians watched the camp-meeting excesses with incredulity, irritation, and disgust. In some places, mobs stoned or egged noisy Adventists.

In other places, Adventists more quietly prepared for the end. Some gave their property away to show their faith in its uselessness. Others sold their goods to liquidate their debts and to support the movement. Poor people called their bound-out children in from their masters in order that the family might all "go up" together. Some went about making last minute pleas to unconverted friends.

Even more heat has been generated in Adventist publishing houses over the matter of "ascension robes," to be worn in the "going up," than over whether Miller set the exact day. For some reason beyond ordinary understanding, this is an incredibly sore point—but there can be no doubt in a disinterested mind that generally speaking such robes, usually of white but occasionally of black to show humility, were prepared and worn as a very natural piece of symbolism. A similarly sore point is whether the Millerites ascended to high places to await the Coming—and be it said that every Millerite expected the point of the Arrival to be within the circle of his own vision.

In the early 1920's, Clara Sears, who had long lived in the cooled hotbed of the old Millerite culture, and who had written scholarly books, decided as a historian and as a sympathetic student of Adventism to see what she could learn on these matters. Advertisements in New England papers brought her an avalanche of letters from people who in childhood had been in families or neighborhoods of Millerites—and indeed from some who had been adults at the time of the "going up" and who remembered both robes and high places. Still living was one old lady who freely confessed that she had made many such robes, and her picture is in Miss Sears' book, *Days of Delusion*, published by a staid and irreproachably conscientious firm, which gives many of these letters.

One congregation supplied itself with large baskets in which to sit for the trip into the air. One Believer painted his buggy afresh, just in case Jesus should require transportation. People mourned for their faithful animals which must die in the flames. A neighbor of Miss Sears' grandfather came to him and begged him to repent while he still could— and in token of that, her unconverted grandfather helped keep the man from want the rest of his life since he had given his property away.

The joyous day came. Some congregations met at their churches, or by neighborhoods in homes to fast and pray and await the end. One group gathered on Gallows Hill at Salem where the witches had died. Others sought other high places, either symbolically or, as non-believers liked to say, to make it handier for them "to go up." In Boston, the "saints" gathered into the Millerite temple which they believed would be taken up with them in it—a temple not yet completed but insured, only a few months before, for a year, against fire! All up and down New England, people, following the example of Zaccheus, climbed into trees, and in the case of at least one old man there was later enormous difficulty, involving the entire neighborhood, in getting him down after he had become "cast" from long perching there.

Cemeteries were popular places for gatherings, that night of April 23, since people wished to be near their friends who were to rise, so that they might thus go up together, or if worse came to worst, say goodbye. Now, Millerites had been promised eternal life in the flesh—but in 1840, three years before the expected holocaust, Miller had resigned himself to die from typhoid fever, but recovered, and what must have later been some embarrassing letters by him from those days have survived. For years, in fact, Millerites had been dying, which indicated hidden weaknesses, but their living relatives still had hope for their salvation. During the last few days of the dispensation, dying saints were in places left unburied so that when the resurrection came they would not find themselves under six feet of New England dirt.

Here and there, the night of the 23rd, Millerites were frightened or awed or sent into rejoicing by distant fires—and terrible frights were dealt non-Millerites by those same fires, as Miss Sears records. One of her correspondents reported that her unbelieving family went out into the snow to watch a glow that lighted all the sky some miles away—and after it began dying down the hired girl suddenly recollected that she had left her new teeth in the house. And what, she demanded, much upset, would God have thought of her had she suddenly been summoned before him without her teeth!

The tricks and unfunny jokes which should have been expected—the blowing of trumpets, and such—by unbelievers, were perpetrated, and sometimes with spectacular results, for the Millerites were at breaking pitch as they watched the heavens from their windows, their yards, their hilltops.

But morning approached. The sun rose. The night was over. There was poverty to be faced, and the ridicule of the world, and the stunning realization that somebody had erred. Many nonbelievers, doubtless including some ready to repent just in case, had gathered to watch the Adventist groups and they often could not contain their hilarity. In the following days, the common greeting to the stunned Believers was, "Why, is that you? I thought you went up the night the world burned!"

Many began saying well, the date was really just to be in April, and the 23rd had been the logical time. Surely the end would come before the month was out—and then the mockers would receive their deserts. But at last the fatal month was entirely gone. Himes had to speak or lose control of the movement which still showed possibilities of life. What was he to say? No one knows how many preliminary

copies and what bales of logic he may have struggled through
—but what he came up with, in the columns of *The Midnight
Cry* after the middle of May, was that it was not the Adventists
but their enemies who had spread the word that the 23rd
was the date!

Stunned old Prophet Miller, who had not given away
his farm which was being busily attended by his sons, re-ex-
amined his figures, and suddenly it occurred to him that because he had not used Hebrew chronology he was a year off!
After all, the next year was the Jewish Year of Jubilee, and
that was further proof that the Advent, which was to occur
in such a year, was to be then. This was the clinching point.
It *had* to be in 1844.

Everywhere the Millerites seized upon this. And
again a new date went round—October 20, 1844, which, in
"Jewish chronology" was the tenth of the seventh month.
Miller and Himes, rushing everywhere to preach, decried
this setting of a date, but everywhere the Adventist slogan
became, "Seventh month, tenth day, year of Jubilee!" Street
urchins and non-believing wags chanted it; it became the
catchword of the day.

A little later, Jewish rabbis began pointing out that
the next year of Jubilee was not 1844, but was some quarter
century away. The Millerites were taken aback but for a
moment. Then they retorted, "Well, its God's Jubilee if not
the Jews'!" and they continued their preparations. The argument had collapsed, but they kept the result of it most tena-
ciously. Their fields lay unplowed and unplanted in the summer of '44. They subsisted however they could, from truck
patches, the charity of new Adventists who had not ruined
themselves in '43, and from day labor.

Miller and Himes hurried home from Ohio as the
eagerly awaited moment neared, each still urging people not
to set their hearts on the 20th, and indeed reminding everyone that it was not the Jewish year of Jubilee. They would
have done better to save their breath. Then Himes received

a letter from Miller who was at Low Hampton, and who had been at the mercy of various "elders." It appears in *The Midnight Cry* for October 12, 1844:

> Dear Bro. Himes:
> I see a glory in the seventh month which I never saw before. . . . Thank the Lord, O my soul! Let Bro. Snow, Bro. Storrs, and others be blessed for their instrumentality in opening my eyes! I am almost home. Glory! Glory! Glory! I see that the time is correct; yes, my brother. . . . Oh, the glory I have seen today. . . . My soul is so full I cannot write. My doubts and fears and darkness are all gone. . . . I will shout when the King of Kings comes. Methinks I hear you say: "Bro. Miller is now a fanatic!" Very well—call me what you please. I care not—Christ will come on the seventh month and bless us all. . . . Then I shall see him— and be like Him—and be with Him forever; yes, forever and ever!
>
> William Miller

Himes too was suddenly carried away by the excitement he had generated. Said he, in *The Midnight Cry:* "We are shut up in the conviction [that is, he was] that the tenth day of the seventh month must usher in the glorious appearing of our great God and our Saviour Jesus Christ. . . . J. V. Himes."

There were new "signs of the times," too. For instance, in Connecticut a woman had died and come back to life and had lived a hundred twenty days without food. And, she said, she would "tarry so" until Jesus came. "You may talk about superstition," said the *Cry,* "but he must be madly unbelieving who does not see and feel that the finger of God is in this thing."

The fiasco of 1843 was repeated. This was enough for many, and in bitter disillusion they turned to other excitements. But there were many who "could not believe the Bible was wrong." What, then, was the explanation of the failure of the prophecy?

While poor Prophet Miller lay eaten up with plagues of boils and carbuncles, the answer was discovered to be that the "great change" was not even supposed to have taken place on earth, but in heaven, and that indeed it had occurred there on the dot of October 20! Miller, being human and earth-minded, had made what was merely a natural and a relatively unimportant mistake.

The world, in short, was in a new dispensation—in the millennium, the thousand years. Some Adventists said, moreover, that it was "a Sabbath" of that length, and that hence they would never work again. What became of them is not recorded. Splinter groups formed to contend for points which seemed worthwhile to them, and some five or six of these groups, each claiming to be the true vine, still exist as national congregations.

It might well have been expected that in the great decade of communalism, groups of Millerites should draw together after the grand fiasco to form colonies. But for whatever reason—perhaps utter poverty of goods was one— this occurred but belatedly. It was in 1861 that one of Miller's elders, a former Quaker named Frederick Howland, established his "Adonai-Shomo" colony—the name meant "The Lord is Here"—at Athol and later at Petersham, Massachusetts.

The fluctuating group of a dozen to thirty members lived in a unitary house on eight hundred forty acres of land, said the Lord's prayer night and morning as "a sacrifice," observed Saturday as a holy day, and, since they were in the millennium, lived eternally in the flesh until, one by one, they died off. Howland went rather early, in fact, when in a runaway he was thrown from a wagon and his head crushed.

There was momentary excitement later when a hopeful gentleman came along, announcing that God had sent him as leader, and, when accepted, tried to institute bizarre sex practices for which they had him indicted by the grand jury. After that, a member named Richards became leader and in 1896, when all the other old people had died and the young ones had left, the latter, as heirs, sued Richards on the ground that he had taken the property for his own use. The courts sustained them and crushed the charter, but in a forced sale the $4390 the estate brought did little except pay Richards' debts.

The other Adventist colony which has survived in history is of interest because of the massive fixation for leadership of its founder, a Millerite preacher named Peter Armstrong, and because of the martydom through which he put his family. After the debacle of 1844, Armstrong felt that the faithful should gather together "in the wilderness" to await the Lord's coming. But the faithful did not seem interested in gathering in the wilderness. Nevertheless, led by heavenly visions, and convinced that he was selected to begin preparing a place for the 144,000 who were to be saved, Armstrong began looking for the predestined spot.

In 1852 he found it in an almost inaccessible area in the mountains of Sullivan County, Pennsylvania, ten miles in the hinterlands beyond the last hut. He knew, despite the drawbacks the place presented, that this was the intended Eden, for he received a warning from heaven not to look for "a more eligible situation." God, he said, could sustain the 144,000 on rocky hillsides as well as in "fat valleys."

He bought twenty-five hundred acres and, lacking other help, pitched in with his wife and seven children to clear ground and provide shelter for the future occupants of his heaven—which indeed he named Celesta. It was not easy to bring in such needed materials, provisions, and equipment as could not be found or produced on the spot. For: "If it were necessary," wrote one man who visited there, "for God's people to hide from the world to prepare for heaven, I know of no more secret place than the one chosen by Armstrong."

For nine years the Armstrongs labored, clearing land,

reclearing it as sprouts took it, and trying to farm while putting up a sawmill and cutting lumber and building houses and outbuildings. Four dwellings and some barns of sorts were erected. Rains gutted sloping fields, and gathering torrents stripped off plowed topsoil in low places.

Finally Richards was broke. He had spent "forty dollars an acre to clear the land; and it was worth about five dollars an acre after it was cleared." Nevertheless, he had no thought of giving up. He was in wide correspondence with prospective members, and it is possible that some of them sent him a little money. At any rate, he hung on, and in 1861, as the Civil War began, a new member or two appeared. Others came in the next two or three years, but few stayed very long and there were never more than a dozen, besides the Armstrongs, at one time.

Armstrong nominally made all residents equal partners in everything. Someone must have brought a bit of cash. Certainly, in some way funds materialized for the printing of three thousand copies of "The Day Star of Zion" to be sent to prospective members. It contained letters from his correspondents and communications from those at the moment at Celesta. One member, acknowledging that people might well have heard of the poverty of the place and the soil, still begged those who would "escape God's judgments to forsake the world and flee to the mountains; neither look back but remember Lot's wife. The objection against the feasibility of 144,000 subsisting here is a libel on God's power, and an ignoring of past examples. If this be God's work there need be no fear; if it is not, it will soon fall of its own weight."

For a long time a difficulty had been that Armstrong could not make people believe that he was offering them anything they did not already have. Since Adventists were living in the millennial dispensation, they were already among the 144,000 who would not taste death. The prophet lacked persuasive fire to make them feel that their salvation depended further on an ingathering at Celesta. Moneyed

Adventists had no desire to come there; ne'er-do-wells knew that they would not be supported unless they shared in the incessant labor that was required for the barest "cornbread living" from the soil of the new Eden.

But then there was a change—uncharitably attributed by some to the increasingly ghastly war which, while distant from New England, nevertheless indicated God's displeasure. Interest in Celesta began increasing among Adventists until "hundreds were ready to sell their property" and go there. No doubt the "Day Star" had some effect toward this. But those who arrived were quickly disillusioned by the primitive conditions and by Armstrong's lack of ability as a leader, although he was admittedly earnest and well-meaning.

Another uncharitable accusation was that a remarkable transaction he made in 1864 was simply a move to avoid the paying of taxes. He and Mrs. Armstrong deeded the place "to Almighty God" that it "might be subjected to bargain and sale by man's cupidity no more forever." This document was recorded at the county seat.

Further, "as representing God's people worshiping at Celesta," Armstrong wrote to the Pennsylvania legislature, pointing out that they had "resolved to peaceably retire from the entanglements of the outside world," and had, "in the name of the omnipotent Jehovah, renounced all allegiance to earthly governments," and that they intended, "in the face of an unbelieving world to gather and make a wilderness preparation for the true Canaan and everlasting rest, which shall be brought to use at the revelation of our glorified King." Not only that, but he wished that "the people of Celesta, now and henceforth, be considered peaceable aliens and religious wilderness-exiles from the rest of the commonwealth of Pennsylvania, and fit subjects for exemption from the war service." He also wrote to President Lincoln and obtained the release from the Union army of a Celestan as a conscientious objector.

All these things were part of a pattern of personality

which repelled the members. One recorded that "we began to see things in Mr. Armstrong which seemed fanatical," and one by one the new arrivals would leave after a few weeks. Further, they wrote to the Adventist papers published in Boston, New York, and Battle Creek and their letters "resulted in effectually deterring the rush into the wilderness."

Armstrong's bitter disappointment did not spoil his hopes, but for the moment—perhaps Mrs. Armstrong simply had had enough and packed her things—he took his family to Philadelphia. He could find no one who would pay even the taxes on the place for the privilege of working the barren ground, and even had it been for sale he was aware that it would not bring "a tenth" of the cash, not to speak of the labor, which he and his family had put into it.

But, he said, "the wealth of the world could not purchase our interest here." And since the place had been deeded to God, with some logic he decided that the state might look to God for the taxes, if it wished to press the point on religious property. Accordingly, he thenceforward paid not a stiver. Thus, in the automatic course of events the land was sold for taxes and was bought by one of Armstrong's sons. But Celesta was never revived.

It remains to follow the trail of Elder Himes. He continued prominent in Adventist circles for thirty-six years after the going-up. Then abruptly he went West and in South Dakota was ordained as an Episcopal rector which was about as far as a man might have swung from Adventism. He served in the hamlet of Elk Point for fourteen years, apparently with little and perhaps no reference to his career as an Adventist.

Toward the end, he requested that he be buried in Sioux Falls because the cemetery there was on a hill and he wished to be on such an eminence when he rose to meet Jesus. And there he was in fact buried. Meanwhile, the old fire horse had been further alerted in him during his final months by a controversy in *The Outlook* magazine concerning the ascension robes. Just before his death, he declared in the issue of October 29, 1894, fifty years and a week after "the great change":

> I *know* the whole story of the Ascension robes to be a concoction of the enemies of the Adventists, begotten of religious prejudices, and that there is not a scintilla of truth in it. When these stories first started, and while I was publishing in the interests of the Adventist cause, I kept a standing offer in the paper, of which I was editor, of a large reward for one well-authenticated case where an Ascension robe was worn by those looking for the Lord's return. No such proof has ever been forthcoming.

Indeed, he said, he had refuted the story "hundreds of times" in the *Cry* and the *Advent Herald*. Adventists still cite this communication of Himes's, but they seem never to tell where one may find either a notice of the "large reward" or of one of the hundreds of refutations he mentions. Certainly, in the almost complete files of the *Cry* and the *Advent Herald* in public libraries, experienced researchers are unable to find even one instance of those things which, there in Elk Point in his ninetieth year, the old elder thought he recollected having printed.

. . .

No more again, no more again,
Shall Jesus, in sweet Yessa, pass from men.
He shall appease the hunger of the eyes,
    By sight, that satisfies.
He shall appease the hunger of the breast,
    In-breathing there His rest.
Lo, men shall look, to see his wounded side,
And Yessa shall glide forth, and beam, the Bride!
Lord, even so abide.

. . .

We consecrate to Him the winding stair.
    By Him, if any dare,
They shall arise to Hymen's chambers fair:
    The Bride shall carol there.
The Bride's pavilion, mystic, purple, dim,
In silken curtains and soft vails of white,
We consecrate to Him, by all delight;
While the low-breathing love-winds hush their hymn,
And She, whose beauty overflows the night,
    Touches the eyes, to see
The floating vision of Her mystery;
Touches the hearts, that thrill,
And tremble into one, and so are still.

—THOMAS LAKE HARRIS. *This poem exemplifies part of Harris's sexual mysticism, and touches upon his concept of the male-female "twain-one" godhead which was given adoration by The Brotherhood of the New Life. "Yessa" was the "female counterpart" of Jesus, and was otherwise known as Queen Lily and the Bride.*

CHAPTER SEVENTEEN

THE MAN WHO BECAME GOD

Soul-life and sex-life are at one,
In the Divine their pulses run.

—THOMAS LAKE HARRIS

SEVERAL cults had had their avatars and deities. It remained for the hinterlands of New York, the spawning ground of more than its share of religious enthusiasms for seventy-five years after the Revolution, to produce one with not merely an avatar—a deity incarnate—as its head, but with in addition a sort of love goddess, Queen Lily, the Bride, who lived in a heaven-in-the-skies called Lilistan. Intellectually and emotionally, if not physically, this "arch-natural" cult established by Thomas Lake Harris gave us the most sex-ridden religion ever dreamed up in this country.

Lily herself, in fact, came regularly down to the colony of The Brotherhood of the New Life to visit Harris

319

in the privacy of his bedroom where he spent many of his nights writing sensuous poetry to her. From these visits she bore children for him—he said—up in Lilistan and often, while in trances, in which he roamed to far planets and other universes, he visited her and the youngsters—a boy, Chrysanthile, and a girl two years younger, who was not weaned, he remarked, until she was past two. They allowed Jesus to select her name—Artalilla.

Harris celebrated the birth of the boy, who apparently was destined to be a messiah, in poetry:

> *Babe upon my Lily's breast,*
> *Blessed one, in pureness drest* . . .
> *Swifter far than bird or bee,*
> *Is thy flight, Chrysanthile;*
> *Swifter still than bee or bird,*
> *Joy-birth of our Bridal Word!* . . .
> *If, perchance, a child is born,*
> *Saturn-like for earth forlorn,*
> *He shall people air and seas,*
> *As with new divinities.* . . .

It was in 1867 that the people around Brocton, on Lake Erie in western New York, learned to their surprise that they had not, as they supposed, seen everything in the way of religion—for they heard that God and a hundred or so close followers were to settle nearby on sixteen hundred acres of small farms which a crew of bearded, long-haired, poorly dressed men had bought and thrown together as an estate.

Soon the similarly hirsute but expensively and immaculately groomed deity, Harris, arrived in a splendid equipage—once the hunting coach of Louis Napoleon. As a traveling companion he had a woman, generally described as queenly, bedecked in jewels and silks—the only woman of the colony permitted such folderols. This was Miss Jane Waring, who had humiliated her socialite family by be-

coming Harris's rapt disciple. She had in fact given him upwards of a quarter million dollars which he had already
spent in a cultist enterprise which failed to pay its way.
He was now using money from some English disciples. Miss
Waring served as Harris's private secretary and, moreover,
as a sort of "platonic" wife—for the angels had told Harris
that the Mrs. Harris of the flesh was a bit off her rocker,
and she was kept locked in her room much of the time.

At any rate, Harris told the press that he did not
consider himself divine—that he was only a well-intentioned
Christian businessman. However, he frequently told the
press things that were not true—and many of his people believed him to be divine. Certainly he was at least progress-
ing in his own mind toward self-deification through such
phases as "the Primate of the Earth, the Pivotal Man of the
Universe."

Besides his streak of poetic ability, Harris had a massive oratorical and rhetorical brilliancy, not to mention an
impelling black eye which went well with his hawk nose.
Further, at the moment, he possessed a windfall of upwards
of a hundred thousand dollars, partly in cash and partly in
treasures of art and furniture and jewels, all of it given to
him by a pair of English disciples just as the last of Miss
Waring's fortune disappeared. In return, he had granted
them eternal life on earth—or at least they were at the moment working out harsh penances as his serfs in hope of at-
taining that immortality.

On the Brocton estate—purchased in part with the
funds and from the labors of his lesser followers, some sixty
adults, besides children, at this time—he and Miss Waring
raised a thirty-room mansion for themselves. He piped
water to it from a spring two miles away, with the overflow
going to the flower garden—for Queen Lily would not visit
the place unless there were flowers.

Harris named the mansion Vine Cliff. Cynical
worldly farmers of the neighborhood soon dubbed it "the
Harem"—for while Harris permitted the several "most spir-

itual" of his disciples to live there with him and Dovie, as he called Miss Waring, it chanced that all these were women.

The colony was called "the Use" because each person in it was to be used as God saw fit. And each person was given a spiritual or Use name, on the order of Miss Waring's. Harris was Faithful. Others were Steadfast, Golden Rose, and Viola. Laurence Oliphant, the English lord, novelist, and adventurer who had given Harris the current hundred thousand which had built Vine Cliff, and who at the moment was living in a pigsty, was Woodbine. He wrote to a friend concerning the Master:

"Yesterday he moved into the house which he is going to make his home. It is a sad reflection upon all of us men, that not one of our states is sufficiently advanced to enable Faithful to bear us living with him yet. I constantly think of it with shame and regret." Indeed, "in spite of all my efforts" Oliphant had not come into a "state" which had permitted him even to speak to Harris, whom he regarded as his savior, since entering the colony months before—nor was he to be permitted to live there even after his wife was taken into the inner circle.

Despite the vaunted rule of celibacy at the Use, gamey stories were soon abroad, scattered by hired hands and servants and dissident, departing colonists, of orgies conducted in honor of the Bride, the Lily Queen. Jane Waring was accused by indignant parents of young girls of being a procuress for Father Faithful. And public sport was made of "the essential mystery of the universe," which, it seems, was Harris's "mystic union" with the Bride.

It had all begun in England in 1826 when Harris, at the age of three, began having visions. He was taken to New York at five by his rigorously religious parents. His mother died and a harsh stepmother made him happy to leave home to go to work at nine. As a young man he could compose poetry extemporaneously "by the mile." At eighteen he had visions of his mother. In 1847, at twenty-one, his magnetism and his gift for oratory won him the pulpit of a fashionable Universalist church in New York City—for he had rejected the bitter doctrine of election held by his forebears, which as a child had terrorized him with the fear of hell. He wanted no part of the evangelical denominations.

All through the forties, spiritualism and table rappings were the national enthusiasm. Harris became famous overnight after angels began putting him in trances and dictating sermons to him. He recorded that he delivered the first of these angelic discourses "in the mystery of vibrating intelligence, quivering with love, calm as the stillness of a great night in midsummer; while from eye to eye it seemed as if the hushed melted audience diffused an atmosphere to hold the dew of tears."

The text was "Suffer little children." At the end of the sermon, Horace Greeley rose and with the iron still hot started the movement which led to a rescue house for children—the New York Juvenile Asylum. But New York could not hold a man who could make such gaudy arrangements of words as Harris. Presently, when his young wife died, leaving him with two infant sons whose lives in their manhood he was to make completely hellish, he went on tour, holding seances and preaching.

One of his "controls" was St. Paul from whom, through table rappings, he learned that the site of the Garden of Eden was at Mountain Cove in what later became West Virginia, and that Jesus would soon return to earth there. With two associates and a hundred followers, Harris established an agricultural commune at the holy site, treating some of the brethren as slaves and some as guests while he spent the funds of all. In two years the place was bankrupt, Jesus had not appeared, and the project disintegrated.

Harris went awandering again and in 1855, in what he later claimed was a platonic marriage, he acquired a new wife, a New Orleans girl who believed passionately in him and his spiritualistic powers. She shared his belief in fairies, and indeed later declared herself the recipient of a revelation that she was queen of the rabbit fairies, after which she always desired to be addressed as Lady Pink Ears. A peculiar irony, when the character and beliefs of Harris be understood, was that the prophet thought this odd of her and was even irritated by the matter.

Some five years after this marriage, just before the outbreak of the Civil War, Harris was rescued from a petty existence as a preacher-spiritualist by Jane Waring. On her money he established The Brotherhood of the New Life at Wassaic, New York, with a bank and other commercial projects. By 1865 Jane's fortune was swallowed up, despite the Civil War boom which was bringing prosperity to the Icarians and other Utopians. Bankruptcy was imminent.

Harris and Jane went junketing to England, with Mrs. H. tagging along—but for whatever reason, that lady soon deserted them with tears and hard words and returned to the States, though it was four years before she rejoined the colony. In London, heaven delivered its tastiest remaining prize to Harris—Laurence Oliphant and his mother, Lady Oliphant. England was aghast that an MP, a celebrated wit, author, and world traveler, should believe that Harris was Deity. But he did believe and so did his mother —for in some way Harris had told them things about themselves "which no mortal man could know." Further, "Christ is actually descending with power and great glory a second time to dwell with us"—and those who would "give themselves up to Him" would be regenerated. The Oliphants went off to America to a menial existence in return for regeneration and eternal life on earth.

Lady Oliphant was promptly put in a shed and set to mending the garments of field hands, some of whom had once been affluent people. But the canny Harris whetted Laurence's eagerness by keeping him on probation outside for a while—for, still a bachelor, Oliphant was notorious for his project to "know" a thousand women in the Biblical sense. London gossip was that he really desired to fall into the arms of Jane Waring and not into her hands.

On admission, he was given a stable loft with a straw pallet and not even his mother was permitted to speak to him for more than a year. Harris communicated with him by notes—notes which "permitted" him, after his four A.M. to eight P.M. stint, perhaps to haul water until midnight for next day's use. If this chanced to be in zero weather, so much the more glorious, for Harris impressed upon his people that labor was a high form of worship. And he made his pronouncements the more impressive by his ability to speak "in two voices, near and far." The "near voice" was vivacious. The other, which seemed to come from some spot away from Harris, was deep and solemn.

Even after Harris moved the Brotherhood to Brocton on Oliphant money, the lord and his mother were kept in their harsh probation, and the Primate continued the development of his religion—one which very nearly refutes the view that no creed is any more peculiar than any other.

Harris required some forty-five major works, partly of poetry of epic length, partly of involved and even incomprehensible, if often beautiful, prose, to explain his tenets. He believed in demons—indeed, they tempted, cajoled, and tortured him in droves in attempts to persuade him to throw his weight on their side in the war between heaven and hell. He believed in a special race of fairies called fays which inhabited the bosoms of women—those in the left breast being kings and queens, and those in the right priests and priestesses. These creatures, the result of "the nuptial relations of our Divine Lord and Lady," were the seeds of a future deathless race of people. They had cities and governments within the women. They passed their lives in love making and other delights and rejoiced in the "conjugial" activities of men and women. Sometimes they came out and held dances on the exterior of the breast and their voices "might be frequently heard in a faint, exquisite music, responding to the high and holy inspiration of the Divine Love."

Strangely, for the prophet of a sex-ridden religion, Harris had a fear of the cosmic element of femaleness, and a supposed fear of women. The most terrible demons of hell, in his revelation, were female; and one should have frequent contact with the earth in order to "demagnetize" himself of female influences. Complicating all this was his great attraction for women and theirs for him.

But the foundation stone of his religion was the principle of "Internal Respiration"—a stone resting upon and well mortared up with sexual connotations:

> Soul-life and sex-life are at one,
> In the Divine their pulses run.

This internal respiration was "the breathing of the atmosphere of heaven, not only into the spiritual but also into the natural lungs." This "arch-natural" breath was the very breath which God was taking simultaneously into His lungs and which, through the Holy Spirit, was shared with those "sufficiently regenerated to receive it, and was originally possessed by the entire humanity of this planet." The elect were thus made one with God. They formed "the arch-natural society," and only they could remain alive after the Apocalypse.

The first hope of a member of the Brotherhood, then, was to receive the Breath—and doubly so because until then celibacy was not merely a matter of theory but a hard fact for him. In Harrisism, the greatest of errors was indulgence in the pleasures of "the natural marriage bed." However, that left the legitimate indulgences of the "arch-natural" marriage bed for the elect—those more devout recipients of the Breath to whom Lily might decide to award soul mates or "heavenly counterparts."

And it was here that gossip reared its head and puffed its scandalized breath across the Brocton countryside: Behind the system was Harris's bisexual deity, with Queen Lily as the female counterpart of God—while at the same time she was the counterpart of Harris. Jesus-Yessa was the bisexual messiah, Yessa also being Lily, the Bride. If the Holy Spirit had a counterpart, she seems to be lost beyond the reach of reasonable research in Harris's turgid volumes; but it seems safe to conjecture that if she is there, she is Lily, under whatever name. For instance, later, when Harris, in a furious pique at Oliphant, dropped "the Jewish religion" and took up "the Eastern religion," Yessa not only became Issa, the great earth mother, but "the Lotus Queen" as well. Also behind the theory of counterparts was the inescapable point that Adam at first had been the bisexual he-she, Adam-Eve, until his female counterpart was removed from him.

Well, then. Apparently everyone eventually would have a counterpart—but it was unlikely that any except the "children of the Bride" would ever get together with theirs, for somehow time had got out of gear for most people and their counterparts probably had lived in a previous age and were now in the afterworld. Or perhaps they were there waiting to be born. But if a person had the Breath, then Lily might, through revelation to Harris, make it known that she would allow him to make spiritual contact with his counterpart—and these spirit mates often become incredibly real to their earthly partners. One ecstatic spinster confided to her diary:

> I heard the strangest little noises in my breast, and everything there all day long has seemed to be in a flutter, as if little wings were moving, and something keeps singing to me In your breast love will build his nest. I cannot even write this without the tears filling my eyes. Every time I wake at night or in the morning, I always feel flowing into my body my counterpart. Wonderfully beautiful it all is, and beyond imagination to have someone inside of you. I scarcely know what to call

it, this which within me dwells, and with all my being
dwells, angel, husband, friend, or lover, "Sweet my
sweet, my own dear wife," 'tis what he says, "call me love
and husband ever." I kiss my hands for very joy when
love's own life is in them.

And at one point she bursts out, "The lovely simplicity of our father Harris is just like that of a child, I feel as
if I wanted to put both my arms about him and kiss him."
Queen Lily had provided for such eventualities as
that, too. Under the system, some man's female counterpart
might come down and invade not only his body but that of
some woman in the Use. In such case, it would be perfectly
proper—and indeed, perhaps was required—that he commune with his counterpart by communing in private with
the flesh-and-blood sister. At the same time, the woman
might be communing with some other man who had been
invaded by her male counterpart, and if the counterparts
should go skipping around, as they reputedly did at times,
the obvious changes might have to be made. During the
supposed orgies, said recusant members or those expelled
for some offense, "husbands and wives were changed all
around," and one man declared that Harris required him to
commune with five different women in one day.
So much for gossip. When confronted with the reports
by the press, Harris angrily declared that while the theory
had been given him in revelation, the fact was that Lily had
not allowed any counterparts to so invade the colony and
that there were no grounds for public outrage. And, while he
finally was to flee the state to avoid the legal consequences of
tales of ravaged girls, and the complaint of a well-thought-of
family of his disciples that Harris, whom they had looked
upon as God, had tried to "marry" their young daughter, he
apparently was for the first several years at Brocton telling
the truth about the "orgies" among his followers. For such of
these as may have occurred were undoubtedly confined to
Harris and his little circle of women in the mansion.

The first to be added to his and Jane's menage was "Golden Rose"—Mrs. James A. Requa. Requa had been Harris's right-hand man, his business manager—but suddenly he died, although he had been granted eternal life on earth.

Harris first said that he had died "through the infernal magic of counter respiration, in direct antagonism to the Divine Breath." But later he said that Lily had called Requa away because, by a rare chance, it had turned out that the Requas were counterparts. It was thus necessary that one of them be taken to heaven to act as guardian angel over the other, and heaven had chosen the husband. A Swedish hired girl reported that she saw Harris comforting the prostrated Golden Rose with kisses.

And in *The Wedding Guest,* Harris wrote: "The wife who remains . . . Lily selected for the matron of her house. To her she first made, and since has most fully and continuously made, the demonstrations of her presence. The first nuptial celebration of the marriage of the earth and skies, after our own [Harris's and Lily's] was in our home, when this luminous one [Lily] came to be bridally involved into the outward of that heroic, long-suffering, ever-faithful 'Golden Rose.' "

Mrs. Requa bore up, partly to strengthen Harris who, too, was crushed by Requa's death, for the prophet was extremely responsive to the "states" of those around him, and to "spheres of influence" in the world in general. Indeed, in his early career he once was suffering from the rising of "hellish spheres" around him "too terrible to narrate." Writing of it in the regal plural, he declared that he would have died had not the "Divine Father-Mother caused Lily to become ultimated to us." She "made her way through the obstacles, and by the involvement and distillation of her precious life, brought the saving external aid." Thus, apparently, he received Lily as his counterpart in the first place.

But he was a thoroughgoing hypochondriac. Once he became convinced that his entire colony might somehow become infected with syphilis and, regardless of the odor, he required everyone to wear a bag of balsam cofaiba to ward off the disease. Now and then, under strong provocation from unappreciative people, or invisible demons, he would have "convulsions," punctuating his contortions with impromptu songs such as "Be brave, little Faithful, be strong, fight hard." People who became weary of the spectacle reported that he merely suffered from "fits," spasms, and hysteria.

Nevertheless, he convinced his people that he was highly sensitive to their states. It became a usual occurrence for some nearby household of his serfs to be routed out in the middle of the night and forced to move to the farthermost empty house or to some barn in the colony because they were in "a bad state" which was draining him of the strength which he automatically poured out to them in their need.

Laurence Oliphant, the English lord, wrote that "These are the moments when persons' states get tired, for at such a time the harmony has to live unbroken through all the inevitable petty annoyances incidental to so many being tumbled anyhow into an unfurnished house." And, regarding the sex scandals, after he married and his wife and mother were forming part of the feminine circle around Harris, Oliphant wrote to disciples in England that they must cease writing doubting letters and holding doubting thoughts concerning Harris—that one must "believe, despite appearances," and that doubt caused much pain to Father Faithful.

But it must not be supposed that Oliphant was completely insensible to his own condition. One evening, hauling in a load of potatoes, he "felt as though something in me would break if I did not have some sort of outlet."

The outlet was to whip up the horses and clatter down the road in the heavy wagon, shouting and screaming. "I never enjoyed a better quarter hour," he declared. The colony turned out behind as he passed the houses, everyone thinking there was a runaway. When they caught up, Oliphant was in the barnyard, calmly feeding the team.

Soon afterward, Oliphant was instrumental in bringing some wealthy Japanese to the Use for a free-spending sojourn. They were acquaintances from his diplomatic days in Japan where he had very nearly been killed by a blow on the head in a lion-like defense of the British embassy against a mob. As a reward for bringing the Nipponese, Oliphant was promoted to the position of fruit butcher to meet the trains at the depot, and there he underwent much rough teasing from travelers who knew who he was.

Then in 1870, money low, Harris permitted Oliphant, whose name was worth excellent fees, to go to Europe to cover the Franco-Prussian war for the London *Times,* the money to come to the primate. In France, Oliphant was occultly protected from Prussian bullets by Harris's influence—but the primate, not thinking to protect him from women, was astounded and enraged when he received an apologetic, pleading notice that Oliphant had fallen in love with an English girl, Alice le Strange.

He did not even answer Oliphant's plea for permission to marry—for after all, Oliphant knew that no sexual indulgence was permitted at the Use. Oliphant's hope, however, was that Harris would receive a revelation that the lovers were counterparts, which would permit such indulgence. But presently Harris learned that the girl was an heiress, and in possession of an extensive dowry, whereupon the platonic wife, Miss Waring, informed Lady Oliphant that she might write her son that a marriage was forbidden—unless the girl could give Oliphant up "utterly to God and enter upon what discipline is before her to prepare herself for the place and use in God's new kingdom, upon which He will bring them together when and as He will, if they are for each other."

In other words, Alice had to surrender her fortune to Harris—and the couple had to agree not to consummate their marriage until Harris should give consent. That is, until he should receive a possible revelation that they were counterparts.

It required some two years for Alice to reason herself into accepting Harris as her savior, and to addressing Miss Waring as "mother," but because of her love for the long-haired, long-bearded Oliphant she managed it and surrendered her fortune. Harris married the pair and allowed them to room together—but after many months the primate received a revelation that the two were not counterparts. That, indeed, a beautiful young friend of Lily's, by name Alawenie, residing in Lilistan, was Oliphant's counterpart. Oliphant's feverish hope then was that Alawenie would invade Alice's body—but this did not occur. Hence the Englishman "learnt self-control by sleeping with my beloved and beautiful Alice in my arms for twelve years without claiming the rights of a husband." He said that that was a considerable trial, inasmuch as he was "a passionate lover."

As a matter of fact, Oliphant did not spend much of the twelve years in Alice's arms, for, he being the only man of any particular ability in the Use, the prophet kept him much in New York attending to business and speculative enterprises, and in England getting out books, the profit of which of course came to Harris. And meanwhile, the gentle, beautiful Alice—her photographs show an unreal, ethereal quality —was taken into Vine Cliff.

What actually went on there is anyone's guess. By day, Harris sauntered in the great flower gardens which were in honor of the Bride, or rode out in his coach to inspect the colony. He did not scruple to smoke expensive cigars in the presence of his people, who were denied tobacco, just as Jane wore her silks which were not permitted them. Indeed, Jane smoked, too, using the clay pipes which Harris smoked once and discarded. He might stop to chat approvingly with people who, in their labors, lisped in baby talk in their attempts to "become as little children," but he viewed only coldly the actual children who were brought up in unschooled ignorance away from their parents in the Bird's Nest, or "the roost," as it was facetiously called.

In the evenings, he and his ladies met at the fine table which had come from the Oliphant house in London, and dined from Oliphant heirloom china with Oliphant heirloom silver. Places and chairs were provided for Lily and her children, but Harris tolerated only with poor grace similar ones for the fairy rabbit royalty who Mrs. Harris, in her role as queen of the rabbit fairies, insisted were present. These had such names as Prince Wisdom, Sir Sunbeam Courage, and Lady Precious Pearl.

After supper, while girls hired from without the colony cleared up, "the family" gathered around the organ for a few of Harris's sensuous hymns to Queen Lily, in whom they considered themselves spiritually united:

> *Perchance to thrill the outward ear,*
> *Celestial love-birds warble near.*
> *Perchance, encircling, hand in hand,*
> *Glides the irradiant Sister Band.*

> *This marriage chamber, edged with thorns,*
> *Holds light of Love's eternal morns:*
> *Comforts and healings from it glide*
> *To bless the children of the Bride.*

And:

> *—I saw the Holy Grail:*
> *The cup was in our Lady's hand:*
> *I saw our Lord beside her stand.*
> *He pressed the blossom of Her breast;*
> *The milk-white love-wine was exprest;*
> *And, as the sacred cup it filled,*
> *All Fairyland for joy was thrilled.*

The sex scandals became so notorious that the colony was on the verge of being crushed by the legislature as a public nuisance. To soothe public opinion—for the winery was making money a little faster than other departments were losing it and the enterprise was worth saving—Harris fled to California with Mrs. Requa. His excuse to the press was that Queen Lily wished him to establish a new home where the goddess might come to enjoy flowers the year round.

A new colony was founded at Santa Rosa and "the more spiritual" disciples were brought from Brocton. Harris included the younger Lady Oliphant among these, but Oliphant and his mother, sick with disappointment, were left behind to help manage the old estate. Also taken was Harris's daughter-in-law, but the son who had married the girl against the prophet's wishes was left. Apparently Harris had never permitted them to live together. The primate had quarreled stormily with both his boys, publicly cursing and reviling them. He had crushed the love affair of the second one and got rid of the girl in the case, and had later driven the boy from the colony. This son went West, and later Harris paid hush money to people claiming to be the boy's illegitimate children.

At Santa Rosa, vineyards and a winery were soon flourishing at the new Fountain Grove colony—and Harris assured the world that the beverage was beneficial to the consumer because by special dispensation it contained Divine Intelligence.

A "Commandery" was built to house the men, with capacity for an eventual one hundred. A bath house was in the basement and soon dissidents and expellees were scattering stories of mixed nude bathing and wife-swapping. As usual, Harris stoutly denied all such allegations. He asked where the children were who surely would have resulted from such doings—for the gossips seem never to have suggested that any babies were born. Critics pointed to the Oneida Community, where indiscriminate mating was a social affair and where, through the restraint practiced by the men, there were no unplanned babies. While restraint seems not to be in the spirit of orgies, it is true that the popular contraceptive method of the day, widely publicized by Robert Dale Owen and others despite religious and legal opposition, was that of *coitus interruptus,* and the Brotherhood could not have been ignorant of it.

As a matter of fact, the Free Masons of Santa Rosa, in after years when the gossip was thicker than ever, satisfied themselves that no one had proved anything and invited Harris to address them. He had thought to have to refuse because of throat trouble of years' standing—but he was miraculously healed in time to make the address, one which he classified as perhaps the greatest given on earth since the Sermon on the Mount.

At any rate, the wine-bibbing public but little cared for the morals of those who produced the drink. Thus the prophet continued prosperously until he made the blunder of quarreling with Alice Oliphant. Either he expelled her or she left. To his irritation, instead of her crawling back after allowing him to sulk a while, she went into the mountains and taught miners' children for a living. After several months of her defection, Laurence came to California to see her in defiance of Harris's orders—but Harris ordered him to let her be until she had shown repentance. Following a three months' wait during which she failed to seek a reconciliation with Father Faithful, Oliphant returned to Europe without having got in touch with her.

Despite his pusillanimity, Alice suddenly joined him in Europe and they went on a writing tour of the Continent —with their earnings going regularly to Harris. For the end of the world was approaching, and Oliphant did not wish to be left out of the number to be saved alive. Harris had just settled down to the writing of a new book of his philosophy when, in 1880, Oliphant appeared at his door again, unheralded. On a litter, he had brought his mother who was dying of cancer, and they were expecting a miraculous healing. Coldly Harris admitted that he had healed people by the laying on of hands—but because of the disobedience of the Oliphants in not staying in the East he refused to cure Lady Oliphant.

Presently Jane Waring entered the room and on her finger Lady Oliphant saw the engagement ring given herself many years before by Laurence's father, and which she had surrendered to Harris to show her worthiness to be his disciple. Abruptly, she seemed to wake from a long, cloudy dream. Before she died several days later, she had a promise from Laurence that he would sue for recovery of the Oliphant property.

Courts had frequently held that gifts to messiahs were not recoverable. But despite Harris's alternate cajolery and warnings, Oliphant instituted suit. Harris wanted no airing of his affairs in court. Failing in an attempt to have Oliphant locked up as insane, he announced that Lily had advised him to settle—but he added that only the theft of important papers by Oliphant had spoiled his case so that he could do no less. He gave Oliphant the major interest in the Brocton estate and made over the remainder of it to other disciples there to prevent suit by them. Though disgruntled that Oliphant had received his own share and much of theirs, too, they nevertheless accepted him as their new prophet.

To Harris's unbounded irritation, Oliphant began receiving revelations not only from his soulmate Alawenie, but from Lily herself! The international press caught up the story. Ignoring the laughter, Harris announced that Queen Lily was not communing with Oliphant—that the English lord was being hoodwinked and hypnotized by Alice who was in reality a female demon posing as Lily. In fact, he said, Alice had been sent out of hell by Satan in the first place to disrupt the Brotherhood—and he confessed that he had known of this while she was still with him in California. One night he "sank to sleep, with Lily involved, and watching in my external frame. Lily roused me in the night, and as I began to return to the outward of my body, I found that my respiration was almost lost. I encountered a current of deadly magnetic force, sharp as a spear, and entering my breast. Looking for its source, I saw with my bodily eyes a materialized spectre, made to imitate Lily, even to the color of eyes and hair. This image stood near the foot of my bed. Through it, from the deep magic of the most deadly spirits, flowed a suffocating poison, sufficient to destroy natural life. My love and I fought this terror, till its powers waned, and it began to recede. As it receded, I followed it with my eyes, and saw it re-enter the body of Alice Oliphant who was in the cottage close by. It then mingled its elements in her magnetic body, and was wholly lost to sight, being drawn into the interiors of her person. It is this image that afterwards passed over from Alice to Oliphant that is sometimes about him, but at other times involved in his magnetic body, and which he calls the 'Lily Queen.' "

This trickery of Alice's upon himself, the prophet said, was The Second Great Betrayal—the first having been the betrayal of Jesus by Peter.

At any rate, Oliphant was considered by his followers to be the new "pivotal center of the universe." Drawing the income from Brocton, he and Alice opened a brotherhood in Palestine for Jewish repatriation, and, continuing to receive messages from both Lily and his own counterpart, Alawenie, Oliphant wrote incomprehensible books which appear to use Harris's basic philosophy, but with a scantily veiled change of terms and catchwords.

Alice died rather suddenly, apparently without ever having consummated her marriage with Oliphant, but from Lilistan she dictated literary works to him. Harris wrote an incredibly bitter tirade about her, "the siren of the snake," after her death, which, he hinted, was the natural and inescapable result of her having crossed him and Lily:

> *Let the sword fish, as he noteth,*
> *Strike against our beak of steel:*
> *He shall strangle, till he floateth*
> *As a corpse beneath the keel.*

> *For the Woman of the Waters*
> *In her oceanic hand*

Bears our social barque, through slaughters,
To the Blithe and Blessed Land.

Did the subtlest soul of magic
Sting your hearts to bleed and ache?
By a doom-stroke, swift and tragic,
Died the siren of the snake.

Soon after Alice's death, Oliphant, in 1887, stupidly set up an experiment in Paris in which he persuaded some young unmarried men and women to engage in experiments that would "teach them the habit of self control." This led to a great and scandalous hullabaloo, for they were of good families.

In America to recruit members for his Palestinian brotherhood, Oliphant enrolled Rosamond Owen, a daughter, no longer young, of Robert Dale Owen. On the voyage to England, where they were to stop over, he persuaded her to marry him. She wrote that she had long prayed for "a stately mate" but found herself a handmaid to the dead Alice and the "other" heavenly counterpart, Alawenie.

Yet, she felt that she could draw Laurence closer to the dead wife who wanted him to have a female on earth— for Alice became worn out in helping him deal with the many women with whom he came in contact. She wanted an assistant—for, it seems, beings in "the invisible" become tired just as do those in the visible. Added Rosamond, who occasionally did have intercourse with Oliphant as a sacred rite: "We realize that our union, instead of separating my husband from Alice has, in truth, bound him only the more closely, for she has become so atomically welded with me, that we, the wife in the unseen and the wife in the seen, have become as one; her life is poured through me as an instrument doubling my own affectional consciousness."

But Oliphant did not take Rosamond to the Holy Land—where, to the fury of Harris, he declared Jesus was going to land, rather than at Fountain Grove in California.

A few days after the wedding, Oliphant was struck down with cancer of the lung. Harris had already told him that he might consider that they were in a match of afflicting each other through the occult—and as he died Oliphant said that he had no doubt that "the Harris devils have been at me." He was resigned to death, even though he had thought to live forever and regenerate the world. And in California, Harris boasted that it indeed was he who had killed Oliphant.

Protecting her dead husband's name, while admitting that he had perhaps erred, Rosamond Oliphant tried to explain away the "temptation" experiments in Paris before she knew him. She and a niece, with a young man named Templeton who had been involved in those experiments, lived at the Palestinian colony, its sole occupants, and for a time formed "a little paradise" in Paris.

Templeton married the girl, who was his counterpart, and after her death in childbirth he was told by God, at thirty-three, to marry the forty-five-year-old semi-invalid Rosamond, which he did. Two years later God told him to drown himself. He did that, too, jumping off a ship near Haifa—sacrificing his life, Rosamond said, for "humanity's sake." He had gone on "to join his celestial partner."

Still supported by funds from the grudging Brocton trustees, Rosamond died in 1937, at the age of ninety, to the end agitating for "sexual purity" and for a Palestinian Zion in memory of Oliphant.

The defection of his Brocton followers shook Harris deeply. He announced his disgust with the Hebrew-Christian "proprium" and turned to the religions of India which were in great vogue in this country at the time. After demolishing their tenets in a five-hundred-page book, he began receiving revelations concerning a religion on which those of India were obviously based, springing from a Mother Lotus—Lily, again—and Father Brahm, a one-twain being, with the elect of humanity forming the Society of the White

Lily. All this was at least to the profit of his muse of sensuous poetry. His lyrics—which alone almost make his career worth-while—continued to pour out:

> *I sun myself in the tropic band*
> *Of thy unzoned Indian charms:*
> *My Aryan Bride, in the star-flower stand;*
> *O! Love me deep in the lotus land,*
> *And flow through my petalled arms.*

> *My Bridal Girl, whom the Golden Lord*
> *Led forth from the gleaming shore;*
> *Wake joy in my heart by the deeper chord;*
> *O, love me deep in the Vedic Word—*
> *In the flower that Brahma bore!*

Lily rewarded him with the revelation that he was to have seven stages of life. He was then in the sixth, she said, in which he was to be called King Chrysantheus. The Apocalypse would come soon, probably in 1881. He would then be in "the Seventh House," and would be God. Already the heavens were sinking near the earth. When they should touch it, all who did not share the mystic breath of God with him would smother.

Harris issued notices that God and His Lady were dwelling at Fountain Grove. They were not yet receiving friends but those who wished to write them might, if gentlemen, address communications to T. L. Harris, or, if ladies, to "Mrs. Lily Harris." The Queen, the Bride, Lily, Issa, Mother Brahm, the Lotus Goddess, had become Mrs. Harris!

Celebrating his new status in *The Lyre of Helios* is his egomaniacal:

> *I am the minstrel of the law,*
> *Pure, absolute, without a flaw,*
> *That Brahma, from his Orient, saw.*
> *The Powers reveal as they create;*

They who declare originate:
As is my song, so is my fate.

As "King Chrysantheus," he decided to give his new religion to all the earth. With "Lady Dovie" he retired to his cottage, Lin Lilla, in the mountains to write about it. He almost died in a severe illness there, but "Issa" kissed him "from her celestial marriage bed," as he said in a letter to the papers, and brought him back to life. This was the Resurrection. He was at last a full-fledged deity—but apparently he voluntarily gave up some attributes of godhood that he might associate with people on the human plane.

He decreed establishment of a new calendar, with a "Luminous Year." The months were to have such names as Love, Adoration, Peace, Thanksgiving, Dove, and Consummation, with similarly fanciful names for the days. In the new dispensation, each member of the Brotherhood would have a counterpart—in the flesh. At the beginning of each new year, all marriages would become null, and in a demagnetization ceremony, each person would step out of his old skin, which at that time would have conveniently split down the back. The skins would be saved for parchment—and each person, according to sex, would be married either to Harris or "the Mother," and afterward to his or her own counterpart.

Somehow, the world was not attracted by all this. The sex scandals grew in frequency. Harris was sixty-eight. He was tired. The conversion of mankind—and the wine business which was in difficulties from competition—required that he travel. He could no longer travel alone because of infirmities, nor yet could he face the hullabaloo which the public created when he fared forth with Mrs. Requa to New Orleans, or across the continent with Jane.

Accordingly, in 1892, after some exceedingly gamey publicity from a lady journalist who said Harris tried to make her "Queen of the East" and to seduce her, the prophet married Miss Waring. Poor Lady Pink Ears had died several years previously. Harris's sons were dead—one of them of tuberculosis, just a day's journey from Santa Rosa, which he was trying to reach. He had wanted to do two things before dying—to see his wife who had been kept from him for so long, and to kill his father whom he considered a monster.

Quarrels had so riven the Brotherhood that Harris felt he was alone except for Dovie. With her he settled in New York City to manage his wine outlets there. Then it was revealed to him that he was to stay there, for New York, it seemed, had been visited by St. Paul at the time of Henry Hudson and proclaimed the center of "the Mother's Kingdom." In this term may be seen Harris's growing preoccupation with femaleness, and the dwindling of importance of the male half of divinity in his mind. Too, he issued proclamations concerning the end of the dispensation. Twenty-five million people were to be saved at the end, most of these being—at various times—Japanese or French or other national groups. The world government would be housed in "the occult space under the Dome of the Capitol at Washington." Officials were to be Washington, Jefferson, Lincoln, King Alfred, Cromwell, George Fox, Adonai, and "the Adepts of the Rock."

Jane had to stay with Harris constantly in public—for he caused scenes by grabbing strange women and kissing them if she was not about to prevent it. But he was not entirely senile. He sold the California colony to some of the members there for a quarter million dollars and made shrewd investments in Florida real estate. For, he said, the fairies who traveled with him liked Florida—and indeed he vacationed there frequently on their account. Too, he wandered over the earth in his trances, returning to tell his little circle of disciples that he had preached that day in England or China. He called himself Theos (God) Lilistan most of the time. But on occasion to denote his duality as the divine Father-Mother of mankind he changed it to Theos-

Thea. Again, in divine simplicity, he made it Him-Her and He-She.

Still, life was not easy. Devils came nightly from hell to pester him, offering bribes and making threats to win him to their side in their war against "Divine Motion." Nevertheless, declaring that he was the only force which prevented their winning that war, he did not yield to "the Infernals," even though they punished him with anguishing bodily pain and even more acute pain of the spirit. Yet, he told Jane they eventually would kill him—it was ordained.

And on the night of March 23, 1906, they did so while he slept.

Jane and his latter-day disciple, Edwin Markham, tried to keep the news from the papers since they did not recognize what had occurred as being death. They waited three days, expecting Harris to rise. But by then the bodily changes were so great that it was clear he had been borne away to Lilistan by the Bride that he might no longer be tortured by the demons.

Jane kept a fitful correspondence going among the surviving faithful here and there over the country and in England. But one by one these were gathered to "the Upper Kingdom." In 1916 she died—the last of those who had helped form the Brotherhood the year before the Civil War began.

CHAPTER EIGHTEEN

GOD'S CHILDREN AND SOME OTHER ELECT ONES

Three wise men of Gotham
Put to sea in a bowl.
If the bowl had been stronger
My song had been longer.

—MOTHER GOOSE

i.   AMONG THE ELECT ONES

OFTEN when the communitarian movement has threatened to become dull or repetitious, some particularly wild-eyed prophet has livened it again. For instance, it has been seriously proposed in this century to organize the world into a single commune, move the English royal family to Canada, and establish Jesus as world ruler in Buckingham palace. While waiting for the minor details to be worked out, the New York woman who dreamed up the idea would take charge from Washington, D. C. Another scheme of the same order, and similarly reminiscent of the proposal of the Fifth Monarchy Men in Cromwell's day, was hatched about 1930 in California—a state to which we are much indebted for almost a century of wonderfully zany stuff from prophets, mahatmas, and world savers of all kinds.

Not all these are of communitarian bent. Some charge merely a straight fee—as in the case of the lady who intercepts messages from other planets and forwards them to subscribers for good round sums. But these gentry lack éclat, flair.

The Purple Mother had flair, to an extent. Before the death of William Judge, the theosophist leader, at the turn of the century, he made mysterious references to a great disciple, variously known as The Light of the Ledge, The Promise, and The Veiled Mahatma. After he died, one Katherine Tingley, an often-married New Englander, announced that she was this person, The Purple Mother. She went to California well-supplied with funds, saying that she desired to build "a White City in a Land of Gold beside a Sunset Sea." And so she began the Theosophical Community near San Diego.

She put up forty buildings, some fantastic with color. The architecture was a mixture of Moorish and Egyptian, "with something belonging to neither," to use her own understatement. The whole thing, with hidden buglers to announce the approach of visitors, and with her three hundred people of two dozen nationalities floating about in flowing costumes, was as colorful as The Purple Mother's prose. Her people tended chickens, silk worms, and vegetables, but the big business was the receiving of love offerings from the tens of thousands of theosophists who came to sit at the feet of the Mother. Soon there was a theater, a college, a temple of the arts, and all the appropriate theosophical lectures. The Mother ruled everything with a whim of iron.

California has spawned other cults, some of them messianic, with hordes of neurotics chasing after shrewd operators, eager to hand over money in exchange for a moment of attention, but these are beside the communal point.

In the communitarian field, farther east, prophets have gained attention as divine or Biblical personages.

Elijah has been a popular reincarnation through ancient, medieval, and modern times—as for instance in Jemima Wilkinson's retinue. More recently, there was "Elijah the Restorer," otherwise a Scot, Alexander Dowie, who founded Zion City, Illinois, in 1901, after a successful career as a faith healer. He was driven from power in Zion City after his cult became wealthy. The place later achieved prominence under Wilbur Glenn ("The World is Flat") Voliva whose religious and scientific pronouncements diverted a generation of newspaper readers. He reached his peak when he proclaimed that Jesus would arrive in Zion City "on or about September 10" of 1934, with the usual resultant excitement and disappointment among his followers.

The Lake Michigan country has for a century had more than its share of avatars—incarnated divinities—such as Strang finally came to be. Perhaps the most interesting of these was the Invisible Presence, otherwise Cyrus Spragg, whose cheerful career is wreathed with mists of legend. Some say Spragg is a folk-projection of the Strang story, while still others declare that Spragg was real and that the assumption of legend comes from the fact that both Spragg and Strang were Mormons, communitarians, deities, unorthodox sexualists, and most of all from the similarity of their names. People still living declare they remember hearing of the Invisible Presence and his offspring, "God's Children," in Illinois in their childhood before the turn of the century. A prominent author of today says that his family was lastingly embarrassed because relatives became disciples of the Presence.

Anyway, Spragg was driven from a Mormon stake in Michigan. He took some followers with him and established a commune in which he enjoined the practice of nudism and abolition of private property. He forbade polygamy.

Later he led his people on a rambling hegira into the Illinois hills where intimations of messiahship came upon him. He spoke prophecies—including one of a deluge. He built an ark which was to save his people—but when the flood did not materialize he announced that he was the supreme deity of the universe who had come down to bless those who would believe in him.

Henceforth he was to be known as the Invisible Presence. Since he was not to be seen again by human eyes he retired into the ark. However, he still had human necessities. His food was to be placed where he could get it without being seen. Through the window which had been cut for letting out doves, he handed out directions for conducting the affairs of the commune, which was called New Jerusalem.

One night there was a new revelation: A virgin of the colony was to produce a messiah who would save mankind. She would have to be impregnated by deity in the tradition of the virgins of the various Eastern religions who had brought forth young. In this case she would have to visit the Invisible Presence. Since it was not to be revealed just which young lady might produce the true messiah, the Presence recommended that each who might possibly be old enough get in line and provide herself with one these scions which were to be called "God's Children."

Things rocked along with prospective messiahs being born to these erstwhile virgins. The girls were forbidden to marry and in order to miss no opportunity to produce what might be the messiah, they continued visiting the Presence in the darkness of the ark.

If all that seems a little thickheaded on the part of their parents, one need only remember the noble Roman matron of whom Josephus tells—she who was designated for special attention by a god who sent word by priests of his temple that if she would be in a back room of the sanctuary, come night, he would descend to her. And he regularly did for quite a number of nights. Her family took massive public pride in this until to her indignation and that of her husband it turned out that the god was really only an old admirer for whom bribed priests were making the arrangements.

Spragg was finally murdered by a jealous lover who, happily, escaped. An enterprising pair of young men secretly disposed of the body and as secretly assumed the place of the Presence. Though they fulfilled their chief function in darkness, for some reason some of the more experienced virgins grew suspicious and exposure followed. This rather put a damper on Spraggism. New Jerusalem fell apart but central Illinois reputedly still has a quota of the grandchildren of God's Children.

Researchers point out that no one can tell where New Jerusalem and the ark were located. Nevertheless, if the Spragg story is not true it certainly should be, for there is no other quite like it in the communitarian saga.

ii.   KING BEN

> *Benjamin was born in 1861*
> *Which was the year the Civil War begun;*
> *Perhaps he felt at home*
> *'Mid the environment of war*
> *For he had been a warrior*
> *In the war of heaven, before.*

So wrote a follower of "The Younger Brother of Jesus," otherwise known as "The Seventh Messenger," or "King" Benjamin Purnell—or, in cosmic simplicity, merely as Benjamin, as in the above "poem." Notwithstanding the homage and adoration paid him, King Ben impressed some as a scoundrel of the first water. He began his career by deserting his wife and baby to contract a bigamous marriage, and he ended it in a courtroom, exposed as the systematic ravisher of the girls of his House of David at Benton Harbor, Michigan.

His first wife, a neighborhood girl he married near Maysville, Kentucky, said that he "liked to lie around in the sun, or go visiting where all he had to do was eat and sleep." He and his spouse didn't get along. He ran off, took up preaching, and married another woman, all before he was twenty. He wandered about with a mule-drawn house on wheels, his hair and beard growing, and though he announced himself as "the Second Son of the Virgin Mary" he was so unimpressive that he had to make brooms to eke out his income from preaching.

Drifting into Detroit, he and his wife joined a local heaven conducted by "Prince" Michael K. Mills, who soon died in the jail where he was held on complaints of assault from some indignant sisters of the flock. Mockers said the indignation really was from the fact that each of these women belatedly learned he was assaulting others besides herself.

The immortal prince had vanished, but Purnell's eyes had been opened to the value of a religious colony and a royal title. Opportunely, he was informed by the "Holy Graph," whatever that may have been, which came down from heaven, that he was the "Seventh Messenger" of the books of Malachi and Revelation. Purnell said the six preceding angelic messengers had all been English or Australian, and he named poor, mad Joanna Southcott as number one. Apparently it was beside the point that her own information had been that she was "the woman of Revelation 12." At any rate, Purnell was number seven. He was "the angel flying in the midst of heaven," and when he "should begin to sound, the mysteries of God should be finished." In other words, the end of the dispensation was at hand, and would be accomplished when Purnell "should begin to sound." Benjamin and those he gathered unto him would be preserved forever in the flesh. All others would have to experience death.

The Holy Graph told Purnell to adjourn to Benton Harbor and begin the "ingathering" of "Israel," which was to say the 144,000 descendants of the "lost tribes" who were to be saved in the flesh. Miss Southcott had "sealed" great droves of the 144,000 lucky ones of Revelation almost a century before, charging what the traffic would bear, from a penny to a pound, and other prophets had similarly obliged other hordes, but it does not appear that Purnell was to make numerical adjustment for these. It didn't make a lot of difference. He never had a thousand followers at any time, even by including the shaggy and not always too-devout ballplayers who wandered about the country in his name.

The Purnells took the titles of King Benjamin and Queen Mary, apparently most informally. Officials of the commune today refuse to discuss or answer questions about the royal role of the prophet. People flocked in, eager to live forever in the flesh, and gave all they owned to Purnell. 1903 began the new dispensation, and accordingly was renumbered as the year 1. Buildings were put up, with such names as Shiloh, The Ark, Bethlehem, and Jerusalem, the entire establishment being The Israelite House of David. The members worked hard, in adoration of the leader.

They were enjoined to celibacy and to the use of vegetables, rather than meat. Liquor was forbidden. But the most striking thing from the public standpoint was the long hair and full beards of the men. The hair was cultivated because "the pictures of Jesus all show him with long hair," and because the Bible says man is the head of the woman, and that it is a shame for the head of the woman to be uncovered. Other sects use this text for requiring that a woman have long hair and cover it in daily life, or in church, or both.

The House of David theology is otherwise remarkable in that it says the snake in the Garden was not really a snake but a preacher created by Satan of himself for the purpose of tempting Eve. He became the father of Cain. Adam then sinned in having relations with Eve after her slippage from rectitude. This was the fall of man.

It was pretty rough going at first in the House of David, but that was unimportant because King Benjamin said his older brother, Jesus, would arrive in 1906 to begin the millennium, with headquarters at the commune. Those who had "ingathered" would be the blessed, while the rest of mankind would receive its just deserts. When 1906 was over, with no evidence of the millennium having begun, Purnell said the fact was that the proper date was 1916—that the stenographer had misunderstood him when he gave the original revelation.

Ordinarily, little errors like that did not trouble millennarian converts too much, but this and a series of misunderstandings moved an untoward number of his possibly three hundred followers to attempt to recover the possessions they had contributed. The disgruntled were got rid of as quietly as possible. New hopefuls were pouring in until Benjamin presently had eight hundred to work the farmlands, to labor in the shops, and to live in miserable dormitories.

With growing prosperity, the Seventh Angel may not have been seen very often in the midst of the heavens, but he was seen all around Benton Harbor, and in fine clothes, a broad hat, and flashy equipages. He acquired a public amusement park, a restaurant, and other enterprises which poured money into his pockets, so that in the privacy of Shiloh house he and Queen Mary lived in splendor.

Jesus didn't come in 1916, either, but there was too much going on in the world for this to be particularly noticed. The great war in Europe proved that if 1916 was not the exact date, it could not be far wrong. In some way, a whispering campaign developed that while Benjamin preached celibacy, he was keeping a harem of the more comely damsels in the house called Shiloh. This talk grew so persistent and circumstantial that a Federal investigation was attempted, but Purnell successfully fought it off.

However, a rift had by then developed within the commune between the king's adherents and his detractors. In 1920 the latter brought a deluge of lawsuits against him. That of a couple named Hansel came to trial at last as a test case. The Hansels presented proof that they had given Purnell five thousand dollars, and with their children had labored nine years for him. The court awarded them a judgment of $26,000—which was suddenly but a small matter in the news, for the trial had uncovered evidence pointing to the real reason that some marriages were being permitted by Purnell.

The stories were that the king kept girls clothed in silks in "Oriental" style around him, that he "initiated" these into the mysteries of sex, and that he conducted orgies with groups of them. Should one chance to become pregnant, she was forthwith married to one of the young men of the colony. It was claimed there was once a mass ceremony in which twenty-four of these girls were married simultaneously—which seems to be quite a few girls.

Several were finally found who would accuse Purnell, but before the warrants could be served he disappeared into the tunnels and secret rooms of his network of buildings—or perhaps he left town. Either way, he remained out of sight for several years until one of his erstwhile alleged paramours betrayed him for four thousand dollars in Judas money. His indignant adherents cried that he was God. In court, pleading for mercy, he said, "I am a poor, broken, dying old man."

That was exactly what he appeared to be. He was found guilty of various fornications, and the House of David was thrown into receivership. In the midst of the legal maneuvers, while appealing the verdict, Purnell died—or he seemed to. His gold collar studded with diamonds was placed around his neck and his richest robes were placed upon him, with his ruby ring upon his finger. His long brown wavy hair was combed out upon the pillow. He was expected to rise in three days.

The king had no more permitted embalming than he had permitted education—"Dung is more useful to mankind than education"—but though the three days passed the body still appeared natural. A year went by and finally three of them. The body still looked "as if it might rise tomorrow." Abruptly, then, it disappeared, and in after times an undertaker declared he had not only embalmed it immediately after death but had been called in at frequent intervals to reembalm it—a thing necessary because of its exposure to the air.

Meanwhile, the dissolvement decrees had been reversed and the charter allowed to stand. A division was permitted, however, between the wrangling factions. Queen Mary obtained half the assets and two hundred followers and established The City of David in her share of the buildings. The other faction continued as The House of David.

Then the scandals quieted. Queen Mary established the King David Hospital and Clinic and busied herself with other humanitarian enterprises as well as continuing farming and dairy operations. The other side went into lumber and other businesses, continued to operate the park, a motel, and entertainment enterprises. It even lifted the ban on liquor and tobacco for the Davidites who had decided in the second generation, with prosperity, that those indulgences were not sinful. Wealth multiplied all through the depression until each faction was worth millions. This splinter group finally admitted it did not expect the king to appear again in the flesh. Queen Mary would have none of this, declaring the resurrection was bound to come. However, she refused to set a date.

She was still waiting for the king's rising, and the visit of his older brother, when she died at ninety-one in August of 1953. The House and the Kingdom still go on getting richer by the day and proclaiming that "Thousands now alive will never see death."

iii.   KORESH

It was to Cyrus R. Teed and his science of the Cellular Cosmogony that the world became indebted back in the 1880's for the knowledge that it is only to the "unilluminated" mind that the earth appears to be a sphere on the outer surface of which man lives. He wanted it known that this is a gross error. The earth is a sphere all right, he agreed —but it is hollow and man lives inside it with his feet pointing outward from the center and with the horizon curving upward on all sides instead of downward.

A man like Teed could not reasonably be expected to be satisfied with such a conservative name, and soon the ex-physician, who was in the comfortable tradition of being immortal in the body and of confabulating with God, took the name of "Koresh" because God always so addressed him. Referring to himself in the regal plural, he announced "from the authority vested in us and under the light of divine illumination" the revelation of the "true astronomical and religious system." These were either the same or were so mingled as to make small difference to the unilluminated mind.

The keepers of the Index Librorum Prohibitorum had quietly allowed Copernicus to slip from the list in the 1830's. In 1870, the thirty-year-old Dr. Teed was forced to begin his own veto of both the enlightened fathers and Copernicus, not to mention Pythagoras and Ptolemy. This he did without apparent regret.

He christened the new system "Koreshanity," after his new name, Koresh. God called him Koresh, he said, because it was the Hebrew equivalent of his name, Cyrus. "anity" was added to Koresh to designate the new heaven and new earth and the new philosophy which would "replace all churches and governments." Koreshanity consisted in part of his cellular cosmogony which was concerned with man's living inside the earth.

A logical objection to the unilluminated seemed to be the matter of the heavenly bodies at their inconceivable distances—distances in excess of the diameter of the earth which he said was actually only seven thousand miles. But the problem was more apparent than real, Teed declared— and he revealed that there are no stars: what people suppose to be such bodies are really reflections of the planets, and the assumed distance of these from the earth is an illusion. In fact, Teed said, even the planets are not planets, but luminous mercury discs floating around inside our earthly sphere.

He added that this was not a matter of controversy but a demonstrable fact—one easily proved to anyone of open mind. He was also willing to demonstrate "the contradictions and absurdities" of the Copernican system and he established a "scientific staff" from among his disciples, providing them with fanciful instruments which proved all his contentions beyond doubt to any stern realists in his train. These instruments consisted of a hollow globe, a telescope and charts, and, most importantly, a "rectilineator." This would show anyone that the earth "curved upward eight inches to the mile" instead of downward, from the viewer.

For fifteen years or so "Cyrus the Messenger" preached his doctrine. Finally in 1886 in Chicago he established "The College of Life" which was to further the teachings of "the Koreshean Unity." Somewhere along there he formed the "Society Arch Triumphant."

Disciples increasingly flocked to him. There had been a world-wide religious conclave in Chicago and in the wake of it the city had many dabblers in "Eastern" religions— pseudo Hindus, Taoists, Buddhists, and so on. These were certain they were filled with "the wisdom of the Orient," and somehow the new religion of Koresh appealed to many of them.

In 1894 the *Chicago Herald* reported the progress of the "smooth shaven little man of 54 whose brown, restless eyes glow and burn like live coals. He directs the destinies of a 'new race of men,' the 'sons of God.' He exerts a strange, mesmerizing influence over his converts, particularly the other sex."

It was notable that three-fourths of his followers were female, but male and female alike they agreed to abstain from sex indulgence just as they freely gave him their property. He had a reputed four thousand followers, and he may well have had, for large sums of money came to him.

Presently, he established a commune near Chicago in which rulership was supposed to be vested in a board of trustees, but the *Herald* declared that Teed "is the absolute, irresponsible, immaculate and inviolate high muck-a-muck if ever there was one. He is addressed with awe and trembling. Neither his acts nor his motives are inquired into and his word is law—the only law."

Koresh retorted that "since the established churches have completed their work and have nothing left to recommend them to the favor of the world," people were called to "come out" and join Koreshanity, which would be all things to all men. He said that as soon as he should have located the proper spot, he would establish a world capital which would be the greatest city in existence. It would be "located at the point where the vitellus of the alchemico-organic cosmos specifically determines. The position of the sign marks the head of the coming dispensation and will define the location of this greatest of all cities."

Presently the vitellus was located when a disciple named Dampkohler gave Teed 320 acres of land in the sparsely settled coastal area of southwestern Florida—that is to say, looking out over the Gulf. There, at Estero, Teed began establishing his New Jerusalem. Streets were platted four hundred feet in width, which Teed thought modest enough for the projected greatest city on—rather, in—earth. More land was to be acquired, of course, to accommodate the expected 8,000,000 inhabitants—and indeed the prophet soon snapped up a tempting offer of several thousand acres for $12,000. The chief drawback proved to be that the acquisition was subject to frequent overflow and was accordingly worthless. Meanwhile, when the few advance colonists were not busy laying out parks and streets and such, they erected preliminary habitations for men and others for women. A sawmill, printery, and other shops were put up.

In the upshot, Teed lacked 7,999,800 of achieving the expected population—but the two hundred people who finally did gather in supported him in fair style most of the time. Fortunately, there were contributions from distant members of the "Church Triumphant," as the "Arch Triumphant" was commonly called, so that when there were brawlings and withdrawals of the celibates he did not suffer unduly. Recusants told the press that nothing at the place was conducted with any degree of sanity, that for months at a time everyone might go without actually enough to eat—except for Teed and a few of his favorites who, it chanced, were female—and that nothing made money except the trinket shop which rooked tourists and the printery which sent out a paper to nonresident members.

These departing rebels at first tried suing Teed for the return of their property, but the precedents were too strong. Mostly, the courts gave them only the back of a hand. Tradition in the area became that an undue percentage of the Jerusalemites committed suicide in despair, but history seems not to say whether Dampkohler, who donated the original 320 acres, was among these. Certainly the courts dealt with him more generously than with some who sued: he got back half his land, and most fortunately so, as it proved, for his lawyers took it for their fee and called everything even.

Soon the Messenger was impelled to establish a lesser order of membership in which those weak in the flesh might indulge in marriage, since he could not otherwise keep enough of his people to support him properly. But like their more exalted brethren, it still appears that those of the lesser order were to live forever. Teed said that matrimony was all right for them for the time being, since they were in the "investigative stage." But he recommended celibacy for them as they advanced. He embraced this tenet himself, he said. And while his wife lived in the recommended austerity in the women's quarters, he led a flashy existence, driving frequently to Fort Myers with three young women of his colony. For a time, he was much taken up by Fort Myers society, and it is a moot point whether he made an ass of society or whether the élite permitted him to make an ass of himself with his pronouncements in having him at their functions.

Many people saw him as a corrupt and foolish man—even an insane one. Various Florida papers castigated him. The national press picked up the story which became a great one of the day. All of Koresh's doings were chronicled. The state threatened to quash him and under the general pressure he became so spiritually beaten down that just before Christmas of 1908 he died.

He had not failed to provide for the retention of his grip on his people even after that event. In the tradition of Shadrach Ireland, he told them that he might appear to pass on—but that he would rise again and take all believers with him directly to heaven. Accordingly, it behooved them to remain faithful. Everyone gathered around the body for a prayer meeting. On the fourth day officers appeared and ordered the putrid remains to be buried. Under pressure, a bathtub was brought and the prophet was got into it and carried to a tomb on Estero Island.

Thirteen years later, while his son and the other faithful still awaited his appearance and the journey to heaven, the tomb was found empty—understandably so even to the Koresheans, for in a hurricane the sea had cut into it. Some say the body was never found. Others declared it was washed up on the beach, which seems unlikely since there had been no embalming, and was secretly buried by the colonists.

With Teed's death, the newspapers forgot the commune. The dwindling membership continued living inside the earth, subsisting largely by farming and fishing. If any of them wondered why a boat sailing out into the Gulf disappeared hull first as if sailing down over a sphere instead of up its slope, they seem not to have said so in their newspaper, *The American Eagle*, which they continued publishing.

The commune survived Teed's death by forty years. Finally, in 1947, the dozen or so remaining members fell to quarreling and to suing each other, and most of the property passed at once into private hands. Now Estero caters to tourists who stop to see the museum. There, among other objects of interest, one may still see the scientific instruments which Teed used to demonstrate that Estero was at the vitellus of a hollow earth.

. . . . . .
Where the pure currents flow
From all gushing hearts together,
And the wedding of the Lamb
Is the feast of joy forever.
           Let us sing, brothers, sing.

We have built us a dome
On our beautiful plantation,
And we all have one home,
And one family relation;
We have battled with the wiles
Of the dark world of Mammon,
And returned with its spoils
To the home of our dear ones.
           Let us sing, brothers, sing.

When the rude winds of wrath
Idly rave round our dwelling,
And the slanderer's breath
Like a simoon was swelling,
Then so merrily we sung,
As the storm blustered o'er us,
Till the very heavens rung
With our hearts' joyful chorus.
           Let us go, brothers, go.

So love's sunshine begun:
Now the spirit-flowers are blooming,
And the feeling that we're one
All our hearts is perfuming;
Toward one home we have all
Set our faces together,
Where true love doth dwell
In peace and joy forever.
           Let us sing, brothers, sing.

—ONEIDA SONG

CHAPTER NINETEEN

ONEIDA AND THE
PERFECT RACE

TO EVERY MAN HIS OWN DISH AT THE MARRIAGE SUPPER. I CALL A
WOMAN MINE. SHE IS YOURS. SHE IS DEAR IN THE HAND OF THE
STRANGER.

ONE day in the summer of 1846 a letter was received by
Harriet Noyes at Putney, Vermont—or rather at the
Kingdom of Heaven on the outskirts of the town. It was a
love letter from a married man who, since he has relatives
who might still be embarrassed about the whole matter, shall
be known here as Charles George, which is close enough.
He was an associate of the lady's husband, John Humphrey
Noyes, who was prophet of the inhabitants of the Kingdom
—a group of "Bible Communists" who called themselves Perfectionists. This meant that they strove to live sinless lives.
Many frankly felt themselves to be doing so.

The fifty people of the hill farm were having a difficult time and George was in the field to contact sympathizers

who it was hoped would contribute to keep the commune going until all might be gathered in. Lonely, he wrote not his own wife but the prophet's. Mrs. Noyes took the letter to her husband who was producing copy for his proselytical newspaper. The thin, jut-jawed man of thirty-five read the missive and Harriet confessed that she returned George's feeling.

Noyes did not rebuke her nor speak of a serpent in his Eden. He had long declared that no one could call himself a Christian unless completely unselfish, and that this included the sharing not only of labor and goods with one's fellows, but of spouses. So far, though, Noyes had done nothing about this beyond theorizing, and trying to keep fervent converts from putting the theory into practice before he deemed the time had come.

Perhaps the fact that George was a timid soul made the letter more striking. Noyes took it as indication that God was ready for the establishment of complex marriage under which all the men of the commune would be husbands to all the women. He and his wife had been successfully practicing birth control, so he knew sex indulgence could be departmentalized. Most contacts would be on "the social plane," which he said would lead to a closer spiritual understanding between the men and women of the Kingdom. Socially, couples would mate rather at will, while propagatory contacts would be controlled, with couples scientifically paired to produce an increasingly superior race.

He called George back to Putney that he and the Noyeses might meet together. Noyes had had quite a bit of trouble in the past on George's account, for the latter's wife, Mary, had been prone to practice complexity with one of the male pillars of Perfection, an erstwhile jackleg preacher. As a matter of fact, Noyes himself had brought her to Putney from the hinterlands of her temptation so he might keep an eye on her, for he had seen in her "a Magdalene" who might blunder around and condemn her soul if he left her unshepherded.

The couples convened and proceeded to some self-dramatization. Someone read George's letter aloud. Mrs. Noyes (so Mrs. George recorded) said she was pleased by it and that her heart was drawn out toward him. George, the only handsome person of the quartet—a dark-haired man of moody and changeable nature—was still of the same mind as when he mustered enough spunk to write to Mrs. Noyes. After he expressed himself, Noyes asked his leave to tell Mrs. G. that he loved her.

According to Mrs. George, her husband "heartily consented." She then shyly confessed that she loved Mr. Noyes no end, and had done so for a long time. In fact, she had loved him so much she "was afraid he would find it out." However, Noyes suspected some of the angels of his heaven were not psychologically ready for complex marriage and he decreed that actual establishment of the doctrine should be postponed while he prepared the minds of the others.

So, says Mrs. George, the couples considered themselves only "engaged" for the time being, expecting to live in conformity to the laws of "the world." But the effect of confessed affection was "most refreshing" to their spirits. Their love, they knew, was of God because it was destitute of selfishness—the selfishness of wishing to retain a mate exclusively to oneself. They had formed a circle which she said it would not be easy for the devil to break.

Noyes was probably in his early teens when he first heard of Perfection, a sect embraced by many in millennial fervor. Much of the early work had been done by Charles Finney, a lawyer turned preacher, but in time he begged that he no longer be called Perfectionist because of the scandals which had come to be connected in the public mind with the term.

There were two chief groups, the New York and Massachusetts, each with congregations in several states. Noyes said the New York church was "wild and barbaric like Esau," and the other, to which he belonged, "like Jacob, more intellectual and civilized." Finney declared both had become antinomian, holding themselves above the laws of the Bible, and that in their freedom from law they were nothing but religiously veiled free lovers.

The quarrel was aired in the press and Noyes said that Finney was a liar. Finney reasoned, Noyes said, that if *he* were above the law he would promptly plunge into whoredom—and accordingly was certain that those who were released from the law had done so. A bit later, when complex marriage had been instituted in the Putney group, assurances were still given by the brethren, while attempting to win young female converts, that no free love was going on. After exposure was made by defecting angels of the Kingdom, it was explained that free love did not exist there, for that implied freedom "to love today and leave tomorrow," while complexity required the continued protection of the man for his numerously shared wives and their children.

Even in Finney's administration Perfectionists had become overweeningly concerned with hitting upon the mode of sex activity which would please God. They felt nothing would be right about their religion if they were off the track in that department. Finney sternly said celibacy was the only answer. He was so fervent in his stand that entire classes of young men and women ministerial students under him at the new Oberlin Theological Seminary took vows of perpetual celibacy.

So did many of his converts—sometimes whole congregations among the "hundreds" of churches he established. These vows were perhaps the easier to take in view of the momentarily expected end of the dispensation. There is no record of how well they were kept.

Splinterings, regroupings, resplinterings were rampant. Some Perfectionists, for instance, sought "perfect love," and were pleasantly hazy as to just what the phrase might mean. Some were pretty sure it had to do with more than spiritual love.

Now, it came to some of Finney's avowed celibates in New England that there was small virtue in maintaining perfection of character unless this was done in the face of temptation. Untempted, who could not remain stainless? Some congregations might concentrate on refraining from temptations of murder or covetousness or gossip, but these were bored with twiddling with milk-and-water enticements which even a moderately striving Perfectionist might conquer. For those who had learned to run, strong meat was required.

Their solution was ingenious—or ingenuous: Perfectionists should deliberately tempt themselves with sex. Then by refusing to indulge, they would gain virtue, as well as strength for withstanding temptation in the future. But they did not counsel casting pearls before swine: The tempting was to be done strictly within the congregation, which circumstance would have the additional advantage of allowing two Perfectionists at a time to overcome temptation.

They judged there must have been a reasonable degree of temptation in the Holy Kiss which had been exchanged wholesale at the love-feasts of Christians in St. Paul's day, else it would not have led to such grave scandals and the thunderings of the Fathers of which there were clear echoes in the Bible.

And so a deal of holy kissing went on at some of the Perfectionist meetings, but something stronger was clearly needed. The eager believers then recollected another custom of the early church which had caused even more commotion. This was spiritual mating, in which households of brethren took *agapetae*—"beloved ones"—with whom they lived, bound by love vows and by oaths of celibacy.

Accordingly, some of the celibates took spiritual mates. They felt that they might most strongly tempt each other in bed, and at night, which would provide privacy for the bashful and at the same time not waste the Lord's daylight. The custom was simplified by the fact that meetings were commonly held in the homes of members. Too, it was just as easy to return to one's own house next morning as in the middle of the night after preaching.

Now, bundling was probably not new in New England, where it presumably was instituted to save candles and to provide opportunity for rest for a young man who had come a distance to see his girl, and who must be back at work at daylight. In 1781 Samuel Peters had discoursed on "The Advantages of Bundling" in his *General History of Connecticut*. He said that because of the great modesty of the females there it would be rude for a gentleman to speak before one of "a garter, knee, or leg, yet it is thought but a piece of civility to ask her to bundle—a custom as old as the first settlement in 1634. It is certainly innocent, virtuous, and prudent, or the puritans would not have permitted it to prevail among their offspring. . . . If any man . . . should bundle with a young lady in New-England, and behave himself unseemly towards her, he must first melt her into passion, and expel heaven, death, and hell from her mind. . . ; if he escapes with life it will be owing to the parents flying from their beds to protect him."

On the other hand, Washington Irving did not believe the young ladies quite so fierce as all this toward their bundling mates. He said this fine old custom had produced in New England "a raw-boned hardy race of whoreson whalers, wood-cutters, fishermen and pedlars, and strapping corn-fed wenches."

Bundlers had also been scorned in verse:

> *Deep down in hell there let them dwell*
> *And bundle on that bed,*
> *Then turn and roll without control*
> *Till all their lusts are fed.*

Perhaps the Perfectionists with their great knowledge of history, did not expect the impossible of their holy bundlers who indeed were not to have a board between them but were to stimulate, though not feed, their romantic impulses. They provided a remedy: If a couple should ruefully report to the congregation that no matter how hard they had tried to maintain the ultimately proper distance under the blankets, it had been impossible not to indulge in a bit of fornication, this was viewed as a sign from heaven that they were not entirely suited to each other as spiritual mates.

They then canvassed the congregation for individuals who might better strengthen their spiritual sinews. Perhaps understandably, all this created a hullabaloo in those quarters where it was not realized that the worshippers were tempting themselves strictly for the kingdom of heaven's sake.

It was this lunatic fringe of periodic celibates, holy kissers, and spiritual lovers which had outraged or delighted a decade of newspaper and church-journal readers before Noyes began preaching Perfection in the middle 1830's. His parents were Congregationalists, religiously conservative, and the last thing either he or they would have expected was that he might become involved in any of the roaring evangelical movements—especially this one.

His father, a slow-courting merchant, was forty when he married Polly Hayes—a lady through whom the future prophet became a cousin of a future President. The wedding might not have occurred when it did had not Polly, who was seventeen years the younger, told Noyes, Sr., to fish or cut bait, for he had taken up five years of her time already without her being able to bring him to the point by subtler means. This was in 1804, and following a succession of daughters, John was born in 1811 in Brattleboro, Vermont. Polly prayed that her new baby might grow up to be "a minister of the Everlasting Gospel," but John showed none of her interest in religion until he was eight, when he was converted at a revival.

His father had made a financial killing in the War of 1812, meantime, and had retired to Putney, Vermont, to become a private banker. He was sent to Congress against his will, and he found the experience drudging and unpleasant, though he could not entirely fail to enjoy the honor itself.

John desired to go to Yale but he was sent off to

Dartmouth instead, where his father once had tutored Daniel Webster in order to earn funds for his own schooling. John's mother feared Yale might prove dangerous to the morals of a young man. His innate stubbornness, of which he eventually would need all he could muster, is shown in his wearing the already-purchased Yale collars, despite the jeering of his Dartmouth fellows.

Scared of the girls, he applied himself to his books, kept a journal, and was elected to Phi Beta Kappa. Then his personality changed, and he wrote that he went "through the mazes of dissipation," whatever that meant to him, after which he was again overtaken by "virtue, honor and the dictates of conscience." His binges may not have been extensive, for three or four years later, in trying to pacify an outraged sweetheart—probably the only woman he ever burningly loved—who was humiliated by scandal in which he was involved, he declared himself still a virgin. However, like Thomas Lake Harris, he was likely to have a private definition, opposite to the generally accepted one, for words to apply to himself and his acts.

Despite his physical homeliness, Noyes had a strong and pleasant personality and when he returned from Dartmouth to Vermont to study law with his sister's husband, he found plenty of girls waiting to be squired. In the winter of 1830, when he was nineteen, another revival struck. These were the days of Lamarck and the Transcendentalists, and the freethinking young law student went to scoff—and to court, for church attendance was necessary if one wished to spark the daughters of the better families.

He remained to be engulfed by a veritable fever of religion—and a demand from God that he preach. He refused. He was struck down by violent illness and, near death, agreed to become a minister if God would let him live—and his mother was tearfully overjoyed.

Up and around, he was presently off for Andover seminary where he was amazed at what he considered a coldness of spirit among the ministerial faculty and the students. To him, religion had become life and not merely a phase of it. He and several other fervent young divines banded together privately, compacting to become missionaries to Asia—where, indeed, some of them did go. Two were eaten by cannibals in the Pacific islands.

The important thing about these meetings at Andover, where they vowed to remain "young converts forever" —which was to say, fervent ones—was the "mutual criticism" of each others' defects. The victim stood before the others while they dissected his moral and spiritual character and scathed his shortcomings. Though he be brought to tears, he was not allowed to speak back. This was to be the system of government in Noyes's as-yet-undreamed-of religious colonies.

For his second year, Noyes transferred to Yale where his younger brother George was a student. But the atmosphere in the seminary was fully as cold as that at Andover. Disappointed, he settled down to studying his Bible, preaching on Sundays at a local chapel and in a country church or two as a licensed student minister.

He had taken it for granted that the dark peoples of the earth were the ones needing missionaries, but one day he was struck by the staggering realization that New England was worse off because the people there were sinning in the face of knowledge. Despite the cries of betrayal from his Dartmouth friends, he remained with his resolution to save New England first.

About this time, his searchings of the Scriptures convinced him that God wanted no part of the sin-repent-sin-repent cycle of living which even preachers declared was not only inevitable, but necessary in view of man's fallibility. Even the Perfectionists, who made a point of being as perfect as was humanly possible, were convinced that a reasonable amount of sin would be incurred by the best of them.

Noyes announced that God had meant what He said in commanding men to be as perfect as the angels. He explained that this was entirely within human abilities because, as was evident from biblical history and prophecy, Jesus had returned to earth at the destruction of Jerusalem in 70 A.D. and had instituted a covenant which made it possible for Christians to be perfect and which secured their eternal salvation, besides "giving them full freedom from written law and human instruction." In other words, guaranteed safe from error, they might make their rules as they went along. Noyes further announced that he himself was living a sinless life.

The faculty was marvellously irritated by all these pronouncements. Uncowed, Noyes disputed with them freely and was faced with dismissal. He mollified the reverend gentlemen a bit by stating that although he was sinless, he realized his outward actions might not appear at all times perfect to others. Largely on his brother's account, he was allowed to remain a few weeks to get his degree, but his preaching license was lifted.

Said Noyes, "I have taken away their license to sin and they continue to sin. They have taken away my license to preach, and I shall continue to preach." Nor had he any patience with his father's warning that unorthodox preachers such as he would be "whipped into the traces." His family was embarrassed. As he said, his friends fell away, his good name was lost before the world, but he "rejoiced and leaped for joy," thinking all that a small price to pay for salvation.

Besides, Abigail Merwin, one of his New Haven converts, was loyal. She was older than he by several years, but he loved her, the first woman he had ever loved, as she was quite possibly the last, at least so far as unquenchable, eating, passionate, all-forgetting emotion was concerned. But then Noyes caused a rift in an escapade of his in New York. Falling into a period of self-doubt, his apologists said, he went into the rum shops and brothels of the slums for several days. By his own account, he went into those places to preach to the downfallen. However, when his friends rescued him he was in such a dirty and only semi-coherent condition that no one believed him.

There is a bit of a puzzle here. In his writings he says that during his career in "legal religion"—the religion of ordinary Christians, with their laws of conduct—he had practiced temperance. But having become a Perfectionist, he felt impelled "to assert practically my liberty from the rules of my old bondage." Accordingly, "I drank ardent spirits, that I might reprove the spirit of legality which still hovered about me, and that I might practically transfer the keeping of my soul from the temperance pledge to the Spirit of God."

Also: "The turn which my mind took in regard to sexual morality had much influence on my subsequent course. . . . I did nothing of which I had occasion to be ashamed, but I lost reputation with those who saw only externals. . . . I was loosed from the moorings of ordinary prudence, and set adrift once more with no pilot but God."

It seems possible, then, that he could have invaded the beds of the ladies in the Five Points and have remained, by his mode of reckoning, quite virginal—which is what he assured the angry and humiliated Abigail Merwin that he was when he returned to New Haven. He had to send his assurances by letter for she refused to see him, the scandal having been widely noised. This letter and subsequent ones went unanswered, though he made a bemeaning spectacle of himself by standing outside her house day after day for hours at a time. Abigail married another suitor and moved to Ithaca, ignoring even the final missive in which Noyes told her that some day he should have her—God had assured him of that.

Then began what he called "three years of wandering, both physically and theologically," three years of misery of spirit, of frustration in thinking of Abigail who became an obsession with him. Had he been able to marry her as a student, there is little telling what direction his career might have taken, for he "had no thought of being a leader" in

those days when his ideas of sex and marriage seemed orthodox. But it must be remembered that his own escapade,
stemming from perhaps a severe nervous disorder, drove
him to the wrecking of that courtship. Even had he won Abigail, his bent might have led him to an off-trail course.

The New York incident humiliated and alarmed his
family at Putney. He fell into difficulties with his parents
who thought he should go to work and support himself,
while he felt they should contribute "to the work of God" by
financing a religious journal he and a friend published at
New Haven in the beginning of his "three years of wandering."

The venture faded. He went on a tour of Perfectionist congregations in New Hampshire with a young friend.
There, apparently, he had his first experience in the organized unconventionalities of some of the splinters. At a meeting in Brimfield several young ladies—"well versed in the
Scriptures, but forward"—kissed and hugged him. He refused to reciprocate. Leaving his friend, he journeyed to
another town, fortunately being away when the "Mary
L—— scandal" burst at Brimfield.

What this amounted to was that Mary L—— and
another damsel, Maria B——, invaded the friend's bed
one cold February night and stayed with him until morning.
They intended no harm, meaning only to test their virtue.
"But as usually happens in such presumptuous experiments," Noyes declared, "in the end the flesh triumphed
over the spirit."

This was not what Mary and Maria declared the
morning after it happened. They would not confess to any
weakness of the flesh. A general quarrel ensued and Mary
seems to have slapped her protesting father. What the young
man said during all this is not recorded. The scandal was
noised outside the congregation, which was obviously not
converted to the strength through temptation theory.

Meantime, to turn the talk to something else, Mary
announced that God had warned her He was going to de-

stroy Brimfield that night and only those who fled with her
to a certain mountain top were to be saved. Her prophecy
found little honor in her own country. Only another girl,
a friend of hers, went with her. They became mazed in the
brush in the darkness, at last found their way to a farmer's
house, and spent the night there. Next morning Mary announced God had spared Brimfield because she had taken
the sins of the town upon herself.

Newspapers declared that the girls pranced about
naked on the mountain top at daybreak, and some people
said they shed their garments on the way to the mountain to
appease God. It seems well to recollect that a February blizzard was brewing and to accept the official Perfectionist version that they merely "lost some of their shoes" in the darkness.

On Noyes's return to Brimfield he attended a meeting in a Perfectionist home. The daughter of the household
gave Noyes "some passionate kisses" and she and others of
the well-Scriptured girls complained that he was too standoffish. They felt his holier-than-thou attitude unbecoming,
and that he was boorishly suspicious of their motives. Accordingly, he exchanged a few holy kisses and sat on a bench
in meeting with his arm around one of the damsels. His
good sense then got the better of him. In the night God
warned him that he should leave. Departing at daylight despite the blizzard, he traveled afoot through snow and zero
cold the entire sixty miles to Putney.

News quickly reached there of the scientific moral experiment of the girls in the young stranger's bed. In the gossip Noyes was made a chief participant in a religious sex
orgy. Presently Noyes's friend and a preacher named Weld
arrived at the Noyes home. The latter added to the gossip, as
it later developed, by talking behind John's back.

Noyes refused his father's demand that he "track
down and refute the base lies," and "after a warm discussion," as he says, the old gentleman more or less invited him
and his two friends to live elsewhere. They moved in with a

Perfectionist farmer nearby. John did write the woman at whose home the scandal had occurred and her matter-of-fact account by return mail absolved him.

Strangely, despite that, new stories sprang up and John finally realized that Weld, a chief priest of Perfection, was at the bottom of them. He kept quiet for the time being about his discovery. This man had dominated him spiritually for some time past, Noyes giving in to his leadership despite Weld's pussyfooting preachments which dealt too lightly with sinners lest they cease their financial contributions.

On a new tour, Weld did all the preaching as usual, until one day Noyes had opportunity to deliver a sermon. In it, he allowed Weld to realize he knew of the slanderous stories the man had told. Then he turned the other barrel loose on both Weld and the congregation, which was one of Finney's groups who believed a little sinning would pass muster—if repented—since it was inevitable.

Noyes told them bluntly they were children of the devil. Then, he recorded, "there was a strange sound."

It was from Weld who sat "with his eyes closed, his countenance black with horror, his hands waving up and down, lungs laboring with long and rattling breaths." The congregation was in such great agitation that not even fascination could hold some who, in terror, as if the fiend were present, left the building.

Weld's breathing "became a frightful roar." Then he grew quiet. "Gleams of joy appeared on his countenance. He gazed slowly around with an eye of angelic brilliancy. He fixed his gaze upon a young man with whom he had lately disputed the doctrine of holiness," which was to say, Perfection. "There was a lion in his eyes. The young man quailed. In the same way he singled out another opposer of holiness, and he too quailed. Finally, his eye met mine. I looked at him steadily. His countenance softened into a smile and he dropped his eye."

And then another seizure took him. Finally recovering, he stated both attacks had been brought about by Noyes's words which "were like fire to his spirit." And God had said to him in good King James English, "Touch not mine anointed, and do my prophet no harm."

Strangely, though Noyes's status as a prophet had been announced through Weld, the man continued circulating "improbable and foolish" stories about him, making him a monstrous lecher. Finally Noyes challenged him to a Biblical disputation on a sort of winner-take-all basis. Apparently one would make a statement or ask a question. Then indefinite time would be given for preparation of an answer which of course had to be proved from the Bible. After many days of what Noyes calls "hair splitting" argument, he had driven Weld by littles into an impasse. Taking that as a sign of God's favor, he promptly cut Weld off from the faith forever.

Such, then were the things occupying Noyes's mind in the early days of his prophetship. But Abigail Merwin was in his thoughts, too, and he had been perhaps unconsciously seeking a sanctified way to have her, but without waiting for her husband to disappear from the scene.

He set off on a wandering journey which led in the general direction of Ithaca. He was in an orgy of depression and doubt such as had struck him at the time of his conversion, when he ended by becoming a preacher, and again on his journey to New York. Traveling seemed to relieve his mind. He kept up a correspondence with his friends, and as he neared Ithaca he paused to write to one a document which became known as "the Battle-Axe letter." Also, he told him to show it to others or not, as he pleased:

"When the will of God is done on earth, as it is in heaven, there will be no marriage. The marriage supper of the Lamb is a feast at which every dish is free to every guest. Exclusiveness, jealousy, quarreling, have no place there, for the same reason as that which forbids the guests at a thanksgiving dinner to claim each

his separate dish, and quarrel with the rest for his rights.
In a holy community, there is no more reason why
sexual intercourse should be restrained by law, than why
eating and drinking should be—and there is as little
occasion for shame in the one case as in the other. God
has placed a wall of partition between the male and
female during the apostasy, for good reasons, which will
be broken down in the resurrection, for equally good
reasons. But woe to him who abolishes the law of the
apostasy before he stands in the holiness of the resurrection."

Noyes never made any bones of the fact that by "the
resurrection" he meant the resurrection of conversion to
Perfection or Holiness, as his friend well understood. He
continued:

"The guests of the marriage supper may have
each his favorite dish, each a dish of his own procuring,
and that without the jealousy of exclusiveness. I call a
certain woman my wife—she is yours, she is Christ's, and
in him she is the bride of all saints. She is dear in the
hand of a stranger, and according to my promise to her
I rejoice. My claim upon her cuts directly across the
marriage covenant of this world, and God knows the
end."

What may have given him the basic idea of the sharing of mates can now never be known. He would have said
from the Bible in its commands for sharing. If he had read
Goethe's novel of mate-swapping, "Selective Affinities,"
among two couples, a book which had shocked Europe, he
might even have got it from there.

At any rate, in Ithaca Abigail refused to see him,
though he renewed his habit of standing outside her home.
Printers proving agreeable to advancing credit until sub-

scription money should come in, he decided to stay and establish a paper to spread Perfection.

Meantime, his friend had confidentially lent the "marriage supper" letter to others and a Perfectionist woman, who later became harmlessly deranged, was convinced God wished it publicized. She chanced to give it to an editor, however, who was Noyes's worst enemy, Theophilus Gates of Philadelphia, a Finney Perfectionist who published a paper called *Battle-Axe and Weapons of War.*

Possibly he thought the letter a spurious plant to cause him to expose himself to a lawsuit, so in printing it to bring discredit on the non-Finney-ites, he left off Noyes's name, knowing it would be laid to the authorship of the non-celibate group. But it was too juicy a morsel to be left to the religious press. Papers everywhere reprinted it as joyously as those of the twentieth century would recount the discovery of new nests of polygamists in the golden West. In the public mind Perfection had fallen to a new if interesting low, for the public did not distinguish between the splinters of the sect. Many Perfectionists withdrew in disgust. One remarked that he would "spear the tallest Archangel" if he caught him meddling with his wife.

For some reason, the letter was credited to—or blamed upon—a friend of Noyes's, with no suspicion toward its real perpetrator. Promptly Noyes rescued his friend by acknowledging authorship in his own *Witness* at Ithaca. He defended his position with logic, but the net result was a rehashing of the entire thing in the national press. However, it didn't increase his own subscription list, and, worse, the scandal removed his last hope of being received at Abigail's house. He owed his printers and his landlady. He could obtain no cash or credit and was unwilling to call on his father. He knew any attempt to leave town would end with debtor's prison.

Just then his prayers for succor were answered. One of his disciples, Harriet Holton, back in Westminster, Ver-

mont, was directed by inspiration to talk her grandfather
out of eighty dollars and to mail it to Noyes—the "exact
amount" he needed.

Harriet was three years older than Noyes, and no
handsomer in the face. She had his same strong mind, and
was of the same aristocracy as he. She had had a chance at
marriage, had persuaded her fiancé to change to her church,
as a condition, and then had dismissed the bewildered fellow
when she became converted to Noyes's religion. The truth
was that she had fallen in love with Noyes, had visited in
Putney and made acquaintance with his mother and sisters,
and was not aghast at the Battle-Axe letter. Her grandpar-
ents, who thought Noyes's ideas wild, had repented once of
interfering in her life and now they delivered no ultima-
tums, for after all she was nearing thirty and presumably
knew her own mind.

Much depressed, Noyes returned to Putney and for a
time went into seclusion, but then he went wandering again.
From one of his few followers still remaining faithful,
Abram Smith, who lived on the Hudson River, he learned
to his bursting joy that Abigail and her husband had separated. Life promised new meaning. Noyes wrote her instantly and gave Abram the letter to deliver—or possibly
only to post. Either way, by carelessness or design, Abram
put the letter aside and she never received it, but it was
many months before Noyes knew this.

Meantime, anxious, distracted, and finally despairing
as no answer came from her, Noyes made a decision. He had
become convinced that he must get Perfection out from
under the cloud of sex notoriety which constantly shadowed
it or see his religion "swallowed up by the devil." And this
was to be done, he said, "not by preaching and stirring up
excitement over a large field, as we had done at the beginning, nor by labouring to reorganise and discipline broken
and corrupted regiments as in the past, but by devoting myself to the patient instruction of a few simple-minded, un-

pretending believers . . . of sober and timid honesty. This I found in the little circle at Putney and this proved to be to me, and to the cause of holiness, the beginning of better days."

The little circle, consisting most largely of his brother George and their sisters Harriet and Charlotte, was about to have an addition. He abruptly dispatched a letter to Harriet Holton (who, over his protest, had sent him further offerings of money), for he was convinced Abigail had decided not to answer.

He proposed marriage to Harriet, but he carefully coppered the arrangement by explaining that if she accepted "we can enter into no engagements with each other which shall limit the range of our affections. . . . I desire and expect my yoke-fellow will love all who love God, whether man or woman, with a warmth, a strength of affection which is unknown to earthly lovers, and as freely as if she stood in no particular connection with me." He said that marriage "would set us free, at least myself, from much reproach and many evil surmisings which are occasioned by celibacy in present circumstances." Obviously, the gossip had not stopped for a minute concerning Banker Noyes's son.

There was a great deal more of the letter. In a subsequent one he assured Harriet's worried grandfather that things were going to be better for him financially—he felt it in his bones, and anyway he was heir apparent to a considerable sum of his aging father's money. Delicately he avoided mention of Harriet's similar hopes from her grandfather.

Harriet wrote that she had had some dreams of marrying Noyes—"the morning star," she called him—but had not dared think she would have the opportunity. Further:

"In gladly accepting this proposal for an external union, I agree with you that it will not 'limit the range of our affections.' The grace of God will exclude jealousy and everything with which the marriage state is defiled as we see it in the world. I only expect by it to be placed in a situation where I can enjoy what Harriet and Charlotte and your mother are now blessed with, your society and instruction as the Lord pleases and when he pleases.

"And I will say frankly, that there may be no mistake between us, that so far from regarding the act of sexual enjoyment as in itself unholy, I am sure there is no sacrifice except that of the heart, that is more acceptable to God."

Harriet's grandfather gave them a wedding present of money and provided them with an allowance for the future. They bought a press and types during a brief honeymoon and hastened to Putney to resume publication of the paper Noyes had begun at Ithaca—*The Witness.* They moved onto a farm at the edge of Putney and with John's sisters and brother had great fun learning to set type and print without a teacher. Noyes frankly hoped that the paper would bring in large contributions to further the teachings of Perfection. It didn't.

They were not at all without humor, but it was not in jest that they named their place the Kingdom of Heaven. The Kingdom was established because of God's promise, which Noyes had discovered in the Bible, that such a kingdom would be founded on earth. In Perfectionist theology it was apparently not the same as "the kingdom of God" which is what is ordinarily referred to by others as heaven.

Soon a few like souls joined them and it was only natural that they should work and share alike. For income, a store was opened on the Putney square at the edge of the farm, and there a chapel was erected where outsiders were welcome. Most who applied for membership in the Kingdom were under the impression that the colony was a pious stew and were promptly turned away. Gradually some earnest souls were received, and more houses had to be built.

While it would grow boresome to dwell on how they

slopped the hogs and got out the paper at Putney, rather than to enlarge on the romantic aspects which the country found it so intriguing to speculate upon, it must be emphasized that for some seven years after the founding of the commune there was no complex marriage. Noyes dealt sternly with those detected in flagrancies, for he saw not only social difficulties but sin in dalliances occurring outside the rules and regulations he was to establish. He might of course have decreed complex marriage from the first, but this long wait, as well as showing his quality of caution, makes a certain commentary to charges that he was merely a holy lecher.

In short, he seems really to have been convinced that a "community of wives" was a correct and necessary basis of thoroughgoing Christianity. Certainly many of his disciples —particularly, perhaps, his personal converts—were convinced. Extreme respect, love, and even adoration were paid him, and while some may have at first merely been along for the ride, the later time of persecution did not cause any to abjure the faith.

In the fledgling years Noyes worked out the system of government through "mutual criticism" and "fellowship." There was a reasonable approach to an anarchy, with each person in such a spirit of cooperation that little rule was needed. Yet rules were implicit in the system of fellowship, which meant that the young in age or new in faith were ordinarily to defer to the opinions of those older in years or of longer conversion.

There were three degrees: In "horizontal fellowship," one was in association with those of his own general age or spirituality. On the descending plane, one associated with his inferiors, always of course setting a good example which would elevate them while taking care not to be drawn down. Ascendingly, one learned from his superiors. Thus from moment to moment an individual might find his status of fellowship changing. Noyes was freely granted position as the superior being and consequently within the group he might have only descending fellowship. Horizontally, he communed with Abraham and the patriarchs, and ascendingly, with Jesus.

Still, errors were committed, offenses given, and something was needed to restore the individual to tractability. Noyes used the method of his seminary days at Andover. The recalcitrant or erring one either offered himself or was called upon to stand before the gathering, and while he remained silent he was told of his shortcomings. This was such an intense experience that it was found it often would cure a sick person, apparently by rousing all his feelings to such pitch that the illness was sloughed off. Accordingly, illness was seen to be the result of sin, and a patient might well expect to have his room invaded by a dozen or so of his friends to give him a criticism. In the same tradition, new ideas, plans, and projects were submitted to the membership for criticism.

Noyes's greatest grief was his wife's terrible suffering in her miscarriages. It was then that he decided to become celibate instead of to decree complexity on the sly ground of relieving her from danger while he associated with other women. But since celibacy was not working out, Noyes began experimenting with "male continence." He explained this as the art of prolonging an act of intercourse as greatly as possible without exposing his wife to the risk of pregnancy. This was, however, at the expense of his own climactical pleasure which under the Noyes system was supposed to be avoided. He wrote that he so perfected his art that Mrs. Noyes experienced "great satisfaction." The system was to make possible the general sexual freedom in the commune, without impinging upon the "stirpiculture," or scientific production of children of the complex years, and it was so generally important to Noyesite Perfection that in time notice of it was carried on the masthead of the paper.

While the ordinances of fellowship, mutual criticism, and general "Bible Communism" were being worked out at Putney, Noyes and other missionaries went out on preaching tours. Early in the 1840's, Mrs. George, a schoolteacher in Brooklyn and the mother of several small children, became a convert. Her husband worked in the publishing department of a society which was dedicated to eradicating vice. One of the activities of the society was the collecting of books and objects having to do with depravity. Exhibitions of these were in demand, along with suitably horrified and unctuous lectures, at ministerial conferences that gentlemen of the cloth might better know how to root out sin.

Another project of the society was the printing of the names and addresses of prostitutes in the society's magazine. This was designed toward shaming the ladies into closing shop. The only noticeable result was hilarity on the music hall stages, and the clamor of the wretched girls to be included in what was commonly dubbed "the whore book."

Perfection was also a major target of the society, which never wearied of exhuming the old Perfectionist scandals. Its opinion of the Putney group—a group accepted by the townspeople of Putney as moral enough at this time—was explicit. There was sudden consternation in the society when the lady who edited its publications became a convert to Noyes. Her attempts to take a new editorial tack were quashed and her resignation forced, resulting in a promotion for George ——.

To his horror, just then his wife Mary became a Noyesite and she gave him no rest until he agreed to live the perfect, sinless life. He was fired but Mary could still write to Noyes with tears of happiness blotting the letter that he was in the fold.

Noyes visited them and George fell deeply under his influence. Presently Noyes mentioned Mr. and Mrs. G. to that same Abram Smith who had failed to deliver the letter to Abigail Merwin. Smith interviewed the now-destitute couple and took them back up the Hudson where Mary was surprised to learn there was a Mrs. Smith, stepmother to Abram's children. Somehow Abram had given the opposite impression. Abram put George to work on one of the farms he managed, and at a distance so that he had to sleep there. He was to receive no pay, for Abram had expansively suggested they have a "Bible Commune" like that at Putney.

Mary stayed at the house to help with the work. Mrs. Smith soon moved out in indignation at what she saw going on. There was talk in the vicinity of mobbing Smith. Someone wrote Noyes and he arrived to find feeling still high, and Abram determined to withstand any mob violence by force of arms. George was brought in and made privy to circumstances. He did not take things well, though he knew that theoretically the resurrected Mary might with propriety put her shoes under the equally resurrected Abram's bed—but he had understood all that was just theory, probably not to be practiced until the next life.

Noyes bluntly disapproved the rushing of things by Smith and Mary, and their not obtaining permission from George; but he pointed out to George that it was obviously only a misunderstanding of the finer points of the creed, with no intent to hurt anyone. The prophet then roundly rebuked George for having "a claiming and legal spirit" in regard to Mary, and reminded him that selflessness was the chiefest thing in Christianity and consequently in Perfection.

In short, Noyes reduced George to such repentance that even Mary and Abram forgave him. Noyes extracted oaths of proper future conduct from Smith and Mary and, in order that the town might simmer down, took Abram to Putney after requiring him to post bond for the support of his wife. This would also give George and Mary opportunity for full reconciliation.

Smith returned late one night and tapped on Mary's door. George was with her. Sulkily he at last permitted the insistent man to come in to make his greetings. Abram assured him there would be no more dalliance. Later, privately, he told Mary that Noyes would approve of their union as long as George, who was yet young in the faith, should not find it out. Mary was uneasy—but then, Abram had been in Perfection a long time. Should he not know the proper thing?

George was not entirely blind. Later he wrote, "I very well understood I could not at that time carry the marriage spirit into the heavenly kingdom, even if Mr. Smith could. Neither could I avoid making the discovery that he was freighting his barge with the commodity I was throwing overboard." George flattered himself there, since it was Mary who was throwing it overboard for him.

Finally, the second exposure could not be postponed even by George. Mary said she was greatly relieved for she had somehow felt she wasn't doing her husband exactly right. The angry Noyes cut Mary and Abram off from the faith and apparently dismissed George from his mind as a nincompoop—or perhaps as one having too claiming and legal a spirit. Abram fired George and the again-destitute couple made their way to New York. From there Mary wrote Noyes:

"I never in my heart turned aside from the promise I made to you last spring. Again and again I asked Mr. Smith if you would be pleased, for I had terrible misgivings. He assured me you would and that he himself would tell you. Guilty as I am, I have been miserably deluded by him. I am reaping the curse of trusting in man, and I deserve it. The instruction I received to lie and deceive began to open my eyes. I do thank God for the judgment that has overtaken me, even if I am to be sent to hell at last, and I wish none to consider me a friend of the gospel until my deeds make it fully manifest."

Noyes was won over by this deep repentance and so George was put to work briefly in the Kingdom's print shop at Putney and then sent on the road, while Mary taught her children and the several others of the commune. Most were too small to learn the three R's, so she read the Bible and told them stories.

Mrs. Noyes, who was her close friend, and the other women cooked enough food to last a day at a time, and people ate when they were hungry. Thus much kitchen slavery was avoided. The people were happy, and Noyes wrote in his paper that if carpers and railers could show any better or more Christian way to live than this, in which each worked for all, he should be glad to adopt it.

Then Abram Smith showed up, wreathed in remorse, and fetching his nubile daughters. He convinced Noyes that he had learned his lesson and should not be shut from the fellowship of the elect. Smith had failed Noyes in the past, but on the other hand he had also been a nominal disciple when almost all other converts were falling away. Perhaps that softened the prophet a little. So now he called Mary in and had a plain talk with the two, and then drew up articles of peace for them to sign:

"The transaction between Mrs. George and Mr. Smith was characterized by two vices—licentiousness and deception. I judge Mrs. George took the lead and was the principal agent in the licentiousness, and that Mr. Smith took the lead and was principal agent in the deception. She kindled the fire and he excused and justified it and concealed it. This is exactly in accordance with the respective tendencies of the two sexes. Woman is strong in the department of susceptibility; man in that of intellect. . . ."

Like the gentleman he was, Smith penned at the bottom: "I do subscribe most fully to the above and do wish to take on myself most of the evil."

And Mary: "I think Mr. Noyes is correct in his judgment; and that I took the place of Eve in tempting and seducing man, who is made in the image of God. I sincerely ask Mr. Smith's forgiveness for having dragged him down into sensuality. M. G."

Harriet's grandfather was called to his reward, leaving her a considerable sum which was put into support of the commune. Old Mr. Noyes distributed his money to his heirs before dying, the four of his children at the colony receiving some $20,000 among them. This too went into the common fund.

When Mr. Noyes died, his widow went on an extended round of visits to other towns. John declared himself the head of the family. His mother had expected to make good marriages for Harriet and Charlotte, but he married them to men she considered nobodies—members of "the Putney group." Mrs. Noyes was beside herself.

Soon George wrote his letter to Noyes's wife and the two couples arranged to swap spouses when the prophet should direct. Part of his reason for waiting was to see that the men of the Kingdom had a clear understanding of "male continence," and would agree to create no pregnancies without the consent of Noyes and of the ladies involved.

Moving cautiously, Noyes soon learned that Mary had now been dallying with John Miller, to whom the prophet had married his sister Charlotte. His sister Harriet, whom he had married to an ex-Quaker named Skinner, had also been in a mild intrigue with Miller. Charlotte was deeply hurt. Noyes scolded her for her "legal" spirit toward her husband and for her pique toward Mary and Harriet, and she promised to try to do better. Mary wrote that she felt unhappy at being an apple of discord in the family which had done so much for her—but that alas, that seemed to be her fate.

Mary had an inquiring mind and was always eager for instruction from Noyes. One evening as he rested from his literary labors he and she wandered by chance into the woods while he discussed a theological matter of which she had asked. Dropping upon a large stone to rest, they suddenly discovered the appointed time had come.

Noyes recorded that he said to himself, "I will not

steal!" He "got a signal" they should consult with their spouses. "After a moment we rose and went toward home. On the way we took some liberty of embracing, and Mrs. George distinctly gave me to understand that she was ready for the full consummation." However, Noyes was not minded to make love so informally and he refused until they should first go home. "On reaching George's house, I called a meeting of the four, related our doings, and offered the transaction for criticism."

For some reason, possibly because he supposed matters had gone farther in the woods than he was being told, George became sulky. But then he thawed and "we gave each other full liberty, and so entered into marriage in quartette form. The last part of the interview was as amicable and happy as a wedding, and a full consummation . . . followed."

A small "inner circle" was made privy to this. Gradually the marriage circle enlarged. There were all sorts of problems to be solved and rules to be formulated. Should there be any public kissing or courting—that is, even before others of the community? No. This would be distasteful to all. Other problems were not so easily settled: What was the proper etiquette in courting another man's wife? Who was to initiate the young women and young men into the marriage circle? How were jealousies and frustrations to be handled? Supposing some person loved another who did not reciprocate enough for "full consummation"—who was to be pleased in the matter? What was to be done with those who wished to remain in the Society but not to practice complexity?

And there was Noyes's brother-in-law, Miller, who apparently was not much taken with the idea of male continence, and who viewed complexity as no more sacred than the same pleasant adultery he might have found outside. Noyes noted with concern the intrigue that still flourished between his sister and the man. Instead of seeing Harriet, he wrote her a note about Miller, warning her "to hold yourself aloof from him, or at most coquette with him, and don't allow him to feel free with you until he openly avows our principles and submits to my instructions." For, he added, complex marriage was licentious in Miller's mind, and as long as he felt that way, there was "damnation" in his practice of it.

He remarked that the man had "embraced Mrs. George last evening." The extent of the embrace is not detailed, nor does Noyes mention what warning he may have given the lady concerning Miller's damnable practices. Harriet apparently took her brother's advice, for Miller presently made full avowal of the principles and with the final permission of his wife and of Harriet's husband joined with his sister-in-law in the enlarging circle of complexity.

Mrs. George named her twins Victoria and Victor Noyes, apparently with no objection from the prophet. The girl lived only a few days.

By the time they were born, a considerable storm brewed in the countryside over the sacred discoveries of Noyes concerning marriage. The inmates of the Kingdom were keeping their practices quiet and unblinkingly lying about the suspicions voiced against them—but no doubt in their antinomian philosophy these lies were not lies since their pilot was God and they were above sin as well as law. The fact was that they were trying to inveigle several local families into permitting girls to join the commune, and to win them they had to give assurance that the sex practices were orthodox. They gave it.

Still, one family balked, even when it was proposed to win their fifteen-year-old daughter by marrying her to George Noyes. Her family shipped the maiden to relatives in another state. She wept and the anticipative males of the Kingdom stormed at this brutal interference with the salvation of her soul. One of the girls who was permitted to join presently found her name in the report of a grand jury which indicted Noyes for doing with her "what would be adultery had she been a married woman."

This came about from the gabbling of a disgruntled pair of male angels of the Kingdom, their names best forgotten, who, but fledglings under the rules of fellowship and spirituality laid down by Noyes, were not allowed as much freedom among the maidens as they felt their degree of piety justified. Noyes was arrested in October of 1847 and taken before a Putney justice of the peace. He was released under $2000 bond after exchanging witty sallies with the justice.

His humiliated mother was fortunately out of town. His sister and brother without the fold came in horror and unbelief to attempt the reformation of their four brothers and sisters of the Kingdom. Noyes downed them with theological argument and the others were so cheerfully stiff-necked that the interference was a failure.

Noyes was at first ready to go to prison to prove his sincerity. Then he said that on second thought that would not stop the persecution of his people. Other indictments, naming both men and women, were handed down, and Noyes and others fled the state. He took Mary and her youngsters, including Victor Noyes, to the place where his mother was visiting, and he expressed hurt and wonder that Mary was met by Mrs. Noyes with coolness.

They went to Brooklyn. From there, Noyes fanned out, preaching and observing. And so he came to the home of a starveling convert named Burt at Oneida, in the center of the state. Two families of Perfectionists lived in a cabin at the sawmill on the farm, and others were scattered through the area. Noyes buoyed up their hopes and told them all about the fine points of complex marriage, for they were not well up to date.

He explained that the union of men and women with God was the most important of all considerations, and union with each other the second most important. In fact, the two were so intertwined that neither union might be fully achieved without the other. He recognized "the natural timidity of women," but at the same time wished them to realize what a "scanty and monotonous fare" they as well as their husbands were condemned to by monogamy.

He was preparing to write a book on the general subject and he tried out some other ideas on his audience: Woman was an endless mystery, just as God was unfathomable. She could not be known by knowing just one woman in the biblical sense. Intercourse of the sexes was a form of worship when done under Noyesian auspices. And so on.

Some of the Oneida saints were taken aback, but only Mrs. Burt was hostile. Noyes felt pretty sure that in time the true spirituality might seep into her nature and he was lenient, merely emphasizing to her that the act of physical love was the sign of inward grace—of "the resurrection." And that one who could not love husband or wife and be happy at seeing him or her loved by others had no place in the Kingdom and was fit to be only "with the potsherds of the earth." One wonders what, exactly, he supposed a potsherd to be.

In general, his reception at Oneida was so enthusiastic that he gave Burt five hundred dollars with which to start building more shelters. The people dribbled in from afar while George quietly beat the Perfectionist brush for money to get the new heaven on proper footing. In a cellar, Noyes labored on his marriage book, scorning afresh the onanism of Robert Dale Owen's marriage manual which permitted satisfaction of a sort to the husband while protecting the wife, and the similar method of a notorious book by Dr. Charles Knowlton.

It was in 1832, while the country was still twitching with condemnation of Fanny Wright, of free love, and of Owen's contraceptive methods, that Knowlton had written *The Fruits of Philosophy; or The Private Companion of Young Married People*. Abner Kneeland, publisher of *The Boston Investigator*, brought out the booklet which advo-

cated contraception for medical and economic reasons. Kneeland was arrested, ostensibly for libeling and profaning God
in his freethinking paper, and indicted on such a charge.
But when he came to trial, the prosecution talked mostly of
his championing of contraception—and God knew that if the
women of the country generally knew of any sure method,
the homes would no longer be safe, and so on, and so on.
The gentlemen of the jury apparently felt as unsure of their
wives as did the prosecutor. They convicted Kneeland of
profaning God, as charged.

For five years the publisher kept the case in the
courts but after a series of hung juries and a second conviction he spent two months in jail. All this made for a wonderful sale of the book, but Kneeland was bitter. Ironically,
from his jail window, he watched the raising of the Bunker
Hill monument—a monument to human freedom—all during his incarceration. As for Dr. Knowlton, he was fired from
his professorial job at Taunton, and for three months was
locked up in the workhouse at Cambridge in the shadow of
Harvard College. Soon after the release of Kneeland, the
publisher and his First Society of Free Enquirers—a name
remindful of Frances Wright—founded a little colony, Salubria, of no special interest, in Iowa.

Even as Noyes blasted Owen and Kneeland, so he
condemned "the lecherous bachelor's earth and bachelor's
heaven" of Swedenborg who had been much taken up by
mystics of the Thomas Lake Harris and the Brook Farm
variety—although by and large, like the Brook Farmers,
most Swedenborgians seem to have been more wistful than
dynamic concerning that philosopher's ideas.

While the new storms of words lashed the Oneidans,
money and converts came in. There were several hard seasons, with people sleeping in barn-like quarters part of the
time, privacy furnished by curtains between the closely-or-
dered beds. This excited the imagination of the world and
attempts were made to drive the Perfectionists out. Some of
the women were taken before a grand jury and asked every

obscene question the prosecutor might think of. The neighbors of the community testified that the Noyesites were quiet, pleasant, industrious people. The grand jury refused to indict and the commune was left in peace for many years.

A large, unpretentious frame "mansion house" was completed for the adults, with a connected "children's house." In the course of three years the group had grown from fifty to more than two hundred. In time, counting two minor subsidiaries, the cult edged the three-hundred mark. All the women, except those pregnant on arrival, ceased bearing children until money should be plentiful, but there always seemed to be a considerable crop of youngsters because of the arrival of converts.

Why did people join the movement? They joined early Perfectionism because they were approached with it, in fervently evangelical times, by some preacher who made them like the idea of striving for perfection on earth, even though that perfection be admittedly not quite attainable. Noyes's extreme movement, based on the tenet that perfection was attainable, clearly did not at first challenge many into activity—other than the activity of getting away from him as quickly as possible. And no doubt curiosity and the desire for sensationalism attracted some into the holy-kissing groups.

The real question is whether the people were attracted to Noyes's commune by sex or by true religion—but it should be remembered that for Noyes the question answered itself in the latter way since the two things had become part of the same thing and of each other. Certainly he turned away many applicants who seemed to think Perfection was sex only and unlimited. He had, in other words, a sharp religious test, as divorced from sex, which the applicant must pass. And no doubt just one leer or unwary joke, one untoward remark in parlor or boudoir, concerning the "family life" of the community would have brought expulsion.

Just as many groups ringed themselves around with constitutions, elaborate rules of conduct, and religious rituals to cover their mental poverty and to make their actions important, so at Oneida it was endlessly affirmed that the foundation stone of Christianity, which only they possessed, was the ultimate selflessness of sharing mates. Certainly their sacrifices in the "starving times," and in the facing down of public opinion, were a high price to pay for sex adventure if that was all they wanted. One can scarcely take their sincerity, as religiously motivated people, at less than their own evaluation of it. Still—

A Noyesite writing under the name of Alan Estlake states that the newcomers were always prepared mentally for the new life—or so they thought. Nevertheless, it came as a shock when they really lost control of their children to the keepers of the youngsters' quarters. An unweaned baby stayed with its mother. After weaning, it stayed with her only at night, and then not at all when it began to run and play, except that it might visit her once or twice a week in her room.

There was a large sitting room where the adults met in the evening for a brief discussion of business or to hear a "home talk" by Noyes. Then there was socializing, or perhaps music or a play by colony performers. Sometimes the glee club came from Hamilton college—but perhaps the oddest entertainments were exhibitions of dancing by the Shakers. There seemed a peculiar respect between these celibates and the Oneidans.

On most evenings, there was socializing only. There were no rules against the gathering of small groups in public or private quarters, but the formation of cliques was sharply put down by criticism. In the big parlor there was conversation. Some might play cards or have an impromptu dance, or see if the spirits would do a bit of table tipping. At a planned dance, youngsters might be brought from the children's house to exhibit their talents. The room was supplied with reading matter, too, and women might knit or sew.

No doubt there was some tacit courting in all this but overt public courting was frowned upon. Those becoming seriously interested in each other were expected to pursue their discussions in private. This usually meant in the lady's bed-sitting room. Since "special visits" at bedtime were always made by the man to the woman, the ladies had individual quarters. Ordinarily the man returned to his own room, which he usually shared with another, for the remainder of the night.

Poor George, for instance, for the good of his soul, was required by the prophet to occupy even the same bed with Abram Smith. At first he found this a trial but then he realized that "it was just the medicine" required for his old "unbrotherly feelings" toward Smith—his old comrade in arms, as he said, against the world, the flesh, and the devil.

Estlake noted that while the men were usually able to surrender their wives to the marriage circle with good grace, having worked up to that in their minds before arrival, it was hard for them to relinquish all authority over their erstwhile spouses. It had been decided that no one need "receive the attentions of one they do not like," and a woman was free to refuse her former husband, as she was to join in a criticism and tell him things she had longed to for years. Usually families adjusted and made good Oneidans, but occasionally, and in most such cases because of the husband's attitude, Noyes would advise withdrawal of a family for a while.

As much confusion as curiosity exists concerning the mode of arranging for "special visits." Certainly it would have been indelicate for the gentlemen to parade the halls, accosting each passing dame or damsel with proposals of such a highly personal nature. One writer would have it believed that the men stood placidly by, waiting to be beckoned by the women. Too, it was commonly declared that a committee of men and women received applications from those desiring certain persons; that if they considered the pairing suitable they arranged the meetings or obtained a refusal which was relayed to the applicant.

For a little time during the scientific breeding program something like that was tried for the productive matings, but it was superfluous since Noyes in the long run had to pass upon the pairings himself. Apparently the rule through most of the complex days was that a romantic male should make the approach through a third person—"preferably an older woman," as Estlake says, and he was there. Thus if there was a refusal there was less embarrassment than if the proposal were made directly.

So much for the rule. One may suspect that it was honored largely, as it were, in the breach. Men and women constantly associated and were free to visit in each other's rooms. It seems unlikely that a burst of romantic feeling might be interrupted while someone trotted off to find a go-between. Indeed, Noyes pointed out that the advances in nature always came from the female, and that it was quite proper for a lady Oneidan to approach any desirable male. But, as he said, a smile or a flash of the eyes was really all that was necessary—gestures so plain as not to be mistaken, but so unobtrusive that no hurt need be felt if the gentleman pretended not to understand. Quite likely it was this statement of Noyes's that gave rise to the belief that the men were to await until summoned.

Anxious apologists for Noyes are wont to declare there was "more to Perfection than sex." There was also more to the Mississippi than the palace steamers, but it was those craft that brought the world rushing to the bank to goggle. And it was the amatory customs of Oneida which interested the public. This is not strange, since it was the central point of interest of these "Bible Communists" themselves, coloring their entire existences, as one remarked, with "a rosy glow," even for individuals whose powers had cooled. This was true because life for all adults, excepting the few celibates who were permitted to remain, was a series of overlapping courtships, each with the hope of fulfillment. Too, in the children's quarters marriage fodder was sprouting higher by the year to brighten one's maturer existence.

This was particularly true because of the way in which Noyes arranged the associations of the young married set. At "the age when young people begin to canvass these matters among themselves," they were given fitting instruction "by Mr. Noyes who taught them that there was nothing unclean about their sexual organs, and nothing sinful in their sexual desires." "Stickiness" and partiality toward individuals were rooted out from the cradle onward and young adults knew that disappointment was likely to be the chief result of falling in love with each other.

For "the girls were taught that, as their first impressions of sexual experience were naturally the more momentous it was of the greater importance that they should receive those impressions through those members who would be more likely to elevate them with the consciousness of having innocently exercised a pure and natural function on the spiritual plane, than would men to whom self-gratification would be a greater temptation; and that it was important that the more mature should give instruction in this particular before the young were allowed a freedom among themselves that they might otherwise unwittingly abuse."

Since the prophet fathered the lion's share of the children in the later breeding experiments, it may be supposed that he took a reasonable view of sacrificing himself in these earlier instances of elevating the young ladies with a proper amatory consciousness on the spiritual plane.

Meanwhile, the boys of proper age were initiated by women past the menopause. Theoretically, the older people held that sex, like everything else, should be kept on a proper plane of fellowship and that it were best that the young make love with their spiritual superiors—which being interpreted, meant the old.

Strong disapproval was heaped upon the young who

sought too much love on "the horizontal plane"—that is, with those of their own ages; or on "the descending plane," with those still younger. The difficulty in such cases was that there was not likely to be a "spiritual link and chain" of ascending fellowship on either side "to connect the experience with God." In a word, having the spiritual welfare of the young ever in mind, Noyes generally forbade the dalliance of young with young, at least until the later days when procreation was permitted which tended, however, to foster a great deal of "falling in love" and "exclusiveness," and even there disparate ages were favored.

This "special love" for one person was the worst of Oneidan sins. Nevertheless, one almost suspects Noyes may have liked Mrs. George more than he did most women, for he and his wife and the Georges began spending much time in Brooklyn at "Willow Place," which consisted of two neighboring houses they had joined together to make a publishing center. However, visits were made regularly to Oneida and to a branch commune at Wallingford, Connecticut, and the print-shop personnel of both sexes was regularly changed so that there was opportunity for some variety in mates.

Noyes felt that his writings were the best means of winning money and converts—and this despite a chronic annual deficit in the printing department. Still, enough money drifted in to keep him hopeful, and his publications did give him contact with the strongly interested. Some of these he called on occasionally—people as far distant as Illinois where, for instance, one Luther Guiteau was such an enthusiast that he required his family, on sitting down at table, to say, "I confess Christ in this food, and I thank the Lord for John H. Noyes and the Oneida Community, and I confess my union with the Community." Luther was never able to join the community, but his boy Charley did join and sleep with various ladies before God called him, as he said, to his crowning work of shooting President Garfield.

While the print-shop deficit mounted, various shifts were made for income. Abram Smith began a boating enterprise which proved profitable. One summer day in 1851, having delivered a load of stone at the Brooklyn docks, he desired to take a couple of the Willow Place women back upstream to cook for him and his two crewmen. A girl named Eliza Allen was chosen and it was then suggested that Mary go along to see if her cheerful presence might give a different outlook on life to one of the men, Francis Long, who was protractedly moody, despite all the helpful criticism he had received.

The quarry was near Smith's old farming enterprises. Mary and Eliza had great fun cooking for the gentlemen and going on nature excursions through the woods with them. Mary wrote her husband that she liked the seafaring life and that the sight of Smith's place brought back the "days of old." She asked him to "tell Mr. Noyes the angels are watching over us."

Then the angels napped—or perhaps it was only the blundering of the steersman, Francis Long, who was on duty as they went back downriver. Despite Smith's repeated warning, the man let the helm get too far over while the other four were below. The men rushed up, thinking a squall had struck. The boat was already turning over. Trapped below, the women drowned.

But grief had no place in Perfectionist philosophy. At midnight, trying to find the exposed mast of the sloop to relight the lantern which had gone out, Noyes and the others "cheerfully hailed the spirits of our dead." Almost a month later the bodies were recovered and buried in the Episcopal churchyard a mile above Hyde Park. They were left in the garments worn in death—the short dresses and pantalettes the Oneida women had adopted as a fitting complement to their short hair—"to which the younger women usually gave a curl." Shortly afterward, when it was obvious that Miss Saphronia Tuttle was dying at Willow Place, despite all the divine healing Noyes could bring to bear, he and his wife and George and others sent messages by the dying girl to Mary in heaven.

At last even Noyes was impressed by the $40,000 deficit the press had piled up, a deficit which was dragging the Community into bankruptcy. The Brooklyn people moved to Oneida for a less strenuous publishing program— but the Willow Place name was taken along and given to a little village that was started on Oneida land. Members circulated between the two by whim, or even went to Wallingford for a change. Too, members might be sent from the place they preferred to another village to break off stickiness or special love.

Noyes continued as president of the Community and editor of the paper. It carried his home talks, news, arguments for his beliefs, the regular notice of "male continence," and "humorous" advertisements:

To Jewelers—a single Pearl of Great Price! This inestimable Jewel may be obtained by application to Jesus Christ, at the extremely low price of "all that a man hath!"

To Brokers. Wanted.—Any amount of Shares of Second-Coming Stock, bearing date A.D. 70, or thereabouts, will find a ready market and command a high premium at this office.

Magnificent Restaurant!—In Mount Zion will the Lord of Hosts make unto all people a feast of fat things. . . . Isaiah xxv., 6-8.

Sinless life was the standard of the community. Many felt that they had achieved this and were ready to fling at doubters, "I say unto you, which one of you convicteth me of sin?" It was felt that when "good influences" were on the ascendancy, there was a near approach to perfection in the commune. On February 20, each year, the anniversary of Noyes's discovery of the possibility of perfection, was celebrated "The High Tide of the Spirit." To keep in mind that temptation must be guarded against, six months later recognition was made of "the high tide of the flesh," and it was apparently customary to refrain from sex at that time. Apologists applaud the fact that Noyes sometimes forbade all sex activity for weeks at a time—but some of his followers privately felt that this was not so much an indication of spirituality as of the fluctuating condition of his aging interests.

Unlike many communitarians, the Oneidans were not willing to live on an agricultural basis. They worked hard at making traveling bags. They spun silk thread and invented several contrivances handy in that industry. Their peddlers journeyed far to sell their goods. But the financial doldrums were not escaped until the colony began the manufacture of the traps of Sewall Newhouse, who had contributed himself, his wife and children, and his talent for making spring steel to Perfection. At first he jealously guarded his smithing secret and made only a few traps in private for the community, but at last he agreed to teach others and soon Oneida dominated the trap market of the entire country, with no apparent regard for the suffering their product created.

A great new Mansion House was built of brick and about this time, in the late 1860's, Noyes decided that there was enough prosperity to permit the bearing of children. About one hundred forty had been brought in but all had been conceived and born in the ordinary, haphazard way, most of unregenerate parents.

Many of the women had by now gone beyond bearing age. It was not known whether the men, under Noyes's system of birth control which theoretically prevented the loss of seminal fluid, had remained fertile. The later verdict was that they were highly fertile. Noyes decreed that all who wished might attempt to become the parent of one child, if able to find an agreeable partner who would be acceptable, in that pairing, to the prophet; but only superior specimens might become multiple parents.

Quite a number of young men and women signed a fervent document that placed them at Noyes's disposal to breed in whatever combinations he might choose, or not at all if he did not think them fit "stirpicultural" stock. There is little doubt that most of those women hoped for the high honor of being chosen by the prophet for himself.

Noyes never exhibited any pretensions to being a little Christ, but nevertheless he was given some adoration. A letter survives to him from one of the women who was mated to him—"how joyfully, you know!"—and in it she dwells on her secret attachment for him as a girl, working beside him in the trap shop when she was beginning to have some inkling that things went on in the big house of which the inmates of the children's house but little dreamed.

Physically, no reason for the attachment is evident in the pictures of this "whopper jawed" man, as one of his sons affectionately described him, with his scraggly beard. He was sixty. His hearing was failing and an old throat trouble, perhaps induced by too much preaching in the early days, seldom permitted him to speak above a whisper. His other powers seemed adequate, however. Out of fifty experimental births he fathered nine "stirps," as the scientifically planned babies were called.

It was admitted that there were among these or perhaps in addition to them some "accidents." But those were accidental only in that some young couples, in love and bitter that they were not permitted to have children together, took matters, as it were, into their own hands.

Not all were so inconsiderate of the prophet's wishes, either then or in the earlier days of mere social sex. For instance, an anonymous member, a lawyer, noted that the secret of John H. Noyes's character was "a consuming lovesick passion for Christ." The lawyer was only a probationary member. Since he was unable to close out his worldly affairs it was understood that he was to make no advances "of a sexual character." For five years he labored as cook, baker, farmhand, laundryman, and in other lowly occupations, "never discontented" for "my peace was like a river."

"It is a commentary on the purity of the Oneida Community," he declared, "that a strong healthy man in the prime of life could live five years in their midst and get such reinforcement of his spiritual nature from their environment that he never once yielded to temptation in any way that involved a breach of the confidence reposed in him."

Not that he failed to fall in love. He was "struck with the charming spirit of a young girl—so different from the young women of the world." Obviously she reciprocated. The lawyer went uneasily to "Mother Noyes," the prophet's wife, and she said she wasn't surprised, for no one could help loving so good a girl. She advised him to do nothing that would put any restraint on the girl "and in God's good time I should surely find a rich reward."

He loved on in silence and if "the object of my affection" found pleasure with other men, it only made him happy. Finally he was admitted to full membership and sure enough he found the rich reward. Even then he avoided any "avowal of special love that if reciprocated would estrange her from the central love in the Community, and that, if rejected, could not be other than distressing to us both."

By "special love" he meant a love for her alone or one greater than he felt for any other woman. Had he spoken of such a love the young lady would have been obligated, if true to her religion, to haul him up for public criticism. Boudoir secrets were against the rule.

This placid lawyer perhaps served as inspiration for a younger member of the community who shared a violent love with Miss B—— of his own age, but who, in Oneida idiom, was "of singularly noble character." "Frequent criticism was necessary to strengthen them against temptations that might militate against their loyalty to Christ," that is, against circulating freely in a wide circle of mates. It was

decreed that "she should become a mother by some other
husband of her choice and that [her admirer] would choose
some other sweetheart to woo for the purpose of maternity."

The trouble was, selfish people like this young man
and Miss B—— would be rather likely to produce a selfish
child, a consideration important to stirpiculture. So the young
man "never harboured a jealous thought of the man who
was united to the same woman; on the contrary, their
common love was a bond of union, and after the child was
born he loved it as tenderly and cared for it as devotedly as
if it were his own."

One man indeed wrote that Miss B—— was "a young
lady of great beauty. Her easy grace, her kind disposition
and fine accomplishments made her very much beloved in
the family. Motherhood ripened her into a most charming
woman and my friendship gradually grew into courtship."
He was visiting her one evening when the baby was so fretful
that everyone in the area must have known the courtship was
not at the moment getting anywhere. But the door opened
and Miss B——'s forsaken young lover, taking the child from
its crib so quietly that they were scarcely aware of his presence, carried it into his own room.

Not all, even of the older men, were so amenable, but
only one person was ever forcibly driven from the commune.
This disgruntled disciple complained to Noyes that the
ladies were cold toward him and that Noyes was discriminat-
ing against him in permitting him to initiate none of the girls.
The man had a particular eye for his own daughter, who
was fifteen and whose maturity had already brought her into
the marriage circle.

Instead of being pacified or expelled, the father was
counseled to be patient and have faith in eventual happiness
—for everything else aside, no one else could keep in operation the dishwasher he had invented and built. His work in the
kitchen brought him in contact with a bevy of his daughter's
friends, and he found that these young girls were glad to

come up to see him because of the candy he somehow contrived to procure.

The pretense was that they were coming to see his
daughter who visited him in the afternoons. Apparently no
harm came from any of this, beyond a great deal of talk concerning love and sex in which the girls recounted their experiences with the men of the commune. Certainly that is
the official account, despite his later talk of "orgies" to the
press of the outside world. Noyes took alarm at his cozy con-
claves. One night the man was heaved bodily out into a
snowbank and his clothes flung after him. He talked. He
brought a lawsuit. He had to be bought off. The Oneidans
considered it a cheap riddance.

Difficulties like this were damaging to the commune
and to the prophet's power. Many young men and girls were
weary of the first fruits of romance being hogged up by gaf-
fers and beldames. At Oneida there was no restriction on
education so long as it was not to glorify an individual but
for the good of the group. Young people were sent away to
college and this led to broad thinking, sophistication, agnosticism, and acquaintance with the ways of the world.
Noyes thought it would all work out for good. Indeed, he
foresaw a time, in the perfection of the world, when "the art
of sexual intercourse" would be taught young men and
women in colleges as part of the curriculum.

The observations of the young people led them more
than ever to desire the marriage customs of the world where
people were allowed to fall in love and not required to cultivate a specious enjoyment at seeing their loved ones bandied
through a wide circle of holy hands. They questioned openly
Noyes's teaching that any normal man loves any normal
woman, and vice versa and that jealousy is an artificial emotion people display because it is expected by society in the
case of love trespasses.

Attacks were coming from the world's clergy. Some of
the ruling clique at Oneida thought Noyes should give up a

little of his power, for he was old and decrepit. The leader
of this group was named Towner, a lawyer from Cleveland.

It was not enough for Towner that he should be a
minor official. He hoped to become head of Oneida, but in
1877 the prophet stole a march by turning the presidency
over to his legitimate son of Putney days, Theodore Noyes,
and moving to Wallingford to leave him a free hand. Theodore had been educated as a physician and had turned agnostic. His religious and social ideas had already made a
coldness between him and his father, and as master of the
community he was soon disliked by a large segment and
finally by almost everyone. With some this was because he
and his wife were "exclusive," holding themselves aloof from
the marriage circle.

Eventually they moved out of the Community but
continued to rule. The climax was a decree that everyone
should fill out blanks accounting for the hourly activity of
each day so Dr. Noyes and his wife might have a close check
on affairs. It was commonly felt Theodore's wife was back of
this. Soon the situation was so explosive the old prophet had
to return and resume the presidency.

Perhaps he was touched with senility by then. Possibly it was only that his sexual powers were dulled or gone.
He began saying, well, with all those demon clergy led by
Dr. Mears howling at the gates, perhaps they would have to
give up complexity in order to survive. That is, give up the
practice but never the belief in the rightness of the principle.

He reminded his followers "that I have frequently
said within the last year that I did not consider our present
social arrangements an essential part of our profession as
Christian Communists." He certainly had not said that in
the years when he feared Mrs. George might "become a
Magdalene" if he didn't save her.

He took fright—too easily, many thought—at the danger of jail and allowed himself to be persuaded to go to
Canada, in the belief that with him away the slavering Dr.

Mears would cease attempting to destroy the commune. Smelling blood, Mears pursued the harder. Confiscatory legislation threatened. Noyes wrote his people that he thought they had been lucky to be suffered to practice complexity for thirty years. His advice was that they give up this phase of Perfection to preserve the rest of their way of life. A lofty moral tone was taken and virtue made of necessity. His abdication had shocked some. Now these were reduced to a period of mental numbness. Some of the girls who had happily borne children by him were bitter at what they looked upon as his denial of the rightfulness of the former life.

In point of fact, it was probably fortunate for the Community that they were forced by outside pressures to make the reorganization which followed—for internal pressures from the formation of cliques as to how affairs should be conducted, and from the cries of many young people for change in the customs of romance, would soon have blown the colony into oblivion. This may be said because almost certainly there would have been suits and counter suits, such as plagued some disrupted groups, which would have consumed everything.

As it was, industrial, financial, and marriage reorganization all came together, while the people could still work as a group—even if a two-party group of conservatives and modernists. Oneida was changed into a joint stock company. Shares were issued on the basis of age, status, and length of time in the commune. Provision was made for children. The enterprise was worth $600,000—no great sum when divided among three hundred. Some sold their shares to others and left. Some departed with their shares, leaving instructions that dividends be mailed to them in plain envelopes—and mistakes in this particular led to anguish in many a small town off and on during the next several decades.

The amount of child support and the income from the shares was so small that it was necessary for almost everyone to work for wages in the Community enterprises. Monthly rent now had to be paid on apartments in the

Mansion House, and meals in the dining hall required cash. Everyone was allowed a certain amount of furniture and clothing in the great division, and the surplus was auctioned off to the members. Many people who had grown up in the Community were handling their first money and the bidding was wild.

Meanwhile, the old firehorse in the exiled Noyes roused a little. He recollected that he had adherents in other places. He advertised a mass meeting to be held in Chicago for the establishing of a new commune, complete with complexity. He invited many of his former correspondents in the Midwest. Only one man appeared for the meeting and sadly Noyes went back to his home which overlooked Niagara Falls from the Canadian side. A harem of Oneida ladies, including Mother Noyes, trotted off to keep him company. A fledgling cutlery factory, begun by a son of the Georges at Wallingford, was moved to the Falls, on the American side for cheap power, and the prophet was revered by the workers there. And so he settled down quietly to a final six years of life.

At Oneida, the real heartbreak of the situation was under completion. Noyes, for instance, had fathered children by nine girls and married women. Some women had children from as many as four or perhaps more men. The plan adopted called for the married couples to settle together in a return to the "scanty and monotonous fare" of monogamy. The woman usually kept the children begotten to her, by whomever. Effort was made to find a husband among her husbands for the single women who had become mothers. Often such men were already married. But some of these girls did find Oneida husbands. Others were so disillusioned in the crushing of everything they had been taught from babyhood that they did not marry at all. And as for the teen-agers, they often drifted into courtship with each other and many of these young Oneidans eventually married and settled in the Mansion House where indeed a few of them still survive.

There was rough going the first few years after the break-up, with quarreling and backbiting between cliques, and with losses from incendiarism. Foolish internal politics had led to the selection of poorly qualified managers which led to severe losses. Finally the young people seized control at a stockholders' meeting. Business improved. The group gradually developed what seems to have been a contented and even happy existence.

Certainly this is the present case for the children and their children and grandchildren who still live in the Mansion House. Some of the youngsters went out into the world and made good in various commercial and artistic fields, and in public service. Those who remained brought the silverware business back to the neighborhood and managed it, as the inhabitants of the House still do.

Meanwhile, in 1886, the prophet took to his bed, still cheerful despite his failing voice, sight, and hearing. He died, and those at the Falls would have buried him there, fearing a rebuff at Oneida, but a cordial telegram from the Community asked that the body be returned. And so the prophet lies among those he had brought there from Putney. A modest stone bears only his name and the two dates, 1811-1886.

CHAPTER TWENTY

THE SONG IS DONE

THE SHADOW AND THE SUBSTANCE

We wither, from our youth, we gasp away
Sick, sick; unfound the boon, unslaked the thirst
Though to the last in verge of our decay
Some phantom lives such as we sought at first
But all too late, so are we doubly curst.
Love, fame, ambition, avarice;—'tis the same;
Each idle,—and all ill,—and none the worst
For all are meteors with a different name
And death the sable smoke where vanishes the flame.

> —From the journal of James J.
> Strang as a young man.

OF SUCH stuff is the communitarian story. It would be pointless to moralize upon it, but some questions suggest themselves. For instance, what did it all prove? According to those prophets whom the world ranked as failures— Owen, and Brisbane and all his Fourieristic tribe, for example—nothing was proved so far as their individual systems or philosophies were concerned. The failures were always seen as stemming from the lack of preconceived necessary conditions, despite which the communes had been optimistically begun, or from the shortcomings of inmates, or from the intervention of the unforeseeable. By the same token, the communitarian principle itself was seen as unscathed by the failures.

A notable thing is that almost invariably the unsuccessful prophet was ready, given the means, to establish another colony upon the ashes of his last. Even Charles Lane would have plunged into another Fruitlands had he been able to get a bit of ready money out of the bearded Palmer —this despite his ability, in time, to ask, "When it is impossible for two families to get along in the same house, how can it be expected that many families shall?" The Shakers and others—including Noyes, if in a somewhat unusual way —ingenuously settled the matter of quarreling families by decreeing that in their communes there was only one large family. Lane might further have reflected upon the dead weight which men like himself so casually placed upon many colonies—men who felt that they should be, not do.

Leaning upon the unpublished manuscript of the itinerant observer, MacDonald—the man who was admonished against the eating of salt—Noyes made a study of the causes of failures of communes. Speaking particularly of the vanished Fourieristic ones, he noted that only Brook Farm ended in harmony, if sadness. All the others fell apart under blame-casting and recrimination.

Basically, Noyes found, the all-covering thing behind the quarreling and the failures was "depravity." But there were contributing faults—things which brought out the depravity in frightened, hard-pressed, or generally demoralized people. For instance, Noyes found too much land, too much preoccupation with agriculture, injurious to a commune. For, he said, in the eagerness of communitarians for land, or the taking for granted that they must farm, and in their blindness to the fact that farming was "a long road to fortune," they were led into the wilderness where land might be had cheap. This then made it impossible for them to get into manufacturing because of the distance to markets where they might profitably compete.

He thought that communes should build near cities and get into the making of things. But most of the groups had no factories, except that, "It is really ludicrous to see

how uniformly an old saw mill turns up in connection with
each Association, and how zealously the brethren made use
of it; but that is about all they attempted in the line of
manufacturing."

This is to ignore such facts as that the Rappites thrice
became prosperous by manufacturing in the wilderness, and
that the products of Oneida were sold in far places. Of
course, both groups did have cheap water transportation at
their doors. But more importantly, Noyes was ignoring the
fact that some of the communitarians were fleeing the machine and its horrors, deliberately repudiating the hurly-
burly of the machine age, which promptly overtook them
again in one way or another. In the same way, in the late
1940's people fled the cities of America to establish fruit
and chicken farms and such in the safety of the hills where
populations were too sparse to justify the atom bombs to
blow them up, even could planes penetrate so far. The casual
answer of fate for many was bankruptcy. The nuclear age
itself presently gave a more potent answer in the hydrogen
bomb, the ICBM, and the promise of the cobalt bomb to
wipe out entire geographical areas.

Noyes also pointed out the menace of indebtedness
which could slay a commune aborning. But "GENERAL DE-
PRAVITY," as he put it emphatically, was the villain-in-chief.
MacDonald had assiduously interviewed the survivors of fallen communes and had recorded of the Sylvania Association,
or phalanx, at what is now Greeley, Pennsylvania, that
"greedy and idle people" seized more than their share of
supplies. Of the Clarkson, in Monroe County, New York:
"Ignorant of Fourier's principles, and without plan or purpose, save to fly from the ills they had already experienced
in civilization. Thus they assembled together such elements
of discord, as naturally in a short time led to their dissolution."

The Haverstraw "lacked honest managers, and men
and women of skillful industry, sober and honest, with a
knowledge of themselves and a disposition to command and

be commanded." Further: "The sole occupation of the men and women was parade and talk." The Coxsackie "had many persons engaged in talking and law-making, who did not work at any useful employment."

Expressions MacDonald used of others are, "Ignorant of principles of Association. Too crowded. Too many idlers, bad management and dishonesty. Almost wholly a gathering of worthless adventurers. Some came with the idea that they could live in idleness and these ideas they practically carried out. Most came for a mere shift. Quarrels among the women led to a lawsuit. All lived in clover so long as a ton of sugar or any other such luxury lasted."

The exception to the rule among philosophers of readiness to try another village was John A. Collins, the man who held the hundred communitarian meetings which he turned into anti-slavery conventions, and who eventually founded an ill-fated village. His conclusion was that "the theory of Communism" could not be carried out in practice until some more opportune, far-distant time when a set of ideal conditions and of ideal humanity should appear upon the earth: "There is floating upon the surface of society, a body of restless, disappointed, jealous, indolent spirits, disgusted with our present social system, not because it enchains the masses to poverty, ignorance, vice and endless servitude; but because they can not render it subservient to their private ends. Experience shows that this class stands ready to interpret license for freedom and insists that every member shall make their strength, skill and talent subservient to the movement, then the cry of tyranny and oppression is raised against those who advocate such industry and self denial; then the enterprise must become a scapegoat, to bear the fickleness, indolence, selfishness, and envy of this class."

Noyes, who was preoccupied with sex, was suspicious that the brethren of the fallen communities were universally hiding a potent source of dissension. For, said he, not one word had been said about "the woman question" in any breakup:

"The terrible passions connected with distinctions of sex, which the Shakers, Rappites, Oneidans, and all the rest of the religious communities have had so much trouble with, and have taken so much pains to provide for or against, are absolutely left out of sight. . . . Can it be . . . that Owen had such conflicts with whiskey-tippling, but never a fight with the love-mania? that all through the Fourier experiments, men and women, young men and maidens, by scores and hundreds were tumbled together into unitary homes, and sometimes into log cabins seventeen by twenty-five, and yet no sexual jostlings of any account disturbed the domestic circle? The only conclusion we can come to is, that some of the most important experiences of the transitory Communities have not been surrendered to history."

In the light of the general love of people in that day to spread scandal, the conclusion seems far drawn, despite its logic.

In the very beginning, long before he came to America, Robert Owen put himself far ahead of his age by declaring that the interests of all classes were identical. The German Von Gentz answered bluntly that the German upper classes had no desire that the masses have a sufficiency, "at ease and independent of us. All government would then be impossible." Greeley was certain that Fourier's system, which was to benefit all men and not some class, would effect "the Renovation of the World, the Elevation of the degraded and suffering Masses of Mankind. . . ."

But presently, disillusioned as to men and means, he had his biting comment concerning the fact that the movement seemed only to attract those general failures who still "are sure to jump into any new movement as if they had been born expressly to superintend and direct it, though they are morally certain to ruin whatever they lay their hands on." In passing defense, he remarked that in the same period many banks and factories as well as communes had gone bankrupt. But, ruefully: "The fact stares us in the face that the ignorant, poverty-stricken Shakers" had established a constantly growing prosperity. So with the Rappites and others—and all the exceptions, he found, were religious.

Noyes felt that the saving, binding element of the successful Associations was a common religion among the inmates—and he further thought that the "tests of earnest religion" might be the very thing to keep out "the floaters and scamps" who might ruin any enterprise. Further, in the religious commune there was respect for authority, and he believed that to be a bedrock necessity for success, even though he certainly was no dictator. The nonreligious colonies under Owen had failed. The semireligious under some of the Fourieristic leaders had failed. If one wished to discuss the meager success of the Icarians, the fact remained that to them communism was a burning religion.

All this of course is to conveniently ignore the failure of Strangism; of the various Orders of Enoch set up by Joseph Smith and Brigham Young under Mormonism proper, and the communitarian failures of Sidney Rigdon, Smith's righthand man; of the swift collapse of the Dorrilites, and of other religious communes. And it indicates a lack of omniscience on Noyes's part concerning the doom which changing times would bring to the Amanists, the Zoarites, the Keilites, the Oneidans themselves, and others. Irony, indeed, lurks in the turning of Oneida into a stock company, and with the approbation of Noyes, at that—for he had sneered at the joint-stock arrangements of the phalanxes. After all, he demanded, does a father sell stock in the household to his wife and children, or do all work and share together out of love?

But there was solid ground for stressing that the conspicuous successes of the communitarian movement were the religious colonies. Noyes confidently predicted that the movement was virtually finished unless the churches of America might be roused to take it over.

Another question which the philosophers wistfully considered was whether the movement had been sufficiently worthwhile to justify itself. In any event, it seems to have been inevitable, and it did represent an honest effort to move away from poverty and war and to benefit all people. In the 1830's, Harriet Martineau, who found the Shakers "conceited and inert," still was able to declare that the communitarian principle was the most important question then agitating society. Of course, in Europe those who were getting ready for the Manifesto of 1848 and who were crying for revolution and not transformation, and the Chartists who demanded class war to the bitter end, thought the Associationists were childish and silly and blind with their milk and water methods and their pious wishes to benefit all men.

As to the matter of the worthwhileness of communitarianism, one may scarcely do more than point to the things which were part of the same ferment, though outside community life proper, that were accomplished by some of the leaders. Certainly Frances Wright did not live to see women vote—nor Negroes freed and raised to positions of equality with their former masters. Cabet did not see social security nor old age pensions established. Owen did not see universal free public schools. But on those and other scores, if the shades of some of the prophets are hovering near perhaps they feel a little pleased, a little smug—and certainly that is their due even though all those advances would have been made had not those particular agitators been born. They did hasten the day.

In his heart, Noyes must have felt that "Association" was a completely dead issue. And up to today, at least, he would have been essentially correct, even though on into this decade men and women have continued to found an occasional colony. The excuses and the undoubtable reasons have been the same as ever and the pattern of mortality and survival similarly identical to that of a century ago. The two or three communes which at the moment are "successful" are religiously based—and in most ways they strike the outsider as stultifyingly narrow.

The remaining question is whether religious or economic conditions will ever again lead any large number of those in search of the good life into the founding of communes. The world still has its millennialists, premillennialists, and postmillennialists, its viewers-with-alarm toward Armageddon, its sects who cry that Gabriel may herald the end tonight—some of whose members indeed act as if they believe that, at least during their annual revival meetings.

And the world still has its philanthropists and altruists, its people who burn to be leaders, and those who want to be told what to do. It has its hordes who want aid, not trade; relief, not labor. It has its Ann Lees, Thomas Lake Harrises, John Humphrey Noyeses—its psychopathic personalities, some obviously of latent homosexual tendencies, and its paranoiacs whose delusions take the messianic or social-reform or just plain meddling bent. It has its millions who are eager to follow after any towering new superstition of religion or economics.

All these things together might at first glance seem to provide the conditions necessary for commune founding. But the Owens of these days have no interest in establishing share-the-wealth villages, and the reformer may very well get his outlet by serving in Congress, by turning revivalist, or by founding a dues-paying club or society, preferably with password, ritual, and secret handclasp, with himself as high Mogul and his photograph reproduced in each issue of his inevitable journal. Or by becoming a free-lance gadfly against whatever the government is or is not doing, or against some element of our population—again with a suitable amount of dues-collecting from the local chapters he organizes. Nor does the fact that representatives of all these types may be fit subjects for consideration by the abnormal psychologist militate against their success, for often the paranoid or psychopathic personality has brilliant gifts of oratory, conversation, and persuasion which win allies among those who an hour before had not dreamed of him or his works.

Of course, all those outlets were similarly open to the reformer of Owen's day. Altruists could and did endow

schools. Lodges and secret societies were numerous, and the
hate element was often used as a binding force. Anti-Jack-
son, anti-Mason, anti-Catholic, anti-Irish, anti-foreigner
causes were popular in Fanny Wright's time, along with the
positive agitations for women's and children's and laborers'
rights, and no doubt some of the advocates of all of these
things did, in their mental and physical gyrations, sooner
or later take up the communitarian cause.

But the difference today is that people seek the solution to social problems in politics which is now dominated by
the maneuverings of massive religious, trade union, racial,
and other ax-grinding entities. Mencken declared that a politician was one who if he found cannibals among his con-
stituency would promise them missionaries for Sunday dinner. The situation has not markedly changed since Menck-
en's pronouncement, and there is no indication that it had
changed between his time and that of Elder Evans who in
the 1820's, in his pre-Shaker days, plumped for "the right of
the man to the soil—vote yourself a farm!" That is, he
wanted a homestead law, and there was a sufficiency of politicians willing to grant it, in return for office, to make it in
time a reality. Evans and the "Fanny Wright Party" advocated a labor lien for wages and that mails should run on
the Sabbath. It was the power of the vote not of altruists
but of a mass of people who wanted those same things that
brought them into being and eliminated them from campaign platforms before Evans died. The vote was that of the
illiterate and unpropertied who were literally voting themselves a farm.

In this century, the Democratic and Republican Parties have taken over and made commonplace the platform of
the scorned Socialists of 1900. Indeed, Norman Thomas wistfully ceased running for President when both Democrats and
Republicans, tuning in on him accidentally, supposed he was
someone speaking for their parties. Economists now say that
if socialism in America continues at its present pace the na-

tion will be entirely socialistic before the year 2000; that we will, in effect, have become one vast phalanx.

Subtly, perhaps even ironically, that would be to prove to the popular mind that Owen and Fourier and Frances Wright and Evans were right in their basic premises. And it would of course eliminate all thought of village communes, except, conceivably, those of religious nature. But the fact is that preachers who turn messianic these days commonly don't receive revelations to withdraw their converts from their jobs.

Too, a difficulty from the standpoint of a prospective communal village member is that in a commune he would be expected to work. And there is no reason to think that those who intend to work have changed—they have always preferred to do it where they would have definite wages. And today, those who don't want to work prefer to be where they can take advantage of the welfare provisions of our present society.

What a massive depression with its possible revamping of social legislation might bring about is conjectural. But at the moment, with the military to sop up young men, whom child labor laws, until induction, keep in an often stupid and irritating idleness that leads to delinquency, and with social security and old age benefits, pensions, farm price supports, tariffs and other subsidies to manufacturers, subsidies to airlines, and other similar developments, innovations, and leveling contrivances, it seems unlikely that we shall again see any great promulgation of the village commune.

The song is surely done.

BIBLIOGRAPHY

GENERAL

These references deal with the social, economic, and religious backgrounds out of which communitarianism developed and with studies of the movement as a whole. As noted, some of the books may be consulted in reference to various specific communes.

Arnold, J. I. *Cooperative Citizenship.* Evanston, Ill., 1933.

Bell, T. *Pioneering Days.* London, 1941.

Bestor, Arthur Eugene, Jr. *Backwoods Utopias; The Sectarian and Owenite Phases of Communitarian Socialism in America: 1663-1829.* Philadelphia, 1950. (This book is highly documented and is valuable not only as an unsurpassed piece of scholarship, but as a bibliographical source.)

Bishop, Claire Hutchet. *All Things Common.* New York, 1950.

Brummer, E. de S. *Village Communities.* Garden City, N.Y., 1927.

Clough, Shepard Bancroft, and Cole, Charles Woolsey. *Economic History of Europe.* Boston, 1952.

Cross, Whitney R. *The Burned-Over District.* Ithaca, N.Y., 1950.

Dickens, Charles. *American Notes for General Circulation.* London, 1842.

Fromm, Erich. *The Sane Society.* New York, 1955.

Granlund, Laurence. *The Cooperative Commonwealth.* 1884.

Grimm, Harold J. *The Reformation Era.* New York, 1954.

Gide, C. *Communist and Cooperative Colonies.* New York, 1930.

Harbison, E. Harris. *Socialism and American Life,* ed. D. D. Egbert and Stow Persons. Princeton, N.J., 1952.

Hertzler, Jouce Orame. *The Story of Utopian Thought.* New York, 1923. (This book is an excellent source on the theoretical utopian philosophers, from Plato, More, and Bacon, on down to Bellamy Partridge who wrote *Looking Backward* (Chicago, 1887), one of a genre of utopian books which project the characters into the future.)

Hillquit, Morris. *History of Socialism in the United States.* New York, 1903.

Hinds, William Alfred. *American Communities*. Chicago, 1902. (A member of the Oneida Community, Hinds visited many of the villages of which he wrote. He also depended on printed and manuscript sources and personal interviews and has valuable material on most of the better-known communes of the nineteenth century.)

Holbrook, Stewart. *Lost Men of American History*. New York, 1946.

Holyoake, George Jacob. *The History of Cooperation in England: Its Literature and Its Advocates*. London, 1875. (Contains a valuable account of Owen, "the founder of cooperation," and of various communitarian experiments in which he was involved after New Harmony—the Rappite base of which Holyoake refers to as "a Shaker experiment"—and of the Chartist movement which (1837-48) sought to ameliorate the condition of the English laboring classes.)

Infield, Henrick T. *Cooperative Communities at Work*. New York, 1945.

Laidler, Harry W. *Social-Economic Movements*. New York, 1944. (An excellent survey of socialism, communism, cooperation and utopianism.)

Madison, Charles A. *Critics & Crusaders: A Century of American Protest*. New York, 1946.

Martineau, Harriet. *Retrospect of Western Travel*. 2 vols. London, 1838.

Miller, Ernest L. *Some Tennessee Utopias*. Unpublished thesis. University of Tennessee, 1941.

Mumford, Lewis E. *Sticks and Stones*. New York, 1924.

———. *The Story of Utopias*. New York, 1922.

New York Society for Promoting Communities. *An Essay on Commonwealths*. New York, 1822.

Nordoff, Charles. *The Communistic Societies of the United States*. New York, 1875. (Nordhoff visited communes from the east to the west coasts, and while he was anxious to avoid controversy, he has produced an invaluable account, full of human interest.)

Pettit, W. W. *Case Studies in Community Organization*. New York, 1928.

Randolph, Vance. *Americans Who Thought They Were Gods; Colorful Messiahs and Little Christs*. Girard, Kans., 1943. (A little book containing brief sketches of various well-known messiahs besides some others, obscure but interesting, and still others not written of elsewhere.)

Reid, W. Stanford. *Economic History of Great Britain*. New York, 1954.

Rochefoucauld-Liancourt, François Alexandre Frédéric, Duc de la. *Travels Through the United States of North America in the Years 1795, 1796, and 1797*. 2 vols. London, 1799. (As cited in the text, Rochefoucauld visited Jemima Wilkinson's Jerusalem and some other communes and wrote of them objectively.)

Russel, Frances Theresa. *Touring Utopia: The Realm of Constructive Humanism*. New York, 1932.

Saxe Weimar-Eisenach, Karl Bernhard, Duke of. *Travels Through North America During the Years 1825 and 1826*. 2 vols. Philadelphia, 1828. (Saxe Weimar visited New Harmony, the Rappites' new Economie in Pennsylvania, and other villages.)

Sweet, William Warren. *Religion in the Development of American Culture*. New York, 1952.

Tuveson, Ernest Lee. *Millennium and Utopia*. Berkeley and Los Angeles, 1949. (Traces millennial preachments from Luther's time onward; shows preachers and scholars correlating history with Apocalypse.)

Winstanley, Gerrard. *Works of Gerrard Winstanley, with an Appendix of Documents Relating to the Digger Movement*, ed. George H. Sabine. Ithaca, N.Y., 1941.

Wooster, E. S. *Communities of the Past and Present*. Newllano, La., 1924.

THE SHAKERS

Nordhoff, in his *Communistic Societies* (above), has a long account of Shakerism in the 1870's, after the spirit but not the letter had vanished. For an earlier view—the "authorized" one— see the Shaker publication, *A Summary View of the Millennial Church, or United Society of Believers, Commonly Called Shakers* (New Lebanon, 1823). Modestly without an author's name, it was written by Calvin Green and Seth Y. Wells. The later official picture is that of Elder Frederick W. Evans in his *Autobiography of a Shaker and Revelation of the Apocalypse* (New York, 1869).

All these works are highly sympathetic, and uncritical viewing of the Shaker saga today is customary. It was not always so. Spurious and otherwise, early writings bitterly castigated everything connected with the Believers. This attitude is patent in the titles of some of the following works, which give a fairly balanced picture of what is available.

A Brief Statement of the Sufferings of Mary Dyer, Occasioned by the Society Called Shakers, Written by Herself. Boston, 1818. (An "inside view." Mary Dyer Marshall, the same author, thirty years later published *The Rise and Progress of the Serpent from the Garden of Eden to the Present Day, with a Disclosure of Shakerism* (Concord, N.H., 1847).)

Dow, E. *Portrait of the Millennial Church of the Shakers*. Orono, Maine, 1931.

Haskett, William J. *Shakerism Unmasked, or the History of the Shakers.* Pittsfield, Mass., 1828.

Melcher, Marguerite Fellows. *The Shaker Adventure.* Princeton, N.J., 1951.

Neal, Julia. *By Their Fruits.* Chapel Hill, N.C., 1947.

Rathbun, Valentine. *A Brief Account of a Religious Scheme Taught and Propagated by a Number of Europeans . . . Commonly Called Shaking Quakers, . . . The Whole Being a Discovery of the Wicked Machinations of the Principal Enemies of America.* Boston, 1781. (This was concerned with the spy charges against Mother Ann.)

Sears, Clara Endicott. *Gleanings from Old Shaker Journals.* Boston, 1916.

Smith, James. *Shakerism Detected: Their Erroneous and Treasonous Proceedings, and False Publications . . . Exposed to Public View.* Paris, Ky., 1810.

SHADRACH IRELAND

Material on Ireland is scarce. The only work of any consequence is that by Henry S. Nourse, *History of the Town of Harvard, Massachusetts, 1732-1893* (privately printed, 1894). This is based upon documents and legal records.

Clara Endicott Sears, in her *Gleanings from Old Shaker Journals* (above), gives an account of Shadrach's sojourn at the Square House, and random notes appear elsewhere.

THE DORRILITES, PILGRIMS, AND WINCHELLITES

These sects are discussed by Zadock Thompson in his *History of Vermont, Natural, Civil, and Statistical* (Burlington, 1853); William H. Tucker, *History of Hartford, Vermont* (Burlington, 1889); and in a later era by Henry S. Lee, *Uncommon Vermont* (Rutland, 1926), and David M. Ludlum, *Social Ferment in Vermont* (New York, 1939). It was Thomas Nuttall who recorded the end of the Pilgrim's sojourn at the Mississippi. See his *Journal of Travels into the Arkansa* [sic] *Territory During the Year 1819* (1821. Reprinted in Reuben Gold Thwaites, ed., *Early Western Travels, 1748-1846.* 32 vols., Cleveland, 1904-1907.)

JEMIMA WILKINSON

The chief account of the "Jemimakins" has long been David Hudson's *History of Jemima Wilkinson, a Preacheress of the*

Eighteenth Century (Geneva, N.Y., 1821). Hudson was a real-estate operator in the Jerusalem vicinity and had bitter collisions with Jemima's people and his history is presumably biased.

Since it appeared, the Friend has of course appeared in many communitarian accounts, but most of these depend upon Hudson's work. However, Hudson was not the only one critical of her—as see the cited passage from Rochefoucauld who repeated the story, common in her lifetime, that she inveigled estates from testators to the damage of the natural heirs, and who spoke of her high style of living.

More recently, Robert P. St. John has disparaged practically everything that is anti-Jemima. (Proceedings of the New York State Historical Association: *Quarterly Journal,* April, 1930.) He mentions accounts by Wilkins Updike, historian of Rhode Island, 1847; and S. C. Cleveland, editor of *The Yates County Chronicle,* Penn Yan, 1869, and says that Dr. John Quincy Adams of Geneva "critically sifted" their material and Hudson's and prepared a "brief but scholarly biography"—*i.e.,* one that is pro-Jemima, one gathers. It is on this that St. John largely depends. Curiously, he is in general agreement with the usually cited happenings in Jemima's life but his interpretations are counter to Hudson's. Hudson accuses her of breaking up families and of preaching celibacy. Not at all, says St. John—although in preaching she did somehow give "such an interpretation of Christian duty" that converted wives and husbands often left each other. Other similar examples might be cited from the treatise.

THE OWENS, FRANCES WRIGHT, FATHER RAPP, COUNT LEON, AND JOSIAH WARREN

Until Arthur Eugene Bestor, Jr. published his *Backwoods Utopias; The Sectarian and Owenite Phases of Communitarian Socialism in America: 1663-1829* (above), the only full account of the Owenite movement was that of George B. Lockwood, *The New Harmony Movement* (New York, 1905). Bestor's account is superior to Lockwood's in scope and documentation and (despite its formidable scholarship) in human interest. Lockwood has an excellent account of Warren and his enterprises and writings and a competent section on the Rappites.

Bole, John. *The Harmony Society: A Chapter in German American Culture History.* Philadelphia, 1904.

Flower, George. *History of the English Settlement in Edwards Co., Illinois.* Chicago, 1882.

Knowlton, Charles. *Fruits of Philosophy. A treatise on the population problem.* Boston, 1833. (The work on contraception which got the author into legal difficulties, and which perhaps helped bring forth the book of Robert Dale Owen (below). The latter inspired much invective and gossip concerning Owen and Frances Wright.)

Owen, Robert Dale. *The Life of Robert Owen, Written by Himself.* 2 vols. London, 1857-58. (This work carries his life only to 1820. He wrote for, edited, and published many periodicals throughout his career, but his life is best seen, after 1820, in secondary works.)

————. "Frances Wright, General Lafayette, and Mary Wollstonecraft Shelley," *Atlantic Monthly.* v. 32, pp. 448-459, October, 1873.

————. *Twenty-Seven Years of Autobiography: Threading My Way.* New York, 1874.

————. *The moral physiology; a treatise on popular questions, or means devised to check pregnancy. By a physician.* New York, 1836.

Perkins, A. J. G., and Wolfson, Theresa. *Frances Wright, Free Enquirer.* New York, 1939.

Trollope, Mrs. Frances. *Domestic Manners of the Americans.* London, 1832.

Waterman, William R. *Frances Wright.* New York, 1924.

Williams, Aaron. *The Harmony Society, at Economy, Penn'a.* Pittsburgh, 1866.

BROOK FARM AND THE FOURIERISTIC MOVEMENT

Perhaps as good a brief account of Fourier and his philosophy as may be found is in Hertzler (above, in the general bibliography). Hinds and Noyes give excellent accounts of the Fourieristic movement in this country in their historical works, and Noyes includes a long treatise on the failure of the individual phalanxes. Madison, in his *Critics & Crusaders* (above), has a good discussion of Brisbane, Fourier's American disciple, and of Brisbane's association with Greeley. He also discusses Margaret Fuller at great length, including, of course, her connection with Brook Farm.

Brisbane, Albert. *Social Destiny of Man; or, Association and Reorganization of Industry.* Philadelphia, 1840.

Hawthorne, Manning. "Hawthorne and Utopian Socialism," *New England Quarterly,* XII (1939), pp. 727-729.

Hawthorne, Nathaniel. *The American Notebooks,* ed. Randall Stewart. New Haven, 1932.

————. *The Blithedale Romance.* Boston, 1852.

Haraszti, Zoltan. *The Idyll of Brook Farm.* Boston, 1937.

Journals of Ralph Waldo Emerson, ed. E. W. Emerson and W. E. Forbes. 10 vols. Boston, 1911.

Higginson, T. W. *Margaret Fuller Ossoli.* Boston, 1882.

Letters from Brook Farm, 1844-1847, ed. Amy L. Reed. Poughkeepsie, N.Y., 1928.

Peabody, Elizabeth Palmer. "A Glimpse of Christ's Idea of Society," *The Dial,* October, 1841.

Pellarin, Charles. *The Life of Charles Fourier.* New York, 1848.

Sears, John Van Der Zee. *My Friends at Brook Farm.* New York, 1912.

Southeran, Charles. *Horace Greeley and Other Pioneers of American Socialism.* New York, 1915.

FRUITLANDS

Brief accounts of the commune appear in the standard biographies of Louisa, and there are mentions in Emerson's published journals and letters. Nourse (see Shadrach Ireland, above) has some discussion of them in his history of Harvard, Massachusetts, and Mrs. Alcott confided some remarks to her journal which appears in *The Journals of Bronson Alcott,* ed. Odell Shepard (Boston, 1938). The girls' diaries are quoted in the various works by or concerning the family. Perhaps the best single volume on the commune is that of Clara Endicott Sears, who later was instrumental in preserving and restoring the Fruitlands house: *Bronson Alcott's Fruitlands, with Transcendental Wild Oats by Louisa M. Alcott* (Boston, 1915). This latter thing is Louisa's scarcely disguised account of the season her father gave to saving mankind.

THE STRANG STORY

Legler, Henry E. *A Moses of the Mormons.* Nos. 15 and 16 of the Parkman Club Publications. Milwaukee, 1897.

Quaife, Milo M. *The Kingdom of Saint James; a Narrative of the Mormons.* New Haven, 1930.

Riegal, Oscar Wetherhold. *Crown of Glory, the Life of James J. Strang, Moses of the Mormons.* New Haven, 1935.

Williams, Elizabeth Whitney. *A Child of the Sea; Life Among the Mormons.* Harbor Springs, Mich., 1905.

The general Mormon background is so thoroughly covered in numerous bibliographies that, in addition to the above, only those works touching upon Strang, or upon the United Order of Enoch, are cited here:

Allen, E. J. *The Second United Order Among the Mormons.* New York, 1936.

Ancient and Modern Michilimackinac, Including an Account of the Controversy between Mackinac and the Mormons. St. Ignace, Mich., 1885.

Anderson, N. *Desert Saints; the Mormon Frontier in Utah.* Chicago, 1942. (Includes an excellent account of attempts to establish the Order in Ohio, Missouri, and Utah.)

Geddes, Joseph A. *The United Order among the Mormons.* New York, 1922.

Morgan, Dale L. *"Church of Jesus Christ of Latter Day Saints (Strangite)."* n. imp. (Reprinted from the *Western Humanities Review,* v. 5, no. 1, Winter 1950-51, as the second in a series of bibliographies of the lesser Mormon churches.)

Russell, O. D. "King James I of Michigan," *American Mercury,* March, 1939, v. 46.

The scurrilous works by Beadle and Bennett are also of interest:

Beadle, John H. *Life in Utah; or the Mysteries and Crimes of Mormonism.* Philadelphia, 1870.

Bennett, John C. *The History of the Saints; or an Exposé of Joe Smith and His Mormons.*

THE HARRIS-OLIPHANT STORY

Although Harris and Oliphant were the subjects of many accounts, scurrilous and otherwise, in their day, the entire matter has strangely been skipped or barely mentioned in the utopian histories. What will probably always remain the definitive work is *A Prophet and a Pilgrim,* by Herbert W. Schneider and George Lawton (New York, 1942). Their objective awareness is indicated in the subtitle: "Being the Incredible History of Thomas Lake Harris and Laurence Oliphant; Their Sexual Mysticism and Utopian Communities Amply Documented to Confound the Skeptic." This is a huge and fascinating work and is superior to those below in its objectivity and over-all view. However, there is necessarily much of interest in the others which they cannot include.

Harris's own works, running to several pages—and even in collected form comprising some forty-five volumes—are listed by Schneider and Lawton.

Other primary material includes Oliphant's works which, in addition to his fiction and travel books of pre-religious days, are:

Sympneumata; or Evolutionary Forces Now Active in Man (London, 1885), in which he parroted the Harris philosophy with only a change of terms; *Masollam; a Problem of the Period* (London, 1886); *Haifa; or, Life in Modern Palestine* (London, 1886); *Scientific Religion; or, Higher Possibilities of Life and Practice through the Operation of Natural Forces* (London, 1888). The dead Alice, his first wife, collaborated with him from the spirit world on some of these.

His cousin Margaret Oliphant W. Oliphant, an established writer, wrote a competent *Memoir of the Life of Laurence Oliphant and of Alice Oliphant, His Wife* (2 vols., New York, 1891), in which, despite her embarrassment about the whole thing, she deals sympathetically with his addiction to Harris. She also tries to explain his celibate life with Alice as being at Alice's wish.

Oliphant's second wife, Rosamond Dale Owen, wrote freely of her life with him and of his life with Alice, and of her own relationship and spiritual intercourse with the dead Alice:

Duality; Male and Female Created He Them, by Mrs. Rosamond Dale Owen Templeton (Mrs. Laurence Oliphant). Privately printed. Worthing, Sussex, nd.
The Mediators; a posthumous work by . . . etc. Worthing, 1939.
My Perilous Life in Palestine. London, 1928.
A Trilogy; revised and edited by Charles Anthony Ronzevalle. Privately printed, 1938.

Also see:

Carmer, Carl. *Listen for a Lonesome Drum; a York State Chronicle.* New York, 1936. (Carmer deals with other religious enthusiasms of backwoods New York, with discussions of the Jemimakins, with whom his relatives were acquainted; of Ann Lee; and of the Fox sisters of Rochester.)
Chevaillier, Miss Alzire A. A story on Harris in the *San Francisco Chronicle,* Sunday, Dec. 13, 1891. (This story, accusing Harris of trying to lure her into his colony and to seduce her through great honors and offers, caused him a great deal of difficulty, touching off as it did a new round of muck-raking.)
Cuthbert, Arthur A. *The Life and World-Work of Thomas Lake Harris.* Glasgow, 1908.
Emerson, Rosa. *Among the Chosen.* New York, 1884. (A novel. It was largely bad publicity over Harris's attempt to seduce Rosa, supposedly, that drove the prophet to California.)

Hardinge, Emma. "Spiritual Movements—Mountain Cove," in *Modern American Spiritualism; a Twenty Years' Record of the Communion between Earth and the World of Spirits.* New York, 1870, pp. 207-217.

Hinds, William Alfred. "The Brotherhood of the New Life," in *American Communities.* Oneida, N.Y., 1878.

Hort, G. M., and others. *Three Famous Occultists.* New York. nd.

A Lady in San Francisco to a Friend in England. Ms., usually with diary entry dates in 1881. (Members of the Brotherhood apparently considered it a good exposition of the theory of the counterpartal marriage. Copies exist in various hands at Fountain Grove and elsewhere. Author unknown. While it may be entirely fictional, it has a complete air of naive authenticity. And yet, it smells of Harris's hand.)

Liesching, Louis. *Personal Reminiscences of Laurence Oliphant.*

McCully, Richard. *The Brotherhood of the New Life and Thomas Lake Harris.* Glasgow, 1893.

Munro-Fraser, J. P. *History of Sonoma County.* San Francisco, 1880.

Respiro (C. M. Berridge). *The Brotherhood of the New Life; an Epitome of the Works and Teachings of Thomas Lake Harris.* (Twelve volumes were finally published, in London and Glasgow, from 1896 to 1915, of the sixteen which were announced. They have such titles as *Internal Respiration; The Impending World Crisis; The Second Advent; The Man, the Seer, the Adept, the Avatar;* and *The Evolution of the Cosmos.*)

CABET AND ICARIA

The standard work on Cabet is Albert Shaw's *Icaria: A Study in Communistic History* (New York & London, 1884). However, the Icarian communities have figured in various surveys. Nordhoff (see the general bibliography) visited them in their starveling Iowa days, and Hinds deals with them. A more recent work is *Etienne Cabet and the Voyage en Icarie* by Sylvester A. Piotrowski, a Ph.D. dissertation (Catholic University of America, Washington, D.C., 1935). It is concerned only with Cabet in France, but it contains an exhaustive bibliography on Cabet and Icarianism.

THE MILLERITES

The "authorized" accounts of the Millerite fever appear in the publications of the Review and Herald Publishing Association,

Washington, D.C. The present-day Adventist position is summed up in their book, *The Midnight Cry*, by F. D. Nichol, 1944.

Clara Endicott Sears has given the non-Adventist view in her *Days of Delusion* (Boston, Houghton Mifflin Company, 1924).

Also see:

Branson, W. H. *Drama of the Ages.* Review and Herald, Washington, D.C., 1938.

Dick, Everett. *Founders of the Message.* (The same.)

Spicer, W. A. *Pioneer Days of the Advent Movement.* (The same, 1941.)

Howell, Emma E. *The Great Advent Movement.* n. imp., 1935.

Olsen, M. E. *A History of the Origin and Progress of the Seventh-Day Adventists.* n. imp., 1925.

THE GERMAN COMMUNES

An excellent and adequate study of Ephrata is that of Walter C. Klein, *Johann Conrad Beissel, Mystic and Martinet, 1690-1768* (Philadelphia, 1942). It is a good bibliographical source. Earlier works are the English translation by J. Max Hark (Lancaster, Pa., 1889) of the *Chronicon Ephratense,* by the Brothers Lamech and Agrippa (Johann Peter Miller), (Ephrata, 1786). Julius Friedrich Sachs published three volumes (Philadelphia, 1895-1900) on the Pennsylvania German sects: *The German Pietists of Provincial Pennsylvania, 1694-1708; The German Sectarians of Pennsylvania, 1708-1742;* and, the same, *1742-1800.* Ephrata is discussed in all the communitarian surveys and has been the subject of numerous magazine articles.

The same may be said of Zoar, in Ohio. Nordhoff has a good discussion. More recent is "The Society of Separatists of Zoar, Ohio," American Historical Association, *Annual Report,* 1898, pp. 163-220. This includes excellent background material on the situation in Germany which caused the religious migrations in the early 1800's.

For Dr. Keil's communes, see *Bethel and Aurora,* Robert J. Hendricks (New York, 1933). This is an amateur work, but is a full and friendly account. It scorns the stories of Dr. Keil's early pretensions as a messiah.

Amana has been much written about, but the best thing on the subject is the loving account by Bertha M. H. Shambaugh, *Amana That Was and Amana That Is* (Iowa City, 1932).

ONEIDA

Dixon, William Hepworth. *New America.* London, 1867; and *Spiritual Wives.* London, 1868.

Estlake, Allen (Abel Easton). *The Oneida Community.* London, 1900. (A first-hand account; Easton was a loyal member.)

Eastman, H. *Noyesism Unveiled, a History of the Sect of Self-styled "Perfectionists."* Brattleboro, Vt., 1849.

Noyes, George Wallingford. *Religious Experience of John Humphrey Noyes, Founder of the Oneida Community.* New York, 1923.

Noyes, John Humphrey. *The Berean: a manual for the help of those who seek the faith of the primitive church.* Putney, Vt., 1847.

———. *Bible Communism.* Oneida, N.Y., 1848.

———. *Male Continence.* Oneida, 1873.

———. *Dixon and His Copyists, a Criticism of the Accounts of the Oneida Community in "New America."*

———. *Essay on Scientific Propagation.* Oneida, 1875.

———. *History of American Socialism.* Philadelphia, 1870.

———. *Home Talks.* Oneida, 1875.

Noyes, P. B. *My Father's House, an Oneida Boyhood.* New York, 1937.

Parker, R. A. *A Yankee Saint, John Humphrey Noyes and the Oneida Community.* New York, 1935.

Sellers, Charles Coleman. *Theophilus, the Battle-Axe; a history of the lives and adventures of Theophilus Ransom Gates and the Battle-axes.* Philadelphia, 1930.

RANDOM NOTES

Accounts of the Pantisocracy debacle appear in standard Coleridge biographies. Adequate is that in Maurice Carpenter's *The Indifferent Horseman: The Divine Comedy of Samuel Taylor Coleridge* (London, Elek Books. nd.).

Koresh (Teed) is discussed by Hinds (see above); by Elmer T. Clark in *The Small Sects in America* (Nashville, Tenn., 1937); and by Karl H. Grismer, *The Story of Fort Myers* (n. imp.).

King Benjamin Purnell has been the subject of much periodical writings. The House of David will send various writings concerning him to inquirers. The full "unauthorized" account, with pictures, appears in *The Detroit Free Press* of May 10, 17, and 24, 1942. The Detroit papers at other periods are heavy with Purnell news and may be checked at the dates when he was in the public eye—as at the time of his trial, or the debacle of his end-of-the-world prophecy. Vance Randolph, in *Americans Who Thought They Were Gods* (Girard, Kans., 1943), has a good brief account.

Randolph also has an account of Cyrus Spragg and the Children of God. See also *The Strange Case of Miss Annie Spragg* by Louis Bromfield (New York, 1928).

MAGAZINES

There are as many magazine articles on the communitarians as anyone may want to read in the foreseeable future. For those of the 1800's, see *Poole's Index to Periodical Literature, 1802-1906* (New York, 1938), under logical headings. For others see *Readers' Guide to Periodical Literature* (New York, 1900-55). These source books, of course, are in all libraries.

The following are some of the sort of things available:

"Amana Society Re-organizes," *Christian Century,* June 28, 1933. (p. 837)

Archman, R. F. "Animal Farm," *Nineteenth Century and After,* December, 1945. (p. 255)

"Attempt at a Utopia," *Independent,* July 3, 1913. (p. 7)

Baker, A. G. "True Church Colony," *Woman's Home Companion,* August, 1904. (p. 7)

Bandani, A. R. "From Lyceugus to Lenine, Experiments in Communism," *The Catholic World,* August, 1932. (p. 636)

Boune, P. C. "Shaker Society an Experiment in Socialism," *The New England Magazine,* August, 1910. (p. 668)

Brinsmode, H. H. "Four Dollars a Day and Utopia," *Illustrated World,* December, 1915. (p. 523)

Braam, J. W. "Ruskin Cooperative Colony," *The American Journal of Sociology,* March, 1903. (p. 667)

Brooks, V. "Retreat From Utopia, What Happened to the Brook Farm Colonists After Their Communistic Experiment Collapsed," *The Saturday Review of Literature,* February 22, 1936. (p. 3)

Brown, K. H. "Icarian Community," *Harper's Monthly Magazine,* December, 1904. (p. 141)

Caldwell, W. W. "Equality Colony, a Far Western Experiment in Communism," *The Sunset Review,* February, 1924. (p. 27)

Chapin, F. S. "Utopian Community Experiments," *Science Monthly,* February, 1917. (p. 139)

Copeland, W. E. "Cooperative Brotherhood at Burley, Wash.," *Arena,* October, 1902. (p. 403)

Dallas, W. "Toon O'Maxwell, an Owen Settlement in Lambton County, Ontario," *Canadian Magazine,* February, 1910. (p. 328)

Davis, W. G. "Failure of the Ruskin Colony," *Grunton,* December, 1901. (p. 530)

————. "Passing of the Rappists," *Grunton,* July, 1903. (p. 20)

Dos Passos, K. "New Harmony, Ind., Experiment with a Cooperative Community," *Atlantic Monthly,* November, 1940. (p. 604)

"The Doukhobors and Their Future in British Columbia," *Review of Reviews,* September, 1911. (p. 356)

Ely, R. T. "Amana, a Study of Religious Communism," *Harper's Monthly Magazine,* October, 1902. (p. 659)

"Experimental Socialism," *Independent,* December, 1927. (p. 3118)

Fischer, L. "Communist Puritans," *The Nation,* September 3, 1924. (p. 235)

Fullerton, A. "Doukhobours and Their Utopia," *The Sunset Review,* February, 1917. (p. 31)

Gardner, A. "Communism Among the Mormons," *The Quarterly Journal of Economics,* November, 1922. (p. 134)

Garvin, F. "Arden, a Social Experiment," *American City,* July, 1916. (p. 23)

Gaskine, J. W. "Arden, a Modern As You Like It," *Independent,* August 10, 1911. (p. 299)

Gaston, E. B. "Home of the Single Tax and the Referendum," *Independent,* July 16, 1903. (p. 1670)

Geddes, A. S. "Living From an Acre, Fellowship Farm Association," *Technical World,* July, 1912. (p. 574)

Goodhope, N. "Must the Hutterites Flee Again?" *Christian Century,* November 13, 1940. (p. 1415)

Gruening, M. "Paradise Lost, Review of My Father's House by P. B. Noyes," *The New Republic,* April 21, 1937. (p. 329)

Guthe, C. E. "Shakers," *House and Garden,* March, 1945. (p. 103)

Hayward, V. "Doukhobours, a Community Race in Canada," *Canadian Magazine,* October, 1918. (p. 457)

Hinds, W. A. "American Communities," *Arena,* October, 1902. (p. 440)

"Indian Shakers," *Literary Digest,* March 7, 1914. (p. 496)

"Iowan Utopia," *Literary Digest,* April 1, 1916. (p. 932)

Jeffrey, T. R. "Experiment Fails Twice," *The New Republic,* March 4, 1936. (p. 23)

Knight, M. F. "They Who Shoot the Stars, Three Great Experiments in Communal Existence," *The Christian Science Monitor Magazine,* February 5, 1936.

Lassiter, W. L. "Shaker Legacy," *House and Garden,* March, 1945. (p. 45)

Lippmann, W. "Collectivist Movement in Practice," *The Atlantic Monthly,* December, 1936. (p. 724)

Lockridge, R. F. "American Experiment in Communism," *Travel,* December, 1937. (p. 12)

Marshall, M. "Notes by the Way," *Nation,* August 4, 1945. (p. 110)

"New Hampshire Shaker Village," *Outlook,* January 3, 1914. (p. 40)

Niebuhr, R. "Revival of Feudalism," *Harper's Monthly Magazine,* March, 1938. (p. 483)

Ober, S. E. "New Religion Among the West Coast Indians," *Overland,* December, 1910. (p. 583)

Preston, J. H. "Collective Living," *Harper's Monthly Magazine,* May, 1938. (p. 603)

"Reader's Glossary, Concise Compendium of Characteristic Shakerisms," *House and Garden,* March, 1945. (p. 46)

Rice, M. M. "Eighty-nine Years of Collective Living," *Harper's Monthly Magazine,* October, 1938. (p. 522)

Robertson, C. "The Oneida Community, Nineteenth Century Experiment in Communism," *House and Garden,* August, 1940. (p. 24)

Slossom, E. E. "Home, Washington," *Independent,* April 2, 1900. (p. 779)

Small, J. L. "Mid-Western Experiment in Catholic Community Life," *Catholic World,* March, 1922. (p. 793)

Smart, G. K. "New England Adventure in Idealism," *Travel,* November, 1939. (p. 14)

Smith, A. M. "Amana Community," *Commonweal,* November 5, 1937. (p. 42)

St. Lewinski, J. "Origin of Property and the Formation of the Village Community," *Political Science Quarterly,* September, 1915. (p. 512)

Thomas, I. "Utopia That Prospered," *Travel,* January, 1939. (p. 19)

Thompson, J. M. "Passing of the Shaker," *Harper's Bazaar,* June, 1910. (p. 376)

Thorpe, M. "Collectivism Made in America," *Nation's Business,* October, 1937. (p. 13)

Veregin, P. "The Truth About the Doukhobors," *Independent,* July 3, 1913. (p. 21)

"War Time Uses for the Shaker Colony," *Survey,* December 15, 1917. (p. 325)

"Why All Ruskin Colonies Fail," *Gurton,* May, 1902. (p. 444)

Wilson, E. "Origins of Socialism," *The New Republic,* July 7, 1931. (p. 20)

Wood, G. H. "Anarchistic Communism," *Westminster Review,* February, 1902. (p. 181)

Wooster, E. S. "Inside a Cooperative Colony," *Nation,* October 23, 1923. (p. 378)

INDEX

Abolitionists, 244

Adams, George (Strangite official), 240, 255, 261, 266

Adonai-Shomo (Adventist commune), 312 ff.

Adventism, 306 ff.; *see also* William Miller

Alawenie, 332, 336, 338

Albion, Ill., English colony at, *see* George Flower

Alchemy, 108

Alcott, Anna, 203 ff.

Alcott, Bronson (founder of Fruitlands), 201 ff.

Alcott, Louisa, 202 ff.

Alcott, Mrs. Bronson, 28, 201 ff.

Alphadelphia Phalanx, 192

Altruist Community, 192

Amana (German commune in Iowa), 14, 273 ff.

American Indians, 302; *see also* Lamanites

Anabaptists, 22

Antinomians, 22, 34, 363 ff.

Armstrong, Peter (Adventist leader), 28, 313 ff.

Ballou, Adin, 197

Barbarossa, Frederick, 21

Baumanites, 34

Beaver County, Pa. (home of Rappites), 101

Bedford, Thomas (assassin of Strang), 270

Beissel, Johann Conrad (Ephratan leader), 34

Bennett, Dr. John C. (Illinois politician, Mormon leader), 255 ff.

Bentham, Jeremy (friend of Frances Wright), 119

Big Beaver Island, 239 ff.

Birth control, 123, 157, 162

Bishop Hill (Swedish commune in Illinois), 274 ff.

Blithdale Romance, 177

Bohm, Hans, 21

Books of the Law of the Lord, 241, 262

Bower, Samuel (food faddist at Fruitlands), 209

Brisbane, Albert (prophet of Fourierism), 15

Brocton, N.Y., 320, 339

Brook Farm, 81, 170 ff., 198, 202, 392

Brotherhood of the New Life, 319 ff.

Brown, Apostle David, 270

Brown, Paul (heckler of Robert Owen), 152

Bullard, 97

Bundling, 365

Burlington, Wis., 242

Byron, Lord, 258; verse on Rappites, 105

Cabet, Etienne (Icarian prophet), 11, 223 ff.; his social theories, 226

Carlyle, Thomas, 201
Carthage, Ill., 243
Celesta (Adventist commune), 313 ff.
Channing, Dr., 173
Charles I, 25
Charles II, 32
"Christian Commonwealth", 32
City of David, 353
Coleridge, Samuel Taylor, 90 ff.
Communist Manifesto, 230
Complex Marriage, 4, 361 ff., 381 ff.
Corning, Iowa, 233
Cowdery, Oliver (Mormon official), 97, 251
Cromwell, 25, 258
Crusades, 18

Dana, Charles A., on the aims of Brook Farm, 178
Dark Ages, 11, 17
D'Arusmont, William S. Phiquepal (husband of Frances Wright), 155, 158 ff.
"Day Star of Zion, The", 314
Democrats, in Illinois, 243
Diggers, 25
Dorrilites (early Vermont communists), 94 f.
Dowie, Alexander (founder of Zion City, Ill.), 346

Eastman, Sophia (boarding pupil at Brook Farm), her letter home, 180 f.
Eben-Ezers (Ebenezers), 286; *see also* Amanists
Economie, Pa. (Rappite village), 107
Eliot, John ("Christian Commonwealth" theorist), 31
Emerson, Ralph Waldo, 47, 61, 172, 173, 191 f., 202; refuses to join Fruitlands, 203, 212
Enoch, Order of (Mormon communal society), 248 ff., 262
Ephrata (early German commune in Pennsylvania), 34, 278
Equity store, 166
Equity (village of Josiah Warren), 165 ff.
Estero, 356
Evans, Elder Frederick (reformer, Shaker leader), 15, 70, 162
Evans, George (social reformer), 162
Evans, Mary (friend of Coleridge), 91, 93

Fairies, 324, 325, 333, 342
Feiba Peveli (Owenite commune), 147
Field, Elvira Eliza ("plural" wife of Strang), 241, 259 ff., 272
Fifth Monarchy Men, 25
Finney, Charles (Perfectionist leader), 363 ff.
Flower, George (son of Richard Flower, associate of Owen, Rapp, Frances Wright), 106, 122, 125
Flower, Richard, sells Harmonie to Robert Owen, 106 f.
Ford, Miss, 207
Fountain Grove (colony of T. L. Harris), 334 ff.
Fourier, Charles, 90; his social system, 184 ff., 231
Franklin, Benjamin, his comments on Moravian customs, 35
Free love, 123 ff.
French Revolution, 26, 27
Fretageot, Mme., (educator at New Harmony), 143
Fricker, Edith, 92 f.
Fricker, Sarah, 92 f.

Friends of Association, The, 190

Fruitlands (Alcott's commune), 201 ff.

Fuller, Margaret, 175, 177 f., 183 f.

Gates, Theophilus (enemy of Noyes, publisher of *Battle Axe and Weapons of War,* religious paper), 377 f.

Germantown, La. (site of colony founded by followers of "Count Leon"), 112

Greeley, Horace, 28, 189, 197, 323, 414

Gruber, E. L. (Amanist leader), 282 f.

Guiteau, Charles (assassin), at Oneida, 398

Harmonie, Pa. (Rappite village), 104

Harris, Mrs. T. L., 321

Harris, Thomas Lake (prophet of the Brotherhood of the New Life), 6, 7, 319 ff., 368, 392

Harvard, Mass., 36

Hawthorne, Nathaniel, 174 ff.

"Heavenly Counterparts", 326

Hebert, William (English traveler), his comment on Rappites, 104

Hecker, Isaac (founder of Paulist Fathers), at Brook Farm and Fruitlands, 209

Henry VIII, 23 f.

Himes, Joshua V. (Millerite prophet), 306 ff., 316

Hobbes, Thomas, 26

Hocknell, John (Shaker leader), 46, 54

Holy Hill (Shaker sacred place), 63 f., 72

Holy Roll (Shaker book dictated by angel), 64 ff.

Hopedale ("Miniature Christian Republic"), 197

House of David (cult at Benton Harbor, Mich.), 6, 348; *see also* Benjamin Purnell

Howland, Frederick (founder of Adonai-Shomo, *q.v.*), 312 ff.

Hus, Johannes, 20

Hutterites, 278

Icaria (Cabet's commune), 13, 223 ff.

Illuminati, Order of (secret Strangite fraternal lodge), 257

Inclosures, 24, 27

Industrial Revolution, 8, 27

Inspirationists, *see* Amana

Ireland, Shadrach (communal prophet), 37 ff., 203

Irving, Washington, on bundling, 366

Jackson, Andrew, 117, 122

Janson, Eric, 274 ff.

Jefferson, Thomas, 117, 119

Jemimakins, *see* Jemima Wilkinson

Jennings, Robert (associate of the Owens and Frances Wright), 155 ff., 158, 160

"Jerusalem", 80, 82

Keil, Dr. William (founder of Bethel and Aurora communes), 7, 113, 278 ff.

Kentucky Revival, 54, 56

Kingdom of Heaven, *see* Oneida Community

"King Ludd", 137

Kneeland, Abner (freedom-of-the-press martyr, communal leader), 391

Knowlton, Dr. Charles (contraceptive theorist), 391

"Koresh", 6, 354 ff.
"Koreshanity", 354 ff.
Krausert, Michael (Amanist leader), 283 f.

Lafayette, Marquis de (friend of Frances Wright), 116 f., 119 ff., 125, 231
Lamanites, Indians so-called by Mormons, 261
Landmann, Barbara Heinemann (Amanist leader), 280, 284, 286
Landmann, George, 284
Lane, Charles (Alcott's associate), 202 ff., 411
Lane, William (son of Charles), 202 f.
Lee, Ann (Shaker messiah), 6, 10, 40 ff., 161, 284
Lee, Elder William (Ann's brother), 53
"Leon, Count", 108 ff.
Levelers, 25
Lilistan, 319 ff.
Lily (deity of T. L. Harris's communes), 319 ff.
Livermore, Harriet (prophetess), 301
Locke, John, 26
Lougee, Abigail (paramour of Shadrach Ireland), 36
Lovell, 90
Lundy, Benjamin (Abolitionist publisher), 130
Luther, Martin, 20 f., 274

MacDonald, A. J. (communal theorist, investigator, writer), 193 ff.
Maclure, William (associate of Robert Owen), 124, 143, 153
Macluria (Owenite commune), 146
Madison, James, 117
Malin, Rachel (confidante of Jemima Wilkinson), 85

Markham, Edwin, 343
Marks, William (Mormon official), 248
Martineau, Harriet, her comments on Shakers, 61, 416
McCullough, Dr. H. D. (Strang's enemy), 270 f.
McNutt, Betsy ("plural" wife of Strang), 269, 272
Mears, John W. (enemy of Oneida), 406
Melville, Herman, his comment on Jeremy Bentham, 119
Mennonites, 278
Merwin, Abigail (sweetheart of John Noyes), 370 ff., 376
Metz, Christian (Amanist leader), 274
Midnight Cry, The, 310 f.
Millennialism, 9, 299 ff.
Miller, Charlotte Noyes (sister of John H. Noyes), 379, 387
Miller, William (Adventist prophet), 9, 10, 302 ff.
Mills, "Prince" Michael K. (Detroit cultist), 349
"Modern Times" (anarchy on Long Island), 14, 169
Moravians (German sects in Pennsylvania), 278
More, Sir Thomas, 23, 226
Mormon, Book of, 66
Mormons, 32, 96, 234; see also Strang
Mountain Cove, 323
Mount Lebanon, 55; see also New Lebanon
Mummies and papyrus, 256
Munzer, Thomas, 21

Nashoba (Frances Wright's "free-love" and anti-slavery commune in Tennessee), 99, 116 ff., 122, 125

Natchitoches, La. (site of colony founded by "Count Leon"), 112

Nauvoo, Ill., 230 ff., 243

Neef, Joseph (educator at New Harmony), 144

"Newborns" (antinomian communal sect), 34

New Harmony (Owenite commune in Indiana), 5, 99, 140 ff., 168

Newhouse, Sewall (Perfectionist trap maker), 401

New Jerusalem, 347

New Lanark, 137

New Lebanon (chief Shaker village), 46, 50, 52

New Llano Colony, 198

North American Phalanx (Fourieristic commune), 192

Northern Islander, The, 262

Noyes, George (brother of John H.), 389

Noyes, John Humphrey (founder of Oneida), 7, 28, 220, 361 ff., 411

Noyes, Mrs. Harriet Holton (wife of John H.), 361 ff., 377 ff., 403

Noyes, Mrs. Polly Hayes (mother of John H.), 367

Oliphant, Lady (mother of Laurence), 324 ff.

Oliphant, Laurence (English author, associate of T. L. Harris), 322, 324 ff., 330

Oliphant, Mrs. Alice le Strange (wife of Laurence), 331 ff., 335 ff.

Olson, Jonas (associate of Eric Janson, *q.v.*), 275

Oneida Community, 7, 14, 334, 390

Outlook, The, 317

Owen, Robert, 5, 106, 120, 135 ff., 163 f., 188, 226 f.

Owen, Robert Dale (son of Robert), 123, 125, 158, 160, 162, 335, 391

Owen, Rosamond (daughter of Robert Dale Owen, second wife of Laurence Oliphant), 338 ff.

Owen, William (son of Robert), 123 f., 139

Pacifism, 22, 279

Page, Apostle John E. (Mormon official), 248

Page, Miss, 207

Palmer, Joseph ("Martyr of the Beard"), 208, 210, 219 ff.

Pantisocracy (projected commune of Coleridge in America), 90 ff.

Parker, Squire (disciple of Jemima Wilkinson), 80, 84

Peabody, Elizabeth (Hawthorne's sister-in-law, editor of *The Dial*), 175

Peabody, Sophia (Hawthorne's wife), 175 f.

Peace-Union Community, 196

Peasants War, 21

Peepstones (instruments by which Strang and Joseph Smith, Jr. translated hieroglyphic writings), 250

Perfectionists, 361 ff.; *see also* John Humphrey Noyes, Oneida Community

Phalanx, 186 ff., 192

Phalanx, The (commune in New Jersey), 15

Pilgrims (Bullardites), 97

Plates of Laban (hieroglyphic brass plates shown Strang by angel), 241, 250, 259 f., 262

Plato, 16

Plockhoy, Pieter Corneliszoon, 33

Polygamy, 241, 244 ff., 260, 264

Poor Laws, 24 f.

Potter, William, 80, 82, 84

Prairie Home Community, described by Macdonald, 194 ff.

Pseudosciences, 6, 348 ff.

Puritans, 31

Purnell, "King" Benjamin (prophet of the House of David), 6, 348 ff.

Quakers, 25, 32

Ranters, 25

Rapp, Father George (leader of Rappites), 7, 100 ff., 254

Rapp, Friedrich, 104

Rappites (German communitarians in Pennsylvania and Indiana), 14, 101 ff., 190, 278

Red Oak Grove, 275

Reformation, 16

Requa, James A. (assistant to T. L. Harris), 329

Requa, Mrs. James A. (confidante of T. L. Harris), 334, 341

Richards, Sarah (confidante of Jemima Wilkinson), 79 ff., 83

Richardson, James (associate of Frances Wright), 123, 127 ff.

Rigdon, Sidney (Mormon official, communal leader), 253 ff.

Ripley, George, 173 ff., 176

Rochefoucauld, Duke de la, his comments on Jemima Wilkinson, 83; opinion of Jemima Wilkinson, 87

Rock, Johann Friedrich (Amanist leader), 282 f.

Rousseau, Jean Jacques, 26

Saint-Simon (French social theorist), 90

Salubria (commune in Iowa), 392

Santa Rosa, Calif., 334

Saxe-Weimar-Eisenach, Karl Bernhard, Duke of, discusses Rappites, 107; his comment on New Harmony, 147

Schools, 136 f., 144, 168, 182, 202, 204, 291, 294

Seekers, 25

Shakers, 14, 40 ff., 41, 55 ff., 67 ff., 98, 190, 217 ff., 394

Shelley, Mary Wollstonecraft, plans to come to Nashoba, 130

Silkville, Kans., 274

Sinclair, Upton, 198

Skinner, Harriet Noyes (sister of John H. Noyes), 379, 387

Slavery, 287

Smith, Abram (associate of John H. Noyes), 378

Smith, Hyrum (brother of Joseph, Jr.), 243; murder of, 245

Smith, Joseph, Jr., 66, 97, 230, 240; murder of, 245

Smith, Mrs. Emma (wife of Joseph, Jr.), 248

Smith, Mrs. Lucy (mother of Joseph, Jr.), 256

Smith, William (brother of Joseph, Jr.), 256

Smolniker, Andreas Bernardus ("Ambassador to Christ", founder of Peace-Union), 196

"Snowbound", 301

Social Reform Unity (Fourieristic commune), 193

"Society for Promoting Communities", 89, 138

Society of the White Lily, 339

Southcott, Joanna (English religious fanatic), 161, 349

Southey, Robert, 90

Spiritualism, 61 ff., 66

Spiritual wifery, 241, 249

Spragg, Cyrus ("The Invisible Presence"), 346 ff.

Square House, 38, 50 f.

Stanhope, Lady Hester (prophetess), 301

Stanley, Abraham (Ann Lee's husband), 42

Stewart, Philemon (Shaker leader), 62 ff., 66 f., 67

Strang, James J. (Mormon prophet), 240 ff., 410

Strang, Mary (wife of James J.), 241 ff., 260, 263, 269

Taylor, William (victimizer of Robert Owen), 152

Teed, Cyrus R. (Koreshean prophet), 353 ff.

Thirty Years' War, 22

Thoreau, Henry, 201, 208

"Time store", 166 ff.

Transcendentalism, 171 ff., 368

Transcendental Wild Oats (Louisa Alcott's satire on Fruitlands), 202

Trollope, Mrs. Frances, visits Nashoba, 130 ff., 155 f.

True Inspirationists, 274

Universal Friends, Society of, 80; *see also* Jemima Wilkinson

Un Voyage en Icarie, 226

Urim and Thummim, *see* Peepstones

Utopia, 16, 23 f., 169

Utopia, 23, 226

Utopia (village of Josiah Warren), 164

Vine Cliff, 321 ff.

Voliva, Wilbur Glenn (prophet of Zion City, Ill.), 346

Voree (Strang's town in Wisconsin), 248 ff.

Wallingford, Conn. (site of a Noyesite commune), 398

Waring, Jane (associate, later, wife, of T. L. Harris, *q.v.*), 320 ff., 341

Warren, Josiah (founder of "time stores" and of villages), 140, 154, 165 ff.

Wentworth, Alexander (assassin of Strang), 270

Whigs, in Illinois, 243

Whitby, Richeson (husband of Camilla Wright), 123, 126 ff., 162 f.

Whitefield, George (New Light preacher), 76

Whittaker, Elder James (Ann Lee's successor), 53

Whittier, John Greenleaf, 301

Whitwell, Stedman (Owen's architect, communal theorist), 141, 146

Wight, Lyman (Mormon missionary), 242

Wilkinson, Jemima (messiah, prophet), 75 ff.; description of, 81, 161

Willow Place (Noyesite establishment in Brooklyn, later near Oneida), 398

Winchell (Vermont messianic impostor), 95 ff.; *see also* "Wood Scrape" incident

Wisconsin Phalanx, 192

Woman in the Wilderness, Society of, 33

Wood, Abram (member of Fruitlands), 203, 210

Wood, Nathaniel, 95 f.; *see also* "Wood Scrape" incident

"Wood Scrape" incident, 97, 251

Woollcott, Alexander, 198

Workingman's Party, 158

Wright, Camilla (sister of Frances), 117, 126 ff.

Wright, Frances (founder of Nashoba), 5, 15, 70, 99, 116 ff.;
  plans emancipation of slaves,
  121 f., 142, 151, 155 ff.
Wright, Lucy (early Shaker
  leader), 55 f., 89
Wright, Phoebe ("plural" wife of
  Strang), 269, 272
Wright, Sarah ("plural" wife of

Strang, cousin to Phoebe), 269,
  272
Wycliffe, 20

Young, Brigham, 248 ff., 252

Zion City, 346
Zoarites (German communitarians
  in Ohio), 13, 14, 190, 278